Profits in the long run asks two questions: Are there persistent differences in profitability across firms? If so, what accounts for them? This book answers these questions using data for the 1000 largest U.S. manufacturing firms in 1950 and 1972. It finds that there are peristent differences in profitability and market power across large U.S. companies. Companies with peristently high profits are found to have high market shares and sell differentiated products. Mergers do not result in synergistic increases in profitability, but they do have an averging effect. Companies with above normal profits have their profits lowered by mergers. Companies with initially below normal profits have them raised. In addition, the influence of other variables on long run profitability, including risk, sales, diversification, growth and managerial control, is explored. The implications of antitrust policy are likewise addressed.

Dennis C. Mueller is Professor of Economics at the University of Maryland. He is an editor for the *International Journal of Industrial Organization* and is on the editorial board of the *Antitrust Economics and Law Review*. Professor Mueller's first book *Public choice* was published with Cambridge University Press in 1979.

Profits in the long run

Profits
in the long run

DENNIS C. MUELLER
University of Maryland

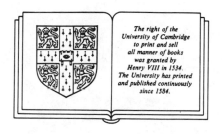

The right of the
University of Cambridge
to print and sell
all manner of books
was granted by
Henry VIII in 1534.
The University has printed
and published continuously
since 1584.

CAMBRIDGE UNIVERSITY PRESS

Cambridge
London   New York   New Rochelle
Melbourne   Sidney

Published by the Press Syndicate of the University of Cambridge
The Pitt Building, Trumpington Street, Cambridge CB2 1RP
32 East 57th Street, New York, NY 10022, USA
10 Stamford Road, Oakleigh, Melbourne 3166, Australia

First published 1986

Printed in the United States of America

Library of Congress Cataloging in Publication Data
Mueller, Dennis C.
Profits in the long run.
Bibliography; p.
Includes index.
1. Corporate profits. I. Title.
HG4028.P7m86   1986   658.1'55   85–12790

British Library Cataloguing in Publication Data
Mueller, Dennis C.
Profits in the long run.
1. Profit
I. Title
338.5'16   HB601
ISBN 0 521 30693 0

to
ADRIENNE *and* JACOB

Contents

Acknowledgments

In 1977, I published an article showing that profit differences across firms tend to persist over time. In 1978, I approached David Qualls, then Assistant Director in charge of the Industry Analysis section at the Federal Trade Commission's Bureau of Economics, to see whether the FTC would be interested in sponsoring an investigation of the causes of these apparently persistent differences in profitability. Dave endorsed the idea and the project was launched. Were it not for his initial vote of confidence, the project would never have been started. As my relationship with the FTC unfolded, I learned to respect David Qualls as an economist and cherish him as a friend. His death in 1984 was a serious loss for the economics profession and a tragic personal loss for all who knew him.

Several people at the FTC were responsible for the project in one way or another over the many years of its history. Special thanks are due them for their patient confidence and support. Particular mention in this respect must be made of Keith Anderson, Ronald Bond, William Comanor, Wendy Gramm, Pauline Ippolito, and Robert Tollison.

In 1981, I took the project with me to the Science Center, Berlin's International Institute of Management. The support of this institution and the confidence of Meinolf Dierkes, Manfred Fleischer, and Bernhard Gahlen are gratefully acknowledged. The views expressed in this book should not be construed as reflecting those of the people mentioned above or their institutions, however.

The *Review of Economics and Statistics* and North-Holland Publishing Company are thanked for permission to reprint parts of Chapter 9.

There must be a law that states that the amount of time required to complete a research project increases exponentially with the number of observations and variables in the data base. In gathering and handling these data, I have been greatly aided by several industrious people. My thanks are extended to Rosemary Morley, Hugh Lederman, Nellie Liang, and Klaus Ristau. Further valuable help was provided in putting the data into computer-usable form by Paul Bagnoli, John Hamilton, Klaus Ristau, and Talat Mahmood. Carl Schwinn was especially helpful in providing some of his data and programs. Ieva

Cucinelli was kind enough to go over the version of the manuscript published as an FTC monograph in 1983 and caught several important data discrepancies. Gail Ifshin has painstakingly drawn the many figures that appear in the book.

David Ravenscraft and Pauline Ippolito made helpful comments on the FTC monograph and some of these are reflected in the current book. Paul Geroski's copious comments on several chapters greatly influenced my thinking and the development of the book. Michael Scherer conscientiously reviewed a first draft and I am extremely grateful for the help his comments provided. Last, but certainly not least, Rebecca Flick wins my applause for preparing the typed manuscript for the publisher. After all of this, I am not sure I can even take credit for the remaining errors, but the better part of six years of my life must have resulted in something I can call my own.

A final note to those who have read the forerunner of this book, which the FTC published in 1983 – Chapters 1 through 3 will look very familiar, but all contain some new material and should at least be skimmed. Starting with Chapter 4, the book replows the structure-performance terrain covered in the earlier work, but in a substantially different way, or asks totally new questions. Thus, starting with Chapter 4, it is really a totally new book.

CHAPTER 1

The persistence of firms

The hypothesis that the competitive process eliminates all economic profits and losses rests on two assumptions. First, in industries where prices exceed marginal costs there is an incentive for firms to cut price to expand their market shares and profits at the expense of other firms. This incentive is usually assumed to be greater, the greater the number of firms in an industry. Thus, the first assumption of the competitive model is that positive profits do not exist in any industry in which the number of firms is sufficiently high and concentration sufficiently low.

Where concentration is not low enough to induce sufficient competition among sellers in a market, profits may appear. These profits are assumed to be a signal for other firms to enter the industry. When they do, prices and profits are driven down. The second assumption about the competitive process is that the free entry and exit of factors and firms assures that profits (and losses) cannot persist, even when transitory market conditions sometimes allow them to exist. The force of the free entry and exit assumptions has been emphasized in the recent literature on contestable markets, where it is shown that even monopolists cannot sustain prices greater than average costs when there is truly free entry and exit (see, e.g., Baumol, Panzer, and Willig 1982).

Given these premises, a normative investigation of the competitive performance of a market economy would logically consist of two parts: a study of the existence, at any point in time, of profits due to existing market structures and other conditions, and a study of the persistence of these profits over time. The present effort is of the second kind.

In contrast, nearly all empirical investigations of the determinants of profitability are of a cross-sectional nature: the regression of firm or industry profits at a given point in time on current or lagged firm or industry characteristics. A criticism that has been leveled against these inherently short-run glimpses at the profit-market structure relationship is that they run the risk of capturing transitory correlations between market structure and profitability and inferring long-run causality (Brozen 1971a, b). Defining the profit variable as a three-

or five-year average and claiming that cross-sectional estimates capture long-run relationships are less than fully satisfactory methods of addressing the long-run nature of the persistence-of-profits question. This study addresses the question directly by using a time-series approach (Chapter 2).

The author has already completed one time-series analysis of the persistence-of-profits question, a study of 472 large U.S. corporations based on time-series regressions over 24 years of data. Companies with higher than normal profits in 1949 were found to have higher than normal profits projected to time equals infinity. Casual examination of those firms that had persistently high profits suggested that many were dominant companies in their markets. Thus, the question of whether profits persist above the norm leads directly to the question of whether market shares and other firm and industry characteristics persist over time. These questions are addressed in Chapter 3.

In attempting to answer these and related questions, our focal point will be the 1,000 largest manufacturing companies as of 1950. This group of companies was the subject of a survey by the Federal Trade Commission (FTC) in the 1950s, which gathered data on shipments by company for each five-digit census product definition for the year 1950 (FTC 1972a). It is the most detailed breakdown of company sales for a large sample of firms that has ever been published.

The FTC has undertaken a follow-up survey of the largest 1,000 manufacturing companies as of 1972. The study actually covers somewhat more than 1,000 companies because it includes some firms from the 1950 1,000 largest still in existence in 1972 but no longer part of the 1972 1,000 largest. These two samples allow us to compute market shares for economically relevant definitions of a market for a large sample of companies for 1950 and 1972 and to test for the persistence of relatively high market shares. The years 1950 and 1972 are the end points of our samples of company data in the time-series portion of the study. In 1972, the 1,000 largest manufacturing corporations accounted for 78.9 percent of total corporate assets (Hay and Untiet 1981, p. 167).

Although the choice of these two years to define our data series was determined by necessity rather than convenience, they constitute not unreasonable end points for an investigation of the economic performance of the U.S. economy. The year 1950 is far enough from the end of World War II that it may be assumed to be free of influences of this great conflict and the immediate postwar transition. It is, however, the first year of the Korean War, and some companies' performance may be atypical for this reason. More directly, our study is affected by this war, because the War Department suppressed the data for those companies heavily involved in armaments production. Thus, our 1950 data on market shares are for somewhat fewer than 1,000 companies.

In contrast, 1972 comes at the close of the Vietnam War. Although the data for this and the immediately preceding years may be somewhat "tainted," limited war and heavy defense expenditures have become such a part of our daily life that a good argument can be made for treating them as normal. The year 1972 has the further advantage of coming just before the price rise by the Organization of Petroleum Exporting Countries (OPEC) and oil crisis of 1973. Thus, our sample covers most of the post–World War II era of rapid economic growth and economic prosperity. Our study seeks to determine whether the forces of competition in the United States were sufficiently strong over this stretch of time and in this economic environment to erode positions of economic profit and market power once they appeared.

From the vantage point of the mid-eighties, the years 1950–72 will seem a long time ago to some. Most graduate students who read this book will not have been born during the first years of the sample period. To many, names like Kingan, Bachmann Uxbridge, Calumet and Hecla, and Godchaux will seem as foreign as Nisson and Renault. Indeed, the major products of the latter two foreign firms are more readily called to mind than for the former four. But Kingan and Co. was a leading food products firm in 1950 – one of the 200 largest, in fact – and the other three were all in the 500 largest.

Perhaps the best way to view this book is as an exploration into economic history, a study of the biggest firms in the most competitive market economy during two of the most prosperous decades that capitalism has ever produced. It asks to what extent persistent differences in profits existed in this particular economic environment and what accounted for them. The relevance of our answers to the present and future of capitalism we leave aside until Chapter 10.

The reigning conceptual framework for explaining the existence of economic profits in the fifties and sixties was the structure-conduct-performance framework most closely associated with the work of Joe Bain. The focal point of the analysis in this framework is the industry. Industry structure determines firm conduct and together they explain profitability. In the early seventies, this reigning conventional wisdom in industrial organization was challenged by Yale Brozen (1970, 1971a, b), Harold Demsetz (1973, 1974), and Sam Peltzman (1977). This "new learning" reinterpreted the previously found positive correlations between concentration and profitability to imply that bigger firms are more efficient and thus more profitable, not that concentration facilitates collusion and thereby greater profits (see Demsetz 1973; Carter 1978). At base, the new learning appears to be arguing that the characteristics of firms are what explain profit differences, not industries. More efficient firms earn higher profits *and* grow to be bigger than the less efficient firms in their industries. The new learning predicts a relationship between profits and firm characteristics, a substitution of firm market shares for industry concentration ratios in a profit equation. Since one of the unique features of the data base is its market share data, it provides a good (if not ideal) data set for testing these new and old ideas about profitability. We do so in Chapter 4 in which we formulate and test two polar models of the firm: an industry-approach model and a firm-approach model. The results of these tests are discussed in Chapter 5. In Chapter 6, the firm-approach model is extended and several additional characteristics of firms that might affect profitability are considered: advertising, patenting, size, growth, diversification, and risk.

A salient feature of modern capitalism is the existence of managerial discretion. Many hypotheses exist concerning the use of corporate revenues, which could, potentially, be reported as profits, to advance managers' personal interests. The effect of managerial discretion on reported profits is examined in Chapter 7, along with the relationship between managerial discretion and managerial income.

Before examining the question of the extent to which profits persist and what accounts for this persistence, a simpler, more basic question must be answered. To what extent did the companies themselves persist? How many of the 1,000 largest firms of 1950 were still in existence as independent companies in 1972?

In its original study, the FTC divided the 1,000 largest companies of 1950 into the 200 largest, 201 to 500 largest, and the bottom 500, and this division is a convenient format for examining the survival issue. Because one company was misclassified, there are actually only 299 firms in the second group and 501 in the third. In all, only 583 of the 1,000 largest of 1950 could be identified as ongoing enterprises in 1972 (see Table 1.1) . These survivors included companies successfully reorganized under the bankruptcy act and firms designated as survivors following a merger. In most cases, the latter were relatively easy to classify as, for example, when Ford acquired Philco. Philco was classified as acquired, Ford as surviving. One might well argue that none of the constituent companies of Norton Simon survived as recognizable entities when this conglomerate (Hunt Foods,

Table 1.1. *Disposition of the 1,000 largest companies of 1950*

	1–200		201–500 (299 firms)		500–1,000 (501 firms)		1–1,000	
	No.	%	No.	%	No.	%	No.	%
Survived	168	84.0	183	61.2	232	46.3	583	58.3
Acquired	31	15.5	110	36.8	243	48.5	384	38.4
Liquidated	1	0.5	4	1.3	14	2.8	19	1.9
No information			2	0.7	12	2.4	14	1.4

Canada Dry, and McCall) was formed in 1968. We have, however, classified Hunt Foods as surviving in the form of Norton Simon. Thus, if anything, the classification scheme exaggerates the number of survivors from the 1950 list. The decision to treat firms like Hunt Foods as survivors was made to avoid biasing the analysis in favor of finding persistent differences in profitability by focusing on an unchanging set of companies, and to maximize the number of companies in the sample. For the same reason, a couple of firms acquired in late 1972 were classified as surviving, if data for fiscal 1972 were available. (The 1,000 largest companies are listed in Appendix A-1 along with our classifications.)

Given that more than 40 percent of the 1,000 largest firms of 1950 disappeared by 1972, a legitimate criticism of the persistence of the profits and market shares results reported in the next two chapters is that they are derived for a subset of companies that were all successful in one important dimension of performance. They survived. In this most fundamental way, these companies were successful, and might be regarded as more successful than the other members of the top 1,000 of 1950. Thus, an artificial stability may be built into the sample. It should be noted, however, that most of the empirical work, starting with Chapter 4, uses a sample of 551, of which 425 are from the 1,000 largest of 1950 and the remaining 126 existed in 1950 but were not among the 1,000 largest of that year. Companies not in existence in 1950 were excluded from the study, however, and the 417 departing companies are present only to the extent that they were acquired by other firms in the 1,000 largest list of 1972.

Most of the companies that did not survive until 1972 disappeared through mergers and acquisitions. Only 19 companies are known to have been liquidated. In determining whether a company survived, we consulted *Moody's Industrial Manual* and the *Standard and Poors'* and *Dun & Bradstreet* corporate directories. Fourteen companies simply disappeared from these references without our being able to determine what happened to them; they are classified as "no information." These were, for the most part, family-controlled companies. Even if we assume that all of them were liquidated, only slightly more than 3 percent of the 1,000 largest disappeared via this route, compared with more than 38 percent via merger.

These figures reveal an important disparity between the description of the competitive process in the industrial organization–microeconomics literature and the way in which this process actually works. Bankruptcy is typically depicted as the harsh penalty for failure in the marketplace, the sword Excalibur suspended over every entrepreneur's neck, awaiting a false decision in the marketplace. But, for firms large enough to make the 1,000-largest list of 1950, the sword of bankruptcy was held aloft by a very thick rope. Less than one firm per year from this group is known to have faced liquidation proceedings between 1950 and 1972.

Some of the companies were acquired in lieu of bankruptcy, consistent with the popular failing firm thesis (Dewey 1961). Our primary concern in this study is with the living, not the dead, so we have not made a major effort to determine why 384 firms were acquired from the 1,000-largest list. In Chapter 9, we do present evidence suggesting that acquired firms performed poorly relative to nonacquired firms from the 1,000-largest list in terms of their ability to retain market shares. But their loss in market shares appears to have taken place *after* they were acquired. In a separate study, I found acquired companies to be no less profitable than otherwise similar nonacquired firms (Mueller 1980a, Chapter 9), and Boyle (1970) obtained similar results. Steven Schwartz (1982) found that target firms had somewhat lower returns on common shares, however. We conjecture that from 1950 to 1972 relatively few of the companies that were acquired faced immediate bankruptcy had they not been merged.[1]

The figures in Table 1.1 do reveal a strong relationship between the likelihood of a company surviving and its initial size. Eighty-four percent of the 200 largest companies survived, whereas less than half of the firms ranked 501 to 1,000 did. The survival rate of the 200–500 largest falls squarely between these two groups. If we think of these 1,000 largest companies as a sample, drawn from the population of all firms over all points in time, and lump being acquired, liquidated, and no information together into not surviving, we can then consider surviving a binary event, and the probability of a firm in the 200 largest surviving is significantly greater than that of a firm ranked 201–500 ($Z = 5.95$). The probability of one of the latter group surviving is, in turn, significantly greater than the survival chances of a member of the bottom 500 ($Z = 4.15$). Taking into consideration that most of the nonsurviving firms were acquired, we can say that the probability of a firm's disappearing through a merger was significantly higher, the lower its size rank as of 1950.[2]

In addition to eliminating a large fraction of the 1,000 largest companies, mergers contributed substantially to the growth in assets of the surviving companies and transformed their asset composition. We examine the effect of mergers on the profits of the surviving companies in Chapter 8. In Chapter 10, the various strands of the analysis are brought together to form a picture of the competitive process as it functioned in the United States between 1950 and 1972.

CHAPTER 2

The persistence of profits above the norm

A. The hypothesis

As George Stigler (1963, p. 1) once observed, the issue of whether profit rates have a tendency to converge on a single, competitive level is fundamental to a normative evaluation of the competitiveness of a market economy. In an economy subject to uncertainty, profits and losses signal the existence of excess demand or excess supply at long-run competitive price. If resources are free to respond to market signals, they should move into areas where profits are being earned and out of areas suffering losses. This movement of resources continues until returns are equalized across all markets (with appropriate adjustment for risk). Of course, each new period brings new uncertainties and new positions of profits and loss, so that a point in time when all firm or industry profit levels are equal never obtains. But if the market is capable of responding to the signals of profits and losses, the long-run movement of individual firm and industry profit rates should be toward a common competitive level. All observed profits and losses should be short-run deviations around this trend.

Despite the central position that the persistence-of-profits issue must have in any normative evaluation of a market economy, it has received surprisingly little attention from economists. Yale Brozen has addressed the issue tangentially in his attack on the positive concentration—profit rate relationship found in much of the literature. Brozen (1970, 1971a, b) presents evidence that the correlation between concentration and profits is unstable over time. But he does not consider whether profits do converge completely to competitive levels (or move only part of the way), and, if convergence is complete, how quickly it occurs. Moreover, by focusing on the profits-concentration relationship, he leaves totally unanswered the question of whether profits due to factors unrelated to concentration disappear over time.[1]

In this chapter, we test the hypothesis that profits, whatever their cause, converge over time on a competitive level. We do not, at this

8

juncture, consider what factors prohibit or slow down the convergence process. Nor do we allow for risk differences across firms. These points will be taken up later. The results in this chapter simply test the hypothesis that all firm profit rates converge on a single competitive level, ignoring risk differences across firms.

The tests in this chapter are conducted using observations on individual firms. Although most studies of profit rate determinants have focused on industry profit levels, the competitive environment hypothesis of convergence on a single competitive level should be equally valid for firm-level profits and for industry profits. For a homogeneous product, all firms in an industry should charge the same price under competitive conditions. Free entry and exit should ensure that only the most efficient firms survive, that all firms have the same average costs as well as price. If all firms in the industry earn profits above the competitive level for long periods, then there must exist a barrier to entering the industry. If only some of the firms in a homogeneous product industry earn persistently supranormal profits, they must have access to a resource, technology, or special managerial talent that allows them to earn these higher profits. The competitive process would then appear to be thwarted in one or more of three possible ways: (1) other firms are banned from using the resource or technology that makes the more profitable firm have lower costs, (2) bidding for this special resource or talent is inhibited so that neither the assets of the firm nor the factor payments rise in value to bring the return on capital into line with competitive levels, (3) the more profitable firms do not exploit their competitive advantage by lowering price and expanding output at the expense of the other seemingly less efficient companies in the industry.

With differentiated products, both the definition of industries and the concept of entry barriers become more fuzzy, the use of firm-level profits more defensible. If a firm with a differentiated product can continually earn profits above the competitive level, other firms must be prevented from selling a sufficiently close substitute or adopting a sufficiently close technology to eliminate the price–cost margin advantage of the more successful firm. If other firms selling close substitutes in what is typically referred to as the same industry are not able to earn returns at competitive levels or suffer losses, this does not offset the fact that the persistently successful firm has some special advantage that others cannot duplicate. Our tests are designed to isolate firms with these special advantages, and to determine how significant they are.

B.   The models

We assume that a firm's returns on total assets at any point in time consist of three components: the competitive return on capital common to all firms; a long-run, permanent rent peculiar to the firm itself; and a short-run, quasi rent, which is also peculiar to the firm but varies over time and converges on zero in the long run. We wish to concentrate on those short- and long-run rents that are related to market structure and competitive forces. But profits can also vary over time because of business cycle factors. In a boom period, short-run rents are higher than average for any given market structure. We shall also assume that the competitive return on capital common to all firms and the permanent rent component of firm i's profits are also higher when business cycle conditions are favorable; that is, if an economy was always at full employment, all firms would earn higher returns on capital and enjoy higher short- and long-run rents, owing to market power advantages, than they would if the economy was continually characterized by excess supply in factor markets. We thus write firm i's return on capital at any point in time t as being proportional to the mean profit rate in the economy:

$$\Pi_{it} = (c + r_i + s_{it})\,\overline{\Pi}_t, \tag{2.1}$$

where c, r_i and s_{it} represent the fractions of average economy profits that correspond to the competitive return on capital, firm i's permanent rents, and its short-run rents, respectively. Subtracting $\overline{\Pi}_t$ from both sides of (2.1) and dividing by it, we obtain

$$\pi_{it} = \frac{\Pi_{it} - \overline{\Pi}_t}{\overline{\Pi}_t} = (c-1) + r_i + s_{it}. \tag{2.2}$$

The hypothesis that all firm and industry profit rates eventually converge on a single competitive level (risk questions aside), which we shall refer to as the competitive environment hypothesis, can now be stated as the twin predictions that

$$r_i = 0 \text{ and } \lim_{t \to \infty} E(s_{it}) = 0,$$

where E represents the expected value.

The deviation of a firm's profit rate from the sample mean at any point in time is composed of two components, the constant $(c + r_i - 1)$ and the time dependent, s_{it}. If s_{it} was assumed to be of sufficiently

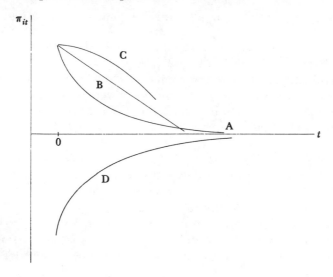

Figure 2.1 Possible profit paths.

short duration that its expected value in any year was zero, we could test the competitive environment hypothesis by simply comparing mean profit rates across firms on the basis of annual firm profits. But the disequilibria in markets that give rise to short-run rents cannot be reasonably assumed to vanish within a single year. A firm earning returns above the competitive level this year can be expected to earn above-normal returns next year without this implying that long-run permanent rents are being earned.

Now consider Figure 2.1. Suppose that i's profits at time $t = 0$ are above the competitive profit rate. If the competitive environment hypothesis is valid, π_{it} must fall to $(c-1)$ as the stochastic component of i's profits erodes. A return to $(c-1)$ along a path such as A is suggested. The two most obvious alternative routes, linear path B and *nonlinear* C, both must be rejected, since each implies a continual decline in profits, even after the competitive rate of return has been reattained. Similarly, less than competitive initial returns can be reasonably expected to return to $(c-1)$ along some path like D.

The curves in Figure 2.1 suggest a specification for the short-run rent component of a firm's profits of

$$s_{it} = \beta_i/t + \mu_{it}, \tag{2.3}$$

where μ_{it} is assumed to be a normally distributed error with the usual error term properties $(0, \sigma_\mu)$. Substituting equation (2.3) into (2.2), we have

$$\pi_{it} = (c-1) + r_i + \beta_i/t + \mu_{it}. \tag{2.4}$$

Since c and r_i are constants, the competitive environment hypothesis can be tested – if we assume the short-run rents are specified as in (2.3) – by comparing the intercepts from the regressions of profits on the reciprocal of time

$$\pi_{it} = \alpha_i + \beta_i/t + \mu_{it}. \tag{2.5}$$

If the competitive environment hypothesis is valid, $r_i = 0$ for all firms, and the α_i $(= 1 - c + r_i)$ should be equal for all firms.

Specifying the short-run rents as in (2.3) presumes that the largest deviation of a firm's profits from their long-run level occurs in the first time period. This specification makes the estimates of α_i sensitive to the choice of time period. This deficiency can be removed by generalizing (2.3) to

$$s_{it} = \beta_i/t + \gamma_i/t^2 + \delta_i/t^3 + \mu_{it}. \tag{2.6}$$

Specifying the short-run rents as in (2.6) allows for the possibility that the peak or trough in the time series occurs at any point in time and allows for two changes in direction for the time path of profitability. Of course, more terms could be added to allow for more changes in direction, but these additional terms tend to introduce multicollinearity, while at the same time eating up degrees of freedom. We confine ourselves to estimating only up to third-order polynomials in time.

Equation (2.6) is only one of many that could be specified having the implication that as $t \rightarrow \infty$, the dependent variable is predicted to approach a constant. For example, one could replace t^2 and t^3 with t^4 and t^6 or with $t^{1/2}$ and $t^{1/3}$. These alternative formulations differ essentially in how rapid an adjustment process is presumed. I tried substituting $t^{1/2}$ and $t^{1/4}$ for t^2 and t^3 in (2.6). This more gradual convergence process gave quite implausible estimates of α. For example, (2.3) and (2.6) yield estimates for α with roughly the same range of values as the individual annual observations, but replacing the cubic and quadratic terms with $t^{1/4}$ and $t^{1/2}$ led to a range of α values far greater than the values actually observed. An examination of the plots of the data indicated that the equations using the simple powers of t fit the data much better than those assuming fractional powers.

This finding points to an important characteristic of equations (2.3) and (2.6). Each imposes on the data the property of convergence to some long-run, constant profit rate for each firm. It could be that the competitive environment hypothesis is valid not because the profit rates of all firms converge on some common return, $(c-1)$, but because they are so volatile that no central tendency can be discerned. By specifying the short-run rents as in (2.3) and (2.6), we presume a long-run central tendency for each firm's profit rate, where none may exist. We might, thereby, be biasing our results away from the competitive environment hypothesis.

An alternative formulation of s_{it} that avoids this characteristic is to assume that the rate of change in s_{it} over time is a function of the size of s_{it} rather than of time, as implied by (2.3) and (2.6). That is,

$$s_{it} = \lambda_i s_{it-1} + \mu_{it}, \tag{2.7}$$

where the competitive environment hypothesis implies $-1 < \lambda_i < 1$, if the process is to converge. The presence of μ_{it}, assumed to be a random error with the usual properties, in the adjustment equation allows for the possibility that profits move away from the long-run rate in any period while remaining on the convergence path. Substituting for s_{it} from (2.7) into (2.2) and writing $(1-c+r_i)$ as α_i once again, we have

$$\pi_{it} = \alpha_i + \lambda_i s_{it-1} + \mu_{it}. \tag{2.8}$$

Using (2.2) to eliminate s_{it-1},

$$\pi_{it} = \alpha_i(1-\lambda_i) + \lambda_i \pi_{it-1} + \mu_{it}. \tag{2.9}$$

The long-run profit rate for a firm can be estimated from the intercept term by estimating (2.9). If the competitive environment hypothesis is valid, the same α_i should be estimated for each company.

This completes our discussion of the models to be used to test the competitive environment hypothesis. Although other specifications for the erosion of short-run rents could be envisaged, the three proposed probably suffice to give a reasonable approximation to most other plausible convergence processes, two making the rate of change in the short-run rent a function of time, the other a function of the size of the rent itself.

Each model gives an estimate of the long-run projected profits of a firm, α_i, that is the sum of the competitive return on capital, and the firm's permanent rents r_i. In a fully competitive market environment, these latter rents should be zero. If we assume that the competitive return on capital is the same for all firms, all should have the same α_i. We test this hypothesis against the alternative hypothesis that there exist permanent rents, r_i, positive and negative, which result in

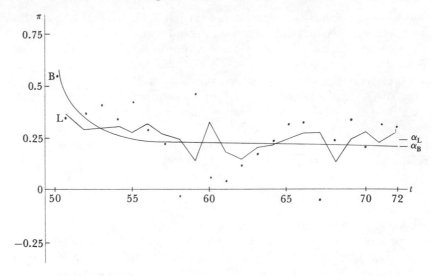

Figure 2.2 Observed and projected profits of Eaton Manufacturing.

systematic differences in the projected long-run profitability of companies.

C.   Some examples

Before we turn to the results for the entire sample, it may be helpful to illustrate the properties of the alternative models and the types of patterns they uncover.

Figures 2.2 through 2.9 present plots of the profit deviations used as dependent variables in each estimated profit projection for eight companies. In addition to the raw profit data (measured again as a relative deviation from the sample mean for each year), the predicted profit rates using the best fit of the three polynomials in $1/t$ (B), and the lagged dependent variable model (L) are presented. The dashes on the right labeled α_B and α_L are the projected long-run profit rates using each equation.

Figures 2.2 and 2.3 present companies that fit one's expectations of how the competitive process works. Both start with profit levels substantially above the norm and converge on profit levels considerably closer to the average, if not right on it. Figures 2.4 and 2.5 present data for companies that converged on the normal return from below. These four companies exhibit profit profiles that all companies

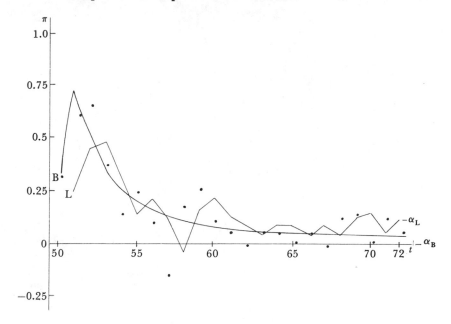

Figure 2.3 Observed and projected profits of Johns-Manville.

are expected to resemble if it is easy to enter into and exit from markets.

But all companies are not like these four. In Figures 2.6 and 2.7, data are presented for two firms that start with above-normal returns and move to levels of still higher returns. As the results in the following section will soon confirm, the profit profiles of Briggs and Stratton and Minnesota Mining and Manufacturing are not atypical. A substantial number of companies start the time period earning above-normal returns and persist in doing so throughout the period. More surprising, perhaps, is the reverse phenomenon – companies like Arden Farms (Arden-Mayfair) and Foster Wheeler persist in earning below-normal returns (see Figures 2.8 and 2.9). Firms like the four depicted in Figures 2.6–2.9 were sufficiently common in the United States between 1950 and 1972 to motivate this inquiry.

Whether the L and B lines fit the data well or not is perhaps a matter of taste. The profit rates they project lie fairly close to one another, and, at least to this observer, indicate more or less where each firm's profit series is going. As we shall soon see, the two projections are highly correlated.

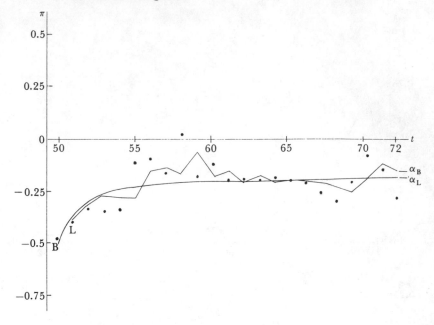

Figure 2.4 Observed and projected profits of Grolier.

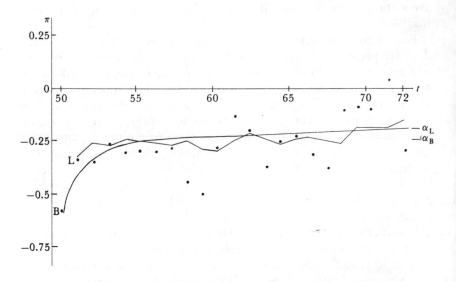

Figure 2.5 Observed and projected profits of Manhatten Shirt.

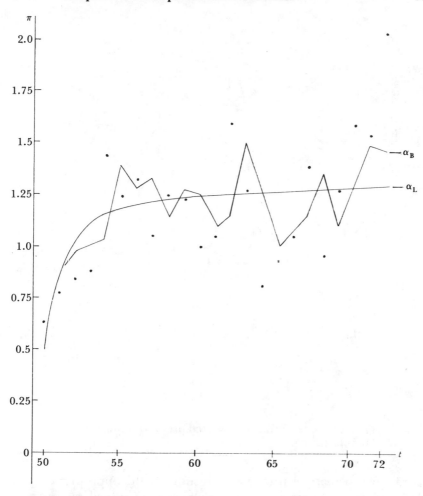

Figure 2.6 Observed and projected profits of Briggs and Stratton.

D.   The results

Long-run projected profit rates for each company were estimated in four ways consistent with the implications of the preceding section. The mean profit rate for each firm over the 23-year sample period, 1950–72, was also calculated (see Table 2.1). A firm's profit was defined as its net-of-tax profits plus interest divided by total assets. In a previous study, both net- and gross-of-tax measures were used, with similar results (Mueller 1977a). Net-of-tax profits have a conceptual

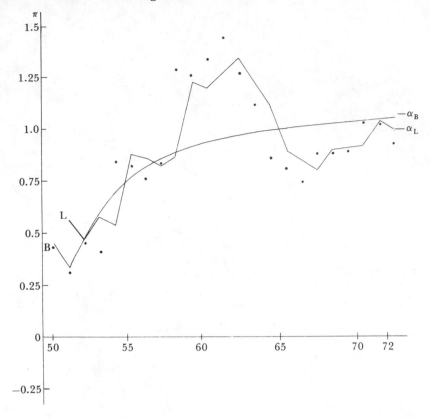

Figure 2.7 Observed and projected profits of Minnesota Mining and Manufacturing.

advantage in that net profits are presumably the appropriate signal for resource movement. Interest payments are added to profits to make the measure of profit independent of the source of funds used to create total assets.[2]

The sample used in this series of tests consists of 600 firms for which complete time-series data are available from 1950 through 1972. The starting point for constructing this sample was the surviving list of companies from the 1,000 largest manufacturing companies of 1950. To this list was added companies for which a full time series was readily available on the COMPUSTAT Tape. Most of these additional firms are in the 1972 sample of 1,000 largest companies. (The companies are listed in Appendix A-1.)

Equation (2.5) was estimated for each of the 600 firms. The full

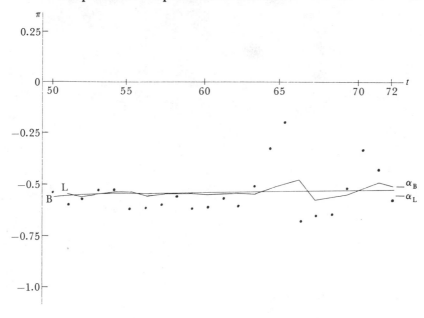

Figure 2.8 Observed and projected profits of Arden Farms.

sample was then divided into six subsamples on the basis of the average profit rates enjoyed during the first three years of the sample period: the 100 companies with the highest average profit rates of 1950–52 in sample 1, the 100 firms with the next highest profit rates in sample 2, and so on. Table 2.2 presents the mean αs and βs for each group. A distinct pattern is observed. On the average, both coefficients are positive and significantly greater than zero in the subsample with the highest initial profit rates and fall uniformly as one moves to subsamples with successively lower average profit rates in the initial three years. In the sixth (lowest initial profit rate) subsample, both coefficients are, on the average, significantly less than zero.

The mean values of $\bar{\beta}$ imply fairly rapid convergence to the long-run projected values for the profit rates. The mean β for the first subsample, for example, implies that although the profit rates for this group were, on the average, 45.5 percent greater than their long-run projected values in the first year of the sample period, they were only 4.55 percent higher after 10 years had elapsed (t being indexed at 1.23). All other mean βs in Table 2.2 imply an even smaller deviation from long-run projected values.

A similar picture emerges when the size of the adjustment in annual

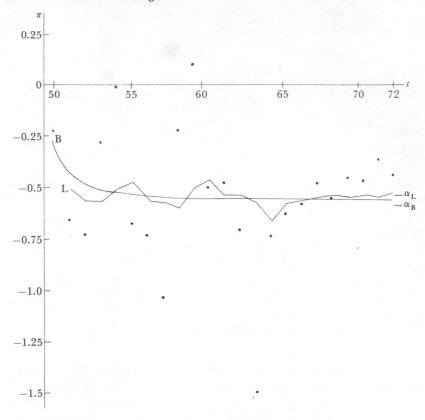

Figure 2.9 Observed and projected profits of Foster Wheeler.

profits is assumed to be proportional to the deviation of profits from their long-run value. Only 7 of the 600 $\hat{\lambda}$s estimated were greater than 1, and none was less than -1. The highest $\hat{\lambda}$ was 1.33. These numbers strongly suggest a process in which short-run rents disappear. Columns 3 and 4 of Table 2.2 present mean projected profit rates and $\hat{\lambda}$ parameters for each subsample. The mean $\hat{\lambda}$s are all around 0.5 and suggest no systematic pattern from subsample to subsample. This pattern is not what one expects to find if all deviations from the norm are short-run rents. If the latter were true, then the λs for companies earning normal returns would be relatively high, in that their normal returns should tend to persist. In contrast, companies with initially very high or low profits should have low λs, since their returns will be converging on the norm. The expected pattern of λs is weakly apparent in the bottom three subsamples, with the

Table 2.1. *Definitions of projected profitability variables*

Projected profitability symbol	Estimating equations	Notes
α	$\pi_t = \alpha + \beta/t + \mu_t$	
α_D	$\pi_t = \alpha + \beta/t + \mu_t$	If DW statistic indicates that the first-order zero autocorrelation hypothesis cannot be rejected (5 percent level, two tail test), $\alpha_D = \alpha$ as estimated from unadjusted data. Otherwise $\hat\rho$ was estimated from $\mu_t = \rho\mu_{t-1} + \epsilon_t$, and α_D estimated from data transformed by subtracting $\hat\rho\pi_{t-1}$ from π_t.
α_B	$\pi_t = \alpha + \beta/t + \mu_t$ $\pi_t = \alpha + \beta/t + \gamma/t^2 + \mu_t$ $\pi_t = \alpha + \beta/t + \gamma/t^2 + \delta/t^3 + \mu_t$	All three equations estimated. Equation with highest $\bar R^2$ chosen as "best-fit" equation. (In about half a dozen cases, highest $\bar R^2$ suggested severe multicollinearity, i.e., large standard errors compared to lower-order equation. "Best-fit" equation then was lower-order equation with highest $\bar R^2$.) Same procedure vis-à-vis autocorrelation applied as well for α_D.
α_L	$\pi_t = \alpha(1 - \lambda) + \lambda\pi_{t-1} + \mu_t$	All $\lambda \geq 0.95$ set equal to 0.95. (This procedure resulted in slightly better fit to data.) Autocorrelation handled as for α_D and α_B.
$\bar\pi$	$\sum_{t=1}^{n} \pi_{t/n}$	

Table 2.2. *Mean αs and βs for two sets of projected profits estimates* $[\pi_{it} = \alpha_i + \beta_i/t + \mu_{it}; \text{ and } \pi_{it} = \alpha_{Li}(1-\lambda) + \lambda_i\pi_{it-1} + \mu_{it}]$

1 Subsample (each of 100 OBS$_i$)	2 $\overline{\alpha}$	3 $\overline{\beta}$	4 $\overline{\alpha_L}$	5 $\overline{\lambda}$	6 $\overline{\pi}$
1	.321 (.061)	.455 (.099)	.305 (.061)	.566 (.029)	.395 (.048)
2	.093 (.037)	.205 (.054)	.115 (.038)	.469 (.032)	.131 (.029)
3	−.018 (.033)	.085 (.052)	.005 (.036)	.514 (.027)	.001 (.026)
4	−.054 (.033)	−.094 (.050)	−.102 (.098)	.483 (.032)	−.067 (.025)
5	−.121 (.031)	−.201 (.042)	−.154 (.033)	.469 (.032)	−.155 (.026)
6	−.228 (.028)	−.448 (.051)	−.189 (.033)	.454 (.035)	−.302 (.022)

mean λ declining as one moves away from the mean, but the decline is very gradual and the differences between adjacent subsample mean λs are insignificant. More important, the highest mean λ in the table is for the highest initial profit group. Those firms that started with the greatest positive deviation from the mean exhibited the slowest average decline toward the mean.

Although both models present evidence of a general pattern of convergence to profit levels closer to the mean than initially observed rates, neither suggests that this process is complete. The mean long-run projected profit rates, $\overline{\alpha}$, for the 100 firms with the highest initial profit figures are more than 30 percent above the sample average under both models. The mean projected profit rates for the second subsample are around 10 percent above the mean, and the mean values of α and α_L both fall steadily as one moves to lower and lower initial profit groups. The lowest initial profit subsample is converging to profit rates that are, on the average, roughly 20 percent lower than the sample average.

Further evidence of both the existence of persistent differences in profitability and the tendency for above- and below-normal profits to converge toward the mean is obtained by comparing the mean values of the profit rates for each subsample over the period 1950–72 (column 6) with the mean projected values (columns 2 and 4). The mean

Table 2.3. *Correlation matrix, alternative projective profits measures*
$(n = 551)$

	α	α_D	α_B	α_L	$\overline{\pi}$
π_{50}	.42	.48	.20	.30	.61
α		.98	.80	.71	.97
α_D			.77	.66	.96
α_B				.55	.73
α_L					.69

profit rates exhibit the same pattern of relative magnitudes as do the mean *projected* rates, except in the highest and lowest initial profit groups, where the projected values are noticeably closer to zero than the simple mean values recorded in column 6. The two models imply convergence to lower (higher) profit levels for the companies with highest (lowest) initial profit ranks than are implied by simply examining the mean profit rates over the entire sample period, but further imply that the convergence process is incomplete.

Equation 5, in which profits are regressed on $1/t$, is the simplest of the time-dependent models by which to judge whether convergence toward the mean is taking place, since there is but one parameter whose sign must be examined. Positive βs are expected when initial πs are greater than their long-run values, negative βs in the reverse case. As indicated in Table 2.2, on the average the $\overline{\beta}$s estimated corresponded to this expectation (column 3). But, as noted above, a second- or third-order polynomial in $1/t$ is more appropriate if the largest deviation in a firm's profits from normalcy occurs at a later point in time in the sample period. The α_B estimates are for the best-fitting polynomial in $1/t$ of the three estimates based on $\overline{R}^2$ (see Table 2.1).[3] Table 2.3 presents the correlation matrix for the various profit projections made, initial profits (π_{50}), and mean profits over the 23-year sample period. These correlations are for a subsample of 551 of the 600 companies on which Table 2.2 is based. The bulk of the empirical work throughout the remainder of this study is undertaken with this 551-firm subsample, and so we make the comparison of different profit projections over this group.

All profit projections correlate fairly well with one another and with mean profits for the sample time period. The profit projections based on the "best-fit" polynomial in $1/t$ have the poorest correlation with both initial profits and mean profits. Thus, the persistence of differences in profitability across firms is less pronounced when one projects

Table 2.4. *Regression of alternative projections of profitability on* π_{50} *(n = 551)*

Dependent variables	Intercept	π_{50}	π^2_{50}	$\bar{R}^2$
α	.019	.461		
	1.18	10.91		.177
α	.725	.725	−.372	
	1.63	8.86	3.75	.196
α_D	.023	.485		
	1.59	12.83		.229
α_D	.030	.739	−.358	
	2.08	10.12	4.05	.336
α_B	.056	.302		
	2.34	4.87		.040
α_B	.053	.207	.134	
	2.22	1.70	.91	.039
α_L	.009	.455		
	.39	7.30		.087
α_L	.016	.704	−.351	
	.67	5.79	2.38	.095
$\underline{\pi}$	.011	.588		
	.90	17.97		.369
$\overline{\pi}$	.018	.815	−.320	
	1.41	12.90	4.18	.387

Note: *t*-values under coefficients.

long-run profitability with the best fit of the three polynomials in $1/t$. Nevertheless, a significant association between projected and initial profits is evident even with the α_B projections. Table 2.4 presents the results of regressing projected profits on initial values for both a linear and quadratic specification. A significant relationship exists between projected profitability and initial profits for all choices of projected profits. For only the α_B projection is the linear formulation superior, however. It indicates that for every 1 percent that a firm's profits were above (below) the average profit rate of all firms in 1950–52, they are projected to be 0.3 percent above (below) the average into the indefinite future.

The negative squared terms in all other equations in Table 2.4 indicate that after a point, the further a firm's profits are from the mean, the greater the percentage movement toward the mean. All

Table 2.5. Z-*statistics for differences between mean firm profits across subsamples*

Subsample comparison	Z-value
1–2	3.84
2–3	4.28
3–4	3.14
4–5	3.18
5–6	2.74

Note: Each firm's mean profit rate, 1950–72, deflated by its standard deviation. For undeflated mean values see Table 2.2.

imply that a substantial fraction of a firm's profits at any point in time are rents, however. For example, the α_D equation implies that a firm earning double the average profit rate in 1950–52, will earn, on the average, 35 percent more into the indefinite future.

The results in Tables 2.2, 2.3, and 2.4 strongly suggest that a significant fraction of above- and below-average profits in 1950–52 represented permanent differences, that is, positive or negative long-run rents. Moreover, the fact that 593 of the 600 $\hat{\lambda}$ parameters estimated using the partial adjustment model fell in the range -1 to $+1$ indicates that profits do tend to converge on a single value for all but a handful of firms.[4] But to some extent the notion of a long-run projected profit rate has been imposed on the data by the choice of model for projecting profitability, at least for the α, α_D, and α_B specifications. How do we know that variations in profitability over time are not so great as to make the idea of a long-run projected profit rate illusory?

As one answer to this question, we divided each mean profit rate for the 23-sample period by its standard deviation and then compared the means as deflated between the six samples, as in Table 2.2. To the extent that profits move so erratically as to make projections of future profitability hopeless, standard deviations around the mean are large, and deflating the means by these standard deviations drives them toward zero. Significant differences between mean profitability figures thus deflated should disappear. Table 2.5 lists the Z-values from comparing the mean profit rates between subsamples after deflating each mean by its standard deviation. All subsample means are significantly different from the adjacent subsample mean(s) at the

Table 2.6. *Fractions of positive αs and βs by subsample*
$(\pi_{it} = \alpha_i + \beta_i/t + \mu_i)$

Subsample	Number of αs > 0	Number of αs significantly different from zero[a]	Number of βs > 0	Number of βs significantly different from zero[a]	n
1	70	71	67	53	100
2	53	64	67	32	100
3	44	60	55	30	100
4	33	71	49	24	100
5	28	67	31	29	100
6	17	69	17	45	100

[a]5 percent level, two-tail test.

1 percent level. The test used allows for differences in subsample variances.

Further confidence in the meaningfulness of our profit projections can be obtained by examining Table 2.6. It lists the fractions of αs and βs significantly different from zero for each of the six subsamples for the full 600 firm sample. On the average, roughly two-thirds of the αs are significantly different from zero. Recalling that $\alpha = 0$ implies a long-run projected return on assets equal to the sample mean, the finding that such large fractions of each subsample have αs significantly different from zero reinforces the conclusion that there are different profit rates to which companies converge over time.

The profit rate variables are deviations from sample means. If, on the average, observed profits contain elements of positive monopoly rents, convergence to the competitive rate of return should be to a return below the average profit rate. The results presented provide two possible ways to estimate long-run competitive rates. First, we might hypothesize that no company can survive indefinitely unless it earns the competitive return on capital. The lowest projected profit rate must then equal the competitive rate. Returning to Table 2.2, we see that both the π on $1/t$ and the partial adjustment model imply an average long-run projected return on total assets for the 100 companies with the lowest initial returns around 20 percent below the sample mean. Under this assumption, the competitive return on capital is some 20 percent below the average and the most profitable firms earn more than 50 percent above the competitive return on capital.

The logic of our second method of estimating the competitive return on capital is as follows: The competitive return on capital is earned by companies that receive zero rents. The profits of these companies differ from the competitive return by a random component assumed to be normally distributed around zero. Firms whose profits equal the normal return plus only a random component should be distributed normally about the competitive return and should exhibit an equal tendency to rise or fall over time. Thus, the competitive return is the long-run projected profits of that group of firms exhibiting equal tendencies for profits to rise and fall. The direction of movement of profits over time is easiest to discern from the simple π on $1/t$ model. Positive $\hat{\beta}$s imply falling profit rates, negative $\hat{\beta}$s rising profits. Table 2.6 reports the number of positive αs and βs for each group, as well as the number that were statistically significant. We are interested in the number of positive and negative βs. There are almost exactly the same number of positive (49) and negative (51) βs in the fourth profit group. This group also contains the fewest statistically significant βs, that is, the fewest equations in which there is a statistically significant tendency for profits to move up or down. Thus, by our second method of determining the competitive return, the average long-run projected profits of the fourth group equal the competitive return on capital. This average lies some 5 percent below the sample's mean profit rate, a figure quite close to the figure we obtained in the earlier study using the procedure, but dividing the sample into eight groups instead of six.

Note also that one-third of the βs of the top group are negative. Thus, in one-third of the 100 companies ranked highest on the basis of initial profits, profits tended to *rise* with the passing of time, a tendency starkly inconsistent with the hypothesis that all of the profits initially observed above the norm were transitory. Similarly, 17 of the lowest-ranked profitability firms witnessed a long-run tendency for their profits to *fall* still further. Although the general pattern of results in Tables 2.2, 2.4, and 2.6 is consistent with an overriding tendency for profits to regress back onto some normal, competitive level, the regression is not complete either in the sense that all firms exhibit such a regression, or that those that do experience a complete return to the competitive level.

E.   Predicting 1980 profitability

The projections of long-run profitability used in this study are based on time-series observations from 1950 through 1972. We stopped our time series in 1972 for several reasons:

1. The market share data are for 1950 and 1972 and we wished to have the profit projections based on data contiguous with the market share data.

2. Each year added to the data base reduces the number of observations in the sample owing to mergers, liquidations, and the other sources of disappearance discussed in Chapter 1. Since an important objective of the study is to try to explain differences in profit across firms with the market share and other data collected, extending the data base in time would hamper this goal.

3. The oil price shock of 1973 and the subsequent reverberations and economic malaise that befell the United States and other Western countries make the seventies a problematic period in which to test for the effects of competitive pressures on corporate profits. More than the normal market forces were at work in the seventies, driving some firms to near bankruptcy while showering huge windfalls on others. By stopping our time-series analysis of company profit performance in 1972, we avoid much of the randomness that seems likely to have been introduced into company profit trajectories following 1973.

4. We also avoid much of the inflation of the seventies that plays havoc with accounting profit rate measures (see Solomon 1970; Stauffer 1971).

Nevertheless, it is important to see what sort of predictors of future profitability the profit projectors are. Data for 456 of the 551 companies to be used throughout the study were available for 1980. Table 2.7 reports the results from regressing 1980 profitability on the various profit projectors. The 1980 profit figure is again the firm's deviation from the sample mean in 1980 divided by the sample mean. If short-run rents are normally distributed around the long-run profit rate, the coefficients on the projections of the long-run profit rate should, in the linear formulation, equal 1. They are significantly below 1. Indeed, there is generally a poorer association between 1980 profits and the projections of long-run profits than there is between the projections and the 1950–52 rates (see Table 2.4). Three factors seem likely to account for this difference. First, the independent variables are estimates of long-run profits and as such are subject to error. These errors in observing the true long-run projected profit rates bias the estimates of the coefficients in the equations in Table 2.7 toward

Table 2.7. *Regression of π_{80} on projected profits and π_{50}* $(n = 456; \pi_{80} = a + bx + cx^2)$

Independent variables x	$\hat{a}$	$\hat{b}$	$\hat{c}$	$\hat{b}\left(1 + \dfrac{\sigma_v^2}{\sigma_X^2}\right)$	$\bar{R}^2$
α	−.012 .55	.256 5.30		.267	.056
α	−.018 .86	.111 1.14	.152 1.72		.060
α_D	−.012 .58	.256 4.90		.309	.048
α_D	−.019 .91	.082 .77	.201 1.89		.054
α_B	−.016 .76	.185 5.14		.209	.053
α_B	−.022 1.04	.046 .66	.111 2.32		.062
α_L	−.005 .24	.143 4.23		.178	.036
α_L	−.011 .53	.255 4.83	−.023 2.75		.050
$\bar{\pi}$	−.009 .41	.269 4.91		.523	.048
$\bar{\pi}$	−.016 .75	.105 .98	.199 1.77		.053
π_{50}	−.0004 .02	.129 2.38			.010
π_{50}	.001 .05	.183 1.72	−.07 .59		.009

Note: t-values under coefficients.

zero. Some allowance for these errors in observation can be made using the standard errors of the estimates of each projected profit rate. If we treat these standard errors as rough estimates of the error in observing the true profit rate, σ_v, and compute the mean $\bar{\sigma}_v^2$ over the sample as a sort of average error of observation, then we can adjust the estimated coefficients in Table 2.7 by multiplying them by $(1 + \bar{\sigma}_v^2/\sigma_X^2)$, where σ_X^2 is the variance in the respective projector of profitability in each equation (Johnston 1972, pp. 281–91). The adjusted $\hat{\beta}$s for the linear equations are presented to the right of the dotted line. They are somewhat closer to 1, of course, but still too far away to allow us to claim that any of the αs or $\bar{\pi}$ is a good predictor of 1980 profitability.

The projections of future profitability made in this chapter are based on the economic history of the fifties and sixties. They are legitimate projections of future profitability to the extent that the seventies resemble the two preceding decades in their economic evolution. As already noted, however, there is good reason to believe that significant structural changes in the seventies reduce the explanatory power of predictions based on the fifties and sixties. The macroevents of the seventies have undoubtedly added errors in our observations of true long-run rates of return of firms, which are several orders of magnitude above the standard errors of the estimates of projected profitability based on data from the 1950s and 1960s.

The third possible explanation for the low coefficients on the projected profit measures is that they may be biased in favor of finding significant differences in profitability across firms. The α estimates are based on the 23 observations from 1950–72 and thus include the years 1950–52. Some slight bias in favor of a positive correlation between αs and initial profits is certainly present. This property should not obscure our vision of the future, however. But, it may be that the αs, like mean profits over the 23-year period, are better statistics of past performance than predictors of the future. The coefficients on the α variables under this interpretation indicate that the process of convergence toward normal levels is continuing. The competitive environment hypothesis is sustained, provided one waits long enough.

Further support for this latter interpretation is provided by the last two equations reported in Table 2.7. The 1950 profitability can explain but 1 percent of the variation in 1980 profits. A company earning double the average profit rate in 1950–52 is predicted to earn about 12.9 percent more in 1980.

If one interprets the results in Table 2.7 as lending support for the competitive environment hypothesis, one is still left with the choice of a glass half empty and a glass half full in evaluating the findings. The earlier results suggested that as much as 70 percent of the differences in profit rates across firms in 1950–52 is transitory; that is, 30 percent or more of any profit differences observed are permanent. Table 2.7 implies that some 75 to 80 percent of these "permanent" differences also disappear over time and that the process of eroding profit differences continues until the job is done. But this process takes a long time. If one had no information upon which to predict 1980 profit differences across companies other than their 1950–52 profitability, one would be better off using this information than making a random guess.[5]

In addition to shedding additional light on the competitive environment hypothesis, the results in Table 2.7 allow us to evaluate the different profit projectors available. The best-fit α is slightly superior to the others because of its ability to predict 1980 profits. In view of this slight superiority in predictive performance, the fact that the equation estimates do provide the best fit to the 1950–72 data, and visual examination of the time-series plots of the data for each firm that suggested that α_B was, on the average, the closest estimate to what one would make oneself simply by looking at the data, we shall concentrate our subsequent empirical efforts on trying to explain differences in α_B across companies. The αs from the simple π on $1/t$ regressions run a close second to α_B. In the previous study, both α_D and α_B were employed as dependent variables, with rather similar results. In the present work, we confine our attention to the α_B variable since it best fits the data for 1950–72, and it best predicts 1980 profitability, even though ever so slightly.

F.   Summary and implications

In this chapter, we have defined and tested the hypothesis that the competitive process eliminates positive and negative rents over time; the hypothesis that the rate of return on total capital for all firms converges on some common competitive rate of return. Several alternative specifications of the possible adjustment paths profits might follow were proposed. All indicated that above- and below-average profits strongly tend to converge back toward the mean of the sample. But all specifications also projected persistent differences in corporate profitability into the indefinite future. A significant correlation existed between these projections and the initial profit rates earned by the companies in 1950–52. Since this starting point was more or less arbitrarily chosen, the present findings imply that an element of the profits of all firms at any point in time is a permanent rent, positive or negative, that the competitive process fails to erode.

These conclusions are based on a time-series analysis of 600 companies over the 23-year period 1950–72. The claim that the projected differences in rates of return across companies derived from this time-series investigation persist is called into question in the previous section in which we observed somewhat disappointing, albeit positive and significant, correlations between projections based on data through

1972 and actually observed profit rates in 1980. The results discussed in that section suggest that it may be necessary to redefine the projected differences in returns as quasi-permanent rents.

Whether the differences in projected returns are interpreted as permanent, quasi-permanent, or merely representative differences that existed for a generation, only to fade during the trying seventies, they are large enough and have lasted long enough to warrant further investigation into their causes. This task will preoccupy us for the remainder of the study.

CHAPTER 3

The persistence of market power

A.   The companies with persistently high or low profits

The previous chapter established the existence of persistent differences in profitability across firms over the 1950–72 period. What causes these differences in profits? To begin to answer this question, we list all companies having projected profits 50 percent or more above the average (Part A, Table 3.1), and all of those with projected returns 50 percent or more below the average (Part B). The projections are the αs from the best fit of the three polynomials in $1/t$ estimated in Chapter 2, since the α will become our dependent variable in all subsequent analysis. The firms are chosen from the 551-company subsample that is employed throughout most of the subsequent chapters.

Only firms with αs at least double their standard errors are included. In addition to the long-run projected profit rates for each company ($\hat{\alpha}$), we have included their profit rates for the first three years of the sample period, π_{50}, and the sales-weighted average of their market shares in 1950, M_{50}. Thus, on the basis of its profit performance over the 1950–72 period, Amalgamated Sugar was projected to earn a return on total assets 53 percent more than the average. Over the three years 1950–52, it earned 12 percent less than the average. Its 1950 average market share was 2.4 percent. Companies with no M_{50} figure were not among the 1,000 largest companies of 1950.

Of the 551 companies, 82 are projected to have profits 50 percent or more above the mean, 70 have projected profits 50 percent or more below the mean. An examination of the names of the companies in each category will undoubtedly suggest different explanations to different readers, and we will want to reexamine Table 3.1 after presenting the main empirical findings. One characteristic of the persistently above-normal profit group stands out to this observer, however. Many of the persistently most profitable firms are the leading and often the dominant companies in their markets – Black and Decker, Campbell Soup, Caterpillar Tractor, Coca-Cola, Kodak, GM, Gerber, Gillette, Hershey, Hoover, IBM, Kellogg, P&G, R. J. Reynolds, Tec-

Table 3.1. *Companies with projected profits (best-fit αs) substantially above and below the norm.*

1950 Name	1972 Name	$\hat{\alpha}$	π_{50}	M_{50}
A. *Companies with significant $\hat{\alpha} > .50$*				
Amalgamated Sugar		.53	−.12	2.4
American Hard Rubber	Amerace Esna	.54	−.51	2.7
American Cyanamid		.56	.03	9.0
American Home Products		1.71	.10	4.8
Arrow-Hart & Hegeman Electric	Arrow-Hart	.81	.48	2.9
Avon Products		2.93	.12	n.a.
Bassett Furniture		1.18	.37	1.2
Beatrice Foods		.63	−.07	3.5
Black & Decker		.69	.17	17.4
Briggs & Stratton		1.33	.76	n.a.
Bristol-Myers		1.51	−.04	5.6
Brown-Forman Distillers		.67	−.07	3.8
Campbell Soup		.56	.05	63.2
Caterpillar Tractor		.72	.05	48.2
Central Soya		.59	.29	3.2
Champion Spark Plug		.62	.71	7.7
Chesebrough Manufacturing	Chesebrough-Pond's	.93	.39	n.a.
Coca-Cola		.98	.34	30.2
Collins & Aikman		1.49	−.37	1.3
Columbia Broadcasting System		.56	−.31	n.a.
Consolidated Grocers	Consolidated Foods	.58	−.44	n.a.
American Snuff	Conwood	.72	−.26	6.0
Corning Glass Works		.76	.27	30.6
Crown Cork & Seal		.55	−.58	3.2
Diamond Match	Diamond International	.63	−.06	19.6
Diebold		.54	−.25	n.a.
Du Pont		.91	.46	23.6
Eastman Kodak		1.42	.13	32.4
Emerson Electric		1.14	−.06	5.5
American Hardware	Emhart	.81	−.53	5.2
Albermarle Paper	Ethyl	.51	−.18	n.a.
Gardner-Denver		.70	.29	6.0
General Motors		.78	.54	47.4
Gerber Products		.92	.18	37.4
Gillette Safety Razor	Gillette	1.58	1.41	43.4
Hershey Chocolate	Hershey Foods	.72	.64	38.1
Heublein		.78	−.41	n.a.
Hoover		.66	−.02	13.1
Inspiration Cons. Copper		.58	.16	2.2
International Business Machines	IBM	1.10	.01	47.9

Table 3.1. *(cont.)*

1950 Name	1972 Name	$\hat{\alpha}$	π_{50}	M_{50}
Julius Kayser	Kayser-Roth	.79	−.47	1.2
Kellogg		1.20	.82	20.5
Eli Lilly		1.61	.27	8.8
Magnavox		1.20	.39	1.8
Maytag		2.37	.96	14.3
J. F. McElwain	Melville Shoe	.78	.57	2.9
Merck		2.12	.10	7.8
Minnesota Mining & Mfg.		1.16	.41	15.8
Monroe Auto Equip.		2.04	−.25	n.a.
Morton-Norwich	Morton Norwich Products	.88	.27	n.a.
National Aluminate	Nalco Chemical	1.14	.50	n.a.
Northwestern Steel & Wire		.99	.33	3.3
Noxzema Chemical	Noxell	.99	1.05	n.a.
Peter Paul		1.00	.06	3.4
Polaroid		.94	.46	n.a.
Procter & Gamble		.86	.37	29.9
Purolator Products	Purolator	1.15	.43	n.a.
R. J. Reynolds Tobacco	R. J. Reynolds Industries	1.11	−.22	23.3
Vick Chemical	Richardson Merrell	.66	.22	2.1
Florence Stove	Roper	.53	−.24	8.4
Royal Crown Cola		.94	.62	n.a.
Schering	Schering-Plough	1.17	−.03	n.a.
G. D. Searle		1.95	1.22	n.a.
Smith Kline & French Laboratories		2.18	.83	2.0
Square D		1.76	.55	6.6
Standard Screw	Stanadyne	.81	.02	3.3
Sterling Drug		1.34	.17	4.5
Stewart-Warner		.59	−.18	4.2
Tecumseh Products		.93	.78	38.7
Texas Co.	Texaco	.52	.24	6.9
Textron		.88	−.67	1.4
Thomas & Betts		1.08	.50	n.a.
United States Tobacco		.97	−.07	10.9
Upjohn		1.43	−1.00	2.0
Vanity Fair Mills	V. F. Corp.	2.60	−.05	n.a.
Walker (Hiram) & Sons	Hiram Walker	.50	.31	8.5
Lambert	Warner-Lambert	1.30	−.46	1.8
Nineteen Hundred Corp.	Whirlpool	.70	.40	14.8
Wm. Wrigley Jr.		.63	.44	52.8
Haloid	Xerox	1.00	−.28	n.a.
Zenith Radio		.97	.33	6.1

Table 3.1. *(cont.)*

1950 Name	1972 Name	$\hat{\alpha}$	π_{50}	M_{50}
B. *Companies with significant* $\hat{\alpha} < -.50$				
American Window Glass	ASG Industries	−.62	−.27	5.6
Alpha Portland Cement	Alpha-Portland Industries	−.76	.11	3.8
Riverside Cement	American Cement	−1.10	.12	n.a.
American Bakeries		−1.09	.05	1.3
American Radiator & Standard	American Standard	−.67	.26	17.3
American Zinc, Lead & Smelting	Azcon	−.60	1.46	8.9
Arden Farms	Arden-Mayfair	−.52	−.55	1.8
Pfeiffer Brewing	Associated Brewing	−1.18	.12	n.a.
Bates Manufacturing		−.62	−.34	1.5
Bethlehem Steel		−.54	−.14	13.4
Bibb Manufacturing	Bibb Co.	−.54	−.51	1.8
Boeing Airplane	Boeing	−.74	−.21	n.a.
Boise Payette Lumber	Boise Cascade	−.52	−.08	n.a.
Brown & Sharpe		−.75	−.61	3.3
Budd		−.55	.09	7.4
Butler Mfg.		−.76	.27	2.2
Carling Brewing		−.58	−.04	n.a.
National Automotive Fibres	Chris-Craft Industries	−.58	.09	8.0
Cincinnati Milling	Cincinnati Milacron	−.84	−.10	8.0
Pennsylvania Coal & Coke	Colt Industries	−.50	−.95	n.a.
Crown Central Petroleum		−.51	−.29	0.5
Curtis Publishing		−.86	−.35	7.1
Universal-Cyclops Steel	Cyclops	−.89	.30	0.6
Elgin National Watch	Elgin National Industries	−.90	−.55	12.4
Fairchild Engines & Airplanes	Fairchild Industries	−.52	−.38	n.a.
Fansteel Metallurgical	Fansteel	−.79	−.12	n.a.
Federal Paper Board		−.70	−.07	0.5
Foster Wheeler		−.57	−.52	n.a.
General Fireproofing		−.96	.50	11.9
General Portland Cement	General Portland	−.75	.77	4.4
General Refactories		−1.11	.13	18.7
General Steel Castings	General Steel Industries	−.82	−.31	1.6
Glenmore Distilleries		−.61	−.19	2.5
Heywood-Wakefield		−.53	−.27	2.1
Edward Hines Lumber		−.56	.52	0.5
R. Hoe		−.53	.23	5.3
Kaiser Cement & Gypsum		−.82	.75	n.a.
Kaiser-Frazer	Kaiser Industries	−.72	.26	2.2
Lehigh Portland Cement		−.92	.10	7.5

Table 3.1. *(cont.)*

1950 Name	1972 Name	$\hat{\alpha}$	π_{50}	M_{50}
Libby, McNeill & Libby		−.59	−.49	6.4
M. Lowenstein		−.81	.04	0.9
National Sugar Refining		−.67	−.42	12.7
Neptune Meter		−.85	.43	14.8
Olin Industries	Olin	−.54	−.68	20.8
Pennsylvania-Dixie				
' Cement		−.84	.44	3.9
Barium Steel	Phoenix Steel	−1.32	−.10	1.4
H. K. Porter		−.60	−.11	n.a.
Publicker Industries		−.97	−.55	13.7
Republic Steel		−.57	−.09	10.6
Revere Copper & Brass		−.82	.16	10.5
Reynolds Metals		−.61	−.26	18.6
H. H. Robertson		−.56	.41	2.5
North American Aviation	North American Rockwell	−.61	.52	n.a.
Sharon Steel		−.66	.09	2.9
Sorg Paper		−.54	−.38	0.5
Sperry	Sperry-Rand	−.52	.98	9.2
Sprague Electric		−1.13	.75	n.a.
Standard Pressed Steel		−.51	.40	n.a.
Standard Railway Equip.	Stanray	−.52	.66	3.5
Sundstrand Machine Tool		−.52	.04	n.a.
Thomaston Mills		−.71	.80	n.a.
Todd Shipyards		−.66	−.47	7.5
United Shoe Machinery	USM	−.61	−.29	4.0
United Aircraft		−.82	−.22	n.a.
United Fruit	United Brands	−.66	.49	n.a.
United States Steel		−.67	−.31	32.3
Ward Baking	Ward Foods	−.64	−.02	3.1
Washburn Wire		−1.35	−.07	0.6
West Va. Pulp & Paper	Westvaco	−.57	.03	3.4
Wheeling Steel	Wheeling-Pittsburgh Steel	−.74	−.17	2.8

n.a. Market share in 1950 not available; company not among 1,000 largest of 1950.

umseh, Wrigley, and Xerox, to name but the most conspicuous in this category. Far fewer of the companies listed in Part B of Table 3.1 are known industry leaders.

Further indication of the importance of market leadership is presented by the M_{50} figures for Parts A and B. The regression results reported in subsequent chapters use projected company market shares in which 1972 market shares receive heavy weight. But, despite the gap between 1950 and 1972, 1950 market shares and projected long-run profits in Table 3.1 appear to be related. Only two of the 70 companies with projected profits 50 percent or more below average had 1950 market shares of 20 percent or more, Olin and United States Steel. Olin engaged in intensive merger activity between 1950 and 1972, including the large, unsuccessful acquisition of Mathieson Chemical Co. in 1954 (see Smith 1963, Chapter 1). United States Steel's market share declined continuously throughout the period (see FTC 1977, pp. 41–82, especially p. 51). In contrast, 16 of the 80 companies with projected profits over 50 percent more than the average had average market shares greater than 20 percent. At the other pole, one observes only 6 of the 82 companies from Part A with 1950 market shares of less than 2.0 percent, and none of these had an M_{50} less than 1.0. Thirteen of the 71 companies in Part B had M_{50}'s under 2.0, and 7 of these 13 had M_{50}'s less than 1.0. The odds of a company with a 1950 market share greater than 20 percent having projected long-run profits substantially above the norm were eight times better than the odds that its profits would be persistently 50 percent or more below the average. The chances that a firm with a market share of less than 1 percent in 1950 would earn profits 50 percent or more above normal were nil.

Thus, evidence of the persistence of profits above the norm raises the question of the persistence of market power. This issue can be addressed in two ways. One can look at *firms* and ask the question: To what extent have firms with high market shares in 1950 persisted in having high market shares in 1972? Or one can look at *markets* and ask the question: To what extent did the same companies dominate individual markets in 1972 as did so in 1950?

Several problems arise when we try to answer the first question. Few firms, even in 1950, operated in only one market, and thus we cannot speak of *the* market share of a company treated as a whole. We can speak either of a company's share within a given industry, or an average of the market shares across all of the markets in which it sells. Since our goal is to explain firm-level profits, an average of market shares across all markets is the logical measure of a firm's market power. But then there are two serious difficulties in making intertemporal comparisons. First, a firm's average market share may change over time, because the industries in which it operates grow at different rates. Thus, a company could maintain precisely the same market share in every industry and exhibit a falling (rising) average market share if the industries in which it has low (high) market shares grow more rapidly than the others. Second, a firm's average market share may change if it diversifies into additional industries, either internally or through merger. In particular, when this diversification is by merger, any changes in average market share that it causes may give a misleading impression of the volatility of company market shares over time. For these reasons, we supplement our investigation of the stability of average firm market shares with an examination of leading-firm dominance in individual markets. We deal with this topic in the following section and then take a closer look at the market share stability of individual firms.

B.   Leadership stability by individual firms in separate markets

Three problems are encountered in attempting to determine the persistence of market leadership: (1) market definitions change, (2) the identities of firms change, and (3) our sample identifies only the top 1,000 companies in 1950 and 1972.

The first problem is relatively serious. The census definitions of industries have undergone a fairly massive transformation since 1950. To give but one example, in 1950 most ethical drugs for human use were to be found in three categories: (a) drugs of animal origin, uncompounded bulk, (b) inorganic and organic medicinals (antibiotics, alkaloids, bulk vitamins), and (c) ethical preparations for human use (products advertised or otherwise promoted to or prescribed by the medical profession). In 1972, a much finer classification scheme was used in which drugs are separated into (a) vaccines and antigens; (b) antitoxins, toxoids, and toxins for immunization; (c) diagnostic substances; and (d) a variety of pharmaceutical preparations separated by their use. There is no way to reconcile these differences without being fairly arbitrary. Thus, many industries that existed in 1950 or in 1972 are not compared owing to the incompatibility of their definitions.

An effort was made, however, to compare as many industries as possible. Thus, several industries in one year could be combined to equal an industry in another, and this was done. In 1950, for example, all farm machinery and equipment, except tractors, were grouped together in a single five-digit industry. In 1972, farm machinery was spread over nine five-digit industries. To compare identities of the leading firms in this farm machinery "industry," we summed the sales of the leading companies in the nine five-digit industries of 1972 and checked the identities of the leading firms in the aggregate against the leaders in the single five-digit industry in 1950.

Numerous cases of slight changes in an industry's definition between the two points in time were simply ignored. For example, industry 36615 in 1950 included recorders, amplifiers, audio equipment, and recording magnetic tapes and wire. This industry was matched against 36514 for 1972, even though the latter did not include magnetic tapes. (A list of the industries matched in the two years appears in Appendix A-3).) It should be stressed, with respect to this first set of data problems, that they all lead to an underestimation of the persistence of market leadership. To the extent that we are not actually comparing the same market at two points in time, it is possible that we will observe a change in the leading companies when no change in the identically defined markets had occurred.

The second difficulty in comparing leading-firm identities in 1950 and 1972 is that the nature of the firms changes through acquisitions and spin-offs. If company A acquired B between 1950 and 1972, and B was an industry leader in 1950, we classified the industry as having the same leader in 1972 if we found that A was the leader in 1972. A more difficult problem is presented by spin-offs, since they are harder to track down. Suppose that A led industry x in 1950 but then sold C, the division producing all of A's x output. If C was then the industry leader in 1972, one might legitimately argue that the industry had the same leading firm in both years. If we had not recorded the sale of the division, however, we would misclassify the industry as having a new industry leader. Again, this problem produces an exaggeration of the number of changes in industry leadership.

The third problem in this section arises because we have data on only the 1,000 largest companies in the two years. If the leading firm in either 1950 or 1972, or both, was not a member of the 1,000 largest of that year, it is possible that the industry has the same leading firm and we have misclassified it as having a new leader. The smaller the industry, the more likely this problem is to occur. In the biggest industries, the leading firms have sufficient sales in the given industry alone to place them in the 1,000 largest. In the smaller industries, a company that specialized in the given industry could dominate it and still be too small to make the 1,000 largest. Thus, although this data problem again biases our findings toward the conclusion that there has been more instability than has actually existed, the bias is less the more important the industry. Nevertheless, the problem should be kept in mind in the following comparisons since in general we do not account for industry size.

Determination of the stability of market leadership is based on the identities of the two leading companies. Theoretical-empirical support for focusing on but the two largest companies is found in Kwoka's (1979) study indicating that a two-firm concentration ratio exhibits the strongest association with profits. A second reason for considering only the two largest companies is to retain in the sample industries for which the comparison can be made. To compare the identities of the two largest companies at two points in time, we obviously need a minimum of two firms in each industry at each point in time. If we wished to compare the three largest, we would need at least three at each point. As more firms are compared, more industries must be purged from the sample because of an insufficient number of companies reporting in one year. Finally, as we increase the number of firms compared, the number of possible ways of defining stability increases at a geometric rate. With two leading companies there are already seven possible categories of change in the leadership of the industry: Both firms may be the same and in the same positions, both firms are the same but have exchanged positions, the leading firm is the same but the second is different, and so on. The seven possibilities are presented in Table 3.2. The column heading "None" signifies that neither of the two leading firms in 1972 was the same as in 1950. Arrows indicate the direction of movement from 1950 to 1972.

Table 3.2 presents the number of industries found in each category classified according to two-digit Standard Industrial Classification (SIC) codes as defined for 1972. One hundred and twenty-five of the 350 industries for which a comparison could be made had two different leading firms in 1972 compared with 1950. The next largest category is the one in which the leader is the same in both years, but the second firm is different. When we combine this with the category in which both leading firms have the same ranks in the two years, we find that there are 142 industries in which the same firm is the leader in 1972 as in 1950; this amounts to some 40 percent of the 350 industries. If we add to these the 13 industries in which the two leading firms have remained the same, but switched places, 155 industries (44 percent of the sample) can be regarded as having a stable leadership structure in the sense that either the same company is the industry leader in both years or the same two companies are the leaders. In 125 industries we have instability in the top two positions, and the remaining 70 cases fall in between. Whether these numbers depict a situation of leading-firm stability or instability on the average is a matter of taste, but this observer regards these numbers as suggesting fairly persistent stability in the identities of the leaders in those industries that could be identified as roughly the same in 1950 and 1972.

The figures by two-digit industry indicate sizable differences in the

Table 3.2. *Classification of industry leadership positions, 1950–72*

Industry, 1972 SIC classification	None	2→2	2→1	1→2	1→1	1→2 2→1	1→1 2→2	Total
20	8	3	3	3	16	1	7	41
21	0	0	1	1	1	0	0	3
22	8	1	0	2	2	0	1	14
23	9	2	0	0	1	1	1	14
24	4	0	0	2	2	0	0	8
25	3	0	0	1	0	0	0	4
26	4	2	0	0	7	0	2	15
27	5	0	0	1	1	0	0	7
28	10	2	2	5	6	1	4	30
29	1	0	1	0	1	0	0	3
30	2	0	0	2	2	0	1	7
31	4	0	0	1	2	0	0	7
32	6	2	0	1	31	1	5	18
33	2	4	1	0	11	1	2	21
34	14	1	1	4	6	1	4	31
35	21	0	4	3	18	4	2	52
36	4	1	1	2	13	2	5	28
37	2	1	0	0	3	0	3	9
38	6	1	2	2	8	0	1	20
39	12	1	1	2	1	1	0	18
Total	125	21	17	32	104	13	38	350

Note: A list of the 350 industries for which the comparison was made, including SIC numbers, appears in Appendix 3.

stability tendencies from one two-digit area to another. In the food and drink industries (SIC 20), for example, 60 percent of the 41 industries had either the same leading firm or the same two leaders in 1972 and 1950, whereas only 20 percent had two different companies leading in 1972. Similar stability was present in paper (SIC 26); stone, clay, and glass (32); primary metals (33); electrical machinery and equipment (36); and transportation equipment (37). In contrast, more than half of each of the following industries exhibited a complete turnover of the two leading firms: textiles and apparel (22 and 23); lumber, wood, and furniture (24 and 25); printing (27); leather (31); and the miscellaneous category (39). These differences in leading-firm stability across industries are stark and invite speculation as to causality. We now examine this question.

C.   The determinants of leadership stability

In this section, we report briefly some results regarding the industry characteristics associated with stable leadership in individual markets.

Given the qualitative nature of the stable leadership categorizations used in the previous section, normal regression techniques are inappropriate. The most straightforward approach would appear to be a binary classification of industries into those with stable leadership patterns, and those without such stability. The three most stable leadership patterns of the seven we employed are those in which the top two firms remain the same, whether they interchange positions or not, and those in which the same firm leads the industry in both 1950 and 1972 (i.e., the three categories farthest to the right in Table 3.2). Any industry appearing in one of these three columns was classified as having a stable firm-leader pattern from 1950 through 1972. All other industries were classified as having unstable patterns.

As explanatory variables we chose the following industry characteristics:[1]

C_4 concentration, $\dfrac{C_4^{50} + C_4^{72}}{2}$

S size, $\dfrac{\text{Sales}^{50} + \text{Sales}^{72}}{2}$

ΔC_4 change in concentration C_4^{72}/C_4^{50}

ΔS change in size, $\text{Sales}^{72}/\text{Sales}^{50}$

ADV advertising intensity, industry advertising-to-sales ratio

Pat patent intensity, industry patent-to-sales ratio.

In addition to the above specification of the concentration and size variables, we tried including the sales and concentration indexes for 1950 and 1972 separately, and used first differences rather than ratios to measure changes. These alternative specifications were either inferior to or no better than the ones reported.

We tested for a relationship between the industry characteristics defined above and leading-firm stability using both the probit and logit maximum likelihood regression techniques. (For a discussion of these techniques, see Pindyck and Rubinfeld 1976, pp. 237–54.) These two techniques gave quite analogous results and so we report only those from the logit technique. SL takes on a value of 1.0 if an industry has a stable pattern of firm leadership (i.e., if it is in the three categories farthest to the right in Table 3.2), and zero otherwise. Under the logit procedure, the dependent variable is $D = \log(SL/1 - SL)$.

When we use the 339 industries for which data for all variables are available, the results are as follows:

$$D = -2.15 + 7.40\ C_4 + .76 \times 10^{-6}S - .37\Delta C_4$$
$$\quad\ \ 4.62 \quad\ 7.41 \qquad 4.51 \qquad\qquad\quad 2.46$$

$$\qquad -.047\Delta S - 3.16\ ADV - 1.22\ Pat$$
$$\qquad\ \ 2.23 \quad\ \ 0.55 \qquad\quad 0.47.$$

Likelihood Ratio   141.2 with 6 degrees of freedom (*t*-values under coefficients)

The likelihood ratio (*LR*) asymptotically approaches a χ^2-distribution with degrees of freedom equal to the number of explanatory variables (six). The *LR* ratio of over 141 implies high significance and strong overall fit for the equation. The concentration variable takes on the highest *t*-value and suggests perhaps that stable leadership patterns are associated with scale economies, if we assume that scale economies explain industry concentration levels over the long run. The positive coefficient on industry size can be given two interpretations. First, to be a leader in an industry with large total sales, a firm must, ceteris paribus, be of large absolute size. Being of large absolute size, it may be better able to adopt more capital-intensive production techniques and have access to cheaper capital in the capital market. These characteristics may make it more difficult for other firms to displace a leading firm in an industry with large sales. Second, we can expect a positive coefficient on industry size because we have data on only the 1,000 largest companies. The probability that an industry leader is not in the 1,000 largest firms in 1950 or 1972 is greater the smaller the absolute size of the industry. Thus, one reason we may observe greater instability in the top two ranks of small industries is that the firms we identify as being at the top in one or the other year were not in fact among the leading two firms in those years.

The negative coefficients on both the change in concentration and the change in sales variables lend themselves to similar interpretations. Industries undergoing rapid structural change, as indicated by large increases in concentration and rapid growth, are more likely to experience turnover in leadership than slow-growing industries with unchanging concentration levels. As Weiss and Pascoe (1983) found in their study of the persistence of market dominance, these results do not support the implications of the dynamic-limit-pricing literature (Gaskins 1971; Kamien and Schwartz 1971). The dynamic-limit-pricing models assume homogeneous products and find that leading firms lose their market share more rapidly the slower the market is growing. A key assumption of this literature is that new entrants cannot enter fast enough to remove the leading firm's advantage in a single period. Given this assumption, the leader's position is "protected" by rapid market growth in that more of the market is left for this company once the maximum possible output of the entrants is taken into account.

Two possible explanations for the observed contradiction to the dynamic-limit-pricing model predictions are offered. First and most obvious is the possibility that their assumptions regarding entry are wrong. Entrants may assume that the leader's ability to satisfy growing demand is relatively weaker, the more rapidly demand is growing. Entry may then be an increasing function of the growth of demand.

In the following chapter, we shall discover that product differentiation is an important determinant of persistent profitability. Rapid growth in a differentiated product market may allow more space for entrants to introduce new products that stand a sufficient distance from the leader's product to secure customers. Indeed, causality in a differentiated product market may be reversed. Observed growth in the market may reflect the introduction of new products by new entrants that are both sufficiently different from the leader's product to win customers, but sufficiently close to it to be legitimately classified as part of the same market. A good example of a market in which rapid growth has been associated with an expansion of the product mix is cereals. (See Schmalensee 1978 for a discussion of this industry and the use of a spatial model to depict product differentiation.) In this particular case, however, the new products have been introduced by the incumbent firms so that the leading firm of 1950, Kellogg, is the leader today (see Chapter 5). An example in which the new products of the nonleading (although still incumbent) firms have been more favorably received than those of the industry leader is cigarettes. R. J. Reynolds and Philip Morris have both been more successful using the new advertising medium, television, to sell their new filter brands, Winston and Marlboro, so that American Tobacco was displaced from the market leadership position it held in 1950.

One might anticipate that large declines in concentration would also be associated with more turnover at the top of the industry than when concentration is relatively constant, that is, that the probability of a stable leading-firm pattern is highest for a ratio of C_4^{72}/C_4^{50} of about 1.0 and low for both rapid increases and declines in concentration. This conjecture was not confirmed. Inclusion of a squared C_4 term in the equation did not change the sign or significance of the C_4 term, nor was the squared term itself significant.

Neither the advertising nor the patent intensity variables took on significant coefficients. This result is quite interesting in that it seems to refute the opposing views of these activities, which claim either that nonprice competition destabilizes industry leadership patterns (see Telser 1964; Nelson 1970; Demsetz 1979; Hirschey 1981), or that these activities lead to entry barriers and thus protection against at least the destabilizing influence of entry (see Comanor and Wilson 1967). Of course, both hypotheses might be partly true and thus offsetting. Heavy advertising and patent activity could protect industry leaders from displacement by new entrants and at the same time lead to more reshuffling among the incumbent leaders. We have not pursued these additional possibilities. Our results indicate that a simple, direct linkage between these two forms of nonprice competition and the stability of industry leadership does not exist.

Given the nonlinear nature of the equation, the marginal impact of a change in any of the independent variables on the probability that an industry has a stable leadership pattern varies with the probability itself. To get a feel for the impact of each independent variable on the probability of an industry having a stable leading firm structure, we make the following calculations: The change in the probability of an industry being classified SL at the mean for SL is computed for changes in each of the significant independent variables from their mean values to a doubling of their mean value:

		Mean of variable	
$\Delta SL/(2\overline{C}_4 - \overline{C}_4)$	$= .542$	0.297	C_4
$\Delta SL/(2\overline{S} - \overline{S})$	$= .170$	9.08×10^5	S
$\Delta SL/(2\Delta \overline{C}_4 - \Delta \overline{C}_4)$	$= .188$	2.06	ΔC_4
$\Delta SL/(2\Delta \overline{S} - \Delta \overline{S})$	$= .064$	5.56	ΔS
		0.442	SL

Thus, an industry with double the average four-firm concentration ratio (0.594 instead of 0.297) would have a 54.2 percent greater chance of being classified as SL if the other characteristics implied an SL of 0.442, which is to say it almost certainly would be classified as having a stable leading-firm structure. The other probabilities can be similarly interpreted.

Taken together, these results imply that industries with stable leading-firm patterns tend to be large and concentrated, and thus that perhaps efficiency advantages or capital market advantages produce stability in industry leadership. Rapid change in industry size and concentration brings with it a greater probability of a change in the identity of the industry leaders. Instability in one industry characteristic is associated with instability in another.

Table 3.3. *Market share statistics for 425 companies in common to the 1950 and 1972 1,000 largest samples*

	1950	1972
Mean	.098	.085
Variance	.012	.007
Minimum	.005	.003
Maximum	.709	.567
N	425	425

D.   The stability of market shares

In this section we consider whether the same companies that had relatively high market shares in 1950 continued to have high market shares in 1972. When asked at the level of the firm, this question must be answered in terms of weighted average market shares for each firm. We first calculated these weighted average market shares using sales as weights and the industry definitions of Appendix 2. We identified 425 firms as being common to both 1,000 largest samples and for which we had complete data to run the persistence-of-profits tests described in Chapter 2. In determining which of the 1950 1,000 largest were in the 1972 sample, we employed the identity changes that followed the mergers recorded in Appendix 1.

The mean weighted average market share of a firm in 1950 was 0.098. The mean market share in 1972 was 0.085. Other statistics of the two samples are presented in Table 3.3. The decline in mean market shares by firm was significant at the 5 percent level using a two-tail criterion.

The simple correlation between weighted average firm market shares in 1950 and 1972 is 0.664, which is statistically significant at all of the usual levels. We can also ask whether firms with high market shares in 1950 were projected to have persistently high market shares at time equals infinity. We do not have annual observations on firm market shares, so we cannot estimate a projected market share for each firm, as we did for profits in Chapter 2. We can, however, assume that an analogous relation holds for market share as for firm profit rates

$$M_{it} = \alpha_i + \beta/t + \mu_{it},$$

Table 3.4. *Mean projected market shares for companies grouped according to their 1950 market shares*

Group	N	M_{ip}	Difference from full sample mean (.084)
1	70	.181	.097[a]
2	71	.101	.017[b]
3	71	.081	−.003
4	71	.060	−.024[a]
5	71	.051	−.033[a]
6	71	.032	−.052[a]

[a] Significant at .01 level, two-tailed test.
[b] Significant at .05 level, two-tailed test.

where M_{it} is the ith company's weighted average share in period t. If we further assume that the observations for 1950 and 1972 fall exactly on the regression line, we can estimate the projected market share M_{ip} of the ith firm at time equals infinity (i.e., α_i) as

$$M_{ip} = \frac{23}{22} M_{i72} - \frac{1}{22} M_{i50}.$$

Obviously, the estimate for M_{ip} is dominated by the ith firm's market share in 1972. The mean M_{ip} for the entire sample is .084 and it correlates almost perfectly with M_{i72}. Nevertheless, it is of interest to run similar tests for projected market shares as were run for projected profits.

To do so, we grouped the 425 companies into six subgroups on the basis of their 1950 market shares. Group 1 consists of the 70 companies with the highest weighted average market shares, group 2 contains the 71 companies with the next highest 1950 market shares, and so on, with each of the other four groups having 71 firms. Table 3.4 presents the mean projected market shares for each group. The average projected market share for the group with the highest initial market shares is almost double the mean of the full sample, a difference that is highly significant. Each successively lower initial market share group has lower projected market shares. The sixth group has mean projected market shares well below half the level for the full sample. Whatever causes the firms to have different market shares in

1950 would appear to continue to affect their relative market power in 1972 and into the foreseeable future.

These results are the more remarkable when it is recalled that no allowance has been made for differences in the relative growth rates of industries or for mergers. Were 1972 market shares weighted by 1950 sales weights, the tendency for market power to persist would most certainly be higher, just as the tendency for profits to persist would most certainly be greater if the effects of mergers, at least, could be netted out. In Chapter 8, we take up the question of whether mergers do tend to produce a regression on the mean effect. The answer is yes, a substantial one. The same is undoubtedly true of market shares. The persistence of high market shares would be more pronounced if we had measured it by firm and market, rather than simply by firm.

E.   Conclusions

The results with respect to market dominance that are reported in this chapter resemble those of Weiss and Pascoe (1983). Defining a dominant firm as one having 40 percent or more of a market, they found that, in the 39 percent of the markets they were able to compare (9 of 23), the same dominant firm existed in 1975 as did in 1950. We found a stable leadership structure between 1950 and 1972 in 44 percent of the 350 industries that we thought were at least roughly comparable. Does 44 percent imply excessive stability? Is 23 years a long enough span of time to anticipate much change? These are questions of judgment I prefer to leave to the reader. If one were to define a fully competitive environment as one in which the probability that any firm with given rank r in 1950 had a given rank of R in 1972 was the same for all firms for which 1950 ranks exist, then the numbers reported in Table 3.2 imply extreme stability relative to this norm. But to expect such fluidity over a 23-year period is to expect too much from the competitive process.

My own view is that these figures reveal an inherent stickiness in market shares and market leadership positions that reflects an attenuated working of the competitive process. Moreover, the bigger – that is, economically more important – the industry, the more stability one observes.

We have established that both profits and market shares tend to persist at above or below average levels over time. In the next chapter, we ask whether these results are related.

CHAPTER 4

Profitability and market structure

In this chapter we begin to explore the determinants of persistent profitability. Over the last three decades, a large slice of the industrial organization literature has sought to explain industry or firm profitability on the basis of various industry or company characteristics (see Scherer 1980, Chapter 9; Weiss 1974). Virtually without exception, this literature has been cross-sectional in nature. The implicit assumptions underlying this research have been that the profit differences observed across industries and firms at any point in time are quasi-permanent differences, and that the cross-sectional estimation procedures capture *long-run* structural relationships. Although the interpretation of cross-sectional regression estimates as measures of long-run slopes and elasticities is rather standard in the literature (see Kuh 1963, pp. 182–6), the permanency of the profits observed in any cross section is open to question. Yale Brozen (1970, 1971a, b) launched his assault on the literature for that reason. The estimates of projected or long-run profitability derived in Chapter 2 should avoid much of the criticism Brozen has raised against previous studies. We use these estimates of projected profitability as the dependent variables in our subsequent work. Our independent variables are drawn from the same sets that other studies have employed, although we place a somewhat different interpretation on some of the variables. The estimating procedures are cross-sectional in nature and we also place a long-run interpretation on the estimated coefficients. Given the long-run nature of the profit measures used as dependent variables and the long-run interpretation of the structural relationships estimated, any support for the hypothesis we find should serve to confirm both the validity of the hypothesized underlying structure-performance relations and our interpretation of the profit projections as measures of long-run profitability of the firms.

As noted earlier, the basic conceptualization of how profits arise and why they might persist in the structure-performance literature focuses upon the industry. Boundaries are assumed to exist, separating one industry from another. Barriers may exist along these boundaries, which impede the entry, and maybe even the exit, of firms. Within an industry, all firms are treated essentially alike. A common technology is assumed for all firms that leads to a unique average cost function available to all firms in the industry. This average cost function is assumed to be U- or L-shaped with first a negatively sloped section up until some firm of minimum-efficient size, and then a horizontal section extending for a long, if not indefinite, range of firm sizes. All firms larger than the minimum-efficient size are assumed to have the same average costs; smaller firms have higher average costs.

The number of firms in an industry or level of concentration determines the degree of collusion in the industry and thereby the average height of prices. Although most studies do not confine themselves to homogeneous product industries, in their treatment of the concentration-collusion hypothesis and the role of product differentiation, they come close to imposing this assumption. Collusion is seen raising a common price umbrella over all firms in the industry. Product differentiation is seen not as a characteristic that differentiates one firm within an industry from another and thereby leads to different prices and profit levels across firms within an industry, but as a characteristic of the industry raising a barrier to the entry of other firms that benefits all companies in the industry alike (see, e.g., Comanor and Wilson 1974).

In contrast to this industry approach to market performance, one can envisage an alternative approach that makes the firm the centerpiece of analysis. Firms differ in the products they sell, their organizational form, and internal efficiency. It is the drive to be different that locomotes dynamic competition of a Schumpeterian sort. Those companies successfully differentiating their products or lowering their costs outpace their rivals and grow to be bigger and more profitable than those rivals. This firm approach to market performance reverses the causal link between size and efficiency. Under the industry approach, when an industry's technology dictates scale economies, the size of the firm determines its costs. Only if it is big enough does it have low average costs. Under the firm approach, efficiency determines size. The more efficient companies with superior products grow to be larger than other firms.

The firm approach to market performance is consistent with the criticisms of the traditional structure-performance literature by Harold Demsetz (1973, 1974) and Sam Peltzman (1977), which emphasize firm-specific efficiency advantages, and with the criticisms of W. Geoffrey Shepherd (1972, 1975), which stress market-power advantages. Both lines of criticism concentrate on the individual firm as the basic unit of analysis.

It is difficult to test the validity of these criticisms of the traditional structure-performance models from the results these models themselves generate, since their very orientation toward the industry rather than the firm serves to obscure the measurement of differences across firms. To sort out the validity of the competing views, we thus develop two models: one that focuses on the industry and treats all firms within an industry alike, with respect to both their product and cost function characteristics, and another that focuses on the firm and allows each firm within an industry to produce a different product at different costs. We begin by developing the industry model.

A.   The industry approach to explaining firm profitability

Each firm in an industry is assumed to sell the identical product at the same price. Since each has access to the same production technology, the same cost function can be assumed for each firm. Since it is necessary to assume some linearity to obtain tractable results when product differentiation is introduced, we also assume linear demand and cost functions in the industry-approach case, although analogous results are obtainable here under rather general demand and cost function assumptions.

Thus, let industry demand be defined as

$$P = A - BX,$$ (4.1)

where P is price, X is industry output, and

$$X = \sum_{i=1}^{N} x_i.$$ (4.2)

We allow for oligopolistic interdependence by positing a "degree of cooperation" among sellers as the weight each firm places on the profits of other firms in its objective function. That is to say, we assume that each firm i maximizes an objective function, 0_i, that includes its profits, Π_i, and a weighted sum of the profits of the other $N-1$ companies in the industry:[1]

$$0_i = \Pi_i + \theta \sum_{j \neq i}^{N} \Pi_j.$$ (4.3)

Perfect collusion implies $\theta = 1$; each other firm j in the industry is given equal weight in i's objective function. Cournot independence occurs when the other firms are ignored, $\theta = 0$. Rivalry implies $\theta < 0$. This approach to modeling oligopolistic behavior differs somewhat from the more familiar conjectural variation approach. The two approaches are contrasted in Section C.

Each firm's total costs are $TC_i = Cx_i$. Substituting into (4.3), we obtain

$$
\begin{aligned}
0_i &= \Pi_i + \theta \sum_{j \neq i}^{N} \Pi_j \\
&= (P - C)\, x_i \\
&\quad + \theta \sum_{j \neq i} (P - C)\, x_j = (A - BX - C)\, x_i \\
&\quad + \theta \sum_{j \neq i} (A - BX - C) x_j.
\end{aligned}
\tag{4.4}
$$

Maximizing (4.4) with respect to x_i, and solving for x_i from the first order condition, one obtains

$$
x_i = \frac{A - C}{B\,(1 - \theta)} - \frac{1 + \theta}{1 - \theta}\, X.
\tag{4.5}
$$

Summing (4.5) over all i, we obtain industry output

$$
X = \sum_l^N x_i = N\left(\frac{A - C}{B\,(1-\theta)} - \frac{1+\theta}{1-\theta} \right) X
$$

$$
= \frac{N}{1-\theta+N+\theta N}\, \frac{A-C}{B}.
\tag{4.6}
$$

From (4.6), we see immediately that $\theta - 1$ yields the perfect collusion industry output $(A - C)/2B$, and $\theta = 0$, the Cournot output $N(A - C)/(N+1)B$.

The profits of any firm i are written as

$$
\Pi_i = (P - C)x_i = (A - BX - C)x_i.
\tag{4.7}
$$

Substituting for $A - C$ from (4.6), rearranging and defining the industry demand elasticity as

$$
\eta = \frac{P}{X}B,
$$

we obtain for the ith firm's profit-to-sales ratio

$$
\frac{\Pi_i}{S_i} = \frac{1}{\eta}\left(\frac{1-\theta+N\theta}{N} \right).
\tag{4.8}
$$

Again, the perfect collusion ($\Pi_i/S_i = 1/\eta$) and Cournot ($\Pi_i/S_i = 1/\eta N$) outcomes emerge, when θ equals one, and zero, respectively.

Equations (4.5), (4.6), and (4.7) imply that the output of any firm and its profit-to-sales ratio are a function of only industry parameters A, B, C, θ, N, and η. The property that each company is of identical size holds for any choice of demand and cost-function structure as long as each firm has access to the same cost-function technology. Each firm, then, has the same objective function and solves a set of symmetric first-order-condition equations.

The implication that all firms in an industry are of the same size is sufficiently at odds with the facts of most manufacturing industries (see Hart and Prais 1956; and Simon and Bonini 1958) to call into question the basic assumptions upon which the industry approach rests, particularly if we assume nonlinear total costs. Although size differences within an industry might exist at any point in time because of historical factors, the freedom to vary plant and firm sizes in the long run should lead firms toward the lowest attainable point on the long-run average cost schedule, given the number of firms in the industry.

Different firm sizes can be reconciled with the assumption that all firms employ the same production technology when the total cost function is linear, as we have so far assumed. Given constant long-run average costs, different size distributions can be predicted to follow from different stochastic-growth assumptions, for example, the log normal from the Gibrat process (Ijiri and Simon 1977). Although postulating constant marginal costs and stochastic-growth processes can rationalize different size distributions of firms, this assumption does not alter the implication of equation (4.8) that all firms have identical profit-to-sales ratios. We thus conclude that the industry approach to explaining firm profitability leads, perhaps not surprisingly, to the implication that *firm* profit rates are a function of *industry* characteristics. All firms in a given industry have identical profit rates on industry sales.

B.   The firm approach to explaining firm profitability

We now wish to allow firms to be different with respect to both their product characteristics and their costs. We write the ith firm's demand schedule in a given industry as

$$p_i = a_i - bx_i - \sigma b \sum_{j \neq i} x_j \tag{4.9}$$

and its total cost function $TC_i = c_i x_i$. Thus we retain the linearity assumption with respect to both demand and cost functions. Each firm's demand schedule has the same slope, but the intercepts can differ. A larger a_i implies a greater willingness of buyers to pay for each unit of output. The a_i parameter is interpreted as an index of the perceived quality of the ith firm's product. The σ parameter is common to all firms in the industry and measures the degree of substitutability of one firm's product for another, $0 < \sigma < 1$. When $\sigma = 1$, an increase in the output of any firm in the industry has the same impact on the price the ith firm can charge as an increase in its own output; the products of all firms in the industry are perfect substitutes. If $\sigma = 0$, the ith firm is a monopolist. The objective function of the ith firm can now be written as

$$0_i - \Pi_i + 0 \sum_{j \neq i}^{N} \Pi_j = (a_i - bx_i - \sigma b \sum_{j \neq i} x_j - c_i) x_i$$
$$+ \theta \sum_{j \neq i} (a_j - bx_j - \sigma b \sum_{k \neq j} x_k - c_j) x_j. \quad (4.10)$$

Taking the first derivative of (4.10) with respect to x_i and solving for x_i, we obtain

$$x_i = \frac{a_i - c_i}{2b} - \frac{\sigma(1+\theta)}{2} \sum_{j \neq i} x_j. \quad (4.11)$$

The first term in (4.11) might be called the quality-efficiency index for firm i. Higher values of this term imply either higher levels of perceived quality for i's product (higher a_i), or lower per unit costs, c_i. Defining $r = \sigma(1+\theta)/2$, (4.11) can be rewritten as

$$x_i = \frac{a_i - c_i}{2b} - r \sum_{j \neq i} x_j = \frac{1}{1-r} \left(\frac{a_i - c_i}{2b} - rX \right). \quad (4.12)$$

The firm's sales are now a function of both industry- and firm-specific characteristics.[2] Firms with higher quality-efficiency indexes have greater outputs.

From (4.9) we can write the ith firm's profits as

$$\Pi_i = (a_i - (b-\sigma)x_i - b\sigma X - c_i)x_i. \quad (4.13)$$

Using (4.12) to remove $a_i - c_i$ and rearranging, we obtain

$$\Pi_i/x_i = bx_i - \sigma\theta bx_i + b\sigma\theta X. \quad (4.14)$$

If we sum p_i over all i, we have

$$\Sigma p_i = \Sigma a_i - (b-\theta)X - Nb\sigma X, \qquad (4.15)$$

or

$$\overline{P}_i = \Sigma p_i/N = \Sigma a_i/N - (b-\sigma)\frac{X}{N} - b\sigma X, \qquad (4.16)$$

with N large $(b-\sigma)X/N \simeq 0$, and

$$d\overline{P}/dX \simeq -b\sigma. \qquad (4.17)$$

We can then define the industry demand elasticity for the case where we have differentiated products as the percentage change in quantity divided by the percentage in mean price and write

$$\eta = -\frac{dX}{d\overline{P}}\frac{\overline{P}}{X} = \frac{1}{b\sigma}. \qquad (4.18)$$

If we now divide both sides of (4.14) by $\overline{P}$, and define $m_i = x_i/X$ as firm i's market share, we can use (4.18) to obtain

$$\frac{\Pi_i}{S_i} \simeq \frac{\Pi_i}{x_i\overline{P}} = \frac{1}{\eta}\left(\frac{m_i}{\sigma} - \theta m_i + \theta\right). \qquad (4.19)$$

The ith firm's profit-to-sales ratio is approximately equal to three terms that include the three industry characteristics, demand elasticity, degree of cooperation, and degree of product substitution, and the one firm characteristic, market share. The firm approach to explaining profitability adds two variables not present in the profit-rate equation in the industry approach, the degree of product substitutability and the firm's market share.

C.   On modeling oligopolistic interdependence

Before examining the empirical estimates for the two models, we contrast the degree-of-cooperation approach to oligopolistic interdependence with the more familiar conjectural variation approach. In the latter, each firm i is assumed to make a conjecture, λ_i, of the aggregate response of all other firms in the industry to a change in its output

$$\lambda_i = \sum_{j \neq i} \frac{dx_j}{dx_i} \qquad (4.20)$$

(see Cowling and Waterson 1976; Dansby and Willig 1979). If we assume a homogeneous product with demand schedule $P = A - BX$, and constant marginal costs C for all firms, as in the industry approach of Section A, then i's profit-maximizing output is

$$x_i = \frac{A - C - B \sum_{j \neq i} x_j}{B(2 + \lambda_i)} \qquad (4.21)$$

and its price-cost margin is

$$\frac{P - C}{P} = - \frac{m_i(1 + \lambda_i)}{\eta}, \qquad (4.22)$$

where m_i and η are i's market share and the industry demand elasticity, respectively. With homogeneous products and identical costs, it is reasonable to assume symmetric conjectures, so that $\lambda_i = \lambda$ for all $i = 1, N$. Then (4.21) and (4.22) imply that all firms are of the same size and have the same price–cost margin as in the results for the industry approach model. Indeed, the same range of price–cost margin predictions emerges with $\lambda = N - 1$ implying perfect collusion, $\lambda = 0$ Cournot independence, $\lambda - -1$ perfect competition (Bertrand independence).

Equation (4.21) implies that the profit-maximizing output of firm i is dependent upon the outputs of all other firms, the conjectured response of all other firms to a change in i's output, and the demand and cost parameters. Should all other firms change their output, i would change its output. Its optimal response would be

$$dx_i = - \frac{1}{2 + \lambda} d\sum_{j \neq i} x_j. \qquad (4.23)$$

In particular, in Cournot's classic duopoly example, if $\lambda = 0$, firm i would respond to an increase in j's output by reducing its output by one-half of j's increase. At the Cournot equilibrium, each firm would hold expectations of what the other firm's output response would be ($\lambda = 0$) that were inconsistent with what their own response would be to a change in the other firm's output, as well as the other firm's response. A rational manager, recognizing the symmetric nature of the duopoly situation, would not choose outputs under the assumption that the other firm will not respond to a change in his or her company's output, while at the same time realizing that in precisely the same situation he or she would respond to a change in the other firm's output.

The seemingly irrational nature of holding inconsistent conjectures has led several writers to impose the requirement that the profit-maximizing response of each firm to a change in output be equivalent

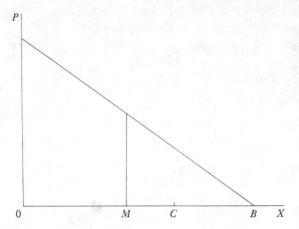

Figure 4.1 Outcomes in a Cournot duopoly game.

to the conjectured response of the other firm(s) (see, e.g., Laitner 1980; Bresnahan 1981b; Perry 1982; Kamien and Schwartz 1983; McMillan 1982; Ulph 1983). Thus, if $\bar{\lambda}$ is the profit-maximizing response of a firm to a change in the output of the other firm and λ remains the conjectured response, consistency requires that $\bar{\lambda} = \lambda$. In the symmetric, homogeneous product duopoly case, the only pair of outputs satisfying the consistent conjectures constraint is at the Bertrand equilibrium ($\lambda = -1$), that is, the competitive outcome where $P = C$.

Despite the obvious appeal of the assumption that rational managers hold consistent conjectures, I find the nature of the equilibria attained under this assumption implausible. Consider the classic Cournot duopoly example. Marginal costs are zero, AB is the demand schedule, M, C, and B are the joint profit-maximizing monopoly, Cournot, and Bertrand outputs, respectively (see Figure 4.1). Should the two firms be at some point to the right of M, say C, each would know that by jointly reducing their outputs they could increase their profits. Each faces a prisoner's dilemma situation, however, so that if one firm alone reduces its output, it is made worse off. Thus, we see the reasonableness of Cournot's assumption that each firm does not expect a cooperative response from the other, so that they remain locked into the noncooperative equilibrium at C.

Now, should the firms hold consistent conjectures, not only would they not try to move from C to M by reducing their outputs in the hopes that the other firms would also cooperate and would they not stay at C on the assumption that the other firm would not move, but *each* would *increase* its output on the expectation that the other firm would *reduce* its output. Thus, a movement from any point to the left of B to B must occur by each company behaving in a manner that is *inconsistent* with the conjectured behavior underlying the justification for claiming B as an equilibrium point, a property I find awkward, to say the least.

I think that the implausible nature of both the equilibria reached and the pseudodynamic movements toward these equilibria under the conjectural variation approach arises from the rather extreme context in which the oligopoly problem is posed. Each firm acts independently of the other, and each speculates on the other firm's output response without directly considering the effects on the other firm's profits. The setting is not unlike that posed by Sweezy (1939) in deriving the kinky oligopoly demand curve, and the results are equally implausible.

At first it might appear that the paucity of information each company is presumed to possess and the independence surrounding the output decision strengthen the analysis. The less one assumes and the more one proves, the stronger the theory is. But with respect to the oligopoly problem, imposing *weak* assumptions about the information available to each seller biases the results against reaching oligopolistic agreements. The more information the oligopolists have, the more likely they are to succeed in restricting industry output to some degree. Similarly, the independence built into the decision process is more compatible with Cournot–Nash–Bertrand outcomes than collusive ones. The emergence of equilibria falling in the Cournot–Bertrand outcome interval under a wide range of assumptions is less surprising than it first appears (see Bresnahan 1981b; Perry 1982; Kamien and Schwartz 1983; McMillan 1982; Ulph 1983).

With these criticisms in mind, modeling oligopoly by assuming a degree of cooperation among firms seems to have some conceptual advantages over assuming interdependence via conjectured output responses by rivals. In the degree-of-cooperation approach, each firm i is presumed to have sufficient information about the components of the demand and cost functions of other firms to allow it to choose its own output so as to maximize the weighted sum of company profits (4.3). The industry equilibrium arises at the set of individual firm outputs obtained from the simultaneous solution of the N first-order conditions. The strength of the assumptions embedded in this approach is now apparent. Each firm possesses enough information about the other $N-1$ companies' demand and cost functions to allow it to solve a set of N simultaneous equations for its own and every other firm's output. In the solution to this set of equations, all firms agree on the weight to be placed on all other firms' profits, θ. As just stated, the assumptions underlying the degree-of-cooperation approach may seem so strong that one is enticed back to positing conjectural variations by the seductive weakness of this approach's assumptions.

Indeed, one might object that the degree-of-cooperation approach presumes detailed information about one's competitors that no firm could possibly have, and if all firms within an industry did have this amount of information they would certainly be able to collude perfectly. This criticism resembles earlier critiques of profits maximization that argued managers do not know their marginal costs and revenues and thus cannot equate them (Lester 1946). The orthodox response has been that what is important in judging a model is whether the actors behave *as if* they had the required information, and the model's ability to describe and predict behavior vis-à-vis alternative models (Machlup 1946). This argument could be used to defend the present treatment of the oligopoly problem. Although no management has the information to maximize a weighted sum of the profits of all firms in an industry, a management that weighed the impact of its output choices on the profits of other firms might behave *as if* it were. Furthermore, in a world of imperfect information and imperfect coordination, the equilibria attained might resemble equilibria that would have occurred had all firms maximized objective functions with some common θ.

In the end, the choice of an oligopoly model from the existing set must be a matter of taste. Each has its faults and virtues. The conjectural variations approach with the added constraint that conjectures be consistent has the virtue of plausibly describing how an equilibrium once attained would be sustained. It has the fault of not describing how one would ever get there. Gone are the reaction curves from traditional duopoly theory since they presume inconsistent conjectured response. Gone, too, is the story about how equilibria are attained.

The degree-of-cooperation approach allows for any possible outcome in the range from perfect competition to full collusion. Any point between *B* and *M* in Figure 4.1 could be an equilibrium. Left unanswered is what it is that leads an industry to settle on a given degree of cooperation, θ, a given point between *B* and *M*.

Those who prefer the conjectural variation approach are reminded that analogous structural equations are derived under this model when the consistent conjectures constraint is not imposed (Long 1982). Initial efforts to estimate conjectural variations have ignored the consistency issue also (see Gollop and Roberts 1979; Bresnahan 1981a; Geroski 1982b; Roberts 1984).

D. Empirical estimates: industry approach

The industry approach yielded an equation (4.8) to explain firm profits, as follows:

$$\frac{\Pi_i}{S_i} = \frac{1}{\eta}\left(\frac{1-\theta+N\theta}{N}\right). \tag{4.8}$$

If all firms were of the same size, $1/N$ would equal the Herfindahl index of concentration, and firm profitability would be a function of demand elasticity, the degree of cooperation, and the Herfindahl concentration measure. The usual assumption is that θ, the degree of cooperation, is also a function of the level of concentration. If we think of the problem of reaching collusive agreement in an industry as analogous to the problem of reaching a cooperative solution to a prisoners' dilemma game, then the most natural assumption to make about θ is that it increases with declining numbers of sellers, that is, that θ is positively related to concentration. This hypothesis underlies the traditional structure-performance literature. In Figure 4-2a, we depict θ as an S-shaped function of concentration, eventually approaching the perfect collusion value of one.

Howard Marvel (1980) has argued that collusion, like pregnancy, is an all-or-nothing affair. Firms either succeed in coordinating their outputs to achieve the pure monopoly industry output or do not, in which case pure rivalry reigns. This view of the collusion game is consistent with a critical concentration-ratio hypothesis (see White 1976; Sant 1978). Figure 4.2b depicts this hypothesis. Paul Geroski (1981) has argued in favor of a generalization of this assumption in which several concentration-ratio intervals are presumed to have different slope coefficients.

Finally, we allow for the possibility that rivalry may increase with increasing concentration, at least over some initial range of concentration levels. This hypothesis concerning concentration and rivalry is undoubtedly most compatible with rivalry in nonprice modes of competition (Cubbin 1983), where rivalrous expenditures on product differentiation can be expected to take the form of an inverted U (Cable 1972; Greer 1971). If nonprice competition is more difficult to coordinate than price competition, rivalry could increase with increasing concentration, at least to some point, and give rise to a U-

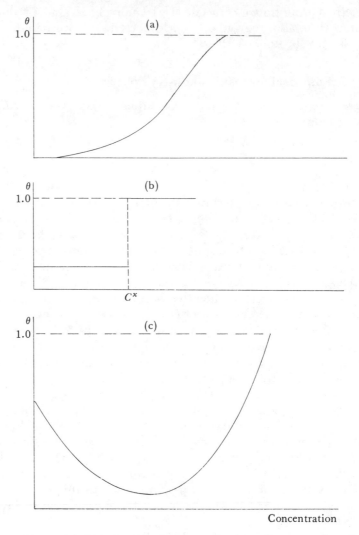

Figure 4.2 Relationship between degree of cooperation θ and concentration.

shaped relationship between concentration and rivalry (see Figure 4. 2c). Although we have not allowed for separate degrees of cooperation on price and nonprice competitive modes, as Cubbin does, it is obvious that the net effect of the two will be reflected in observed profit rates. Thus, if nonprice rivalry is sufficiently strong, we will capture the profit pattern that this mode of competition yields. Nonprice forms of competition lead to product differentiation and thus are incompatible with the industry approach set out here, but we allow for this possibility now for completeness.

A strong form of the structure-conduct hypothesis would assume that a single relationship between the degree of cooperation, θ, and concentration holds across all industries. One could then substitute for θ in (4.8), and using H as the measure of concentration, $H = 1/N$, one would have a relationship between firm profits and but two industry parameters, the price elasticity and concentration:

$$\frac{\Pi_i}{S_i} = \frac{f(H)}{\eta}. \tag{4.24}$$

If each firm sold in only one industry, both the industry demand elasticities and parameters of f could be estimated by regressing firm profit rates on industry concentration levels, assuming enough observations existed for each industry to give reasonable parameter estimates. Two difficulties exist with this approach. First, because almost all firms operate in more than one industry, firm profit rates are a weighted average of the profits earned in each industry. A weighted-average concentration index must be computed for each firm, therefore, but such an index slips in a linearity assumption concerning the concentration-profits relationship, where f might well be nonlinear. Second, f may not have the same functional form for all industries. In particular, the functional form that f takes may vary with the industry demand elasticity.

Equation (4.24) seems remarkably simple compared with the typical structure-performance equations estimated today. Particularly conspicuous is the absence of entry-barrier variables. One reason for their absence is that some variables usually considered as entry barriers (e.g., product differentiation proxies) are incompatible with the homogeneous product assumption underlying the industry approach. Similarly, an estimate of minimum-efficient size is not needed because of the long-run equilibrium assumption we impose, which in turn implies that either all firms are of equal size or marginal costs are constant. An additional problem with the most frequently used measures of minimum-efficient size, those based on the existing size distribution of firms, is that they are not independent of the concentration index (see Scherer et al. 1975, pp. 218–19).

The long-run equilibrium nature of the analysis suggests a more general interpretation of the demand elasticity parameter, η, that would allow for the inclusion of entry-barrier variables through η. The analysis of Section A assumes a fixed number of firms N choosing quantities to maximize objective functions defined with respect to only these N companies; η measures the percentage change in price that follows from a change in quantity supplied by these N firms. If the number of firms in the industry does not change, η is the demand elasticity as usually defined. But we could think of firms outside of the N industry incumbents responding to changes in the incumbents' outputs in the long run, so that the price change that follows a given change in quantity by the incumbents is the result of the total change in quantity occurring, that is, the incumbents' change plus the outsiders' response. The ηs under these assumptions contain the anticipated reaction of outsiders to quantity changes by the incumbents. In this way, the ηs are themselves a reflection of the height of entry barriers. Lower barriers are indicated by larger values of η.

With these considerations as background, we are now prepared to proceed. We follow two paths:

1. We attempt to estimate the η from our data on firms' profits and industry concentration levels.
2. We employ external measures of η and use them to estimate the concentration–profit–relationship parameters.

Consider again (4.8), for example. Rewriting (4.8) with $H = 1/N$, we have

$$\frac{\Pi_i}{S_i} = \frac{1}{\eta} \, (H - \theta H + \theta). \tag{4.25}$$

If we assume that θ has the same functional form for all industries and attempt to approximate θ by the third-degree polynomial

$$\theta = a + bH + cH^2 + dH^3,$$

the term in parentheses in (4.25) becomes the fourth-degree polynomial

$$a + (1-a-b)H + (c-b)H^2 + (d-c)H^3 - dH^4. \tag{4.26}$$

A third-degree polynomial is a sufficiently general functional form to allow us to approximate almost any presumed relationship. Even the discontinuous relationship in Figure 4.1b is approximated fairly well by a third-degree polynomial, as in Figure 4.1a, with the parameters chosen to make the rising portion of the curve quite steep. There are several problems in trying to estimate (4.25) by replacing the term in parentheses with (4.26), however. First, we do not have measures of the Herfindahl index. We can use the market share data for the 1,000 largest companies to calculate a pseudo-Herfindahl index by summing the squared market shares for those companies that are in a given market and in the 1,000 largest companies. For big markets, the leading firms in the market must of necessity have sufficient sales in these markets alone to place them in the 1,000 largest companies. In these markets, our coverage of the leading firms is good and the H one can calculate using the 1,000 largest data is a close approximation of the true H. In small markets, we have but one or two firms and our pseudo-H is admittedly rough. Nevertheless, given that H appears in the equation independently of the θ term, we can simplify the analysis greatly by writing θ as a function of H.

We have individual company sales by five-digit industry for 1950 and 1972. We are thus able to calculate weighted-average Hs for each firm using their sales in each market in these two years. From these, two estimates of the long-run H in the industries for each firm were calculated: a simple average of the 1950 and 1972 Hs, and a projection of H assuming the same type of first-degree polynomial used to project profits in Chapter 2. That is to say, defining $HPRJ_i$ as the long-run projected H for firm i, we write

$$H_i^t = HPRJ + \beta/t. \tag{4.27}$$

Since we observe H for only two points in time, we assume that (4.27) holds exactly for each firm in 1950 and 1972. From the two resulting equations, we can solve for the two unknowns $HPRJ$ and β. For $HPRJ$, we obtain

$$HPRJ_i = \frac{23}{22} H_i^{72} - \frac{1}{22} H_i^{50}. \tag{4.28}$$

Projections of a firm's market share and four-firm concentration ratio were made in a similar way. Since the projected values always performed somewhat better than the arithmetic mean of the 1950 and 1972 figures, we report here only the results for the projected indexes. Given the heavy weight placed on the 1972 H, we simply used this figure for those companies in the sample that were not in the 1,000 largest list for 1950.

1.   Estimates using externally estimated demand elasticities

The simplest method of estimating the parameters in (4.26) is to obtain independent estimates of the price elasticities and to multiply each term in (4.26) by $1/\eta$. This procedure allows us to estimate (4.26) using ordinary least squares and the elasticity-weighted concentration variables. Given that firms occupy more than one industry, the η variable for each firm is a weighted average of the ηs in the industries in which it sells.

Very few studies have employed external estimates of demand elasticities in structure-performance tests and for good reason. Typically, one-third or more of any demand-elasticity estimates are of the wrong sign in any large-scale effort to estimate demand elasticities (see Comanor and Wilson 1974; Houthakker and Taylor 1970). Even when they are of the correct sign, individual estimates often seem rather implausible. For example, several of the estimates made by Pagoulatos and Sorensen (1981) for four-digit food and tobacco industries suggest implausibly inelastic demand schedules, and none of the industry elasticities they estimate exceeds one in absolute value. Given the very long-run orientation of this study, it seems extremely implausible that no food industry has an elastic demand schedule.

Michael Intriligator has kindly made available to me demand-elasticity estimates that he and H. DeAngelo calculated at the four-digit level. When these estimates were of the wrong sign, Intriligator and DeAngelo made new estimates at a higher level of aggregation. Their estimates thus have the twin advantages of spanning all industries in my sample and of being of the predicted sign at some level of aggregation. I have chosen to work with these estimates.[3]

As dependent variable, we wish to use the long-run profit projections from Chapter 2. These projections are rates of return on total assets, whereas (4.8), for example, predicts a relationship between concentration and the profit-to-sales ratio. If (4.8) is multiplied by sales over total assets, the left-hand side becomes profits over total assets, and the right-hand-side variables are all weighted by the ratio of sales to total assets. Our estimates of (4.8) are based on weighting all right-hand-side variables by sales over total assets.

Since the dependent variable is itself an estimated parameter, our confidence in its accuracy as a projection of long-run profitability varies across observations. This variability implies in turn that the variance in errors around an estimated regression line when $\hat{\alpha}$ is used as dependent variable cannot be expected to be constant, with the result that the estimates are inefficient. This problem is removed when each equation is estimated by a form of generalized least squares in which each observation is weighted by the reciprocal of the standard error of the estimate of $\hat{\alpha}_i$ for that observation (see Saxonhouse 1976). This procedure has the intuitively appealing feature of weighting each observation in proportion to our confidence in the accuracy of the estimate of the dependent variable.

Equation (1) in Table 4.1 presents the results from estimating a

Table 4.1. *Estimates of basic industry-approach model using external η estimates*

$$\left[\hat{\alpha}_i = \frac{1}{\eta_i}\,(\beta_O + \beta_1 H_i + \beta_2 H_i^2 + \beta_3 H_i^3 + \beta_4 H_i^4);\; n = 551\right]$$

Equation	$\dfrac{1}{\eta}$	$\hat{\alpha}_i$	β_O	β_1	β_2	β_3	β_4	$\bar{R}^2$
(1)		Best	.087	−.585	1.264	−1.513	1.028	.051
			.47	.35	.23	.21	.31	
(2)		Best	.102	−.571	.652			.053
			5.63	3.81	4.15			
(3)	1	Best	.445	−4.53	15.14	−21.37	11.31	.048
			1.26	1.32	1.29	1.30	1.40	
(4)	1	Best	.132	−.938	1.301			.047
			1.84	2.82	3.70			

fourth-degree polynomial in H using the projected profit rate from the best fit of the first-, second-, and third-degree polynomials using $1/t$ estimated in Chapter 2. All observations are weighted by the reciprocal of the standard error of the estimate of the dependent variable, σ_α. All right-hand-side variables are weighted by an estimate of the average elasticity of demand in the firm's markets and the ratio of its sales to total assets. We can calculate the parameters of (4.25) using the following formulas:

$$
\begin{aligned}
a &= \beta_0 \\
b &= \beta_1 + \beta_0 - 1 \\
c &= \beta_2 + \beta_1 + \beta_0 - 1 \\
d &= \beta_3 + \beta_2 + \beta_1 - 1 \\
d &= -\beta_4.
\end{aligned}
\tag{4.29}
$$

The estimates for equation (1) imply a positive intercept and negative coefficients on all other terms in the θ equation. The degree of cooperation appears to decline as concentration (as measured by the Herfindahl index) increases. The system of equations (4.29) is overdetermined, but both estimates of d are negative. Equation (1) is so obviously plagued by multicollinearity that I did not reestimate it constraining the coefficients as in (4.29).

Both the fourth- and third-degree terms must be dropped to break multicollinearity. The remaining coefficients again imply negative estimates for b and c. The degree of cooperation declines with increasing H at an increasing rate.

Equations (3) and (4) are the same as (1) and (2), except that all firms are given the same $\eta = 1$. The results indicate an only modest decline in $\bar{R}^2$. The same ordering of signs occurs, but multicollinearity appears to introduce more distortion in the estimates of the coefficients. The estimates in (4) again imply declining cooperation with increasing H.

These results are inconsistent with one's expectations concerning the relationship between concentration and cooperation, and one worries whether this may be due to the inadequacies in our measures of H. We therefore estimate polynomials between projected profits and concentration. For 1972, we were fortunate in having Leonard Weiss's (1981) recalculated concentration ratios adjusted for both imports and regional and local market differences. We again tried an arithmetic mean of 1950 and 1972 firm-level concentration ratios and a projected level using the same projection formula (4.27). We used the 1972 figure as the projected C_4 when no 1950 figure was available.

The estimates of the fourth-order polynomials again reveal multicollinearity (Table 4.2), and one observes a flip-flop in the signs of β_1 and β_2 as one drops the C_4^3 term (equations [2] and [3]). Thus, one is somewhat uncertain about the key parameters. The calculations in (4.29) cannot be used to solve for the parameters in the θ function because they are derived from (4.26), in which H plays two roles: as the reciprocal for the number of firms in the industry *and* as an argument in the θ function. It is only with respect to the latter that it is legitimate to substitute C_4 for H. If it were legitimate to use (4.29) to calculate the parameters of

$$\theta = a + bC_4 + cC_4^2 + dC_4^3,$$

then both equations (2) and (3) would imply declining cooperation with increasing concentration, even though profitability would increase over an initial range of concentration levels according to (2). This comes about because the first term in parentheses in (4.26), H, increases with increasing concentration, regardless of what happens to θ, and this can outweigh the impact of θ over some range of C_4 values.

The $\overline{R}^2$ of the equation in which $\eta = 1$ exceeds that for the analogous equation in which the right-hand-side variables have been weighted by $1/\eta_i$ and η_i is a weighted-average demand elasticity for each firm.

Whether this deterioration in performance is due to the quality of the demand-elasticity estimates, our use of a weighted average for each firm as opposed to figures for both profits and demand elasticity by industry, or the inadequacy of the theory itself cannot be ascertained. But both Tables 4.1 and 4.2 suggest that adding externally estimated demand elasticities does not improve the fit of the model.[4] We are thus driven to try to estimate the elasticities internally.

2.   *Industry model with internally generated demand elasticities*

Consider once again equation (4.25):

$$\frac{\Pi_i}{S_i} = \frac{1}{\eta_{ij}} (H_{ij} - \theta_j H_{ij} + \theta_j),$$

where the i stands for firm i and the j for industry j. Suppose that we were to approximate the term in parentheses by a polynomial in H as in the previous subsection. Suppose further that the same functional relationship between the degree of cooperation, θ, and concentration held across all industries, and that each firm operates in but one industry. We could then attempt to estimate both the parameters of

Table 4.2. *Estimates of basic industry-approach model using C_4 and external η estimates*

$$\left[\hat{\alpha}_i = \frac{1}{\eta_i}(\beta_0 + \beta_1 C_{4i} + \beta_2 C_{4i}^2 + \beta_3 C_{4i}^3 + \beta_4 C_{4i}^4); \ n = 551\right]$$

Equation	$\dfrac{1}{\eta}$	$\hat{\alpha}_i$	β_0	β_1	β_2	β_3	β_4	$\overline{R}^2$
(1)		Best	-.264	2.471	-7.766	9.125	-3.159	.080
			1.55	1.59	1.54	1.32	.93	
(2)		Best	-.124	1.114	-3.159	2.686		.081
			1.54	2.07	2.83	3.62		
(3)		Best	.143	-.750	.843			.060
			4.41	4.59	4.92			
(4)	1	Best	-.446	3.791	-9.900	7.910		.082
			-2.69	3.13	3.70	4.37		

the θ function and the industry-demand elasticities by specifying separate dummy variable vectors for each firm (0 if the firm is not in
industry j, 1 if it is), and estimate (4.25) using a nonlinear estimation
technique.

There are several problems in proceeding this way. Perhaps the
easiest of these to get around is the one that arises because companies
operate in numerous industries. To deal with this difficulty, I generalized the dummy variable concept by constructing vectors for each
firm consisting of the percentage of sales in each industry.

More serious is the fact that the sample of 551 firms spans some
775 industries. It is impossible to estimate separate industry-demand
elasticities at this level. I thus aggregated each company's sales up to
the three-digit level, reducing the number of "industries" to 141.

Even so, one could not proceed directly. Estimating more than 140
parameters by a nonlinear regression technique would most likely
have exhausted the International Institute of Management's computer
budget for one year. Moreover, the SHAZAM package with which I
was working had a limit of 100 parameters that can be estimated with
any one regression. I thus had to follow another route.

Assume that the factor in parentheses in (4.25) could be approximated by a polynomial in concentration of, say, the second order.
Using C_4 instead of H because of its superior performance, as evidenced by comparing Tables 4.1 and 4.2, we have

$$\frac{\Pi_i}{S_i} = \frac{1}{\eta_j} (a + bC_{4j}^2 + cC_{4j}^2). \tag{4.30}$$

Now, (4.30) can be estimated using ordinary least squares by estimating a separate intercept term and slopes on the concentration
terms for each industry and using the vector of percentages of sales
for each firm in each industry as a pseudo-industry dummy vector.
If the a, b, and c coefficients in (4.30) are the same for all industries,
then the ratio of the intercept to the slope on C_4 and C_4^2 should be
constants for all industries.

Given that we could not estimate more than 100 coefficients in a
single equation, we first broke the sample of industries into three
groups of roughly equal size: SIC industries 201–266, 271–339, and
341–399. Separate intercepts and slopes were estimated for all industries in the main subgroup, and the remaining two subgroups were
constrained to have the same intercepts and concentration slope. We
then combined all industries having neither an intercept nor a coefficient on the concentration term greater than their respective standard error, and reestimated separate intercepts and slopes across the

entire sample. Multicollinearity across industries did not appear to be very serious, but collinearity between an industry's intercept term and its concentration terms often was. When the concentration terms and intercept for an industry all had standard errors greater than their coefficients, the concentration terms were dropped to see whether the intercept by itself would have a coefficient larger than its standard error.

In all, some 65 of the 141 three-digit industries spanning the sample had at least one coefficient that exceeded its standard error in these first-pass regressions. About one-half of the intercepts were negative and less than $-.30$. Since it is unlikely that the competitive rate of return on capital is more than 30 percent below the sample mean, these negative intercepts can occur only if the η_j estimates for these industries are negative or if $\hat{a}$ in equation (4.30) is negative. But since $\hat{a}$ is presumed to be the same for all industries, if it is negative, then the η_j estimates for all those industries taking on positive intercepts must be negative. But we have defined η_j as the negative of the slope of the demand schedule. Thus, our first-pass estimates imply that roughly one-half of the estimated demand elasticities are of the wrong sign, or that the same $\hat{a}$ and, by implication, the same polynomial in C_4 do not represent the factor in parentheses in equation (4.30).

It is very difficult to accept the implication that roughly one-half of the industries have upward-sloping demand schedules. More plausible is the explanation that holding demand elasticity fixed, the same polynomial relationship between profitability and concentration does not hold across all industries. If this explanation is correct, then it will not be possible to isolate the separate influences of industry demand elasticity and concentration on a firm's profits. A firm having 10 percent of its sales in industry j has its profits shifted some h percent from the sample mean, where this h is determined by a combination of the industry j's long-run demand elasticity, concentration in j, and the degree of cooperation in j, but there is no way to sort out the given effects.

We can attempt to estimate the net effect of these factors, the h_j for each industry, by simply regressing firm profit rates on the vectors of percentages of firm sales in each industry. This technique is essentially an analysis-of-variance approach. We applied it to the 65 industries for which at least one coefficient in any one equation estimated exceeded its standard error. A common intercept was imposed on the remaining 76 industries, and a stepwise regression was employed to determine which of the 65 industries that appeared to be potentially important in explaining profitability would be so on a final pass. A 25 percent probability of significance criterion was used to enter and delete variables from the equation. The results are reported in Table 4.3. Column 1 of the results lists 32 industries that exhibited a 25 percent or better probability of having a coefficient significantly different from all other industries. The coefficient on all other industries is close to zero, so the coefficients as reported indicate roughly the deviation of a firm's projected profitability from the sample mean. The coefficient on the pharmaceuticals industry vector, for example, implies that a firm making 100 percent of its sales in the pharmaceutical industry is projected to earn a return on total capital 127 percent higher than the average profit rate earned in the 109 other industries not singled out in Table 4.3, and 134 percent (127 + 07) greater than the sample mean. All but 5 of the 32 coefficients in column 1 implied plausible projections of profitability differences as a result of participation in an industry; that is, the projections were plausible both with respect to sign (soaps and detergents, and photographic equipment earn above-normal returns, steel mills and railroad equipment below) and magnitude, in the sense that projected values for the industry fall within the range of observed projected values for all firms. But a couple of wild outliers exist. A firm lucky enough to have all of its sales in industry 235 (millinery and hats) is projected to earn more than 1,000 times the average company's return on capital.

Although the preliminary estimations of industry effects indicated that a common relationship between concentration and profitability did not hold across all industries, concentration is one of the industry characteristics that is likely to affect the level of profitability. It is of interest to see, therefore, what happens to the industry coefficients when concentration is introduced into the equation. Column 2 shows the result. Both C_4 and C_4^2 add significant explanatory power to the equation; the same U-shaped relationship between concentration and profitability is observed as was evident in equation (3) of Table 4.2. Two industries (212 and 281) on the borderline to entering the equation in Column 1 drop out, one industry (364) squeezes in. But basically very little change in either the identity of the industries included in the equation or the size of the coefficients follows from adding concentration. The most important exception to this generalization is industry 351 (generators, motors, and engines), whose coefficient and significance level drop sharply when C_4 and C_4^2 are included.

In columns 1 and 2 the right-hand-side variables were weighted by sales over total assets to adjust for the use of profits over assets as dependent variable, rather than profits to sales, as the theory requires.

Table 4.3. *Determinants of profitability, industries with significantly different projected profitability* ($n = 551$)

Industry SIC codes	Industry names	Right-hand-side weighted by S/K		Right-hand-side unweighted	
		(1)	(2)	(3)	(4)
202	Dairy products			−.179 (1.42)	−.152 (1.23)
203	Canned and frozen fruits, vegetables	.184 (3.06)	.168 (2.83)	.396 (3.33)	.347 (2.94)
204	Flour and cereals	.156 (2.04)	.181 (2.43)	.239 (1.81)	.263 (2.04)
206	Sugar and confectionery products	.184 (3.34)	.138 (2.52)	.292 (3.78)	.150 (1.92)
208	Beer and distilled spirits			−.250 (1.81)	−.192 (1.43)
212	Cigars	−.267 (1.17)			
214	Tobacco	3.19 (2.65)	2.34 (2.00)	2.92 (2.79)	1.67 (1.62)
235	Millinery, hats	1098 (3.46)	1218 (3.93)	2518 (3.40)	2711 (3.76)
251	Furniture, wood and metal, mattresses	.208 (1.81)	.235 (2.09)	.363 (1.86)	.429 (2.24)
254	Wood and metal partitions	−2.28 (1.41)	−2.15 (1.36)	−2.43 (1.32)	−2.49 (1.39)
261	Wood pulp	1.59 (1.56)	1.76 (1.77)	1.76 (1.66)	2.00 (1.93)
262	Paper and newsprint	−.668 (2.77)	−.634 (2.69)	−.636 (2.43)	−.561 (2.17)
271	Newspapers	1.06 (1.28)	1.12 (1.38)	1.35 (1.29)	1.39 (1.36)
275	Commercial printing, magazines	.392 (2.61)	.398 (2.70)	.505 (2.88)	.546 (3.10)
278	Bookbinding				−2.03 (1.37)
279	Photoengraving, electrotyping, typesetting	−8.45 (1.69)	−7.66 (1.57)	−12.4 (1.75)	−12.7 (1.83)
281	Inorganic chemicals	−.314 (1.25)			

283	Pharmaceuticals	1.27 (5.91)	1.32 (6.30)	1.40 (5.81)	1.48 (6.28)
284	Soaps, detergents, polishes, toilet preparations	.482 (4.81)	.471 (4.80)	.688 (4.27)	.668 (4.26)
307	Plastic products	.431 (2.40)	.420 (2.35)	.623 (2.52)	.691 (2.80)
313	Nonrubber shoes and boots	8.37 (4.68)	9.08 (5.16)	14.7 (4.37)	15.8 (4.75)
323	Mirrors and other products made from purchased glass	3.87 (2.14)	3.89 (2.21)	3.00 (1.23)	
324	Hydraulic cement	-.937 (2.69)	-1.02 (2.98)	-.722 (2.45)	-.871 (3.03)
331	Steel mill products	-.194 (2.46)	-.176 (2.18)	-.216 (2.33)	-.199 (2.17)
342	Cutlery, razors, hand tools	1.18 (3.70)	1.29 (4.13)	1.57 (3.76)	1.78 (4.38)
344	Fabricated structural metal products	-.218 (1.99)	-.245 (2.29)	-.411 (2.02)	-.460 (2.32)
349	Springs, valves, and pipe fittings	.375 (2.10)	.373 (2.13)	.522 (2.23)	.463 (2.02)
351	Turbine generators, gasoline and diesel engines	.546 (3.41)	.230 (1.37)	.759 (2.90)	
354	Machine tools	.656 (4.09)	.720 (4.59)	.788 (4.23)	.884 (4.86)
358	Laundry and refrigeration equipment	.359 (3.45)	.324 (3.16)	.572 (3.30)	.550 (3.28)
362	Motors and generators, electrical equipment	.569 (2.41)	.581 (2.49)	.804 (2.49)	.753 (2.37)
364	Electric lamps, light fixtures, and lighting equipment		.264 (1.34)		.348 (1.32)
374	Locomotives and railroad equipment	-.451 (1.89)	-.387 (1.66)	-.527 (2.24)	-.414 (1.80)
381	Engineering and scientific instruments	-1.59 (1.62)	-1.53 (1.59)	-1.53 (1.45)	-1.41 (1.37)
384	Surgical and medical instruments	-.905 (1.35)	-.912 (1.40)	-1.04 (1.35)	-.983 (1.32)
386	Photographic and photocopying equipment	.825 (3.83)	.714 (3.37)	1.12 (4.75)	.865 (3.71)
	Others	.071 (5.10)	.113 (1.74)	-.106 (4.89)	.097 (0.74)
	C_4		-1.17 (3.97)		-1.45 (2.70)
	C_4^2		1.52 (4.73)		2.07 (3.81)
	R^2	.286	.322	.291	.330

Columns 3 and 4 report results following the same steps used to obtain columns 1 and 2, but without weighting the right-hand-side variables by S/K. The results are quite similar, with the second set exhibiting slightly higher $\bar{R}^2$s, as was true consistently for the earlier steps in obtaining the final list of industries. More or less the same industries appear with coefficients implying similar differences from other industries. The same industries appear as outliers. Introducing concentration results in an analogous overall U-shaped relationship between concentration and profitability. In addition to a sizable drop in the coefficient and significance of the intercept on industry 351 following the introduction of concentration, the tobacco industry 214 exhibits a decline in significance that is even more pronounced than when S/K is used to weight the variables on the right-hand side.

3.   *Summary of industry model results*

The attempt to estimate an industry model in which firm profits are a function solely of the two industry characteristics, demand elasticity and concentration, has been a mixed success. Imposing an externally estimated elasticity of demand provided generally somewhat weaker statistical fit than assuming all demand elasticities equal one. The multinomial used to approximate the concentration–profit relationship suffered from multicollinearity to the extent that the interpretation of this relationship was sensitive to the number of terms in the polynomial included in the equation. The most reliable estimates appeared to be for the quadratic and cubic specifications. Both indicated a declining portion of the profit–concentration curve over some range of concentration values. Both implied a positive relationship over the higher concentration values.

Trying to estimate the demand elasticities and the parameters in a collusion function from our data on firm sales by industry proved infeasible. But estimating separate intercepts for each industry participation vector did reveal significant differences in profitability across industries. Knowing the fraction of each firm's sales in all three-digit industries enabled us to explain 29 percent of the variation in profitability across firms. Unfortunately, it did not appear possible to determine whether it was demand elasticity, entry and exit conditions, concentration, or the degree of cooperation that accounted for these differences in projected profitability. Some light will be shed on this issue by the results on the firm-approach model.

E.   Empirical estimates: firm approach

Consider again equation (4.23), which we derived to explain a firm's profitability in the presence of product differentiation:

$$\frac{\Pi_i}{S_i} = \frac{1}{\eta}\left(\frac{m_i}{\sigma} - \theta m_i + \theta\right).$$

Let us approximate the degree of cooperation by the quadratic function

$$\theta = a + bC_4 + cC_4^2. \tag{4.31}$$

We now need an approximation for σ, the degree of substitutability among products. One variable frequently associated with product differentiation is advertising. Advertising is both cause and effect of product differentiation. Advertising is profitable only in industries in which some potentially perceivable differences in products exist, and advertising can enhance individual perceptions of the differences in products. We treat the level of advertising as a percentage of industry sales as one index of the extent of product differentiation across industries.

Although advertising is a reasonable index of differentiation for consumer products, it serves less well for producer's goods. Intuitively, one would like some measure of technical complexity or sophistication. There is more scope to differentiate computers than shovels. Although inventive activity is not a perfect index of this dimension of product differentiation, we employ it along with advertising.

The degree of substitutability among products ranges from 0 to 1 and is assumed to vary inversely with product differentiation. If we assume that the effects of advertising and inventive activity are additive, a particularly simple functional form that captures this dimensionality property of σ is

$$\sigma = \frac{d}{d + eA + fRD}. \tag{4.32}$$

When both advertising (A) and inventive activity (RD) are zero, $\sigma = 1$, and the sellers' products within the industry are presumed to be perfect substitutes. As advertising and inventive activity increase, σ falls toward 0.

Substituting from (4.31) and (4.32) into (4.23), one obtains

$$\frac{\Pi_i}{S_i} = \frac{1}{\eta}\left(a + (1-a)\,m_i + b\,(1-m_i)C_4 \right.$$
$$\left. + c(1-m_i)C_4^2 + \frac{e}{d}Am_i + \frac{f}{d}RDm_i\right). \tag{4.33}$$

Equation (4.33) was estimated using projected market shares for each firm calculated in the same way that projected concentration ratios were calculated earlier in this chapter. A weighted-average ratio of industry advertising to sales was calculated for each company using its sales in each industry as weights and Internal Revenue Service three-digit industry advertising figures for 1963 (a point in time chosen because it lies roughly in the middle of the time period and in neither a boom nor a recession year). Two indexes of inventive activity were employed. National Science Foundation (NSF) figures for patents to sales by industry are available for as far back as 1967 and are at the three-digit level for technologically progressive industries. NSF research and development (R&D) expenditures are available for as far back as the mid-fifties (see NSF 1977), but are more aggregated.[5] We tried employing both the 1963 expenditure figures and 1967 patent numbers. Weighted averages for each firm were calculated as with advertising.

Table 4.4 presents results for which all η are assumed to equal one, and the dependent variable, $\hat{\alpha}$, is measured as a return on assets. The model was also estimated weighting all right-hand-side variables by the reciprocal of the Intriligator-elasticities, and by the sales-assets ratio for each firm. Both sets of estimates provided a worse fit, which was quite pronounced when the $1/\eta$s were used, and neither set of results is reported here.

The first equation assumes a linear relationship between concentration and the collusion parameter, θ, and includes only advertising as an index of product differentiation. All coefficients are statistically significant except for the intercept, but the sign on the concentration variable implies that cooperation *declines* with increasing concentration. Both the market share variable and the market share–advertising interaction term have the predicted positive signs.

Equation (2) in Table 4.4 introduces the quadratic term in concentration. It takes on a negative sign and the linear term becomes positive but insignificant. Multicollinearity between the two concentration variables is apparent. The two coefficients on the concentration variable imply rising cooperation to a C_4 of .24 and then falling cooperation. Both market share and the market share–advertising term remain highly significant and of the predicted sign.

Equation (3) drops the linear concentration term, leaving in $(1 - m_i)C_4^2$. The explanatory power of equation (3) is identical to that of (2), and the implication is clearly that cooperation falls, and at an increasing rate, as concentration increases.

Table 4.4. *Firm-model results with* $\eta = 1$ *for all firms, right-hand-side variables not weighted by* S/K, α_i *as dependent variable*

$(n = 551)$

Equation	Int	m_i	$(1-m_i)C_4$	$(1-m_i)C_4^2$	m_iA	$m_i Pat$	$m_i.RD$	$\bar{R}^2$
(1)	.052	.568	−.491		.612			.249
	.95	2.52	3.66		8.11			
(2)	−.180	.859	.632	−1.291	.652			.252
	1.28	3.09	.99	1.79	8.30			
(3)	−.045	.707		−.596	.632			.252
	1.47	3.06		3.97	8.34			
(4)	.062	−.242	−.490		.719	1.48		.275
	1.15	.86	3.73		9.26	4.60		
(5)	−.081	−.032	.199	−.792	.739	1.43		.276
	.58	.09	.31	1.10	9.26	4.36		
(6)	−.039	−.088		−.573	.734	1.44		.277
	1.29	.31		3.88	9.42	4.67		
(7)	−.040			−.583	.718	1.38		.278
	1.38			4.04	12.20	5.44		
(8)	.048	.618	−.435		.624		−.051	.248
	.87	2.23	3.61		7.91		.54	

Equations (4)–(7) add the market share–patent intensity variable. It takes on the predicted positive coefficient and is significant.

The signs and significance of all other variables in the equation remain about as before, except for the market share variable, which now is insignificant. The m_iPat interaction is the fourth, in equation (5) the fifth, variable in the equation containing market share. Something had to give and it was the market share term by itself. The hypothesis that the intercept term and m_i coefficient sum to 1, in contrast to equations (1)–(3), is now rejected.[6] Whether this is because the model is wrong or because multicollinearity exists cannot be determined.[7] Equation (7), dropping market share, including m_iPat and including only the C_4^2 term, provides the best fit to the data of the eight equations in Table 4.4. Equation (8) adds the market share–industry R&D expenditure term in place of m_iPat. It does not have a statistically significant impact on projected profits. Since R&D expenditures and patent activity are highly correlated at the firm level (see Mueller 1966; Comanor and Scherer 1969) and both proxy the

same phenomenon, inventive activity, we attribute the weak performance of the R&D industry expenditure index to the more aggregated
nature of these data in contrast to the NSF patent intensity data.

Returning to equation (4.23) and ignoring demand elasticity, we
see that the determinants of profitability in the firm model consist of
two components: the one, m_i/σ, is related to the extent of product
differentiation, the other, $(1 - m_i)\theta$, to the degree of cooperation.
Product differentiation leads to the introduction of market share and
market share–advertising and market share–inventive activity interaction terms. Collusion introduces the intercept and the concentration–$(1 - m_i)$ interaction term. The collusion term implies that the
coefficient on market share equals one minus the intercept. Since the
intercepts in equations (1–3) are all insignificantly different from zero,
the large, positive, and significant coefficient on market share, entered
as a separate variable in these equations, must be attributed to the
product differentiation part of the story. When market share loses its
significance, it does so because another index of product differentiation is included, market share–patent intensity.

The collusion-related terms make a significant contribution to explaining profitability, but the impact of concentration on firm rivalry
is of the opposite sign from that assumed in most structure-performance discussions. That concentration might have a negative impact
on profitability was already suggested by the results for the industry
model discussed earlier in this chapter. The firm model suggests
strongly that, given a firm's market share, increasing industry concentration increases rivalry lowering profits.

Market share has a positive, marginal impact on profitability in every
term in Table 4.4 having a t-value greater than 1.0. Equation (7), the
equation providing the best fit to the data, implies that, when the
interaction variables are evaluated at their means, an increase in market share of 10 percentage points results in an increase in the long-
run projected return on capital of 20 percent of the sample mean.
(Recall that the dependent variable is the projected relative difference
between a company's returns on total assets and the sample mean.)

F.   Conclusions

The basic assumption of the industry approach model is that all firms
within an industry face identical demand and cost conditions. In the
long run, all firms should choose to be sufficiently large so that average
costs are minimized. If all firms are of the same size, $1/N = H$, the

Herfindahl index, and the basic industry approach equation (4.8) becomes

$$\frac{\Pi_i}{S_i} = \frac{1}{\eta} (H - \theta H + \theta). \tag{4.34}$$

This equation may be contrasted with its firm-approach analogue (4.19),

$$\frac{\Pi_i}{S_i} = \frac{1}{\eta} \left(\frac{m_i}{\sigma} - \theta m_i + \theta \right).$$

The firm approach replaces the industry characteristic H or $1/N$ with the firm's market share and adds industry product differentiation to the equation. If all firms are of the same size and the industry has a homogeneous product, $m_i = H$ and $\sigma = 1$. The firm approach then collapses into the industry approach. One way to judge the relative merits of the firm approach over the industry approach is to see whether firm market shares in conjunction with industry product differentiation add a significant amount of explanatory power to the basic industry-approach model. By this criterion, the firm-approach model wins hands down, as comparisons of Table 4.4 with Tables 4.1 and 4.2 quickly reveal. An F-test of whether relaxing the restriction that $\sigma = 1$ and $m_i = H$ results in a significant reduction in the sum of the unexplained residuals yields an F-statistic of 68.9, safely above the .05 level of critical value.

As an alternative way of allowing for industry-specific determinants of firm-level profits, we conducted an analysis of variance. Some 30 separate three-digit industry definitions proved to be important in explaining long-run differences in company profitability. Roughly 30 percent of the variance in long-run projected returns was explained by the industry participation vectors. Still on the basis of Occam's razor, the firm-approach model is probably to be preferred. The firm model explains some 28 percent of the profitability differences across firms with but four variables (three terms) in the equation.

Nevertheless, three of the four variables in the firm model are industry characteristics, and thus one might reasonably argue that the firm model, as estimated, is in large part an industry model. It must be stressed, however, that the advertising and patent intensity variables play a different role in the firm-approach model than is usually claimed for them in studies in which industry profits are the dependent variable. Typically, advertising in an industry profits equation is taken to be a barrier to entry (Comanor and Wilson 1967, 1974;

Porter 1974). By analogy, a similar role could be attributed to patent intensity (e.g., as in Grabowski and Mueller 1978). Something is inherently wrong with this interpretation, however. A variable's coefficient in a regression equation is usually taken to be an estimate of a partial derivative; that is, in the equation $Y = a + bX$, b is an estimate of the change in Y to be expected from a unit change in X. If X is industry advertising intensity, and Y industry profits, b measures the change in industry profits resulting from an increase in industry advertising. But since industry profits are defined net of advertising, a positive, linear relationship between advertising intensity and profitability under the barriers-to-entry hypothesis must imply that companies in all industries are underinvesting in advertising. Low advertising intensity industries would increase their profitability by advertising more and thereby raising the height of entry barriers. Presumably, even advertising-intensive industries might find it profitable to further heighten entry barriers by increasing advertising.

A more plausible assumption to make about the level of industry advertising is that it is at the optimal level for maximizing profits for each industry. Thus, *any* change in a given industry's advertising from the present level would *lower* its profits. Of course, oligopolistic coordination problems may prevent the firms in an industry from achieving the joint profit maximum advertising level, but if anything, these coordination problems probably lead firms to undertake too much advertising rather than too little, as implied by the entry-barriers interpretation. (For evidence with respect to advertising, see Grabowski and Mueller 1971; and Netter 1982. With respect to R&D, see Grabowski and Baxter 1973; Grabowski and Mueller 1978.) The easiest assumption to defend is, perhaps, that each industry's advertising or inventive activity level is at its optimum, plus or minus some random error with mean zero.

The latter interpretation is compatible with our use of industry advertising and patent intensity in the firm-approach model. Industry advertising and patent intensity capture the degree of product differentiation in the industry. That the cereals industry spends more on advertising than does the vegetable oils industry tells us something about the potential for product differentiation in cereals and vegetable oils. But vegetable oil manufacturers cannot simply advertise more and increase the degree of product differentiation to that of the cereal industry.

In this context, it is important to recall that industry advertising and patent intensity appear in the firm-approach model as interaction variables with firm-market share. It is the combination of the potential for product differentiation, as measured by industry advertising and patent intensity, along with high market share, which indicates success at differentiating one's product, that explains above-normal long-run profits. Thus, the strong performance of these two interaction terms (m_iPat and m_iA) reinforces the interpretation that the firm-specific product characteristics and cost advantages of the firm-approach model explain long-run profitability differences.

Both the firm-approach model and the industry models should include the industry demand elasticity as a multiplicative factor. But in the absence of good external estimates of industry price elasticities of demand, it is impossible to estimate the full firm model as specified in equation (4.23). Since industry demand elasticities appear in both the industry and the firm models, proxying these elasticities by industry intercept dummies does not help us sort out whether the assumptions underlying the firm or the industry model are more appropriate. Moreover, given the important role that product differentiation plays in the firm model, it is impossible to determine whether a separate industry slope or intercept is significant because it is capturing a significant difference in demand elasticities across industries, or a significant degree of product differentiation within the industry. We must base any claim we make that differences in product quality or efficiency across firms within an industry play an important role in explaining profitability differences across firms on the strong performance of market share–advertising and market share–patent intensity in Table 4.4, and on the rather perverse performance of concentration in all of the equations estimated throughout the chapter.

The present study adds to a short but rapidly growing set of studies that has found a negative relationship between profitability and concentration (e.g., Shepherd 1972, 1975; Gale and Branch 1982; Kwoka and Ravenscraft 1982; Ravenscraft 1983). They reinforce the importance of these findings in that they are not drawn from cross-sectional analysis of annual data, but are based on cross-sectional analysis using long-run projections of both profit rates and the key market structure variables. The profit data also do not include the post–oil crisis period, so that the results are not dependent on some unusual consequences of the seventies on accounting profit data or on the long-run structure-performance relationship across industries. Rather, the projections are based on a span of time, 1950–72, that, in retrospect, certainly appears to capture capitalism at its best. Finally, it should be noted that the negative relationship between profitability and concentration is not due to some collinearity between market share and concentration that forces the coefficient on the latter to be negative when market share is included in the equation. The results for the industry-approach model also imply a largely negative impact of increasing concentration on projected profitability. Adding market share to the equation tends only to strengthen this interpretation.

Concentration appears in both the industry- and firm-approach models as a determinant of the degree of cooperation. Its negative impact on profitability in both models implies that cooperation declines as concentration increases. The greater the concentration in an industry, the greater the rivalry. Given the positive impact of the advertising– and patent intensity–market share interaction terms, it is natural to interpret the result that concentration leads to rivalry as implying that *nonprice* rivalry is encouraged by rising concentration. But a modeling of this conjecture would require industry data and an industry approach to nonprice competition and is beyond the scope of the present study.

CHAPTER 5

The results in perspective

The firm-approach model is extremely compact. With industry demand elasticity removed, it purports to explain the difference in long-run profitability across companies with but four variables: two measures of industry product differentiation, advertising and patent intensity, industry concentration, and the firm's market share. Many other variables have been proposed as possible causes of profit differences, and the typical structure-performance model today is a multiequation endeavor with sometimes a score or more of exogenous variables. The next three chapters add a variety of possible explanatory variables to the basic firm-approach model. The main results for this model will prove to be remarkably robust with respect to the addition of other explanatory variables, although some new variables will add significant explanatory power to the equation. Thus, the main novelty of this study, vis-à-vis the structure-performance literature, is already contained in the previous chapter. With this fact in mind, we shall pause in this chapter, before launching into more algebra and econometrics, to consider the results so far obtained, and place them into the context of the existing structure-performance literature.

A major finding of this study is that persistent differences in profitability across companies exist and that these differences are to be explained by a combination of firm- and industry-specific factors. Firms with products that are perceived to have higher quality or those with lower costs have higher profits and market shares and these quality-efficiency advantages become more important as the industry's product structure and technology become more differentiated. In the following section, we illustrate the nature of these results with the profit profiles of several companies. It must be stressed that these firms have been selected because they fit the pattern of the aggregate econometric evidence and are not purported to be randomly selected case studies offering independent evidence in support of the hypothesis. In Section B, we relate our results to other work in the structure-performance literature. In Section C, we begin to consider whether the observed results are an artifact of the use of accounting profits data.

85

Table 5.1. *Concentration ratios in cereals*

Year	C_4
1947	79
1958	83
1967	88
1972	90
1977	89

Source: U.S. Bureau of the Census, as reported in Scherer (1982, p. 195).

A. The profit profiles of selected companies

1. Bakeries, cereals, and cookies and crackers

These three industries have many characteristics in common. They are relatively mature industries, of which the ready-to-eat (RTE) segment of the cereal industry is perhaps the youngest of the group (it has been in existence some 80 years).

The products of each stand high on every American household's shopping list. All are made from processed grains plus various other ingredients using technologies that are relatively simple and widely known. Some methods for transforming grains into the particular forms found in packaged cereals are perhaps the most complicated, but, for the most part, these date back more than 75 years (Scherer 1982, p. 192). Indeed, the similarities are such that several producers appear (or have at one time appeared) in more than one of the industries, and Nabisco (formerly National Biscuit) appears in all three.

But there are also important differences. Cereals and cookies and crackers are much more concentrated than bakery products and more susceptible to product differentiation. These differences allow us to examine differences in industry and firm characteristics and their relationship to profitability at closer range. We begin with cereals.

a. Cereals: The cereals industry, which includes hot and baby cereals as well as RTEs, is one of the most highly concentrated in all manufacturing (see Table 5.1). Thus, it is a prime candidate for collusive pricing under the hypothesis that high concentration fosters cooperation and the industry appears to be characterized by both dominant-firm (Kellogg) price leadership and considerable restraint on the part of the leading companies in pursuing price competition (Scherer 1982, pp. 201–7; Headen and McKie 1966). Figure 5.1 presents the net-of-tax return on profits profiles for five of the six leading cereals producers for the years in our sample period. Several commonalities can be observed. All five companies experience local peaks in profitability in 1954, 1958, and 1970–71, and four of the five enjoy profit peaks in 1961. In part, this common pattern may indicate the more stable sales and profit histories that cereal companies enjoy over the business cycle. Recall that our profit figures are deviations from the full sample mean divided by the sample mean. Thus, in years of low overall profits in manufacturing, companies whose profits do not vary much with business conditions appear relatively profitable. But the pattern is also what one expects of a cartel that stabilizes prices with imperfect success over time. It is interesting to note that the period between the two profit peaks in 1954 and 1958 was one of intense competition among cereal producers using in-pack premiums, a form of rivalry that suddenly came to an end in the summer of 1957 (Scherer 1982, p. 206).

The similarities in profit profiles across companies are revealing, but even more striking perhaps are the differences. Kellogg's profit performance stands apart, averaging more than double that of all manufacturing firms over the entire 23-year period. Kellogg's profits reached their lowest relative value in 1951 when they fell to but 61 percent more than the mean for all companies. Only General Foods profits reached a height in any year greater than Kellogg's profits in its worst year. The numbers used to construct Figure 5.1 are based on the total profits and assets of the companies and not just their earnings and assets in cereals. Thus, caution must be used in interpreting them. The most meaningful comparison is between Kellogg, which had 84 percent of its 1950 sales in cereals, and Quaker Oats, which had 30 percent. Although both companies earn more than the average return for all companies in the 600-firm sample, Kellogg's profit rates are more than double Quaker Oats' returns. General Mills, General Foods, and Ralston Purina had 9.1, 7.8, and 4.2 percent of their 1950 sales in cereals, respectively. The 1970 *Moody's Industrial Manual* reports that 34.7 percent of General Mills' sales are in cereals and snack foods of which cereals would seem to account for over half. Thus, the figures in Figure 5.1 may be more representative of General Mills' performance than the 9.1 percent figure for 1950 suggests.

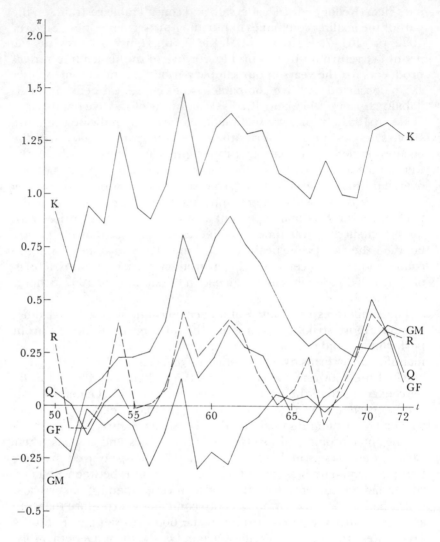

Figure 5.1 Profits profiles of five leading cereal producers, 1950–72.
Key: K = Kellogg, R = Ralston Purina, GM = General Mills, Q =
Quaker Oats, GF = General Foods.

Scherer presents the following average after-tax accounting returns
for the five companies for the period 1958–70; they are based on
evidence collected in the FTC's (1982, p. 211) suit against the cereal
manufacturers.

Kellogg	18.9
General Mills	29.5
General Foods	15.1
Quaker Oats	9.0
Ralston Purina	20.5

Although the Kellogg figure is slightly more than double Quaker's profitability, as in our data, the returns to capital for the other three firms are much higher and more comparable to Kellogg's. It is tempting to conclude from these data that it is presence in the industry that leads to high profits via collusion protected by entry barriers. But if high profitability is industry related, why are Quaker's returns only 43 percent of those of the other four? Nabisco's returns also appear to have been "well below the industry average" (Scherer 1982, p. 211, n. 46). Thus, two of the six leading cereal firms did not participate in the high returns that collusion and entry barriers are presumed to have conferred, and, within the four high-profit companies, General Mills' returns are almost double those of General Foods. It is possible to look at the returns on assets of the individual cereal companies and infer that differences across companies are large and must, presumably, be related to some individual company differences. Our empirical work in the previous chapter suggests that these differences should be related to individual company market shares.

Table 5.2 presents market share data for the six leading cereal producers at various points in time. The three companies with the highest market shares in 1969–70 are among the four with profits substantially above the norm. The fourth and fifth leading firms with market shares at (Quaker) and below (Nabisco) the average for all firms have much lower returns. The major outlier in this pattern is Ralston Purina. Its market share appears to lie between 3 and 4 percent over two decades and yet it earns, according to the figures in the FTC case, more than double the average return on capital. The changes in market shares that occurred over the two decades are also consistent with the impression one gets about the differences in firm characteristics by looking at the profits rate data for individual firms. The big loser in market share was Quaker with a decline between 1950 and 1963 of 15 percentage points, of which 4 were recouped by 1970. The two big gainers are Kellogg and General Mills. The 50 percent increase in the General Mills market share between 1950 and 1970 is consistent with its industry-leading 29 percent return on capital. Figure 5.1 indicates an upward trend in returns for Kellogg from 1950 to 1972 that is consistent with its near doubling of market share. The

Table 5.2. *Cereal producers' market shares*

Company	1950	1963	1964	1965	1966	1967	1968	1969	1970
Kellogg	24.4	43.5	43.5	41.0	41.0	42.5	43.0	43.5	47
General Mills	13.9	20.5	21.0	22.0	22.5	22.5	21.5	21.0	21
General Foods	15.3	21.0	19.0	18.5	18.0	17.5	17.5	17.0	15
Quaker Oats	19.1	4.0	5.0	7.0	7.0	7.0	7.5	8.0	8
National Biscuit	3.9	4.5	5.0	5.0	4.5	4.5	4.5	4.25	4
Ralston Purina	4.2	3.5	3.0	3.5	3.5	3.0	3.0	3.25	n.a.

n.a. Not available.

Sources: 1950 figures are 1950 sales from FTC (1972a) divided by the 1950 sales from the Census of Manufacturing; 1963–69 figures are from Nelson (1966, p. 19 ff. and 1970, p. 32 ff.); 1970 figures are from Scherer (1982, p. 195).

difference between its return on capital and the sample average increased by two-thirds between the 1950–52 period and 1970–72, while its market share in cereals nearly doubled.

Still, one might wonder how it is that General Mills can earn a 50 percent greater return on capital with less than half the market share of Kellogg, and that Ralston can earn roughly the same return with less than one-tenth of Kellogg's market share. One possible explanation is that the figures for returns on capital for just the cereal business are inflated for companies like Ralston, General Mills, and General Foods, which have less than 10 percent of their sales in cereals. The possibility that these companies would underallocate overhead expenses to cereals and thus overestimate their profits in this area seems greater than for Kellogg, with over 80 percent of its sales in cereals, or even Quaker, with 30 percent in cereals. In any event, the figures reported here seem to underline in part the importance of differences across firms in profitability within a well-defined industry, and of the translation of a substantial fraction of these product characteristic–efficiency advantages into market share differences.

A key explanatory variable in the firm-approach model is the interaction term between market share and advertising. Scherer (1982, p. 208) quotes advertising-to-sales ratios for the industry of 18.5 and 10.9, which make cereals one of the half dozen or so most advertising-intensive industries in manufacturing. Economists and the popular press alike often attribute the high profits of the industry to its heavy expenditures on advertising. For example, an article in *Forbes* (November 15, 1963, p. 35) claimed that Kellogg outspent General Foods with an advertising-to-sales ratio of 11.8 percent, as opposed to General Foods' 9.2 percent, and implied that it outspent the rest of the industry. But the reasoning must be partly fallacious. If General Foods could increase its advertising-to-sales ratio to equal Kellogg's and thereby raise its market share and return on capital, presumably it would. If advertising accounts for Kellogg's greater market share and return on capital, then the question is why is Kellogg's advertising more effective than General Foods' advertising, for this greater effectiveness must account for both its higher expenditures and greater market share. Indeed, the same article goes on to discuss Kellogg's cartoon characters and how effective they are in Kellogg's TV advertising.

Without question, it is product differentiation that accounts for the success of those cereal makers that do earn greater than normal returns in this industry. The most significant improvement in profitability for the five companies depicted in Figure 5.1 is for General

Mills. The upward movement accompanies a management change at General Mills that led to increased emphasis "on branded, packaged goods" (*Forbes*, October 1, 1963, p. 22). We have already noted that cereals appear to have become a larger fraction of General Mills' dollar sales than in 1950. But advertising is as much a symptom as a cause of high product differentiation, and companies do appear to differ in their abilities to profit from the potential that high product differentiation offers, as the figures in Figure 5.1 or those quoted above from the FTC cereals case imply.

b. Cookies and crackers: Although less differentiated than cereals, cookies and crackers are nevertheless a product characterized by above-average product differentiation. The advertising-to-sales ratio for the three-digit industry 205 that includes bread and other bakery products as well as cookies and crackers was 0.02, according to IRS data. Since bakery products undoubtedly have lower advertising outlays than cookies and crackers, the advertising-to-sales ratio for the latter must certainly exceed 3 percent.

Figure 5.2 presents the profit profiles for three leading manufacturers of cookies and crackers. Consider, first, National and United. National Biscuit's profits never fell below the average for all firms, whereas United's rose above the average but once, in 1952, and then just barely. United Biscuit was the third leading firm in the industry in 1950 with a market share of 12.9 percent. National Biscuit was the leader in 1950 with a market share of 34.8 percent and is reported to have had 40 percent of the market in 1968, a share several times that of Sunshine and United, now renamed Keebler (see *Forbes*, November 15, 1968). Although "several" is a rather imprecise term, one suspects that both Keebler and Sunshine had lost some of the market share (12.9 and 15.6, respectively) they enjoyed in 1950.

United Biscuit's problems appear directly related to inadequate product differentiation. Formed out of the acquisition of several regional companies over the course of this century, United found itself after World War II with four different brands for the same products, each known only in a particular region of the country. It was thus not well situated for the shift to television advertising and national brands, which took place in this and many other food and beverage industries after World War II. The change in the company's name to Keebler symptomizes its efforts to establish a single-brand image. Figure 5.2 reveals that this effort met with limited success over the period under investigation. The product differentiation advantages that allowed National Biscuit to dominate the industry also allowed it

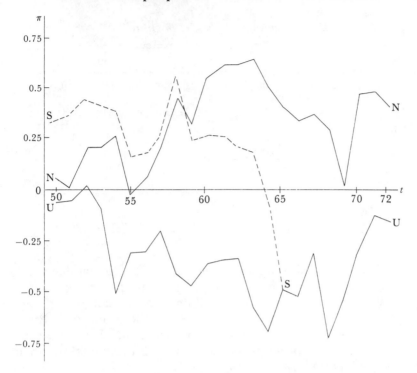

Figure 5.2 Profit profiles of three leading biscuit producers, 1950–72. Key: N = National Biscuit, U = United Biscuit, S = Sunshine Biscuit.

to earn a substantially higher return on capital. It should be noted that the profit rates depicted in Figure 5.2, although they are for the entire company, are fairly indicative of the return in the cookie and cracker business. Cookies and crackers accounted for 71.3 percent of National Biscuit's sales in 1950, 81.6 percent of United's, and 81.2 percent of Sunshine's. Although these percentages probably declined over time, the percentages undoubtedly remained well above 50 percent for all three firms through 1972.

Sunshine Biscuit's profit performance is interesting. It starts the period as the number two firm in the industry with a market share of 15.6 percent, double the average market share for all firms in our sample, but less than half of National Biscuit's market share. Its return on capital exceeds National's, however, and remains above it until 1959. Although the two profit profiles move apart after 1959, Sunshine's returns remain above the average until 1964, and even the

Table 5.3. *Market shares of bakery products*

Company	1950	1963
Continental Baking	5.8	10.0
General Baking	3.7	3.5
Ward Baking	3.1	2.8
Purity Baking	2.9	n.a.
Interstate Bakeries	2.1	3.4
American Bakeries	1.3	3.6
Gordon Baking	1.1	n.a.
National Biscuit	.8	n.a.

n.a. Not available
Source: For 1950, FTC (1972a) and *Census of Manufacturers*; for 1963,
Forbes (March 1, 1964, pp. 16–17).

steep plunge in 1965 brings Sunshine's return on capital down only
to that of United Biscuit. It is tempting to interpret the tail-off in
Sunshine's profits prior to its acquisition to poor management, and
to consider this profit decline the cause of the acquisition. But if
Sunshine's profit history implies bad management, what can one say
of United's, since its profit profile lies beneath Sunshine's throughout
the 1950–65 period?

Although National, Sunshine, and United Biscuit share the same
fairly concentrated industry, with high product differentiation, their
profit performances over the 1950–72 period are quite different.
National, the definite industry leader, has consistently above-average
profits; United, the number three firm at the start, has consistently
below-average profits. Sunshine starts out as number two with a profit
performance resembling that of National and winds up resembling
United just prior to being acquired by American Tobacco.

c. Bakery products: Bread and cakes are products for which brand
image has been less important than in the two previous industries.
Advertising is a smaller percentage of sales and one expects market
share to be a less important index of success. Indeed, market shares
tend to be much smaller here than in the other two industries (see
Table 5.3), although market shares and concentration ratios based on
national figures such as these are somewhat misleading owing to the
local geographic nature of the bakery market.

As with cereals, some industry similarities are evident in the profit
profiles of Figure 5.3. All companies experience profit peaks in 1967,

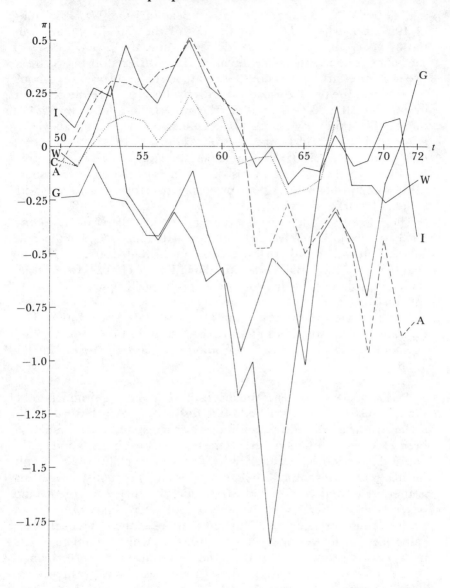

Figure 5.3 Profit profiles of five leading producers of baked goods, 1950–72. Key: I = Interstate Bakeries, W = Ward Baking, C = Continental, A = American Bakeries, G = General Baking.

and all but Ward Baking experience a peak in 1958, Ward's coming in 1957. But where the profit profiles of the cereal companies lie mostly above the zero, average deviation line, the profit profiles of the bakeries lie mostly below the line. These differences between the two industries are conspicuous, but so too are the differences among firms within the two industries. Ward's profits are above the zero line in only 3 of the 23 years, and are below -1 (i.e., the company lost money) five times. By contrast, Interstate's profits remain above average until 1962 and fall below a $-.25$ deviation from the average only in the final year of the sample period. The relatively good profit performance of Interstate is consistent with its increased market share (Table 5.3), just as Ward's poor profit performance is consistent with its loss of market share.

The biggest absolute increase in market share between 1950 and 1963 was by industry leader Continental Baking. Its profit profile follows Interstate's rather closely right up through 1967, the last full year before Continental was acquired by ITT. It is hard – from either the market share growth figure or its profit performance relative to the rest of the industry – to conclude Continental was poorly managed and that managerial inefficiency led to Continental's acquisition. This inference is consistent with ITT's decision to leave Continental's management in charge after the acquisition (*Wall Street Journal*, May 20, 1968).

d. Summary: Despite basic similarities in the types of products sold, these industries have exhibited quite distinctive profit histories. The *average* returns earned in each industry correspond to the rankings in product differentiation; cereals the highest, next biscuits and crackers, and bakery products the lowest. But some cereal firms earn only normal returns for most of the sample period. Particularly interesting is the biscuit and cracker industry, which lies between cereals and bakeries in both advertising intensity and profitability. The profit profile of industry-leading National Biscuit resembles that of the cereal producers in level, and number three firm United could be placed in the bakery products industry on the basis of its profit performance. Above-normal profitability in these industries comes with product differentiation *and* market share.

2.   *Fruit and vegetable canners*

The importance of product differentiation is further illustrated by the profit profiles of five firms that process fruits and vegetables and package them in cans or jars. Two of these companies concentrate their processing activities on specialized products for which they are the dominant firms in their market. In 1950, Campbell Soup had 76.9 percent of the five-digit canned soups and poultry products industry, and Gerber Products had 40 percent of the canned baby foods market (SIC 20336). In 1968, Campbell had 84 percent of the canned soup market down from 89 or 90 percent in 1965 (*Printers' Ink*, September 1968, p. 34, and November 25, 1966, p. 9), and Gerber was reported to have 55 percent of the U.S. baby food market in 1970 (*Financial World*, July 15, 1970).

Although Del Monte (formerly named California Packing), Stokely-Van Camp, and Libby, McNeill and Libby were leading packers of fruits and vegetables throughout the fifties and sixties, they did not dominate their markets the way Campbell and Gerber did. The two most important markets for all three in 1950 were canned fruits (20331) and canned vegetables (20332). Del Monte was the leading fruit canner with 11.6 percent of the market in 1950, Libby was second with a 7.6 percent market share, and Stokely was fourth with 2.7 percent. In canned vegetables, Stokely was the leader with 8.0 percent of the market.

The profit profiles of the five companies are presented in Figure 5.4. The two firms that dominate their respective markets consistently earn profits substantially above the norm; Campbell Soup's profits range mostly from 25 to 75 percent more than the average firm's profit rate, and Gerber's profits fall mostly in the 50 to 100 percent higher range. The other three companies' profits are persistently below the mean. The advantage of dominating a differentiated product's market is clearly illustrated by the differences in profitability for these five companies.

Of course, the markets in which Campbell and Gerber sell are not exactly the same as the markets in which Del Monte, Stokely, and Libby have their sales concentrated. Thus, one might be tempted to argue that it is the markets that make the firm, rather than the firm the market. But the vegetables and fruits that go into Gerber's baby foods are obviously not different from those Stokely, Del Monte, and Libby put into cans, nor would the technology of straining them for consumption by babies seem to be beyond the reach of large experienced food processing corporations. One presumes that soup and baby food have become products with greater product differentiation, products that in America are identified by the names Campbell and Gerber, because these companies have succeeded in stamping their brand image into the minds of consumers.

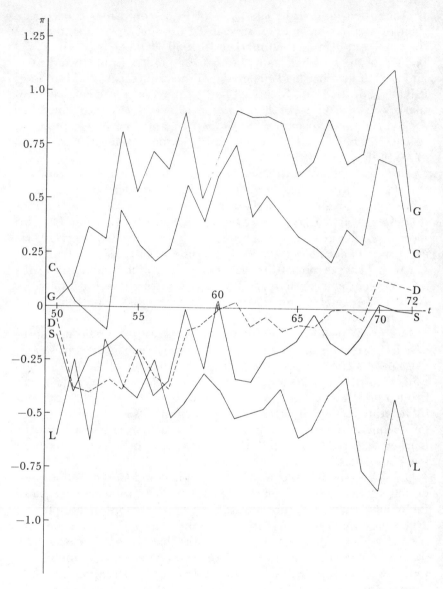

Figure 5.4 Profit profiles of five vegetable and fruit packers, 1950–72. Key: G = Gerber Products, C = Campbell Soup, D = Del Monte (California Packing), S = Stokely–Van Camp, L = Libby, McNeill & Libby.

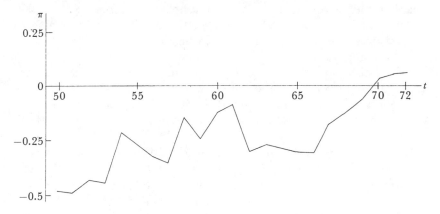

Figure 5.5 Profit profile of H. J. Heinz, 1950–72.

That mere presence in these industries does not lead to above-normal profits is demonstrated by the profit record of H. J. Heinz. Heinz was second to Campbell in soups in 1950 with a market share of 5.5 percent and third to Gerber in baby foods with a 12.4 percent share of the market. Heinz had a steady 5 percent of the wet soup market throughout the 1960s (*Printers' Ink*, September 1968, p. 34, and November 25, 1966, p. 9), and was still third to Gerber and Beech-Nut in baby foods in 1964 (*Forbes*, April 1, 1964, p. 32). Heinz's other major product in 1950 was catsup, in which it was the market leader with a 13.8 percent share, slightly more than Hunt Foods and Del Monte. Heinz remained the leader in catsup in 1967 with a reported 24 percent of the market, where Hunt Foods had 23 percent, and Del Monte was still third (*Business Week*, November 11, 1967, p. 148). Despite its presence in soups and baby foods and second and third ranking, and its industry leadership in catsup in 1950, its profit rate remained below average from 1950 until 1970 (see Figure 5.5), and reached a 23-year peak in 1972 of 0.09 above the norm, which was only slightly more than Del Monte's profit rate in 1972 (see Figure 5.4).[1]

In addition to illustrating the importance of market share, these markets illustrate the subtlety of the product differentiation concept. *Printers' Ink* (November 25, 1966, p. 10) reported Campbell's total advertising in frozen and condensed soups in 1965 as $19,364,000, compared with Heinz's $714,000. Thus, Campbell spent 27 times as much on advertising in 1965 to obtain its 18 times greater sales volume. The importance of advertising in establishing market share appears to be demonstrated. But Campbell Soup spent $2,251,000 advertising its dry soup label, Red Kettle, in 1965 and was able to capture only 8 percent of that market, whereas Lipton, with $3,608,000 in advertising, had 57 percent of the dry soup market.

Campbell's performance in dry soups indicates that whatever advantage it has over its competitors in wet soups (advertising, or product quality, or managerial acumen) is not easily transferred even to a market as close to the market it has dominated for so many years as dry soups are to wet ones.

Campbell entered the dry soup market in 1961 and spent considerably more than Lipton on advertising as a percentage of sales, Campbell achieved a 14 percent share of the market in 1963, which fell to 9 percent in 1964, and 8 percent in 1965 (*Printers' Ink*, November 25, 1966, p. 9). In 1966 Campbell withdrew from the dry soup business (*Printers' Ink*, September 1968, p. 31).

Rather than stemming from managerial talent, product quality, or other efficiency advantages, Campbell's continued dominance of the wet soup market, like Lipton's dominance of the dry soup market, may be evidence of the first mover advantages in establishing market position, which Schmalensee (1982) has recently discussed. Campbell, Lipton, Gerber, and Heinz in catsup have dominated their markets for about as long as these "markets" have existed. Their products are differentiated because consumers have come to associate the names of these companies with the products they sell.

The importance of product differentiation is further illustrated in the profit histories of the three general vegetable and fruit processors. Their profiles remain closely bunched in the early to midfifties, but Del Monte's and Stokely's gradually drift upward to the average profit rate. Libby's drifts away from it. A *Forbes* article (December 15, 1969, p. 43) analyzed the problem: "The source of Libby's long-term troubles was no mystery. Instead of moving into specialty products, as have Green Giant and Campbell Soup, Libby continued to concentrate on its traditional fruits and vegetables, which are seasonal, commodity-type products subject to both sharp price swings and intense competition." My only question concerning this assessment is whether Green Giant and Campbell Soup *moved into* specialty products or made their products special.

3.   *Furniture*

We now look briefly at a consumer product that is definitely less differentiated than most of the food products we have just discussed.

Although almost every American could name without hesitation the major products of Kellogg, Campbell, and Gerber, the names Bassett, Heywood-Wakefield, and Kroehler would be somewhat more difficult to associate with a given product. They share with the above discussed products the characteristic of being consumer products, but they are ones for which media advertising is a much less important source of information. Point of sale assistance by the retailers is much more important (Nelson 1970, 1971; Porter 1974). The advertising-to-sales ratio for household furniture is 0.0125.

Figure 5.6 depicts the profit histories of Bassett Furniture, Kroehler, and Heywood-Wakefield. All three companies had sales concentrated in the two-digit furniture industry (25) in 1972, according to the *Moody's Industrial Manual*, and some similarities in the patterns of profits can be detected. But the difference in the levels of profits between Bassett and the other two firms is quite sharp. Bassett had profits below the mean in but one year, 1950, and had projected long-run profits of roughly double the norm. Kroehler had above-normal profits in only four years, Heywood-Wakefield in none. Both companies had long-run projected profiles below the norm.

In 1950 Bassett had all of its sales concentrated in the four-digit home furniture industry 2511 with a market share of 1.2 percent, a hair ahead of Singer. According to the 1975 *Moody's* (p. 931), Bassett's sales remained concentrated in this industry in the early 1970s with as much as 90 percent sold to retail furniture dealers. If all of these sales were in the 2511 home furniture industry, Bassett would have had a 1972 market share in this industry of 5.7 percent. This nearly fivefold increase in the leading firm's market share is consistent with the profit performance depicted in Figure 5.6. Unfortunately, information is not publicly available to approximate the 1972 market shares of Kroehler and Heywood-Wakefield, although we do know from *Moody's* that they remained concentrated in the two-digit furniture industry. The data in Figure 5.5 suffice, however, to demonstrate that more information than just the industry of origin is necessary to predict the profitability of these companies.

B.   A comparison with other structure-performance studies

At the beginning of the seventies, Leonard Weiss (1971, 1974) put together a couple of surveys of the structure-performance literature in which he emphasized the consistent, positive correlation between profits and concentration that had been found in dozens of empirical studies in the fifties and sixties. At the time that Weiss was compiling

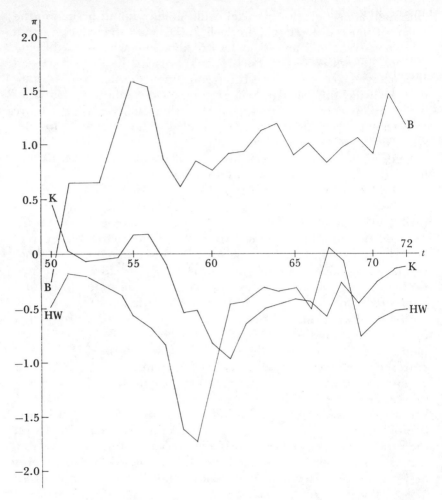

Figure 5.6 Profit profiles of three leading furniture manufacturers, 1950–72. Key: B = Bassett Furniture, K = Kroehler, HW = Heywood-Wakefield.

material for his surveys, the first papers began to appear contradicting the hypothesis that high profits and high industry concentration went hand in hand. Although Imel and Helmberger (1971) found profits and concentration to be positively correlated, they found market share to be more strongly related to profitability than concentration. Writing before the "new learning" challenge to industrial organization conventional wisdom had been launched, Imel and Helmberger did not offer any novel explanation for why market share performed so well, but the first outlines of what would prove to be a striking pattern were clearly discernible in this excellent paper.

The first forthright statement that it was firm market share and not industry concentration that should be the key variable in the profit equation with convincing evidence to support the claim was presented by W. Geoffrey Shepherd in 1972. Shepherd's arguments and results in this article and as subsequently elaborated upon in book form (1975) resemble those of the present study both with respect to the importance placed on firm market position over industry market structure, and the emphasis upon the permanence of market dominance by given firms in many industries. Shepherd places exclusive emphasis on the market power aspects of market share and the ability of a relatively large firm in a given market to raise price. Thus, although his results are consistent with the new learning thesis that efficiency leads to greater size, Shepherd does not hold out this hypothesis as even a possible interpretation to his results. This exception aside, his results and mine are quite consistent with one another.

Several subsequent studies have found that concentration has an insignificant or even negative and significant partial correlation with profitability when market share is present in the equation (Weiss and Pascoe 1981; Gale and Branch 1982; Ravenscraft 1983). Although the variable does maintain a positive and significant coefficient in Harris's (1983) study of consumer good industries, the t-value on market share in Harris's profit equations is much higher than for concentration.

Concentration has typically been found to be unrelated or negatively related to the market value–book value ratio, or the excess of market over book value (Lindenberg and Ross 1981, Hirschey 1982a, b, c; Harris 1984; but see also Thomadakis 1977; Schwinn 1983).

Finally, the strength of the positive concentration-profitability relationship even in the absence of market share does not appear to be sufficiently robust to withstand the recently developed econometric tests of model specification uncertainty (Connolly and Hirschey 1983; Bothwell, Cooley, and Hall 1984). The consensus view that concentration and profits are positively related, which Weiss accurately summarized in the early seventies, has in one decade been totally shattered.[2]

The results of the present study complement these findings in important ways. Whereas previous work has relied on profits defined for a single year or averaged over a few years, the present study uses 23 years of profit data to project long-run profits and rents. Outside of Shepherd's paper (1972), the studies that find that concentration loses its significance or reverses sign when market share is included in the equation use data drawn largely if not exclusively from the seventies (Weiss and Pascoe 1981; Gale and Branch 1982; Ravenscraft 1983; Harris 1984). The seventies was an unusual if not tumultuous decade for many firms and industries. One can legitimately question whether the kind of tacit coordination that is presumed to exist in highly concentrated industries could hold up in the face of price controls, the oil price increases starting in 1973, rapidly accelerating inflation, and the other economic instabilities of this period.

Our profit series ends in 1972, the year preceding the first major OPEC price increase. Our projected profit rates are dominated by observations for the fifties and sixties. Thus, although our results reflect the newly emerging conventional wisdom of the seventies, the data employed are the same as those that generated the structure-performance consensus of the sixties.

The right-hand-side variables of the firm-approach model will look familiar to any student of industrial organization, but our modeling of the firm's decision process packages them in a rather unusual form. Once market share standing alone is dropped from the equation, all variables appear in interaction terms. Interactions are not new to structure-performance models, although they are somewhat rare. Bradley Gale (1972) was perhaps the first to stress the importance of interaction effects between key structure-performance model variables. Gale hypothesized and found a stronger positive link between market share and profitability in highly concentrated industries than in industries of low or moderate concentration. Ravenscraft (1983), on the other hand, found that the market share–concentration term had a negative coefficient in his study using 1975 Line of Business data.

The firm-approach model employed here predicts a negative coefficient for the market share (m)–concentration (C_4) interaction term, *if* concentration's independent effect on profitability is positive.[3] The key term in the estimated equation is $cm(1 - C_4^2)$. If concentration increases collusion that leads to higher profits, $c > 0$ and mC_4^2 has a negative impact. Since $\hat{c}$ is in fact significantly less than zero, my results are actually similar to Gale's.

The other interaction terms in the firm-approach model involve market share and the indexes of product differentiation, advertising, and patent intensity. Ravenscraft (1983) included interaction terms between a firm's own advertising and R&D and market share. Both interaction terms picked up positive coefficients, but only that of the advertising term was statistically significant. Interesting also is market share's insignificant coefficient by itself in Ravenscraft's equations (1983,

Table 2, p. 27); once the market share–advertising and market share–R&D terms are added, the result is the same as the one we obtained. Thus, our results reconfirm some of Ravenscraft's, again for quite different variable definitions and data sets. Moreover, the firm-approach model gives a theoretical rationale for the inclusion of these interaction terms. Market share should be positively correlated with profitability only in those industries in which quality and cost differences are present. Advertising intensity and patent intensity serve as indicators of the potential for product quality and cost differences among firms within a given industry. Thus, one expects these characteristics of industries to be important determinants of firm profitability differences *in conjunction with* differences in market shares.

The results of the previous chapter indicate that both firm and industry characteristics are important in explaining profitability differences across firms. Schmalensee's (1985) recent testing of the relative importance of firm and industry characteristics suggests that industry characteristics dominate. We shall contrast our results and Schmalensee's in Chapter 10, after testing for the influence of other factors on firm profitability.

C.   The use of accounting rates of return

In Chapter 2 we noted the possibility that our measures of projected profitability were not reflecting differences in long-run economic rents, but merely persistent differences in accounting conventions across companies that systematically affect reported profits and assets figures. The results of Chapter 4 raise the further issue of whether specific firm or industry characteristics might be related to differences in accounting rates of return that were not reflective of differences in economic rates of return.

The use of accounting returns to measure profitability raises three issues: (1) the choice of total assets as a deflator rather than sales or equity, (2) the neglect of intangible assets in defining total assets, and (3) the difference between accounting and economic returns stemming from differences in time profiles of returns and depreciation rates across firms. We take up the first and third of these issues in this chapter and defer the second one until we introduce the firm's own advertising and inventive activity (see Chapter 6).

1.   *Sales or assets in the denominator*

The price–marginal cost margin emerges from the first-order condition of a profit-maximizing firm that maximizes short-run profits in an industry with a given number of firms (see Chapter 4, and references cited therein). If marginal costs are assumed constant, the price–marginal cost margin equals the profit-to-sales ratio. Thus, the closest theoretical link between market structure and the profit rate of a short-run profit-maximizing firm is to its profit-to-sales ratio, and this theoretical underpinning has provided the implicit or explicit justification for the choice of profit-to-sales as the dependent variable in numerous studies (for the most detailed defense of this choice, see Cowling 1976).

Profits must exist in the short run to persist into the long run. Thus, the static equilibrium under short-run profit maximization was the starting point for our modeling of the market structure–profit performance equation. But our focus has been on the long-run profit performance of companies. In the long run, profits respond to the entry and exit decisions of firms, and these decisions in turn are going to be based on realized or expected returns on investment. Economic theory suggests that in the long run returns on capital are equalized, not returns on sales. The long-run orientation of the study has dictated the choice of return on assets as the most defensible dependent variable.

But too much should not be made of this choice. We showed in Chapter 4 that a reweighting of the right-hand-side variables, as would be appropriate were profit-to-sales the dependent variable, resulted in modest differences between the results when the right-hand-side variables are left unweighted. Similar results are reported by Long and Ravenscraft (1984). Examination of the results in other studies – for example, those reported in Weiss (1971, 1974) – does not reveal important differences in the relationship between concentration, and by implication market share, and the profit rate, whether that profit rate is defined relative to sales or assets.

That one obtains roughly similar results in a structure-profit performance model when one uses profit-to-sales or profit-to-assets may seem surprising, perhaps even disturbing. Obviously, however, were the capital-to-sales ratio constant across all firms, it would not matter statistically whether one used profit-to-sales or profit-to-assets as the dependent variable; only the size of the coefficients would be affected by the common scale factor of the capital-to-sales ratio. Although capital-to-sales ratios are not constant across firms, they are much more stable than systematic variations in the numerator of the profit-to-X variable that are being picked up by market share and the other variables in the model, with the choice of X proving to be less important than one might have imagined.

2.   *Accounting returns versus economic returns*

Accounting rates of return on assets can differ from economic returns, because the accountant's definition of depreciation differs from true economic depreciation. The size of the gap between accounting and economic returns depends on the time profile of profits from investment and the chosen depreciation formula for measuring profits and assets (Solomon 1970; Stauffer 1971). Thus, accounting returns on assets measure with some error true economic returns on capital. Although this problem has been known to exist for some time, most observers have gone ahead, implicitly lumping this error in measuring the dependent variable along with other components of the error term, and assumed this error to have mean zero and the other usual properties.

Recently, however, Fisher and McGowan (1983) presented numerous examples of how the mismatch of profit streams over time with accounting definitions of depreciation can lead to wide discrepancies between accounting and economic returns (see also Salamon 1983; Salamon and Moriarty 1984). They considered these discrepancies to be so large and so likely to occur that they concluded that " . . . there is no way in which one can look at accounting rates of return and infer anything about relative economic profitability or, a fortiori, about the presence or absence of monopoly profits" (1983, p. 90). If one cannot look at accounting profits and infer anything about monopoly profits, presumably one cannot look at a correlation between accounting profits and concentration or market share and infer anything about whether higher economic profits are linked to these market structure indexes, which we commonly associate with market power. Fisher and McGowan question whether any inferences about market structure and profitability can be drawn using accounting returns on assets.

The Fisher–McGowan paper demonstrates rather persuasively that there *can* be serious errors when accounting returns are used to measure economic returns. Whether there *are* serious errors in fact, and if so, how serious they are, cannot be answered by presenting examples, however. These questions must be addressed empirically (see Long and Ravenscraft 1984).

The basic point of Fisher and McGowan would appear to be that accounting rates of return are essentially uncorrelated with economic rates of return. If our theory predicts a positive correlation between market share and economic returns, we would expect from Fisher and McGowan that our theory might be correct and yet market share and accounting returns would be uncorrelated, so poor is the approximation of accounting returns to the sought-after economic measure. But we have found a rather strong linkage between projected accounting returns on total assets and market share. Given the sizable errors in measuring accounting returns that Fisher and McGowan demonstrate, one must presume that the correlation would be still higher, the unexplained residual still smaller, were we able to measure economic returns more accurately. Thus, the bottom line of the Fisher–McGowan study ought to have been that measurement errors in using accounting returns to measure economic returns result in a serious underestimate of the significance of the profitability–market structure relationship, a significant underestimation of how much of the variability in profit rates one can explain by market structure variables. Yet this is not the conclusion they draw.

What they seem to want to say is that the errors in measuring economic returns by looking at accounting data are such that a positive correlation between profitability, thus measured, and concentration or market share is likely to be spurious. How else is one to interpret "there is *no way* in which one can . . . infer monopoly profits" (emphasis added) in the quotation presented above? But the number of studies that have found a positive correlation between concentration and profitability is large (see Weiss 1971, 1974), and I am not aware of a single study that has used market share data by firm that has not found a significant correlation between market share and profitability (see Section B). For so many studies to have found a positive correlation between profitability and either concentration or market share, despite their wide differences in time periods and sample composition, some *systematic* error must exist in measuring accounting returns, rather than economic returns leading to a positive correlation where none exists, to sustain Fisher and McGowan's conclusion. But they present no evidence or arguments to explain why such systematic errors exist.

The examples Fisher and McGowan present assign return profiles and depreciation schedules to firms more or less at random. Now the time sequence of returns to a given piece of capital is largely out of the control of the firm and may be treated as exogenously given for any firm. But the choice of depreciation schedule for accounting purposes is at management's discretion. Management can, given the time profile of its returns, choose depreciation schedules that systematically over- or understate its return on capital vis-à-vis the true economic return, or it can choose one that would make the accounting returns a reasonable approximation to the true economic returns. The implicit question raised by Fisher and McGowan is whether management might choose depreciation schedules, given their time profiles of returns to investment, such that firms in concentrated industries or with high market shares overstate their true economic returns, and firms with low market shares or concentration understate their returns.

It is difficult to believe that managers choose accounting depreciation formulas or approve the choices of their accountants without considering the impact of this choice on reported profits, the ratio of profits to total assets, or equity and the growth of these variables. Why a firm with a high market share would want to exaggerate its profitability, and a firm with a low market share to conceal it, is hard to fathom. Indeed, if our theory is valid and high market share firms have above-average profits, one might expect firms with high market shares to choose depreciation rates to disguise their true profitability to avoid rousing the suspicions of the antitrust authorities. Similarly, low market share firms that earn below-average profits would be more apt to choose depreciation schedules that inflate their profitability to avoid the criticism of their shareholders, creditors, and the financial community. Thus, if the choice of depreciation rates results in a systematic bias in the correlation between profitability and market share, it is much more likely that the bias is away from finding a positive correlation when one actually exists, than that the choice of accounting profit rates creates a positive correlation when none would exist if the internal return on capital could be used.

The discrepancy between the accounting returns on capital we use as dependent variable and the economist's internal return on capital affects our results in two ways. Certainly, it adds error to our measurement of the dependent variable and helps explain why we cannot explain a greater percentage of the variation in projected profit rates. *Some* of the industry dummies that entered the industry equation in Chapter 4 may capture systematic divergences between accounting returns and economic returns that affect all firms in an industry alike. But I do not believe that all of the projected differences in profitability implied by the industry dummies are due to accounting data paradoxes. The significantly below-average profit performance of the cement firms is not simply the result of an unfortunate intersection of intertemporal profit patterns and depreciation schedules. Nor does the variation in profit rates explained by market share and product differentiation seem to be simply the result of accounting vagaries. If anything, the use of accounting data grossly understates the importance of these factors.

The present study reports the existence of persistent differences in profitability across firms and relates these differences to market share and product differentiation. A look at the list of most profitable firms reveals many companies that dominated their major markets through the time period investigated in this study: Campbell Soup, Coca-Cola, Kodak, GM, Gerber, Gillette, Hershey, Hoover, IBM, Kellogg, MMM, Polaroid, Proctor & Gamble, Tecumseh, Wrigley, and Xerox. Among the firms with persistently low profits, the incidence of market dominance is rare. Fisher and McGowan would have us believe that nothing can be inferred about the existence of monopoly rents from the persistence of accounting returns substantially above the norm and their correlation with market dominance and market share. That the above firms happen to dominate their industries while consistently enjoying accounting rates of return substantially above the average is mere coincidence. Perhaps, but this observer suspects that there is more to it than accounting happenstance.

CHAPTER 6

Profitability and the firm's own advertising, patent activity, risk, and other characteristics

The model estimated in Chapter 4 abstracts from many factors that might affect a company's profitability. This and the following two chapters introduce several firm-specific variables that might be related to corporate profitability. We begin with the company's own advertising and patent efforts. In Section B, the results regarding the firm's own advertising and patent intensities are used to appraise the seriousness of our omission of intangible capital stocks. In Section C, we explore the possibility that differences in risk across firms might account for the profit differences we observe. The relationship between profits and company growth, size, and diversification is taken up in Section D.

A. Profitability, firm advertising, and patent intensity

In Chapter 4, we found both industry advertising intensity and industry patent intensity to be positively related to firm profitability when included as interaction terms with market share. The rationale for including both of these variables was to proxy product differentiation, or in the case of patent intensity, product and production-function differentiation. But it is possible that advertising and patenting are playing some other role in the equation, or that in addition to indexing differentiation, advertising and patenting have some other role to play.

What is perhaps novel in the firm-profitability model is that advertising and patenting as *industry* characteristics explain *firm* profitability, but only when combined with firm market shares. Advertising and patenting intensity index the potential to realize high profits but do not in themselves confer high profitability. It is only those firms that succeed in differentiating their products or lowering their costs and thereby obtain higher market shares that earn higher profitability.

Let us now explore the question of what role the firm's own advertising and patenting might play in explaining profitability. Consider again the linear model in which firm i's price, p_i, is given as

$$p_i = a_i - bx_i - b\sigma\sum_{j\neq i} x_j \tag{6.1}$$

and x_i is i's output and σ parameterizes the degree of substitutability among firm products, $0 \leq \sigma \geq 1$. The most straightforward way to introduce the firm's own advertising into this model is to make a_i, the demand schedule's intercept, a function of own advertising, $a_i = a_i(A_i)$. The intercept indexes perceived product quality. Whether advertising is viewed as information acquainting buyers with a product's quality or persuasion deluding the buyer about a product's true character- istics, it is a_i that should be affected by advertising. Replacing a_i by $a_i(A_i)$, the ith firm's profits become

$$\pi = (a_i (A_i) - bx_i - b\sigma \sum_{j \neq i} x_j - c_i)x_i - A_i. \tag{6.2}$$

The objective function can be written as before,

$$O_i = \pi_i + \theta \sum_{j \neq i} \pi_j, \tag{6.3}$$

which upon maximization with respect to x_i yields precisely the same first-order condition as before and an expression for i's output of

$$x_i = \frac{a_i(A_i) - c_i}{2b} - r \sum_{j \neq i} x_j, \qquad r = \frac{\sigma(1 + \theta)}{2}. \tag{6.4}$$

Maximizing (6.3) with respect to A_i yields the first-order condition

$$a'_i = \frac{1}{x_i}. \tag{6.5}$$

Equation (6.5) implies a positive relationship between advertising and output. But all of advertising's impact on profitability should be cap- tured through the market share term. Equation (6.4) can be solved for the same profit rate–market share relationship as before, and there is no reason to posit an independent effect of advertising on profitability.

The same arguments apply to patent intensity. Patentable inven- tions might shift either the demand function or the cost function. Writing $a_i - c_i = q_i(Pat_i)$, we could proceed as before, solving for op- timal output and patent intensity. But market share depends directly on $a_i - c_i$, so that patent intensity's impact on profitability is reflected through its impact on market share. Once market share is included in the equation, neither advertising nor patent activity should have anything left to explain. Of course, if we could measure the inherent characteristics of a company's product or its advertising or its inventive process that generates the demand and cost function shifts, we could work our way back and solve for advertising, market share, profitability, and patenting, all as functions of these underlying firm-specific characteristics. But in the absence of knowledge of what these characteristics are and how to measure them, we are stuck with the problem that market share, advertising, and patenting all reflect the same underlying differences in demand and cost functions across firms.

An alternative way to try and introduce the firm's own advertising or patenting activity to assuming that these activities affect the demand-schedule intercept or cost parameter is to assume that they affect the degree of product differentiation or the slope of the demand schedule. A more general formulation of the firm's demand equation is

$$p_i = a_i - b_i x_i - \sigma_i \sum_{j \neq i} x_j. \tag{6.6}$$

Both the own-slope portion of the firm's demand schedule and the degree of substitution between its product and the products of all other firms in the industry are now firm specific. The range for σ_i is $0 \leq \sigma_i \leq b_i$. When $\sigma_i = b_i$, the products of all other firms in the industry are perfect substitutes for the firm's own product. When $\sigma_i = 0$, the firm is a monopolist. Assuming that equation (6.6) is the firm's demand schedule, we can rewrite the firm's objective function from Chapter 4 as

$$0_i = \pi_i + \theta \sum_{j \neq i} \pi_j = (a_i - b_i x_i - \sigma_i \sum_{j \neq i} x_j - c_i) x_i$$
$$+ \theta \sum_{j \neq i} (a_j - b_i x_j - \sigma_j \sum_{k \neq j} x_k - c_j) x_j. \tag{6.7}$$

Maximizing (6.7) with respect to x_i yields as a first-order condition

$$a_i - 2b_i x_i - \sigma_i \sum_{j \neq i} x_j - c_i - \theta \sum_{j \neq i} \sigma_j x_j - 0. \tag{6.8}$$

Using (6.8) to replace $a_i - c_i$ in π_i and dividing by x_i, we obtain

$$\frac{\pi_i}{x_i} = (b_i - \theta\sigma_i)x_i + \theta \sum_{j=1}^{N} \sigma_j x_j. \tag{6.9}$$

We can now proceed to obtain an approximation to the firm's profit-to-sales ratio, as we did in Chapter 4. Summing the p_j over all firms and dividing by N yields

$$\Sigma p_j = \Sigma a_j - \Sigma(b_j - \sigma_j)x_j - X\Sigma\sigma_j$$
$$\bar{p} = \Sigma p_j/N = \Sigma a_j/N - \frac{\Sigma(b_j - \sigma_j)x_j}{N} - X\bar{\sigma}, \tag{6.10}$$

where $\bar{\sigma} = \Sigma\sigma_j/N$ and $X = \sum_{j=1}^{N} x_j$.

If we recall that $0 \leq \sigma_j \leq b_j$ and assume that N is fairly large, the middle term in (6.10) is small and we can assume

$$\frac{\partial \bar{p}}{\partial X} = -\bar{\sigma}. \tag{6.11}$$

From (6.11) we obtain as a measure of the industry demand elasticity, η,

$$\eta = \frac{\bar{p}}{\sigma X}. \tag{6.12}$$

The η defined by (6.12) is directly analogous to the measure used in Chapter 4, where all firms were assumed to have a common b and σ. Defining S_i as company sales, $S_i = p_i x_i$, m_i as market share, $m_i = x_i/X$, and if we assume $\Sigma \sigma_j x_j \simeq \bar{\sigma} X$, we can use (6.12) and (6.9) to obtain

$$\frac{\pi_i}{S_i} \simeq \frac{\pi_i}{x_i \bar{p}} \simeq \frac{b_i m_i}{\eta \bar{\sigma}} - \frac{\theta \sigma_i m_i}{\eta \bar{\sigma}} + \frac{\theta}{\eta}. \tag{6.13}$$

This equation is to be compared with that of Chapter 4:

$$\frac{\pi_i}{S_i} \simeq \frac{m_i}{\eta \sigma} - \frac{m_i \theta_i}{\eta} + \frac{\theta}{\eta}. \tag{6.14}$$

Equations (6.13) and (6.14) differ in that the first term of (6.13) is scaled by b_i and the second by $\sigma_i/\bar{\sigma}$. Now, a company's advertising and patenting could conceivably affect either b_i or $\sigma_i/\bar{\sigma}$, or both. Given that b_i multiplies $m_i/\bar{\sigma}$, which we have approximated with interaction terms between market shares and industry advertising and patent intensity, and $\sigma_i/\bar{\sigma}$ multiplies θm_i, were we to try to write both b_i and $\sigma_i/\bar{\sigma}$ as functions of the firm's advertising, we would encounter a plethora of interaction terms in our estimating equations. Our experience in Chapter 4 suggests we would not be able to sort out the separate effects of each variable. We thus proceed less ambitiously.

We first assume that only b_i is affected by a firm's own advertising or patent activity. Defining A_i as company i's advertising expenditures divided by its sales, and A as the weighted-average industry advertising-to-sales ratio for firm i (these and other variables used in this chapter are defined in Table 6.1), then the following four specifications for b_i seem reasonable:

$$\begin{aligned}
b_i &= b + hA_i \\
b_i &= b + h(A_i - A) \\
b_i &= b + hA_i/A \\
b_i &= b + h\log(A_i/A)
\end{aligned} \tag{6.15}$$

with analogous equations for patent intensity possible. Replacing b_i in (6.13) with any of the alternatives in (6.15) would yield the same

Table 6.1. *Definitions of variables used in Chapter 6*

A. *Variables from previous chapters*

$\hat{\alpha}$ Projected returns on total assets expressed as a relative deviation from the mean returns for all companies. Estimated from the best fit of the three polynomials in $1/t$ estimated in Chapter 2.

m_i Projected market share.

C_4 Projected four-firm concentration ratio.

A Industry advertising to sales ratio.

Pat Industry patent to sales ratio.

B. *Variables introduced in this chapter*

A_i Firm i's own advertising-to-sales ratio.

Pat_i Firm i's own patent-to-sales ratio.

$\alpha 15$ Projected returns on total assets adjusted for intangible advertising capital, assuming a 15 percent annual depreciation rate.

$\alpha 28$ As above, assuming a 28.8 percent depreciation rate.

$\alpha 45$ As above, assuming a 45 percent depreciation rate.

β_π The coefficient on mean profits from a linear regression of the firm's annual profit rate on the sample mean.

$\bar{\beta}$ The mean β from the Capital-Asset-Pricing model estimated using monthly stock market returns and averaged over the sample period.

σ_π The standard deviation in company profit rates for the 23 years 1950–72, annual data.

σ_α The standard error of the estimate of $\hat{\alpha}$ from the best-fit time series of Chapter 2.

G_i The growth in assets from 1950 to 1972 of firm i.

$S72_i$ 1972 sales of firm i.

DIV_i A Herfindahl index of firm i's diversification.

IND_i The number of different markets in which firm i had positive sales.

---

equations estimated in Chapter 4, plus additional interaction terms that include m_i, A, and the respective A_i term from (6.15), all as multiplicative factors. All of these variants are tried.

Intuitively, it seems that the functional form for $\sigma_i/\bar{\sigma}$ should be defined in terms of both A_i and A, and should equal 1 when $A_i = A$; that is,

$$\frac{\sigma_i}{\bar{\sigma}} = f(A_i,A) \qquad (f(\ ) = 1) <-> (A_i = A)\,, \frac{\partial f}{\partial A_i} < 0.$$

Two simple specifications for f( ) having these properties are

$$\sigma_i/\bar{\sigma} = 1 - a(A_i - A) \tag{6.16a}$$

$$\sigma_i/\bar{\sigma} = 1 - a \log(A_i/A). \tag{6.16b}$$

Replacing $\sigma/\bar{\sigma}$ in (6.13) and assuming $b_i = 1$ would give us precisely the same equations as estimated in Chapter 4, plus a set of terms that multiply m_i, the appropriate variables from θ, and the respective variables in A_i. For example, defining $\theta = f + gC_4^2$ would require that we add two terms to the equations estimated in the last chapter to estimate (6.16a), $m_i(A_i - A)$ and $C_4^2 m_i(A_i - A)$.

Finally, note that

$$\frac{\partial \pi_i / S_i}{\partial A_i} = \frac{m_i}{\eta \bar{\sigma}} \frac{\partial b_i}{\partial A_i} - \frac{\theta m_i}{\eta} \frac{\partial \sigma_i / \bar{\sigma}}{\partial A_i}$$

(6.17)

If $\theta > 0$, then

$$\frac{\partial \pi_i / S_i}{\partial A_i} > 0,$$

under the most reasonable assumptions about the other two partial derivatives, $\partial b_i / \partial A_i > 0$, $\partial(\sigma_i/\sigma)/\partial A_i < 0$. Assuming (6.13) could be approximated via a Taylor expansion, we simply add terms in A_i, $A_i - A$, A_i/A, and $\log(A_i/A)$ to see whether they have any effect on firm profitability.

Advertising data over the years 1970–72 were obtained for a substantial fraction of the companies for six of the major media: magazines, newspapers, network television, spot television, farm publications, and outdoor advertising.[1] Data for earlier years were available for a much smaller sample of firms and for only three or four media. These were also gathered and scaled up to a six-media approximation by multiplying the three- or four-media figure by the ratio of the six-media total to the three- or four-media figure in 1970–72, on the assumption that these media were of the same relative importance in each company's advertising mix over time. These earlier data were gathered for the years 1955, 1960, and 1965. We then estimated the ith firm's advertising-to-sales ratio in the later years 1970–72 for which full coverage over the six media was available; we also calculated the simple average of the figures for the late and earlier years using the scale factor to approximate the six-media figure in the early years. In the second case, when either the late or early advertising figures were unavailable, the figure that was available was used. Since there are more observations available for the average over time, and the results for this variable are analogous to the results when only the late figures are used, we report only the results when the average advertising intensity over time is used as the measure of A_i.

Table 6.2 presents the results when each of the firm-specific advertising variables discussed above is added to the firm-effect equation. Equation (1) is the basic model, estimated for the 436-firm subsample. The resemblance between these coefficients and those in the previous chapter indicates that the 436-firm subsample is representative of the full 551-company sample. Equations (2)–(7) present the main variants on the model when each firm's degree of product differentiation is assumed to differ and to be related to its own advertising. The pattern of coefficients is generally negative. Given that the degree of cooperation, θ, varies inversely with concentration, the opposing signs on the two terms involving A_i in equations (6) and (7) is appropriate. But the negative coefficient on the first of these two terms implies that the a in text equation (6.13) is negative. The firm's degree of product differentiation relative to the industry average actually declines with increases in the firm's own advertising. This unexpected result may be due to reverse causality; that is, firms with relatively more differentiated products can spend relatively less on advertising. Many of the most profitable firms in our sample not only have large market shares, but also have the advantage of being the first to have introduced their type of product into the market (see Table 3.1). Bond and Lean (1977) found that the first firms to introduce a new drug enjoyed greater product image differentiation, and Buzzell and Farris (1977) report that pioneer consumer products can spend less on advertising than follower brands. Brown's (1978) results indicating greater returns to advertising new products than old are consistent with this hypothesis. In any event, only one of the coefficients involving A_i in equations (2)–(7) is significant. The product of m_i and $(A_i - A)$ in (6) is significant at the 10 percent level.

In contrast, the four terms involving A_i in equations (8)–(11) all have positive coefficients, and two of these, the two involving the ratio of firm to industry advertising intensity in equations (10) and (11), are significant at the 10 percent level. Thus, the level of the firm's own advertising does seem to offer some additional positive explanatory power, particularly when measured relative to the industry. The results in equations (8)–(11) suggest that the negative pattern of coefficients in equations (2)–(7) may again be due to multicollinearity between the terms with m_i and A_i, and the other terms involving m_i in equations (2)–(7). Be that as it may, it is apparent from Table 6.2 that knowledge of the firm's own advertising, given the level of industry advertising, does not add much to the explanatory power of the basic, firm-effects equation. The $\overline{R}^2$ for the latter is .286 and the highest $\overline{R}^2$ of any of the equations involving A_i is but .290, for equation (11). Moreover, the coefficient on the industry advertising–market share variable never has a t-value less than 7.9, whereas the A_i terms never exhibit t-values greater than 1.9. Knowledge of the degree of product differentiation in the industries in which the firm operates allows us

Table 6.2. *Profitability and the firm's own advertising, best-fit as*
($n = 436$)

Variables		Equation										
		1	2	3	4	5	6	7	8	9	10	11
Intercept		−.037	−.047	−.044	−.043	−.046	−.047	−.040	−.036	−.032	−.049	.073
		1.16	1.45	1.36	1.32	1.40	1.44	1.22	1.14	.94	1.49	1.94
$(1-m_v)C_4^2$		−.550	−.511	−.512	−.528	−.514	−.498	−.490	−.586	−.568	−.567	−.555
		3.51	3.22	3.23	3.33	3.24	3.13	2.63	3.72	3.53	3.62	3.55
m_rA		.688	.802	.711	.692	.797	.738	.671	.612	.680	.654	.650
		11.30	8.01	11.28	11.34	7.93	10.68	9.65	7.99	10.78	10.22	10.16
m_rPat		1.562	1.349	1.462	1.424	1.374	1.296	1.510	1.738	1.603	1.684	1.685
		4.98	3.90	4.55	4.12	4.02	3.74	3.88	5.28	4.93	5.24	5.27
$A_i m_rA$			−.015									
			1.44									
$(A_i-A)m_rA$				−.011								
				1.40								
$Ln(A_i'/A)m_rA$					−.042							
					.96							
$m_rA(A_i/A)$						−.064						
						1.37						

	(1)	(2)	(3)	(4)	(5)	(6)	(7)	(8)	(9)	(10)	(11)
$m_i(A_i - A)$						−.209 1.89					
$C_4^2 m_i(A_i - A)$						.063 1.45					
$m_i\text{Ln}(A/A)$							−.090 .48				
$C_4^2 m_i\text{Ln}(A/A)$							.045 .61				
A_i								.013 1.63			
$A_i - A$									.004 .48		
A/A										.033 1.66	
$\text{Ln}(A/A)$											.023 1.89
$\overline{R}^2$	.286	.288	.287	.286	.287	.289	.283	.288	.284	.289	.290

to explain firm profitability, but the additional knowledge of the firm's own advertising effort provides little additional explanatory power.

It is possible, of course, that the effect of own advertising on profitability is being picked up by market share. Firms that do relatively more advertising than their industry rivals have higher market shares. But regressions of projected market share on the difference between own and industry advertising $(A_i - A)$ or their ratio (A_i/A) failed to reveal a significant relationship between these variables.

Patent data were gathered from the *U.S. Patent Index* for each company and its subsidiaries for the years 1950, 1954, 1958, 1962, 1966, 1969, and 1972.[2] Average patent-to-sales ratios for a late period (1962, 1966, 1969, and 1972) and an early period were calculated. All equations were estimated with both the average patent-to-sales ratio over the late period, and the average over the late and early periods, with nearly identical results for each measure. The reported results are over the late and early time periods.

Table 6.3 presents the results with the firm patent-intensity variables. Each equation is specified as in Table 6.2, and the basic firm-effect-model equation is included as equation (1) to aid in making comparisons. All of the coefficients on the firm-specific patent variables have negative coefficients except for equation (8), in which the firm's own patent-to-sales ratio is simply added as a separate term to the basic, firm-effect equation. It, and all other firm-specific-patent terms have coefficients that are insignificant at the 10 percent level. Some collinearity between the term with Pat_i and the m_iPat term is apparent in equations (3) and (4). But the conclusion seems inescapable that, given that we know the firm's market shares and the patent intensity of the industries in which it sells, knowledge of the firm's own patent intensity adds nothing to explaining the long-run profitability of the firm. Only equation (2) has a higher $\overline{R}^2$ (.279) than equation (1) (.278). As with advertising, firm market shares were not found to be significantly related to the relative strength of a firm's own patent activity.

B.   Issues raised by the investment-like character of advertising and inventive activity

Advertising and inventive activity can have an effect on a company's profits beyond the accounting period in which these activities are expensed. This characteristic makes advertising and invention resemble capital investment in that today's expenditures affect profits in future periods. Both advertising and R&D are expensed, however, and no direct allowance in total assets is usually made for the intangible capital stocks R&D and advertising create. Denoting S as sales, C as total costs for wages and materials, K total physical assets, A current advertising, A_k the stock of goodwill from past advertising, and λ_k and λ_A as the depreciation rates on physical and goodwill capital, respectively, then our measure of profits over total assets might be written as

$$\Pi = \frac{S - C - \lambda_k K - A}{K}, \tag{6.18}$$

where the true return on *total* capital would be written as

$$\Pi^* = \frac{S - C - \lambda_k K - \lambda_A A_k}{K + A_k}. \tag{6.19}$$

Two possible biases from the use of Π as opposed to Π^* can be envisaged: The current expenditure A does not equal the depreciation on intangible capital, $\lambda_A A_k$, and total capital is greater than total assets by the amount A_k.

To see the possible problems, consider the following example (see Table 6.4). In period $t-1$, two firms have identical sales, costs, profits, and physical capital and earn the identical return on physical capital of .05, which is the competitive return on capital. In t, each firm spends 10 on advertising that will affect sales only in $t+1$. Following conventional accounting practices, advertising is expensed in period t rather than treated as an investment, and accounting profits (row 6) understate economic profits (row 8) by 10. The advertising allows both companies to increase their prices in $t+1$, raising sales revenue to 110. The value of tangible capital at the beginning of $t+1$ is 10 for each company. Firm L's advertising in t allows it to sustain the price increases indefinitely, however, whereas F's demand schedule shifts back in $t+2$, forcing it to roll back its prices. Thus, F's intangible capital depreciates 100 percent in $t+1$, L's not at all. L's economic return on total capital is .095, F's .048 (row 11). L will earn this supranormal return indefinitely, whereas F's return on capital returns to the competitive level in $t+2$.

This example illustrates the main measurement problems arising from the use of accounting returns in the presence of intangible capital: (1) In periods in which intangible capital is being built up (period t), accounting profits understate economic profits because investment in intangible capital exceeds its depreciation ($A > \lambda_A A_k$ from [6.18] and [6.19]). (2) In the steady state, when $A = \lambda_A A_k$, accounting

Table 6.3. *Profitability and the firm's own patent intensity, best-fit αs* (n = 551)

Variables	Equation										
	1	2	3	4	5	6	7	8	9	10	11
Intercept	-.040	-.037	-.039	-.040	-.038	-.033	-.039	-.046	-.044	-.035	-.051
	1.38	1.27	1.34	1.36	1.30	1.10	1.32	1.51	1.41	1.12	1.64
$(1-m_i)C^{84}$	-.583	-.604	-.574	-.584	-.585	-.698	-.640	-.579	-.585	-.591	-.600
	4.04	4.16	3.94	4.04	4.04	4.17	3.69	4.00	4.04	4.07	4.12
m_iA	.718	.721	.718	.719	.722	.748	.721	.721	.722	.721	.726
	12.20	12.26	12.20	12.19	12.22	12.00	11.45	12.20	11.93	12.21	12.22
m_iPat	1.380	1.658	1.019	1.247	1.509	.696	1.238	1.335	1.315	1.358	1.355
	5.44	5.25	1.32	2.29	4.96	4.82	3.77	5.06	4.00	5.30	5.32
$Pat_i m_iPat$		-2.614									
		1.47									
$(Pat_i-Pat)m_iPat$			-.437								
			.50								
$\text{Ln}\left(\dfrac{Pat_i}{Pat}\right)m_iPat$				-.048							
				.28							

	(1)	(2)	(3)	(4)	(5)	(6)	(7)	(8)	(9)	(10)	(11)
$m_i Pat \dfrac{Pat_i}{Pat}$					-1.238 .77						
$M_i(Pat_i - Pat)$						$-.181$ .11					
$C_4^2 m_i(Pat_i - Pat)$						$-.427$ 1.36					
$m_i \mathrm{Ln}\left(\dfrac{Pat_i}{Pat}\right)$							$-.037$ .38				
$C_4^2 m_i \mathrm{Ln}\left(\dfrac{Pat_i}{Pat}\right)$							$-.017$ .47				
Pat_i								.102 .61			
$Pat_i - Pat$									$-.018$ .31		
Pat_i/Pat										$-.011$ .61	
$\mathrm{Ln}(Pat_i/Pat)$											$-.077$ .98
$\bar{R}^2$	.278	.279	.277	.277	.277	.277	.278	.276	.277	.277	.278

Table 6.4. *The effects of intangible capital on observed profit rates: an example*

Time	Firm L				Firm F			
	...t−1	t	t+1	t+2...	...t−1	t	t+1	t+2...
1. Sales	100	100	110	110	100	100	110	100
2. Costs	90	90	90	90	90	90	90	90
3. Advertising	0	10	0	0	0	10	0	0
4. Accounting profits	10	0	20	20	10	0	20	10
5. Physical capital	200	200	200	200	200	200	200	200
6. Return on physical capital	.05	0	.10	.10	.05	0	.10	.05
7. Depreciation on intangible capital			0	0			10	
8. Economic profits	10	10	20	20	10	10	10	10
9. Intangible capital based on past investment	0	0	10	10	0	0	10	0
10. Total capital	200	200	210	210	200	200	210	200
11. Economic return on total capital	.05	.05	.095	.095	.05	.05	.048	.05
12. Intangible capital based on present value of future profits	0	0	200	200	0	0	10	0

profits as a return on physical capital overstate economic profits as return on total capital owing to the omission of intangible assets from the denominator of the profit rate (Firm L in $t+1$ and $t+2$). Note, however, that, when depreciation of intangible capital is rapid, as for firm F, *average* accounting returns on physical capital (row 6) approximate average economic returns on total capital (row 11) quite closely. Thus, if intangible capital depreciates rapidly, as several writers have claimed with respect to advertising (see Clarke's 1976 survey), then even though investments in intangible capital may vary over time and lead to subsequent changes in profitability, it is the *variance* in the return on capital that is mostly affected by our use of accounting profits, and not the mean. Given that our measure of profitability is a projection based on a time-series estimate, our projected returns should be an accurate predictor of true economic returns on total capital, if intangible capital depreciates rapidly. What will be most affected by the neglect of intangible capital is the *fit* of the time-series regression that estimates long-run profitability.[3]

We tested first for the possible bias from underestimating economic profits by using accounting profits when intangible capital is growing. When intangible capital is growing, the profits of growing firms should be understated relative to those of steady-state firms (see Soloman 1970). To check for this possible bias, we reestimated equation (8) including interaction terms with company advertising and growth in assets, and log growth in assets. The latter gave the better statistical fit, but the interaction term had a *positive* coefficient, contradicting the hypothesis that profits are underestimated for growing firms that do a lot of advertising. The results were as follows, where $\text{Ln}(G_i)$ is the log of i's growth rate:

$$\hat{\alpha}_i = -.044 - .515(1 - m_i)C_4^2 + .698m_iA + 1.68m_iPat - .005A_i$$
$$\quad\quad 1.47 \quad\quad 3.86 \quad\quad\quad\quad 7.60 \quad\quad\quad 4.87 \quad\quad\quad\quad .25$$
$$+ .006A_i\text{Ln}(G_i) \quad\quad\quad\quad\quad\quad\quad\quad\quad\quad \overline{R}^2 = .289.$$
$$\quad 1.09 \quad\quad\quad\quad\quad\quad\quad\quad\quad\quad\quad\quad\quad\quad\quad (6.20)$$

Similar experiments with patent intensity yielded similar results.

Given this failure to find a bias owing to growing intangible capital, the long-run orientation of this study, and the use of projected profits as dependent variable, it is tempting to assume that firms approximate a steady-state equilibrium.

If we assume a steady-state equilibrium in which the depreciation rate for each firm is the same, then the intangible stocks missing from each firm's total capital are proportional to current levels of investment in intangible assets. Thus, the upward bias in measured returns on total capital from neglecting intangible capital should be correlated with the levels of current investment in intangible capital. With respect to Table 6.3, however, we observed that the firm's own patent activity or the level of its activity with respect to other firms in its industry was unrelated to its projected profitability. Thus, at least for intangible capital related to patenting, our reported results for the basic firm-effect model do not seem to be seriously biased by neglecting intangible assets.

But we did observe some positive relationship between the firm's own advertising and its profitability in Table 6.2, although the inclusion of the firm's own advertising added little to the equation's explanatory power in the presence of industry advertising and market share. Thus, we should try to make some allowance for the presence of intangible advertising capital. If we assume that all firms are in a steady-state equilibrium and that all have the same depreciation rate on intangible capital, then we can adjust our measure of a firm's long-run profitability to allow for its intangible capital. Recall that the $\hat{\alpha}_i$ is estimated using annual observations on π_{it}, where

$$\pi_{it} = \frac{\Pi_{it} - \Pi_t}{\Pi_t} \tag{6.21}$$

and Π_{it} is firm i's profits-assets ratio in t, and $\overline{\Pi}_t$ is the sample mean. Assuming that each firm's advertising capital was proportional to its advertising ($A_k = A/\lambda_A$), we can recalculate Π_{it} and $\overline{\Pi}_t$ to allow for advertising capital. We did so using $\hat{\alpha}_i$ as our measure of π_{it}, and 1972 figures for assets and $\overline{\Pi}_t$.[4]

The results we obtain upon adjusting for intangible capital stock are sensitive to the choice of depreciation rate. The lower the depreciation rate, the larger the estimated intangible capital for advertising-intensive firms and the smaller their profit rate. Lowering the depreciation rate lowers the variability in firm profit rates, and thus tends to lower the explanatory power of an equation (see Grabowski and Mueller 1978). Were the depreciation rate zero, all firms with positive advertising would have infinite advertising capital, and the variance in rates of return across firms would be zero.

Using the difference between a firm's market and book values as a measure of total intangible capital and assuming a steady state, Mark Hirschey (1982b) recently estimated a common depreciation rate on advertising capital of 28.8 percent. This rate is lower than that most observers have found. We adjusted our profit rate figures assuming $\lambda_A = .288$, and to test for sensitivity, we assumed λ_A equals .15 and

.45. The results for each choice of dependent variable along with those for the unadjusted α are presented for the basic firm-effect model in Table 6.5. Not surprisingly, the coefficient on the market share–industry advertising intensity (m_iA) drops somewhat after adjusting the dependent variable for intangible advertising capital. More impressive is the increase in m_iPat's coefficient. But the coefficients for all three interaction terms maintain the same signs and high levels of significance for the three choices of adjusted dependent variables. The more plausible depreciation rates, .288 and .45, give results sufficiently close to those for the unadjusted variable that we feel confident in proceeding without worrying that our regression analysis is merely reflecting systematic biases introduced by not adjusting for intangible capital.

This conclusion is somewhat dependent, however, on imposing the same depreciation rate on all companies. Previous empirical work suggests substantial differences in depreciation rates across industries (Lambin 1976; Grabowski 1976; Peles 1971). One interpretation of the significant differences in profit rates for some industries observed in our testing of the industry-approach model in Chapter 4 is that the industry intercepts capture differences in intangible capital stocks. Under this interpretation, the large positive coefficient for the pharmaceutical industry would simply indicate the large fraction of pharmaceutical firm total capital made up by the intangible stocks of drug patents and product trademarks. This interpretation of the observed differences in industry profitability must be regarded as a distinct possibility. In Chapter 10, the industry intercepts and firm-effect model variables are included in the same equation. We shall see that the variables for the firm-effect model remain significant in the presence of the industry intercepts. We defer further discussion of the interpretation of the industry intercepts until that chapter.

Of course, depreciation rates on intangible capital may differ across firms as well as across industries. If we had complete time series on individual firm advertising and R&D outlays, we could, in principle, calculate intangible capital stocks for each company and allow each to have its own depreciation rate (see Bloch 1974; Grabowski and Mueller 1978). But here some caution must be exercised, for there are potentially two missing assets whose value one might calculate and add to the denominator of our profit measures to adjust our measure of total assets to obtain a true measure of total assets: One is the investments in R&D and advertising made in the past that have had lasting effects unaccounted for in accounting assets; the other is all of the characteristics of the firm that are not directly related to past

Table 6.5. *Profitability equations after adjustment for intangible advertising capital* (n = 436)

Dependent variables	Independent variables				$\bar{R}^2$
	Intercept	$(1-m_i)C_i^2$	m_iA	m_iPat	
α	-.037	-.550	.688	1.562	.286
	1.16	3.51	11.30	4.98	
α15	.116	-.674	.565	2.350	.210
	3.15	3.74	8.06	6.50	
α28	.042	-.617	.612	2.004	.235
	1.24	3.68	9.39	5.96	
α45	-.014	-.593	.635	1.857	.251
	.41	3.64	10.02	5.69	

Note: *t*-values beneath coefficients.

expenditures, but that allow it to earn permanent rents. If we are correct in interpreting the estimates of projected profitability, $\hat{\alpha}_i$, as measuring long-run positive and negative rents, r_i, then there must exist some "asset" Z_i, to which these permanent rents are attributable. The value of Z_i is the present discounted value of all future rents, $Z_i = r_i/c$ (c = cost of capital). Add this asset value to the denominator of the profit-to-asset ratios prior to calculating the deviations from sample means, and all deviations from the competitive return disappear. All firms would earn the competitive return on *total* capital, thus defined.

This second measure of a firm's intangible capital stock, the present discounted value of the profit stream this stock generates, should not be added to the denominator of the profits-to-assets ratio for fear that one adjusts away what one seeks to measure, the market advantage that product differentiation brings. The only legitimate adjustment is for *past* expenditures that have lasting effects but that are not included in the book value of total assets.[5] The example of Table 6.4 illustrates the issue. By spending 10 on advertising in period t, Firm L created an asset with a market value of 200. Were one to calculate the firm's profit rate using this measure of intangible capital, L would earn the competitive return on capital (20/400 = 0.05). The legitimate adjustment to total assets is the addition of the 10 spent on advertising in t that leads to the permanent price increase. This adjustment lowers the L's return on total assets from 0.10 to 0.095.

This example illustrates yet another unresolved issue in the literature on intangible capital. The first mover advantages documented in the literature would probably translate into longer-lived (lower depreciation rates) intangible assets (see Bond and Lean 1977; Buzzell and Farris 1977). To calculate intangible capital stocks with firm-specific depreciation rates and not ask why some leader firms like L have very low depreciation rates, and followers like F very high ones, is simply to shift the question of market advantage from differences in observed profit rates to differences in depreciation rates.

The results of Chapter 2 indicate significant differences in long-run returns on capital and significant differences in long-run rents. By definition, some intangible assets must exist to account for these rents. The issue is to what extent these assets are directly related to greater past outlays on advertising, R&D, and the like. Past expenditure differences certainly cannot explain all of the differences in profits observed. Many firms in the sample had projected profits significantly below the norm, and below any reasonable measure of the competitive return on capital. To rationalize these away by attributing them to the omission of intangible capital, one must add negative assets into the denominators of the profit variable. But no firm invests to obtain a negative return. The missing asset here is clearly one whose value must be calculated by discounting the future stream of negative rents.

Nor do I believe that all of the deviations in projected returns on the positive side can be rationalized away on the basis of unaccounted for past investments in advertising and R&D. The profits earned by Campbell Soup from 1950 through 1972 are measured after deduction of its advertising and R&D (see Figure 5.4). Were it possible to buy market share by spending more on advertising, Heinz would certainly choose to buy a bigger market share and enjoy more of the profits Campbell receives (see Figure 5.5). Were it possible to buy market share by investing more in intangible capital, Campbell would be the leading producer of dry soup in the United States today.

A similar point holds with respect to R&D. Although one company's expenditures on R&D can easily be matched by those of another, it is more difficult to match the outputs of the R&D process. The economic value of patents is a positively skewed distribution with most patents having zero value and a few having tremendous values (Scherer 1980, pp. 415–16). The differences in profitability that are associated with high market shares in patent-intensive industries come about because the successful firms have come up with very important patents out of their R&D outlays, not simply because they have outspent their rivals at some time in the past.

C.   Profitability and risk

In testing for the persistence-of-profit differences across firms in Chapter 2, our null hypothesis was that all individual company profit rates converge to a single, competitive level. This hypothesis was rejected using the profit projections we made on the basis of 1950–72 data. We have seen in Chapter 4 that certain industry and firm characteristics are related to observed profit differentials across companies. But the most obvious explanation for why profit rates might differ across companies, and the competitive environment hypothesis might yet be correct, we have not examined. Should the activities of companies differ significantly in their risk properties, the capital market will demand higher returns from the riskier companies. Perhaps much or all of the differences in profitability across firms can be accounted for by risk differences. We test this hypothesis in this section.

Two types of risk measures are most frequently used in the empirical literature: the one based on the covariance of a firm's returns with those of other firms, the other based on the variance of its returns. The logic behind the covariance-type measures is that if owners hold diversified portfolios of assets, it is the risk (variance) of the portfolio that matters to them, not the risk (variance) of the individual asset considered in isolation. Furthermore, an asset's contribution to the riskiness of a portfolio is directly related to the covariance of its returns with that of the portfolio, the slope coefficient, $\hat{\beta}$, from a linear time-series regression of the individual company's return on the return of the portfolio (see Sharpe 1964 and any finance textbook, e.g., Fama and Miller 1972). We calculated two $\hat{\beta}$ measures of risk for each firm. The first is based on a regression of the annual return on total assets for each firm on the mean return for the sample in each year, using the 23 years for which our α's are estimated, 1950–72. Equation (1) in Table 6.6 reports the results from adding this variable to the basic firm-effect model equation. The variable has a *negative* and significant coefficient in the equation, opposite to what neoclassical economic theory leads one to expect. The profits of companies with persistently above-normal returns vary less over the business cycle than do the profits of the average firm. The profits of persistently below-normal companies exhibit greater than normal procyclic variability.

The second covariance-type risk measure is based on the risks experienced by stockholders. For each company, the monthly returns on its common shares were used to estimate βs with respect to the market portfolio of all stocks, for five five-year intervals spanning the years 1949–73.[6] These β estimates are dominated by the cyclical swings in stock prices that occur over short time spans. Moreover, the trend in market returns over much of this period was upward. In equation (2) of Table 6.6, $\bar{\beta}$ is the arithmetic mean of the five βs estimated for the five time intervals spanning 1949–73. Where data were missing so that the βs for some time intervals could not be estimated, $\bar{\beta}$ was calculated from the estimates we could make. In all, $\bar{\beta}$ could be estimated for 472 companies. The coefficient on $\bar{\beta}$ is negative and statistically significant. Although the t value on mean β estimated from stock price data is slightly lower than on the β estimated from the accounting profit data, the coefficient on the former is actually three times higher. Once again, the expected positive correlation between risk and profitability is not observed.

The results in equations (1) and (2) of Table 6.6 are quite important since Harris (1983) has recently shown that the coefficient on market

Table 6.6. *Profitability and risk, best-fit αs as dependent variables*

					Independent variables					
Equation	Int	$(1-m_k)C_4^2$	$m.A$	$m.Pat$	β_π	$\bar\beta$	σ_π	σ_α	n	$\bar{R}^2$
(1)	−.059	−.525	.671	1.40	−.073				551	.297
	2.01	3.66	11.32	5.60	3.99					
(2)	.175	−.527	.607	1.30		−.219			472	.299
	2.79	3.41	9.42	5.01		3.76				
(3)	−.048	−.602	.720	1.38			.198		551	.280
	1.61	4.16	12.25	5.45			1.58			
(4)	−.089	−.591	.725	1.35				.656	551	.284
	2.51	4.11	12.36	5.32				2.40		

Note: All variables weighted by $1/\sigma_\alpha$; right-hand-side *not* weighted by S/K.

share in a price–cost margin equation is biased upward if β is omitted from the equation. All three market share terms remain highly significant with comparable coefficients in both equations.

Following the theoretical work of Sherman and Tollison (1972), Harris predicts and finds a negative coefficient on β in the price–cost margin equation. The logic behind this prediction is that *in the short run* managers choose low prices (price–cost margins), if they face high-risk demand to reduce risk. Given that our dependent variable is an estimate of long-run returns on assets and not short-run margin on sales, as in Harris's study, it is doubtful that this hypothesis explains our results. But the similarity in our findings is noteworthy (see also Bothwell and Keeler 1976).

Some empirical work exists in which the current profitability of a firm (profits over total assets or equity) is used to explain its β estimated from monthly stock market returns (see Ben-Zion and Shalit 1975). This work has found that firm profitability is negatively related to a firm's systematic risk. Share prices and perhaps dividend payouts of more profitable companies would appear to be less volatilely related to movements in the stock market than less profitable companies. This negative correlation between risk and return can only be a short-run, disequilibrium phenomenon, if product and capital markets are competitive over the long run. Our findings of persistent profit differences reject the hypothesis of the long-run competitiveness of at least some markets, however. Perhaps the negative correlation between profitability and risk, as measured by our $\hat{\alpha}$ and $\bar{\beta}$, can be explained in the same way as in the single-year cross-sectional studies. Perhaps it is $\hat{\alpha}$ that is causing $\bar{\beta}$. If investors in the stock market can correctly identify companies with persistently high or low profitability, and if the volatility of the returns of firms with persistently high profits is less closely related to the market's volatility than is true for low-profit firms, then the negative association between long-run projected profits and $\bar{\beta}$ is explained by a reverse causality to that assumed in the equation. Given that our β measure, $\bar{\beta}$, is an average over a 25-year period, and given that our profitability measure is a long-run projection based on 23 years of data, if this reverse causality explanation for the negative association between projected profits and systematic risk *is* correct, then the negative coefficient on $\bar{\beta}$ in equation (2) is further confirmation of the existence of *recognizable*, persistent profit differences, and of the existence of permanent impediments to competition or to the flow of capital to account for these persistent differences in profits. The market's treatment of the shares of firms earning persistently higher returns on total assets was such that the shareholders of these companies were able to enjoy lower systematic risk on the shares they held *on the average for more than 25 years.*

It is perhaps worth remarking that the negative relationship we have estimated is between the long-run profitability of the *real* assets of the firm and the systematic risk associated with its common shares. Once the stock market recognizes that a firm is and will be earning persistently higher returns on real assets, capital should flow toward the firm in the stock market and drive the price of its shares up and the return on them down, until the long-run *positive* relationship between risk and returns one expects in a competitive market is established.[7] The negative relationship we have estimated between the riskiness of common shares and the projected profitability on real assets indicates that the flow of capital toward a firm in the stock market is not matched, fully, by the flow of real capital into the markets in which the company sells.

Our results and the above interpretation of these results are consistent with the findings of Sullivan (1978) and Scott (in Caves et al. 1980, Chapter 13). Sullivan sought to explain βs estimated from monthly stock market data in terms of a firm's market power. Sullivan found market power to be negatively associated with the Beta-risk measure and concluded

that as the prices of securities in the secondary capital market fluctuate due to changing general economic, political and social factors, the prices of the securities of powerful firms fluctuate less because of the ability of the powerful firm to either minimize those general economic, social and political changes that would adversely affect its operations or to minimize the effect on its operations of those systematic changes that might occur. (p. 216)

If market power leads to higher profits, then Sullivan's results dovetail nicely with mine. It must be noted, however, that Sullivan measures market power by the concentration ratio for a firm's most important line of business and company size. Neither of these variables is positively related to profitability in the present study. But given the sample Sullivan works with, his concentration variable and our market share variable may be closely related.

John Scott found that the concentration ratios of a firm's industries were negatively related to the returns its shareholders earned; that is, firms in concentrated industries had to pay their shareholders lower returns presumably because these shareholders experienced less exposure to risk. Once again, if one assumes concentration and profitability are positively related in Scott's sample, as they appear to be (see Caves et al. 1980, Chapter 9), so that concentration plays the same role in his sample as market share does in mine, then Scott's results have precisely the same interpretation as mine.

Bowman (1980, 1982) has also observed a negative association between real returns and various measures of risk. Bowman reviews several possible explanations for this relationship and offers his own, which also involves reverse causality. Bowman speculates that firms with low profitability are forced to take risks to try to raise their profitability levels. We shall see in Chapter 8 that low-profitability firms do engage in more merger activity and that mergers may account for an inverse relationship between these two risk measures and profitability consistent with Bowman's hypothesis.

Whether the proper specification of the relationship between α and $\bar{\beta}$ is as assumed in equation (2) in Table 6.6 or one in which α explains $\bar{\beta}$ will not be resolved here. The results more than suffice to reject the hypothesis that projected higher than normal profits can be accounted for in the context of a competitive market environment by the higher risks these companies experience.

σ_π is the variance in a company's return on total assets over the 23-year period 1950–72. Its coefficient is positive, as predicted by economic theory, but insignificant (equation [3]). The coefficients on the other variables in the equation are unaffected by σ_π's inclusion.

As with β_π, α_π is a combination of cyclical variability of profit rates and long-run trend: Companies that experience significant increases or declines in profit rates will exhibit high variances in profits, even though these trends may have been easily anticipated. As with our β measure, one might prefer a measure of risk that captures only the cyclical or unpredictable variability of a company's returns.

If the capital market makes predictions about the long-run profitability of a company using the same kinds of data and the same kinds of equations that we have used to project the long-run profitability of a firm, then our confidence intervals around our estimates of long-run profitability should correlate with the market's confidence intervals around its estimates of future returns. The standard error of our estimate of α might proxy for the stock market's confidence in its ability to predict the future profitability of the firm.

The equations in this chapter, like those in Chapter 4, have been deflated by the standard error of the estimate of α, σ_α, and thus estimated by a form of generalized least squares. What we report as the intercept is actually the coefficient on $1/\sigma_\alpha$. If we now add a normal intercept term to the equation (i.e., a column of ones), it captures the impact of σ_α on profitability. Equation (4) in Table 6.6 adds this vector of ones. It is positive and significant. The level of projected long-run profitability is positively related to the confidence interval around this projection. If we assume that the market projects long-run profitability in somewhat the same way as we do, then the market does seem to withhold capital from those companies for which it has difficulty projecting long-run returns, that is, for those companies for which none of the three polynomials in $1/t$ provided a fit with a narrow confidence interval around α. The range in σ_α is from .026 to 1.21, so that the coefficient on σ_α in equation (4) of Table 6.6 implies a predicted difference in profitability between the firm with lowest σ_α and the firm with the highest value of more than 80 percent of the average profit rate, a sizable difference.

The weak performance of the variance in a firm's profitability over time as a predictor of the level of its profits is consistent with the findings in the existing literature.[8] The comparably strong performance of σ_α suggests that part of the problem in previous research may have been the use of the "wrong" variance-type measure of risk.

It is interesting that both variance-type measures of risk picked up the theoretically predicted positive sign, whereas neither covariance measure did. The covariance measure of risk is the appropriate one in a world in which capital owners hold diversified portfolios of assets; the variance in the return on a single asset is the appropriate measure of risk when only this asset is held. One possible explanation of our results is that capital ownership is on the average closer to the single-asset-portfolio assumption than to the fully diversified portfolio assumption of the Capital–Asset–Pricing (CAP) model literature. A second is that the CAP model's βs are poor empirical proxies to the risks investors actually take into account.[9]

But it must be kept in mind that our profit rates are long-run accounting returns on accounting values of real assets. Two explanations related to this characteristic of our data were offered for the two different measures. The β_πs calculated by regressing company profit rates on the mean profit rate may have been affected by the downward trend in profitability over the last couple of years of the sample period. Companies with higher than normal projected returns bucked this trend over the last few years. Reverse causality may account for the inverse relationship between β measured from monthly stock returns and long-run profits earned on real assets. Companies with persistently high profits have less volatile returns on shares; companies with persistently low profits have more volatile shares.

Regardless of how one accounts for the differences between the relationships between profitability and the two types of risk measures, it is clear that neither measure's inclusion in the basic equation of the firm-effect model detracts noticeably from the explanatory power of the other variables in the model. Market share, product differentiation, and concentration are not simply proxies for risk in explaining long-run profitability.

D. Growth, size, diversification, and profitability

In this section, we test for the possible influence of three variables used in other profitability studies. Two of these reappear in the next chapter on managerial control, but others have hypothesized a relationship between them and profitability independent of the managerial control literature so we present some results for them here. First, we briefly discuss each variable, and then present the results.

1. Growth

Many studies have included an industry's growth rate in equations to explain industry profit rates on the grounds that in rapidly growing industries demand growth often outstrips supply growth and thus allows incumbent firms to earn short-run above-normal profits. The inclusion of growth in an equation thus rests on the assumption that potential entrants and incumbents on the average tend to underestimate the growth rates of fast-growing industries or face bottlenecks that preclude capacity expansion to meet growing demand.

Whether a firm's growth rate can be assumed to explain its profits by the same sort of hypothesis is less certain, particularly when we are working with a long-run projected profit rate. On the other hand, a firm's growth rate might proxy for various firm-specific characteristics such as superior management talent, a superior product, more efficient production technology, and the like. To the extent that these superior, or inferior (for below-normal profit firms), characteristics are reflected in 1972 market shares, and the projection of future market shares can be accurately made with the formula we use involving 1950 and 1972 market shares, then the equation we estimate with projected market shares and concentration should accurately predict future profitability. But the projections of future market shares and concentration are heavily weighted by the 1972 figures for these variables and are equal to these figures when the 1950 figures are missing. The growth rate of the company could capture product and efficiency advantages not reflected in our projections of market share and concentration, and thus contribute to the explanation of future profitability as projected by our best-fit equation.

Two measures of the growth of company i are employed:

$$G_i = \frac{\text{TOTAL ASSETS of } i \text{ in 1972}}{\text{TOTAL ASSETS of } i \text{ in 1950}}$$

Ln (G_i), the natural log of G_i.

2.   *Size*

Theoretical support for including the absolute size of a company, as opposed to its relative size as measured by market share, is somewhat lacking. One might associate many of the market power advantages often mentioned in references to conglomerate size with size per se. That is, absolute size might be viewed as a sort of interaction term between market share and diversification. In particular, a corporation's ability to exert political pressure and win profitable favors from the national or local legislatures might be most closely related to its absolute size. On the negative side, larger firms might suffer from greater internal control and information loss and bureaucratic inefficiencies of other sorts, what typically goes under the heading of X-inefficiency. This latter explanation begins to resemble the link between size and profitability predicted by the managerial theory of the firm, which we take up in Chapter 7.

The earliest tests for the effect of size on profitability in the United States found a positive effect (Hall and Weiss 1967). Empirical work in Europe has more typically uncovered a negative coefficient.[10] Thus, we make no sign prediction for the size variable. Two measures of size are employed:

$S72_i = $ 1972 sales for company i
Ln$(S72_i) = $ the natural log of $S72_i$.

3.   *Diversification*

Several hypotheses in the literature predict a positive association between diversification and firm profits. As usual, these break down into those predicting greater market power for diversified firms, and those hypothesizing greater efficiency. Market power advantages might arise through the exploitation of an advantage in one market in some other market, for example, if a firm with monopsony power were to force one of its suppliers to purchase one of its products as a condition for purchasing the supplier's product.[11] Efficiency advantages can be claimed for diversified firms because they are able to avoid some of the imperfections of the capital market. Promising investment opportunities in one market can be funded by drawing capital away from other markets, without jeopardizing the profitability of the investment by having to reveal its characteristics to raise capital.[12] Some initial, empirical work has found a positive association between diversification and profits.[13]

We employed two measures of diversification: DIV a Herfindahl-type index of diversification,[14] and IND a raw count of the number of industries in which the firm operated. If S_{iI} is firm i's sales in industry I, S_i its total sales over the m markets in which it sells (that is, $S_i = \sum_{I=1}^{m} S_{iI}$), then

$$DIV = \sum_{I=1}^{m} \left(\frac{S_{iI}}{S_i}\right)^2$$

and

$$IND = m.$$

We constructed DIV and IND indexes for both 1950 and 1972 and then computed a projected DIV and IND index in the same way that we projected market share and concentration. The results for projected DIV and IND resemble those for 1972 DIV and IND, and we report only the latter.

4. The results

Table 6.7 presents the regression results from adding each of the above variables to the firm-effect model. Only $Ln(G_i)$ is significant and it is highly so. Market advantages leading to rapid firm growth do seem to be positively related to projected profitability over and above what our market structure variables predict. The same holds for market disadvantages. The intercept term, when log growth is included, is five times lower than without it and becomes highly significant. The performances of $(1 - m_i)C_4^2$ and m_iA are strengthened by log growth's inclusion in the equation, but the coefficient and t value on m_iPat falls. Log growth appears to be picking up some of the influence of market success in technologically progressive industries. The marked difference between G_i's performance in the equation and that of $Ln(G_i)$ implies a tail-off as one moves into the higher growth rates of the relationship between additional growth and projected profitability.

The two size measures are of opposite signs and do not approach

Table 6.7. *Profitability, growth, size, and diversification, best-fit αs* ($n = 551$)

Equation	Int	$(1-m_t)C_4^2$	m_tA	m_tPat	G_i	$Ln(G_i)$	$S72_i$	$Ln(S72_i)$	DIV_i	IND_i	$\bar{R}^2$
(1)	−.044	−.588	.721	1.36	.0005						.277
	1.48	4.07	12.23	5.36	.77						
(2)	−.210	−.636	.758	1.12		.100					.321
	5.25	4.53	13.20	4.48		6.00					
(3)	−.039	−.572	.716	1.41			-36×10^{-5}				.277
	1.33	3.91	12.15	5.42			.53				
(4)	−.054	−.587	.718	1.37				.002			.277
	.68	4.02	12.19	5.36				.19			
(5)	−.034	−.572	.726	1.36					−.031		.277
	1.06	3.90	11.84	5.30					.45		
(6)	−.043	−.582	.718	1.38						.0001	.277
	1.26	4.02	12.19	5.41						.15	
(7)	−.033	−.562	.724	1.39			$-.34 \times 10^{-5}$		−.030		.276
	1.02	3.79	11.78	5.28			.52		.44		
(8)	−.053	−.586	.718	1.37				.002		$.037 \times 10^{-4}$	.275
	.61	3.96	12.18	5.35				.12		.04	

statistical significance. Both diversification variables have the pre-dicted signs (lower *DIV* implies increasing diversification), but neither is significant.[15] Combinations of the variables did not alter the picture; two examples of these are presented as equations (7) and (8).

E.   Conclusions

In this chapter, we have made several modifications to the basic firm-effect equation specified in Chapter 4. Allowing for the possibility that individual firm demand schedules have differing slopes and for different degrees of substitutability across products did not lead to a significant increase in our ability to explain long-run differences in firm profitability. A slight increase in explanatory power was contrib-uted by knowledge of the firm's own advertising relative to industry advertising.

The covariance of a firm's profits with the profits of other companies and of a firm's monthly return with the return on the market portfolio proved to be negatively and significantly related to profitability. The sign on this variable is not what one expects from the high risk-re-quires-high-return hypothesis, and suggests a reverse causal relation-ship. High-return firms are less risky investments. Two variance measures of risk are positively related to profitability, although less strongly so than the covariance measures.

Of the other firm characteristics we tried, only the log of the com-pany's growth rate proved to have a significant (positive) relationship to projected long-run returns on assets. This positive relationship was interpreted as a correction factor for our firm-effects equation. The projected market shares, concentration ratios, and industry advertis-ing and patent-intensity variables under- (over-) estimate long-run profitability for rapidly (slowly) growing companies.

None of the variables examined in this chapter detracts seriously from our conclusions of Chapter 4 as to the role market share, con-centration, industry advertising, and industry patent intensity have in explaining long-run profitability, nor does adjustment of the pro-jected profits variable to allow for intangible capital. The impact of the new variables is largely additive. Firm advertising detracts a bit from the explanatory power of the industry advertising variable; firm growth detracts from the patent-intensity variable. Adjustment for intangible advertising capital detracts from the advertising variable, while enhancing the measured impact of patent intensity. But the variables in the basic model have a consistent, strong relationship to profitability. The new variables taken into consideration in this chapter, if they have any role to play at all, tend to add to our ability to understand and explain the long-run profitability of firms.

CHAPTER 7

Profitability and managerial control and compensation

A.   Background

Since the time Berle and Means ([1932] 1968) first emphasized the importance of the separation of ownership from control in the modern corporation, a phenomenon that today goes under the rubric of principle-agent-problem, a large literature has evolved exploring what managers can do and have done with the discretion they now have. (For surveys of this literature, see McEachern 1975, Chapter 2; Hay and Morris 1979, Chapters 8, 9; Marris and Mueller 1980; Lawriwsky 1984.) By and large, this literature has presumed the existence of pecuniary or nonpecuniary managerial objectives in conflict with the stockholder's presumed objective of the maximization of profits or the present value of the firm.

The pioneering article suggesting a tradeoff between profits and a managerial objective might be regarded as Scitovsky's (1943) classic paper on profits maximization. Although not intended as a contribution to the managerial literature, Scitovsky posited an inverted-U relationship between profits and leisure for the entrepreneur (see Figure 7.1). Given a normal utility function with leisure and income (profit) as arguments, the utility maximization, leisure-income tradeoff involves more leisure and less profits than pure profits maximization. Scitovsky used this figure to draw out the implication that profits maximization implied that leisure was on the borderline of being an inferior good for the entrepreneur, an implication suggesting the implausibility of a narrow definition of profits maximization, even in an entreprencurial world.

The various managerial theories basically assume the same profits-X-tradeoff as Scitovsky did, with X standing for different goals in conflict with profits in each theory. For Baumol ([1959] 1967), X is sales; for Williamson (1964), staff and emoluments; for Marris (1964), the growth of the firm; for Monsen and Downs (1965) and Caves and Yamey (1971), a reduction in risk; and for Comanor and Leibenstein (1969), X-inefficiency. Each of the managerial theories assumes that profits, or the present value of the firm, are traded away to some degree to achieve whatever managerial goal is hypothesized.

143

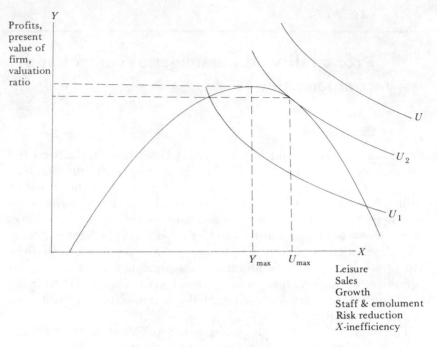

Figure 7.1 The managerial-stockholder tradeoff.

An obvious question raised by the managerial literature is what constrains management from using up all of the profits and perhaps real assets of the firm in pursuit of its own goals. Marris (1963, 1964) was the first to posit the threat of takeover by some outside group should profits or the market value of the firm fall too far below their maximum potential value,[1] and the literature has by and large followed Marris in assuming that it is the threat of takeover that checks managerial discretion.[2]

Let us define π^* as the maximum possible return on assets the corporation would make were its management to make no use of its discretionary advantage, that is, if $X = 0$. The observed profit rate is then

$$\alpha \equiv \pi^* - X, \tag{7.1}$$

where X is also expressed as a percentage of total assets. Define the probability that the firm is *not* taken over as N, where N is an increasing function of both α and D, the level of managerial discretion, $N = N(\alpha, D)$. Setting aside for the moment what determines D and how it is measured, we can reasonably assume that managers maximize an expected utility function composed of two parts: the utility they expect if their firm is not taken over and they remain its managers (call this U,) and the utility they expect following a successful takeover of their company (call this $\overline{U}$). $\overline{U}$ may be experienced by the managers remaining in the firm taken over, but in positions of reduced authority, by their taking lower ranked positions in other similar firms, or by their assuming the top managerial positions in some smaller or less profitable firm. Regardless of which scenario one assumes for the managers' posttakeover, it is reasonable to suppose that $\overline{U} < U$ at the optimal (otherwise managers would try to bring about takeovers), and that $\overline{U}$ is an increasing function of α. The higher that current reported profits are, the better the manager's position in any future posttakeover situation. Utility in the current managerial position is assumed to be an increasing function of all of the activities making up X. We can then write the manager's expected utility as

$$E(U) = N(\alpha,D) \cdot U(X) + (1 - N(\alpha,D)) \cdot \overline{U}(\alpha) \qquad (7.2)$$

where $N_\alpha > 0$, $N_D > 0$, $N_{\alpha D} \leq 0$, $U_X > 0$, $U_{XX} < 0$, $\overline{U}_\alpha > 0$, $\overline{U}_{\alpha\alpha} < 0$. Substituting for X from (7.1) into (7.2) and maximizing (7.2) with respect to α, assuming D and π^* are fixed, we obtain

$$\frac{dE}{d\alpha} = N_\alpha U - NU_X - N_\alpha \overline{U} + (1 - N) \overline{U}_\alpha = 0 \qquad (7.3)$$

$$N_\alpha(U - \overline{U}) = NU_X - (1 - N)\overline{U}_\alpha. \qquad (7.4)$$

Managers push consumption of X to the point where the increment in the probability of remaining in their current position, if α is increased times the utility differential between this position and the posttakeover position, just equals the expected value of the marginal utilities of X in the two positions. Taking the total differential of (7.3) with respect to α and D, we obtain

$$(N_{\alpha\alpha}U - 2N_\alpha U_X + NU_{XX} - N_{\alpha\alpha}\overline{U} \quad 2N_\alpha \overline{U}_{\alpha\alpha} + (1 - N) \overline{U}_{\alpha\alpha})d\alpha$$
$$= (-N_{\alpha D} (U - \overline{U}) + N_D U_X + N_D \overline{U}_\alpha)dD. \qquad (7.5)$$

The expression in parentheses on the left-hand side is negative by the second-order condition. The expression in parentheses on the right-hand side is positive by the assumptions $N_{\alpha D} \leq 0$ and $U > \overline{U}$. Thus, $d\alpha/dD < 0$. An increase in managerial discretion increases managerial consumption of X and thereby lowers reported profitability, α.

Managerial discretion arises owing to the monitoring costs of observing managerial behavior and the transactions costs of removing management should one determine that managers have engaged in nonzero or excessive X-type activity (see Williamson 1975, Chapter 7; Jensen and Meckling 1976). One must first determine what the level of X is and then engage in the expense of a takeover attempt should X be large enough.

Many corporations are extremely protective of information that would allow outsiders to determine what the potential value of a takeover might be. Any effort by the Securities and Exchange Commission (SEC) to force management to provide more detailed reporting of their own financial association with their companies, or accounting data that facilitate outside monitoring, such as the requirements for divisional sales and profit reporting of a decade ago, is in general vigorously resisted by corporate managements. In this connection it is worth recalling that the SEC itself came into existence to fulfill a perceived monitoring gap between stockholders and managers in the aftermath of the Great Crash, when many managerial indiscretions during the twenties were revealed.[3]

Closer to home, the FTC 1972 market share data this study uses have yet to be released, because of opposition from some companies included in the survey to release of the data. One of the arguments often presented by companies not wishing to have their market share data made public is that it gives competitors a strategic advantage. Similar arguments were brought forward in opposition to SEC requirements for divisional reporting, and the reporting of advertising and R&D data. But this information is often already in the hands of a firm's competitors. Industry trade publications often report estimates of company market shares, and the Economic Information Systems, Inc. (EIS) surveys, to which many companies subscribe, provide market share estimates at the four-digit level. The *Leading National Advertisers'* data this study uses are publicly available. They, like EIS and industry surveys of market shares, are available to those who know they exist and can afford their high costs. Given that a company's competitors often have or could have these data, the obvious group from which the data are concealed is the general public, that is, the stockholders and other potential outside raiders.[4] In Europe, corporate secrecy is considerably more pronounced than in the United States. In Belgium, for example, firms are not required to report sales data, and many do not. In West Germany, many firms choose the GmbH legal form of incorporation apparently because it does not require the detailed reporting of sales, profit, and other data as is required by the SEC in the United States and in West Germany, if a firm chooses the AG (Aktiengesellschaft) form of incorporation.[5]

One explanation for corporate diversification is to conceal market share and profitability information that could be used to gauge π^* and thereby X (see FTC 1972b). The market share of a company operating in a single industry can be calculated simply by dividing its sales by industry sales. If its competitors operate in only this industry, their respective profitabilities can be directly compared to gauge π^* and X. When a company operates in 100 or more markets and reports only total sales and profits, this calculation is impossible. Thus, the protection from takeover secrecy provides can be assumed to be directly related to the size and diversification of a company.

This argument may explain why size and diversification were not found to be positively related to profitability in Chapter 6. Managers of large, diversified companies enjoy more discretion to utilize the revenues of the company to their own advantage.

Size can also contribute to managerial discretion by increasing the transaction costs of bringing about a takeover given any level of X. To take over another company successfully, a challenger must essentially acquire 50 percent or more of the outstanding shares of the target firm to vote the incumbent management out of office. The amount of capital this acquisition of shares requires is directly proportional to the size of the target firm. The challenged management has various legal devices it can resort to, to fend off a takeover bid. In making such a defense the incumbent management relies on the legal staff and other resources of its firm. The bigger the company, the greater the counterattack the challenged management can launch, and the larger the legal effort the takeover bidders have to make to achieve their objective. Thus, both components of the transaction costs of undertaking a takeover are positively related to the size of the company. (See Lawriwsky 1984, Chapters 6, 7, for arguments and evidence linking managerial discretion to company size.)

One way to think of the costs of launching a successful takeover is to envisage convincing successive shareholders to vote against incumbent management. The more heavily concentrated shareholdings are in the hands of outsiders, the fewer the number of individuals one must convince, and the lower the transaction costs of conducting a takeover. Moreover, the amount of information a shareholder possesses about the company is likely to be directly related to his or her shareholdings. Since most of the information needed to estimate X is available to the public at a cost, what protects managers, who claim large amounts of X, is the free-rider problem. No single shareholder has an incentive to gather the information needed to determine X. Given the scale economy properties of information gathering, however, the information held by shareholders should increase, probably nonlinearly, with the magnitude of their shareholdings. A negative relationship between X and the concentration of outside shareholdings is predicted, that is, a positive relationship between α and outside holdings.

There is, of course, one type of shareholder who is difficult to convince of the need to replace incumbent management, a member of management itself. The transaction costs of mounting a takeover should be directly related to the concentration of shares in management's hands.

Although many studies have used the number of shares held by a given group of individuals as a proxy for ownership control,[6] most have not distinguished between holdings by outsiders and management. An important exception to this rule is the study by William McEachern (1975), and also the work of Nyman and Silberston (1978) and Lawriwsky (1984). The distinction is crucial. It is true that a manager who owns 10 percent of a company's shares benefits by a factor of 100 times more than a manager who owns one-tenth of 1 percent of the firm's shares. But the former still receives only ten cents out of every dollar declared as dividends, while receiving a full dollar added to his or her salary or used to purchase some substitute for personal consumption. Given that the latter appear as corporate expenses and are deducted prior to the calculation of the corporate income tax liability, whereas any corporate revenue defined as profit must be taxed at the corporate income tax rate, the incentive to maximize shareholder wealth, provided by even fairly large managerial shareholdings, appears rather weak. On the other hand, a 10 percent holding of outstanding shares by management may suffice to raise the transaction costs of an outside takeover considerably. When management holds 0.1 of 1 percent of outstanding shares, a takeover bidder must acquire 50.1 percent of the remaining shares to be sure of success. When management holds 10 percent, an outsider must acquire 55.5 percent of the remaining shares; and when management holds 30 percent, the outside bidder must acquire more than 71 percent of the remaining shares to secure a majority interest in the company.

These considerations lead to the following predictions: D, managerial discretion, is positively related to the fraction of shares management holds, *MC*, and is negatively related to the fraction concentrated in the hands of a few outsiders, *OC*.

B.   Managerial discretion and corporate profitability

To test for the importance of managerial discretion on reported corporate profitability, we gathered data on corporate shareholdings from the company proxy statements filed at the SEC. Each manager is compelled by SEC rules to report his own personal shareholdings, those of his immediate family, and those of any other companies or trust funds he controls. Thus, figures for the amount of shares held or controlled by management are likely to be fairly accurate. On the other hand, data on the holdings of major outside shareholders seem considerably more spotty. Previous investigations by Burch (1972) and Chevalier (1969) suggest that the extent of outside control of corporations is grossly underestimated by the figures reported on corporate proxy statements in many instances. But we did not have the resources to track down outside ownership interests as these authors did.

A second difficulty with outside holdings is that it is not always possible to determine when an outsider is truly an outsider or at least has an outsider's interests. When a major shareholder has the same last name as one of the managers, it is reasonable to assume this person is a relative of the manager and to lump his or her holdings with management's holdings. When the names differ, the outsider could still be related to management, but sometimes there is no way to tell. Thus, some shareholdings attributed to outsiders may be controlled by management.

Particularly difficult to identify and classify are major shareholders who are *former* managers. If no relatives are now part of management, these former managers are categorized as outsiders. But it is possible that a manager with a large holding of shares, who passes into retirement, does not react to current managerial discretionary behavior as someone who never was part of management. If the retired manager engaged in discretionary behavior as part of management, he or she may cast an understanding eye on similar behavior by current management, so long as it does not exceed the levels the retired manager deems reasonable. Thus, the strength of outside control may be overestimated in some cases.

Institutional holdings by independent trust funds and investment banks are not recorded by the SEC. When another corporation was a major shareholder, its holdings were treated like those of an out-

Table 7.1. *Definitions of variables used in Chapter 7*

A. *Variables from previous chapters*

α   Projected returns on total assets expressed as a relative deviation from the mean returns for all companies. Estimated from the best fit of the three polynomials in $1/t$ estimated in Chapter 2.

m Projected market share.

C_4 Projected four-firm concentration ratio.

A Industry advertising-to-sales ratio.

Pat Industry patent-to-sales ratio.

$S72$ 1972 sales of firm i.

DIV A Herfindahl index of firm i's diversification.

B. *Variables introduced in this chapter*

MC The number of common shares held by the top five managers and their relatives divided by the total number of shares outstanding.

OC The number of common shares held by major shareholders outside of the company divided by the total number of shares outstanding.

MS The average salary and cash bonuses earned by the five highest paid officers in the company in 1972. (When figures for 1972 were not available, the closest year to 1972 for which data were available was chosen and the data converted into 1972 dollars.)

OPT The total dollar value of stock options granted to the five highest-paid directors in 1972 or closest year to 1972.

GAQ Relative growth through acquisition. The assets acquired in year t divided by the firm's assets at the beginning of year t summed over the years 1950 through 1972.

NAQ The number of years from 1950 through 1972 in which the company made at least one acquisition.

IG The internal growth of the firm. Total real growth (G from Chapter 6 deflated by the GNP deflator for investment) less GAQ.

---

sider. We computed two variables. The sum of the holdings of shares by the five top managers of a company, their relatives, and trust funds and companies they control, MC; and the sum of all reported holdings by anyone else, never more than five persons or institutions, OC. The mean value of MC was 0.054 with a range from 0 to 0.870; the mean of OC was 0.015 with range 0 to 0.347. These and other variables used in this chapter are defined in Table 7.1.

We can now proceed to estimate the impact of managerial discretion on projected profitability. From (7.1) we have maximum potential profits, π^*, defined as

$$\pi^* \equiv \alpha + X,$$

where X is the amount of corporate revenue management diverts to its own uses, α is reported profits. From the previous discussion, X

can be written as a function of managerial discretion, which in turn depends on management control, MC, outside control, OC, size, and diversification. We shall measure size by 1972 sales, $S72$, and diversification as the Herfindahl index of diversification, DIV, used in Chapter 6. Thus, we can write X as

$$X = H(D), \quad H' > 0$$
$$D = h(MC, OC, S72, DIV). \tag{7.6}$$

Approximating the compound function $H(h(D))$ as a linear function in its four arguments, we have[7]

$$X_i = b_1 \, MC_i + b_2 \, OC_i + b_3 \, S72_i + b_4 \, DIV_i, \tag{7.7a}$$

where the arguments of the previous section imply

$$h_1 > 0, \quad b_2 < 0, \quad b_3 > 0, \quad b_4 < 0. \tag{7.8}$$

(Recall that increasing diversification implies lower values for the diversification index, DIV, and thus larger managerial discretion, and larger X.) The arguments of the previous section suggest that managerial discretion may increase (decrease) at an exponential rate with increasing $MC(OC)$, and Cubbin and Leech (1983) have shown that under certain assumptions a Herfindahl-type index of shareholdings (i.e., the summation of fractional holdings squared) is the theoretically appropriate measure of control. We thus also experimented with

$$X_i = b_1 \, MC_i^2 + b_2 \, OC_i^2 + b_3 \, S72_i + b_4 \, DIV_i. \tag{7.7b}$$

Equation (7.7b) gave slightly higher R^2s in most applications, so we report only those results.

The hypotheses put forward in Chapter 4, like all structure-performance theories, have to do with the maximum potential profits, π^*, not those profits reported after managers have diverted some fraction to fulfill their own goals. A firm's perceived product quality allows it to charge a given price and achieve the corresponding output along its demand schedule. Its level of efficiency determines the minimum level of average costs it could achieve, if the management engaged in no additional consumption of X, and these minimum potential costs and actual revenue determine what the firm's declared profits might have been in the absence of managerial discretion, π^*. Thus, the proper specification of our firm-effect and industry-effect models is to make maximum potential profits a function of each model's respective structural variables. In the case of the firm-effect model estimated in Chapter 4, this would imply that we should estimate the following equation

$$\pi^* = b_5 + b_6 (1 - m_i)C_4^2 + b_7 m_i A + b_8 m_i Pat. \tag{7.9}$$

We can use equations (7.1) and (7.7b) to eliminate the unobservable π^* and (dropping the i subscripts) obtain

$$\alpha = -b_1 MC^2 - b_2 OC^2 - b_3 S72 - b_4 DIV + b_5$$
$$+ b_6(1 - m)C_4^2 + b_7 mA + b_8 mPat + \mu. \tag{7.10}$$

All of the factors that increase maximum potential profits, such as market share, increase reported profits. The factors that increase managerial discretionary expenditures, X, reduce reported profits.

Estimates of (7.10) are contained in Table 7.2 for the 499 observations for which the control variables were available. The dependent variable is again the long-run projected profit rate from the best-fit equations in Chapter 2, and is a relative deviation from the sample mean. All variables are deflated by the standard errors of the σ_α estimates. The first equation in Table 7.2 presents ordinary least squares results for the basic structure-performance model of Chapter 4. They are quite similar to the earlier estimates indicating that the 499 observation subsample is representative of the full 551 observation sample used in Chapters 4 and 6.

Equation 2 adds the managerial discretion variables. All but $S72$ have the predicted sign, but only the managerial control variable is statistically significant. The inclusion of the four managerial discretion variables does not alter the magnitudes or significance of the four coefficients $b_5 - b_8$ by much.

Although the level of significance of the MC variable is quite high, the performance of the four as a group is weak. One possible explanation for this, which is consistent with the hypothesis that managers have and exercise discretion, is that the estimates suffer from simultaneous-equations bias. Baumol (1959) hypothesized that managers maximize sales; Marris (1964) that they pursue growth. If managers have discretion to pursue their own goals, sales and diversification might be expected to be codetermined variables. To see whether this explanation might account for the wrong sign on sales, equation (2) was reestimated using two-stage least squares treating $S72$ as a codetermined variable and adding 1950 sales as an instrument. The results are reported as equation (3). The coefficient on $S72$ is now of the correct sign and, although insignificant, does manage a t-value greater than 1.4. Diversification and outside control remain highly insignificant, but both the coefficient and t-value on the management

Table 7.2. *Impact of managerial discretion on projected profitability, best-fit αs* (n = 499)

$$\alpha = b_1 MC^2 - b_2 OC^2 - b_3 S{\cdot}72 - b_4 DIV + b_5 + b_6(1 - m)C_4^2 + b_7 m{\cdot}A + b_8 m{\cdot}Pat$$

Equation	Estimating procedure	$-b_1$	$-b_2$	$-b_3$	$-b_4$	b_5	b_6	b_7	b_8	$\overline{R}^2$
(1)	OLS					-.039	-.574	.724	1.68	.306
						1.32	3.87	12.14	6.08	
(2)	OLS	-1.27	.275	.00004	.017	-.033	-.582	.742	1.57	.323
		3.91	.09	.50	.24	.99	3.86	11.97	5.63	
(3)	2SLS	-1.34	-.065	-.00001	.018	-.025	-.526	.735	1.59	.316
		4.11	.02	1.44	.25	.74	3.46	11.79	5.70	

$$\alpha = \frac{b_5 + b_6(1 - m)C_4^2 + b_7 mA + b_8 m\,Pat}{EXP\,(h_1 MC^2 + h_2\,OC^2 + h_3\,S72 + h_4\,DIV)}$$

Equation	Estimating procedure	h_1	h_2	h_3	h_4	b_5	b_6	b_7	b_8	Likelihood ratio
(4)	NL	2.44	-2.60	-.0001	-1.06	-.083	-.867	1.45	2.52	-1315
		3.17	.10	1.80	3.70	1.88	3.58	4.34	4.36	
(5)	NL	2.86	2.06		-.760	-.064	-.650	1.04	1.79	-1317
		3.85	.11		3.11	1.83	3.77	6.52	5.27	

control variable increase in absolute value. Thus, it would appear that our conjecture that sales and the other discretionary variables may be interacting seems plausible. The remaining variables in the equation remain as before.

It should be noted that sales are measured in millions of dollars, so that the coefficient of $-.00001$ in equation (3), although appearing quite small, implies an elasticity at mean sales of -0.80, which is quite comparable to MC^2's elasticity at its mean of -0.94.

Given that MC is included as a squared variable, the amount of deviation between maximum potential profits and reported profits increases sharply with rising MC. At MC's mean value of 0.054, for example, equation (3) implies that reported profits are less than maximum potential profits by but .4 of 1 percent of the average profits for the sample, taking into account all other factors. Should management hold 50 percent of all outstanding shares, however, reported profits would be 33.5 percent below their maximum potential value owing to the increased level of X.[8]

Equations (6) and (7) make the level of discretionary expenditures, X, dependent upon the amount of managerial discretion, D, but not upon the level of potential profits, π^*. A more plausible assumption is that X is positively related to both π^* and D. Managers of firms with cost or market power advantages can enjoy more on-the-job consumption or claim higher incomes than managers of inherently weak-performing companies. Palmer (1973b) has stressed this point. La-wriwsky (1984) also emphasizes that managerial discretion should be made contingent on market power, among other factors. Let us thus write

$$X = (1 - \gamma)\pi^*, \tag{7.11}$$

from which, via (7.6),

$$\alpha = \gamma\pi^*. \tag{7.12}$$

Since X and therefore $1 - \gamma$ are positively related to managerial discretion, D, γ must be inversely related to it. In choosing a functional form for γ, we would like it to exhibit the properties that when managerial discretion is nil ($D = 0$), reported profits equal maximum potential profits ($\alpha = \pi^*$), and then decline with increasing managerial discretion, that is, $0 \leq \gamma \leq 1$, $(D = 0) \leftrightarrow (\gamma = 1)$, and $\partial\gamma/\partial D < 0$. A relatively simple functional form exhibiting these properties is the exponential

$$\gamma = e^{-D}. \tag{7.13}$$

From (7.6) we write D as

$$D = h(MC, OC, S72, DIV), \tag{7.14}$$

or in linear form as

$$D = h_1 MC^2 + h_2 OC^2 + h_3 S72 + h_4 DIV \tag{7.15}$$

by analogy with (7.7b). We assume that the values of the variables and parameters are such to maintain $D > 0$. Substituting for γ and π^* in (7.12), we obtain

$$\alpha = \frac{b_5 + b_6 (1 - m) C_4^2 + b_7 mA + b_8 mPat}{EXP(h_1 MC^2 + h_2 OC^2 + h_3 S72 + h_4 DIV)}. \tag{7.16}$$

Equation (7.16) was estimated using the SHAZAM nonlinear regression option, which employs a Gauss–Newton maximum likelihood procedure. An additive error was assumed and both sides of (7.16) were deflated by σ_n as done throughout the study; that is, the entire right-hand-side expression was deflated by σ_α, not each individual variable. The results are presented in the bottom half of Table 7.2.

The data provide a relatively good fit to the model with a highly significant likelihood ratio. $S72$ again has the wrong sign, and is significant at the 10 percent level. But the other three variables have the predicted signs, and both management control and diversification are significant at the 1 percent level. The multiplicative formulation of the model uncovers a strong relationship between diversification and managerial discretion of the predicted sign (recall that DIV declines as diversification increases).

The appearance of 1972 sales with the wrong sign in this equation again suggests the presence of simultaneous-equations bias. But removing simultaneous-equations bias from a nonlinear equation is no simple task. I attempted to do so by regressing $S72$ on the other right-handed variables in (4), along with 1950 sales and 1950 profits, and then replacing $S72$ in (4) by its predicted value, but the moment matrix invariably turned singular during the iteration process. Eliminating simultaneous-equations bias from equation (4) appears to require a more complete specification of a simultaneous equations model, including the managerial discretion variables. Equation (5) in Table 7.2 shows what happens when $S72$ is dropped from the equation. The coefficient on MC^2 rises, the coefficient on OC^2 reverses signs but remains insignificant, and the coefficients on all other variables retreat back toward their values when all managerial variables are excluded from the equation. Thus, the determination of the exact quantitative impact managerial discretion has on projected profitability is de-

pendent to some extent on the elimination of the simultaneity properties of equation (4). But the performance of the MC and
diversification variables does suggest that managerial discretion has
an important effect on reported profitability.

The large improvement in the performance of the diversification
variable in going from the linear to the nonlinear specification of the
managerial discretion model may seem to be cause for some concern.
In industrial organization, we work almost exclusively with models,
which are linear or linear in logs. In these models a large movement
in a coefficient following, say, the deletion or addition of a variable
usually signals some underlying econometric-data problem, for example, multicollinearity or an outlier observation. The movement of
the coefficients on $(1-m)C_4$, mA, and $mPat$ back toward their values
in the linear model, when $S72$ is dropped in going from equation (4)
to (5), may be due to these traditional problems. But the shift from
the linear to the nonlinear specification of the managerial discretion
model is not analogous to the typical marginal modifications. The
nonlinear model posits an interaction between the managerial discretion variables determining D and all of the market structure variables.
Given the magnitude of this change in the specification of the model,
the change in results can simply be interpreted as reflecting the differing economic logic underlying the two models.

Despite its complexity, the nonlinear specification of the managerial
discretion model is to be preferred. Shorey Petersen (1965) pointed
out 20 years ago that the possibility of inefficiency arising because of
managerial discretion is attenuated to the extent that markets are
competitive. The market is the most effective control mechanism for
checking managerial diversions of corporate revenues. Only in conjunction with market advantages that allow managers the potential of
earning above-normal profits can one expect to find the extent of
managerial discretion playing a role in explaining actually observed
profits. Thus, the proper specification of the managerial discretion
model is in an interactive form.

Given the nonlinear nature of this form of the managerial discretion
hypothesis, the economic implications of the coefficients in the managerial discretion component of the model require comment. Once
again, since MC enters as a squared term, the impact of management
control of outstanding shares becomes pronounced only at higher
values of MC. When management controls the average 5.4 percent
of outstanding shares, reported profits are 0.7 of 1 percent of the
average less than maximum possible profits. When it controls 20 percent, reported profits are 10 percent of the mean below their potential

value; when it controls 50 percent, they are 61 percent lower. The mean value for DIV is 0.30 with a range virtually from 0 to 1.0. An increase in diversification lowering DIV from .30 to .20 results, ceteris paribus, in a 10.6 percent reduction in reported profits from their maximum potential value.

Although these results suggest that managerial discretion has an important impact on profitability, they do not indicate where these profits go: salaries, staff and emoluments, growth, X-inefficiency? Among the most obvious places for management to direct corporate profits is toward their own pockets. We examine next the impact of managerial discretion on managerial incomes.

C.   The determinants of managerial compensation

If managers are hired by the owners of the firm to maximize the latter's wealth, the logical compensation contract is one tying managerial income to the owners' incomes, that is, a sharing contract between managers and the owners of capital (Stiglitz 1974; Sutinen 1975; Shavell 1976). Writing managerial income as MY, we can then postulate a compensation formula for the case where ownership is in control of

$$MY = a_1 + y\alpha, \tag{7.17}$$

where α stands for the long-run reported profits of the firm.

One of the "iron laws of hierarchy" is that supervisors get paid more than subordinates and, therefore, that a manager's income is directly related to the number of strata in the hierarchy, which in turn is directly related to the size of the company (Simon 1957; Williamson 1967). But there is no obvious reason why *owners* would choose such a compensation formula, absent a positive relationship between size and profitability. Owners have no interest in seeing the size of the company increase unless this increase generates at least sufficient revenue, above other input costs, to pay for the additional managers and the additions to managerial incomes due to the expansion of the hierarchy that increasing corporate size brings about. Owners have an interest in seeing the company expand, however, if the company is earning above-normal returns *and* if the additional capital and sales also promise to bring in above-normal returns. Thus, owners might have an incentive to make y a function of company size, where there is no obvious reason why they would make MY directly a function of size. We posit the simple linear relationship, $y = a_2 + f(S)$, S standing for size. Substituting this expression into (7.17) we obtain

$$MY = a_1 + a_2\alpha + \alpha f(S). \tag{7.18}$$

If we recall that α is measured as a deviation from the sample mean, (7.18) implies a positive relationship between company size and managerial income for those firms earning above-average returns, if $f' > 0$. The assumption that ownership hires managers to pursue ownership's interests implies that a_1 and a_2 are positive along with f'. Increasing profitability increases managerial income, and increasing size does also, for those companies earning above-average returns.

We have argued above that managerial discretion varies directly with the size, diversification, and fraction of shares held by management, and inversely with outside control. If we simply assume an additive impact of managerial discretion to what one predicts in the absence of managerial discretion, we obtain

$$MY = a_1 + a_2\alpha + \alpha f(S) + a_4 S + a_5 DIV + a_6 MC^2 + a_7 OC^2. \tag{7.19}$$

In addition to the managerial discretion variables previously discussed, three other variables were tried. Size plays such an important role in the managerial theories, both as objective and as means for fulfilling that objective by providing discretion, that we also included two measures of growth in size. GAQ is the cumulative growth from 1950 through 1972 in acquired assets as a percentage of company assets at the time of acquisition; IG is an estimate of the internal growth rate obtained by subtracting GAQ from total real growth 1950–72; and NAQ is the number of years between 1950 and 1972 in which the company engaged in at least one acquisition. (These variables are discussed in Appendix A-4.) NAQ is regarded as an index of the proclivity of management to engage in mergers, and GAQ measures the relative volume of assets acquired. GAQ can be large because of a few relatively large mergers, or many small ones. NAQ can be large only if the firm was active making acquisitions over much of the sample period.

We did not have the resources to calculate the total compensation for each manager for our large sample. Two components are examined: direct compensation as salary and bonuses, and stock options. Lewellen's (1968) work indicates that income from stock options made up the largest component outside of salary and bonuses during the fifties and sixties. Although we do not have a measure of the income earned through stock options, we do have figures for the total dollar value of stock options granted in the respective years for which we gathered compensation data. This figure, defined as *OPT*, should be highly correlated with the income earned from these options.

The other income figure, managerial salaries and bonuses, *MS*, is the biggest component of total managerial compensation and is highly correlated with it (see Lewellen and Huntsman 1970). Most data are for 1972, but when we could not get the 1972 figures, we chose the closest year for which data were available and converted the figures to 1972 dollars. The figures are averages for the five highest-paid officers in the firm, or for the maximum number less than five for which data were reported.

Three specifications for *f(S)* were tried: linear, quadratic, and the log of *S*. The log of *S*, defined as 1972 sales, proved to have the best statistical fit. Given that we chose log (*S*) as the specification for *f(S)*, we also experimented with replacing sales in the managerial discretion portion of the equation with log (*S*). Again, the nonlinear specification was superior, thus implying that managerial discretion, insofar as it affects managers' incomes, increases at a decreasing rate with size.

Equation (1) in Table 7.3 presents the results for (7.19) using log (*S*) and adding internal growth and growth through acquisition. The only statistically significant coefficient in the equation is for log sales, and it is highly significant. Managers of large companies earn substantially higher salaries than do managers of small firms. The hypothesis that ownership dictates the terms of management's contract is not confirmed. Managerial salaries are not tied to reported profits, and the relationship between salaries and sales is not dependent on the level of profitability. The only other variables to have *t*-values above 1 are outside ownership control (wrong sign) and internal growth (correct sign). The size of the company is the dominant characteristic determining managers' salaries. The substitution of *NAQ* for *GAQ* as an index of merger activity changes nothing in the equation.

The previous section presented arguments and evidence implying that managerial discretion determines reported profit as a residual from maximum potential profit after deducting management's discretionary claims on profits. Extra salary income is potentially one of those claims, and reported profits, α, and managerial salaries are most appropriately treated as codetermined variables. To allow for α's being a jointly determined variable, (2) was reestimated using two-stage least squares and employing the variables from the basic firm effect model as instruments; $(1 - m)C_4^2$, *mA*, and *mPat*. The results are presented in equation (3) of Table 7.3. The coefficient on α jumps from \$6,513 to \$125,120 and becomes statistically significant. Caution must be exercised when interpreting *t*-values and $\overline{R}^2$ statistics from 2 SLS

Table 7.3. *Determinants of managerial salary income and stock options* (n = 499)

Equation	Dependent Variable	Estimating Procedure	Int	α	αlog(S)	log(S)	DIV	MC^2	OC^2	IG	GAQ	NAQ	$\overline{R}^2$
(1)	MS	OLS	-4345	5895	472	37020	-14306	47982	956810	472	-4359		.107
			.13	.11	.05	7.51	.59	.44	1.34	1.13	.60		
(2)	MS	OLS	-5244	6513	358	37893	-16415	50229	937410	459		-803	.107
			.16	.12	.04	7.28	.64	.46	1.32	1.32		.54	
(3)	MS	2SLS	5700	125120	-22369	36520	-20048	61596	909400	432		-934	.115
			.17	2.13	2.25	7.01	.79	.57	1.28	1.04		.64	
(4)	OPT	OLS	-761300	-459270	94702	160450	-62952	-151020	-1293500	560	58044		.068
			3.78	1.44	1.80	5.33	.42	.23	.30	.22	.22		
(5)	OPT	OLS	-797750	-554630	112630	121720	106500	-215580	-822000	662		34904	.093
			4.04	1.76	2.17	3.88	.69	.33	.19	.26		3.90	
(6)	OPT	2SLS	-882590	-607880	122650	141500	99868	-236260	-810810	2014		31686	.090
			4.41	1.71	2.04	4.48	.65	.36	.19	.80		3.56	

Note: t statistics under coefficients. Equations are undeflated.

estimations, however (see Johnston 1972, pp. 400–9). The other coefficients and t-values in (3) are not changed much from (2). The changes in coefficients on α and $\alpha\log(S)$ between (2) and (3) give strong indication of simultaneous-equations bias in the estimation of (2). The coefficient on $\hat{\alpha}$ in (3) implies that an increase in *maximum potential* profit from the sample average to double the sample average increases each top manager's salary by \$125,120. Equation (2) implies that the same increase in *reported* profits results in a statistically insignificant increase in salaries of only \$6,513. Managerial salaries are far more responsive to changes in the profits their market shares and product characteristics would *allow* them to report, than they are to the profits actually reported. These results suggest that some of the revenue from product differentiation and market shares is siphoned off into management salaries.

If ownership wrote managerial salary contracts, it would reward increases in size for only those cases where the firm was earning above-average profits. On the contrary, the coefficient on $\alpha\log(S)$ implies that managers' salaries are more closely tied to sales the *lower* their maximum potential profitability. Such contracts are most likely to be written by managers.

Stock options are a more volatile component of income than salaries. A company must pay salaries; it need not pay options. Convention may govern in part the height of salaries, but the amount of stock options granted is much more at the discretion of management. But the very discretionary nature of options may make them more amenable to explanation by the managerial variables.

Equations (4)–(6) in Table 7.3 repeat the first three equations substituting the amount of stock options OPI for managerial salaries as dependent variable. The coefficient on sales remains positive and highly significant, but the coefficient on reported profits is negative and borderline significant, and that on the interaction term is positive. Although all managers must be paid salaries, not all must be granted stock options, and thus the discretionary aspect of awarding oneself a stock option is more apparent. This greater visibility of stock options may explain why managers of large firms are more apt to grant themselves stock options if their companies are of above-average profitability.

A stock option is more valuable when the stock's price rises considerably than when it does not. Stock prices should respond to reported profits not potential profits, since dividend payments and reinvested profits come from reported profits. Thus, stock options should be tied to reported profits, and one does not observe a difference between the two-stage least squares and OLS results.

The other variables in the equation are again a washout, except for *NAQ*. This variable, the number of years in which a firm undertook at least one merger, has a positive and highly significant coefficient. Indeed, the coefficient implies an increase in the value of stock options claimed of more than $30,000 for each year a company undertook at least one merger.

The performance of *NAQ* in the stock option equations underscores the importance of managerial discretion in determining the reported profitability and incomes of managers, as well as other variables. Companies that engage in substantial merger activity can be expected to have more volatile share prices, as some merger announcements bring increases, some declines. Having the option to buy company shares at predetermined prices is likely to be a more valuable option for a management of an active acquiring firm. Whether ownership should have an interest in granting sizable stock options to management for engaging in substantial merger activity depends on whether mergers tend to increase profitability and whether for some reason managers are reluctant to undertake mergers that increase profitability without the additional financial inducements stock options provide. Chapter 8 and the literature cited therein cast some doubt on this explanation. But regardless of what ownership's interest in rewarding managers for undertaking mergers might be, managers themselves have a clear financial incentive to grant themselves substantial stock options, if they engage in a significant amount of merger activity.

We attempted estimating multiplicative versions of the managerial income equations by treating *D* as an exponential, as in Section B. But the fit of these equations was too poor to achieve reliable estimates.

D.   Summary and conclusions

The hypothesis that managers have the discretion to divert significant fractions of company funds to their own objectives goes back at least as far as Berle and Means's classic *The Modern Corporation and Private Property* first published in 1932. It was Berle and Means who made the expression "separation of ownership from control" a part of the everyday vocabulary of business economics. Although they highlighted the importance of managerial discretion caused by the separation of ownership from control, Berle and Means had surprisingly little to say about what managers do with the substantial discretion they have. Writing at the time of the Great Crash, when revelations of gross misuses of company funds by managers were an almost daily newspaper story, it is not surprising that they focused upon, although ever so briefly ([1932] 1968, pp. 114–16), the diversion of corporate revenues to the direct pecuniary advantage of management by actions of an illegal or ethically questionable character.

The picture of what managers do with the discretion they possess was filled in with considerable detail in the sixties. Although the managerialists differ in their hypotheses concerning the uses to which management puts its discretion, they agree in the prediction that reported corporate profitability is lower to the extent that management exercises the discretion it possesses.

An important lacuna in the theory of the managerial corporation was filled by Marris's introduction of the threat of takeover as the constraint on managerial discretion. Marris, however, did not devote much attention to the stringency of the constraint, noting simply that takeover raiders were a rare breed in managerial capitalism and thus that a perfect takeover market constraining managers to perform as the neoclassical theory of the firm predicts was "an imaginary world, . . . which could never exist" (1964, pp. 29–45).

Further development of the managerial-agency-cost theories of the corporation emphasize the importance of the transaction costs of monitoring managers and mounting a successful takeover once a potentially profitable displacement of a management team has been found. Some support for the managerial-agency-cost theories of the firm was presented in this chapter. The more shares the incumbent management holds in the firm, the more difficult it is to displace it, and the more discretion it has to divert company funds to its own ends. This hypothesis received consistent support.

When we assumed that the potential for exercising discretion was proportional to the potential level of profits a company can earn, diversification also exhibited a significant, inverse relationship with reported profitability. The more diversified the firm, the more expensive it is to monitor managerial performance, and the greater the spread between actual and potential recorded profits.

Although managerial control of voting shares and diversification performed as the managerial-agency-cost literature predicts, outside ownership of voting shares and sales were essentially unrelated to reported profits. The former variable is likely to be subject to large measurement errors, whereas the latter's coefficient seemed to be affected by simultaneous-equations bias. Nevertheless, the equations presented in Table 7.2 suggest that considerably more work is required to account for the impact of differences in managerial discretion across firms.

A large literature exists that attempts to explain managerial compensation. By and large, this literature has failed to develop hypotheses linking managerial compensation to managerial discretion, and has simply regressed various measures of compensation on sales and profits adjusting for the econometric problems inherent in this specification to varying degrees. (For a survey of the literature that focuses on econometric issues, see Ciscel and Carroll 1980.) A common, but not universal, finding is that sales are directly related to managerial compensation.

The administrative behavior literature provides overwhelming support for the hypothesis that size and salaries should be positively related. To induce someone to manage a bigger company, one must offer a higher salary. What is lacking is an explanation of why ownership would choose such a compensation formula, or, more basically, why ownership would condone an expansion of the firm if it did not result in more profits for managers and owners to share. This point does not seem fully appreciated in the literature. Given that higher-ranked managers must be paid more than their subordinates, and that expansion of the firm requires adding additional layers of management, then there *must* exist either multiplant economies of scale, or some market power advantage from increased size to justify a company's growth beyond a single minimum-sized plant. Constant returns to scale and Gibrat's law are not enough, because additional size brings with it additional layers of management and the associated costs. The evidence, presented in Chapter 6 to show that size is unrelated, or as in Europe, negatively related to profitability, strongly indicates that decisions as to how large the firm grows are not made by ownership.

To ensure that additional size means additional profits, ownership would tie compensation to both size and profitability. Such a linkage was found to exist for stock options in Section C. But managerial salaries exhibited the reverse relationship. The lower a firm's potential profits, the more closely are managers' salaries tied to sales. Although such a compensation formula is easy to rationalize if management dictates the terms, it is difficult to imagine what advantage such a formula has for ownership. Consistent with this conclusion was also the finding that potential reported profits, as determined by the market share and product characteristics of the firm, are positively related to managerial salaries, whereas the actually reported profits are not.

The data for the variables introduced in this chapter undoubtedly have the greatest measurement errors of all the data used in this book. The observations on outside shareholdings are the most problematic. It is the only managerial discretion variable not to pick up a statistically significant coefficient in either set of models tested in this chapter.

The statistical fit of the managerial compensation equations suggests these results should be interpreted with caution. In part, the weak explanatory power of the managerial discretion variables may arise because compensation is but one of the directions in which management can divert company revenues, and perhaps not a very important one at that. The results in Table 7.2 do imply that reported profits are lower when managerial discretion is high. The results of Table 7.3 suggest that some of the revenues managers can allocate at their discretion go into their own salaries. But managers can benefit from their discretionary power to allocate corporate revenues in numerous other ways less conspicuous than putting the money in their own pockets. The rather weak statistical fit to the equations in Table 7.3 may come about because additional managerial compensation is a sufficiently minor channel for corporate revenues, so that the relationship between it and the indexes of managerial discretion is obscured by random elements.

Despite these statistical and data problems, the results in this chapter rather strongly imply that reported profits understate those that could be declared given the market share and product characteristics of the firms. Thus, we tend to underestimate the real magnitudes of the persistent rents earned by the most profitable companies.

CHAPTER 8

Mergers and profitability

The present study differs from much empirical work in industrial organization in its long-run orientation. It examines 600 firms over a 23-year time period. This long-run perspective raises an issue, however, that does not come up in the usual cross-sectional industrial organization study: To what extent is it legitimate to think of a given firm in 1972 as being the *same* firm that existed in 1950? In particular, this question applies to a firm such as Xerox, which in 1972, as today, was the leading photocopier manufacturer, but in 1950 was a small photographic paper manufacturer named Haloid, or to a firm like Textron, which added numerous new lines to its product mix through acquisitions between 1950 and 1972 *and* abandoned its original, primary line of business in textiles.

In trying to determine a criterion by which to define when a company at one point of time can be legitimately regarded as the same company that existed at an earlier point, one could take a fairly loose posture and simply say that, as long as a given company is the same legal entity, it is the same company regardless of how its product mix or name has changed. Alternatively, one could say that only when the same legal entity produces essentially the same types of products is it the same firm. Under this more stringent criterion, General Motors and United States Steel would be the same firms in 1950 and 1972; Xerox and Textron would not be.

We have chosen the looser definition. Indeed, in a handful of cases, we have even defined a company as surviving when it was acquired by a smaller firm not in the 1,000 largest of 1950. We have done this for three reasons: first, to preserve as many firms in the sample as possible, and thus make our results as representative of the whole manufacturing sector as we could; second, to avoid having to divide by some arbitrary line the set of surviving companies into those that are comparable over time and those that are not; third, to bias our findings away from the likelihood of observing persistent profit differences across firms, if a bias must be introduced. Had we chosen a narrow definition of firm identity, our results showing persistent differences of profits across firms might be called into question on the grounds that we had built stability into the sample through the selection process by focusing on an unchanging subsample of companies, and that the finding of profit stability is unsurprising and unrepresentative of what occurs across all firms. Our definition of a firm tests for the persistence-of-profitability differences across the largest sample of surviving companies from 1950 that it is possible to construct.

It should be noted that whatever white noise is introduced by the broad definition of a continuing company used, it should not have a large impact on our independent variables in the firm- and industry-approach models. Industry sales weights in calculating industry dummies and industry advertising and patent intensity are based on 1972 sales. Market shares and concentration are projections for which 1972 figures receive heavy weight. Furthermore, when changes in product composition result in wide variations from year to year in a company's return on assets, the fit of the time-series regression is poor, and the observation is given less weight in the cross-sectional regressions through the practice of weighting each observation by the reciprocal of the standard error of the estimate of projected profits.

A.   The effects of mergers on profitability

Of the many factors that might change a firm's "identity" over time, mergers are by far the most important. Over the last century, mergers have transformed the corporate landscape. There is scarcely a corporation among the current lists of largest firms that has not experienced considerable growth through merger at some point in time, be it United States Steel at the turn of the century, General Motors during the century's first few decades, Occidental Petroleum in the sixties and seventies, or General Foods throughout the last 100 years.

We observed in Chapter 1 that almost 40 percent of the companies in the 1,000-largest list of 1950 had been acquired by 1972. Each company in the sample of 551 firms used in previous chapters acquired a cumulative amount of assets equal on the average to some 44 percent of their size, measured at the time of acquisition.[1] This average conceals a range, however, from 0 to almost 13. That is, some firms have acquired a cumulative total amount of assets several times more than their assets at the time they made the acquisitions, whereas others have made no acquisitions at all. These acquisitions have changed the basic character of numerous companies, and the question arises as to what effect they may have had on the tendency of profit differences across firms to persist.

Two distinct possible effects of mergers on profitability must be considered. First, mergers can raise or lower the profits of the two merging companies from what they would have been had they not merged. Let A be the acquiring firm, B the company bought, and C the combination of A and B. Then, we can define G, the profit gain from the merger as

$$G = \Pi_C - \Pi_A - \Pi_B, \tag{8.1}$$

where Π_A and Π_B are measured prior to the merger. Most hypotheses as to why mergers occur assume that managers maximize profits (see Steiner 1975, Chapters 2–5; Mueller 1980a, Chapter 2; Scherer 1980, pp. 138–41). The managerial theory of the firm can account for negative Gs, if managers pursue corporate growth at the cost of some profits (see Marris 1964; Mueller 1969, 1977b, 1980a, Chapter 2). From the perspective of the theory of the firm, the key question is whether G is positive, negative, or zero. The literature that attempts to test competing theories of the firm by estimating the effects of mergers on profitability has, or should have, tested to see whether mergers have increased the profits of the combined companies over what they were, or would have been, in the absence of the mergers. For a particularly good attempt to measure the change in profits over two merging firms, see Meeks (1977). The country studies in Mueller (1980a) seek to measure effects in the same way. The literature measuring the effects of mergers by looking at changes in share prices surrounding the mergers assumes that these share price changes reflect the anticipated Gs arising from mergers (see, e.g., Mandelker 1974; Dodd and Ruback 1977; Firth 1980).

The present study measures profits as rates of return on total assets. Given this definition of profitability, mergers can have a second, averaging effect on profitability in addition to changing joint profits by G. In our sample, we designate the combined company following a merger as the acquiring company. Thus, projected profits are based on observations for firm A before a merger, on firm C afterward. Assuming that only the profits of the companies are affected by the merger, so that the assets of C, K_C equal $K_A + K_B$, then a merger increases the return on the acquiring firm's assets if

$$\frac{\Pi_C}{K_C} - \frac{\Pi_A}{K_A} > 0; \tag{8.2}$$

(8.2) implies

$$\frac{\Pi_A + \Pi_B + G}{K_A + K_B} - \frac{\Pi_A}{K_A} > 0 \quad \text{or} \quad K_A(\Pi_B + G) > \Pi_A K_B. \quad (8.3)$$

Now if the premerger rate of return on assets of A is higher than the return on B (i.e., $\Pi_A/K_A = \lambda\Pi_B/K_B$, $\lambda > 1$), G could be positive and the return on capital for firm C would be lower than for A, as (8.3) reduces to

$$\Pi_B + G > \lambda\Pi_B. \quad (8.4)$$

Thus, for sufficiently large differences in premerger rates of return on assets, the averaging effects of mergers could swamp any gains or losses generated by changes in market power or efficiency.

This averaging effect is compounded by the likely changes in asset values that surround a merger. If the acquiring company includes the assets of the acquired firm in its books at their market value, rather than at their premerger book value, then the postmerger return on the acquired company's assets should equal the competitive return on capital plus or minus any gains or losses generated by the merger, since the market price of a firm adjusts to the level appropriate to provide stock- and bondholders a normal return on investment. What is more, if the premium paid for an acquired firm adjusts to reflect the anticipated gains, G, from the merger, as often claimed (see Mandelker 1964; Dodd and Ruback 1977), this profit from the merger is also capitalized into the denominator of our rate-of-return measure. Thus, even if the acquired company continues to earn a large positive or negative rent after its acquisition, its return on total assets may be recorded as a normal return on capital when averaged in with the acquiring firm's returns. We expect, therefore, a systematic averaging effect of mergers driving all rates of return on assets toward the mean. We seek to measure this averaging effect in this chapter.

It must be stressed that the attempt is not to measure whether mergers have generated gains or losses in the sense of G as defined above. To measure G properly, one needs premerger data for *both* merging firms and postmerger data for the combined firm. Such data for *all* mergers between 1950 and 1972 are available for only a handful of companies in the sample. Since the aim of this study is to identify the determinants of long-run profitability rather than the effects of mergers as such, attention is confined to trying to make sufficient adjustments for mergers so as not to cloud our vision with regard to the persistence of profits and their causes. (For the effects of mergers on accounting rates of return, see Meeks 1977; Mueller 1977b, 1980a.)

In the process, some light is shed on the effects of mergers, however, in both this chapter and the next.

B.   Estimates of the effects of merger activity on long-run profit projections

In this section, the effects of adding merger activity to the basic firm-effects model are explored. To measure the extent of merger activity, we obtained for each year the FTC lists of companies acquired and checked them against the histories of each company reported in *Moody's Industrial Manual*. For all acquired companies with assets of $10,000,000 or more, the FTC reports the assets of the acquired company; it also gives figures for many smaller acquisitions. When no figure was available, an estimate of the acquired company's size was made using FTC figures on the size distribution of all acquired companies. (For details, see Appendix A-4.) We then divided the assets acquired by each firm for each year by its asset figures at the beginning of the year. This gave us a measure of its real percentage growth in that year by merger. We then summed these figures over the 23 years of the sample period to obtain

GAQ = the cumulative real growth in assets by merger from 1950–72.

Table 8.1 defines the variables used in this chapter, and Table 8.2 reports the results when GAQ is added to the basic firm-effect equation.[2] When GAQ is added separately (equation [1]), its coefficient is positive with a t-value greater than one. Although GAQ's coefficient is not significant at normal confidence intervals, one might claim from equation (1) weak support for a synergistic effect of mergers. But Weston and Mansinghka (1971) have shown that the heavy acquirers in the 1960s, the so-called conglomerates, had significantly lower profit rates than other industrial companies prior to launching their intensive acquisition programs. Equation (1) is consistent with a pure averaging effect of mergers when acquiring firms tend to have lower initial profits than nonacquiring companies. To allow for the averaging effect of mergers, the impact of mergers must be measured relative to the initial level of profits of the acquiring firm. Equation (2) adds π_{50}, the initial profit level of the acquiring firm, and the product of π_{50} and GAQ. The coefficient on $GAQ \cdot \pi_{50}$ is negative and significant, and thus implies a significant averaging effect. When initial profits π_{50} are above average (positive), merger activity lowers projected profitability. When they are below average, mergers raise projected profits. Addition of GAQ to equation (2) results in no increase in explanatory power. When added to the basic firm-effect model,

Table 8.1. *Definitions of variables used in Chapter 8*

A. *Variables from previous chapters*

α Projected returns on total assets expressed as a relative deviation from the mean returns for all companies. Estimated from the best fit of the three polynomials in $1/t$ estimated in Chapter 2.

m_i Projected market share.

C_4 Projected four-firm concentration ratio.

A Industry advertising-to-sales ratio.

Pat Industry patent-to-sales ratio.

GAQ Relative growth through acquisition. The assets acquired in year t divided by the firm's assets at the beginning of year t summed over the years 1950 through 1972.

π_{50} The deviation of a firm's profit rate from the sample mean, divided by the sample mean, and averaged over the years 1950, 1951, 1952.

B. *Variables introduced in this chapter*

ACQ Assets acquired in a given year divided by the total assets of the acquiring company at the start of the year.

Π/K Profits net of taxes and interest divided by total assets.

$\Pi G/K$ Profits net of taxes plus interest divided by total assets.

---

mergers have solely an averaging effect on profitability.

The coefficient on π_{50} in equation (2) is large and so too is its t-value. After allowing for the averaging effect of mergers, and for the other variables in the firm-effect model, nearly 33 percent of any difference between a company's return on assets in 1950–52 and the average is seen to persist indefinitely. This large, positive coefficient on π_{50} implies that there are factors associated with a given company that lead it to earn persistent returns above or below the average but do not translate into market share differences or are not related to industry concentration or product differentiation. Alternatively, the coefficient on π_{50} might capture the firm-specific effect of using accounting profits rather than economic profits to calculate rates of return as discussed in Chapters 5 and 6. In this context, it is important to emphasize that, although the inclusion of π_{50} detracts somewhat from the explanatory power of the two market share–product differentiation interaction terms (while enhancing that of $[1 - m_i]C_4^2$), all terms from the basic equation remain highly significant with comparable coefficients.

These alternative explanations for the positive coefficient on π_{50} allow us to construct an alternative estimate of the averaging effect of mergers. Assume that the initial profit rate variable, π_{50}, captures all permanent rents, either real or merely due to accounting conventions, existing in 1950–52 that cannot be explained by its market share, product differentiation, and the like. Assume further that these rents

Table 8.2. *Effects of mergers on projected profitability, best-fit profit projections*
($n = 551$)

Independent variables	Equation						
	1	2	3	4	5	6	7
Intercept	−.059	.003	.0001	.005	.015	.035	.014
	1.84	.11	.00	.17	.95	1.73	.95
$(1-m_i)C_4^2$	−.575	−.653	−.637	−.649			
	3.98	4.69	4.57	4.68			
$m_i A$	.729	.651	.659	.641			
	12.29	11.35	11.47	11.17			
$m_i Pat$	1.39	1.24	1.24	1.24			
	5.48	5.08	5.06	5.09			
GAQ	.045					−.068	
	1.39					1.69	
π_{50}		.328	.271		.385	.478	
		6.74	6.47		8.23	8.68	
$GAQ \cdot \pi_{50}$		−.148				−.270	
		2.27				3.19	
$\dfrac{\pi_{50}}{1+GAQ}$				.368			.521
				7.10			9.13
$\bar{R}^2$	.279	.333	.328	.338	.108	.122	.131

are somehow tied to the assets that the company had in 1950. If the company continued to sell the same products, or type of products, stayed in the same industry, and so on, we would project the company to earn β percent above or below the sample mean indefinitely, β being the fraction of rents observed in 1950 and assumed to persist indefinitely. Now assume that the firm acquires additional assets equal to GAQ percent of its 1950 assets, or GAQ percent of whatever level its 1950 assets have grown to while still earning the same β rents. On the newly acquired assets we expect a return equal to the sample average, that is, a return of zero. Thus, the observed return on assets is a weighted average of β and zero, with the proper weights being one for the initial assets and GAQ for the acquired ones. We can adjust for this averaging effect on the return on the original assets by replacing π_{50} by $\pi_{50}/(1 + GAQ)$ in the equation. The coefficient on this adjusted variable captures the fraction of 1950 rents that are projected to persist indefinitely in the absence of any profit-diluting mergers. To judge the dilution effect, we first reestimate the basic equation adding the unadjusted π_{50} (equation [3]) and then substitute $\pi_{50}/(1 + GAQ)$ in equation (4). The coefficient on π_{50} is significantly smaller than on $\pi_{50}/(1 + GAQ)$, and the $\overline{R}^2$ for the equation with the latter variable is higher. Mergers are again observed to have had a substantial averaging effect.

The results for equations (2)–(4) are important for two reasons: (1) they substantiate the proposition that mergers have a significant averaging effect on observed profitability; (2) they demonstrate that the results for the basic firm-effect model are not substantially changed by accounting for the effects of mergers. But, with respect to the averaging effect, it should be recognized that equations (2)–(4) must *under*estimate this effect to a considerable degree. These equations estimate the effect of mergers holding constant market shares and the other explanatory variables. But mergers must also have an averaging effect on these other variables. Firms with high market shares are likely to acquire firms with lower market shares than themselves; the reverse is true of companies with initial market shares below the average. Similar arguments hold for the other variables.

To get an idea of the magnitude of the gross averaging effect of mergers on long-run profitability, we regressed the projected profits variable on π_{50} and GAQ alone, dropping all other variables from the equation. Equation (5) in Table 8.2 simply regresses projected profits on initial profits; 38.5 percent of any deviation in a company's return on assets in 1950–52 is projected to persist indefinitely. Equations (6) and (7) allow for the averaging effect of mergers in the two ways discussed above. Both equations imply a significant averaging effect. In the absence of any mergers, between 48 and 52 percent of the differences in profitability observed in 1950–52 would have persisted indefinitely. One-quarter of these persistent differences is concealed by the averaging effect of the acquisitions that companies undertook between 1950 and 1972. Including the averaging effect, only 38.5 percent of 1950–52 profit differences appear to persist. It is also worth noting that equation (6) presents evidence of a slight *negative* synergy effect from mergers over and above the averaging effect. A company acquiring a total amount of assets equal to its preacquisition size has its projected profits reduced by 6.8 percent of the average return on capital.

C.   The effects of mergers on profits: individual cross-sectional results

Tests for the averaging effect of mergers of the type conducted at the close of the previous section can be conducted on individual cross

Table 8.3. *Levels of acquisition activity and profitability, individual cross sections*

Time period	ACQ	π/K	$\pi G/K$	n
1947–49		.051	.097	463
1950–54	.0047	.017	.040	588
1955–57	.0099	.036	.082	598
1958–61	.0061	.020	.059	602
1962–64	.0089	.032	.092	602
1965–67	.0142	.033	.109	601
1968–69	.0187	.044	.172	601
1970–72	.0052	.024	.112	597
1973–75		.026	.117	506

sections, since they do not rely on data for market shares, which are available only in 1950 and 1972. Since acquisitions are rather lumpy investments, several years were combined to form each cross section. In choosing which years to combine into a single time period, I tried to form periods that were similar with respect to both level of merger activity and level of business activity. Thus, the first time period of modest merger activity runs for five years, 1950–54, whereas the peak of the wave years 1968–69 is treated as a single time period.

Mean values for the annual levels for each variable are presented in Table 8.3. The two periods of weakest merger activity are the first and last cross sections. At the peak of the 1960s wave, 1968–69, the average volume of assets acquired per firm relative to its own size (ACQ) was almost four times greater than in the first and last cross sections. The next two variables are profits net of interest and taxes divided by total assets (π/K), and profits net of taxes but gross of interest over total assets ($\pi G/K$). The latter measure of the profit rate corresponds to the measure used throughout the book. The reason for including profits net of interest in this section will become apparent shortly. Although the measure of profitability used to calculate the $\hat{\alpha}$ projections used throughout the book are measured as deviations from the sample mean return on assets to adjust for business cycle factors, the choice of cross section itself in this section has been made to control in part for business cycle factors. Therefore the profit variables are not defined as deviations from the sample mean in this section. The last column in Table 8.3 is the number of observations in each cross section sample.

To estimate the impact of mergers on profitability, profits are regressed on past merger activity, and profitability with an interaction term between past profits and assets acquired included to measure the averaging effect

$$\Pi_{t+1} = a + b\Pi_{t-1} + cACQ_t + dACQ_t \cdot \Pi_{t-1} + \mu_t. \qquad (8.5)$$

Previous profits are lagged an additional period to avoid any simultaneity between profits and acquisitions in t, that is, to be sure that the observed change in profits is caused by the mergers. If the mergers had an immediate impact on profitability, this impact might already be reflected in profits in period t and the effect of the mergers would be obscured.

Equation (8.5) was estimated with Π defined as profits net of interest and taxes over total assets (Π/K), and gross of interest ($\Pi G/K$). The cross-sectional time periods are defined with respect to the acquisition activity; that is, for the 1958–61 cross section, profits in 1962–64 are regressed on 1958–61 ACQ and 1955–57 profits. The first and third equations for each cross section in Table 8.4 present the results when just ACQ_t and the respective lagged profit rate are included, that is, without making allowance for the averaging effect of mergers. The coefficient on profits, lagged two cross-sectional time periods, is positive and highly significant throughout the table and thus further indicates the consistency of profit differences across firms. The time spread between Π_{t+1} and Π_{t-1} averages more than six years. The coefficient on the acquisition variable is positive in six of the seven cross sections in which profits gross of interest are the dependent variable, and significant in five of these six. Thus, as in the first equation of Table 8.2, but perhaps even more strongly, acquisition activity on the average tends to raise the returns on total assets over the 1950–72 time period, when no allowance is made for the averaging effect of mergers.

It is interesting to observe, however, that this tendency of acquisitions to raise profitability is *not* apparent when profits are defined net of interest payments, the third equation in each cross-sectional tabulation. Only one of the seven coefficients on ACQ_t is significant when net-of-interest profits is the dependent variable, and it is negative (in the 1950–54 cross section). Thus, the increases in profits to total assets observed when ΠG is the dependent variable must come through expansion of the interest payments part of gross profits. This finding is in line with results reported by Weston and Mansinghka (1971) that the conglomerates experienced much larger increases in debt-to-equity ratios during the period of their major acquisition activity than did industrial companies not engaging in much merger activity. If we assume that this debt was issued largely to finance the acquisitions,

Table 8.4. *Effects of mergers on profitability, separate cross sections*
$(\Pi G_{t+1}, \Pi_{t+1} = a + b\Pi_{t-1} + cACQ_t + d\Pi_{t-1} ACQ_t; \Pi G = Profit + Interest, \Pi = Net Profit)$

Time period t	Dependent variable	a	b	c	d	$\bar{R}^2$	n
1950–54	ΠG	.064(15.94)	.276(7.85)	−.079(.79)		.114	478
	ΠG	.064(15.87)	.277(7.74)	−.059(.31)	−.377(.12)	.112	478
	Π	.031(22.10)	.127(5.93)	−.143(3.55)		.091	478
	Π	.031(22.10)	.135(6.23)	−.086(1.84)	−2.66(2.38)	.100	478
1955–57	ΠG	.041(17.88)	.433(9.78)	.096(2.43)		.141	597
	ΠG	.040(17.07)	.453(9.76)	.166(2.65)	−2.08(1.44)	.142	597
	Π	.012(10.05)	.449(7.92)	−.003(.14)		.095	597
	Π	.011(9.08)	.532(8.93)	.005(.28)	−3.97(4.08)	.118	597
1958–61	ΠG	.057(16.94)	.401(11.85)	.387(4.00)		.203	601
	ΠG	.056(16.23)	.402(11.13)	.402(2.55)	−.216(.12)	.202	601
	Π	.021(16.68)	.294(10.42)	−.025(.61)		.153	601
	Π	.021(15.68)	.317(10.89)	.135(2.01)	−5.14(2.94)	.164	601
1962–64	ΠG	.069(17.62)	.660(11.61)	.139(2.04)		.195	602
	ΠG	.067(16.70)	.680(11.63)	.249(2.44)	−1.07(1.44)	.197	602
	Π	.022(21.03)	.540(14.09)	−.017(.74)		.249	602
	Π	.022(20.44)	.566(13.62)	.017(.55)	−3.56(1.60)	.251	602

1965–67	IIG	.078(13.92)	.954(17.57)	.433(5.78)		.375	602
	IIG	.073(12.10)	1.01(17.04)	.760(4.95)	−3.27(2.43)	.380	602
	II	.007(3.67)	1.16(22.19)	−.0031(.10)		.468	602
	II	.006(2.80)	1.21(22.22)	.132(2.07)	−4.90(2.34)	.472	602
1968–69	IIG	.051(11.40)	.543(14.52)	.125(3.18)		.291	598
	IIG	.031(6.17)	.717(17.03)	.583(8.35)	−2.85(7.77)	.355	598
	II	.002(1.26)	.674(19.15)	.004(.35)		.381	598
	II	.0001(.06)	.731(19.46)	.048(2.89)	−2.04(3.98)	.396	598
1970–72	IIG	.047(10.51)	.389(17.01)	.064(.72)		.367	506
	IIG	.045(9.49)	.401(16.53)	.304(1.63)	−1.13(1.46)	.368	506
	II	.008(5.55)	.389(14.37)	.011(.28)		.289	506
	II	.008(5.56)	.385(13.70)	−.013(.21)	.937(.50)	.289	506

Note: *t*-values in parentheses.

then whatever gains the mergers produced appear to have gone to finance the debt that was issued to consummate them. The income to which stockholders have claim – profits net of taxes and interest – was not positively affected by the mergers.

In the second and fourth rows of each cross section, the interaction term between acquisition activity and lagged profitability is added to the equations. The averaging effect of mergers is evidenced by a negative coefficient on this interaction term, as discussed in Section B. When profits plus interest payments are the dependent variable, the interaction term has a negative coefficient in all seven cross sections. Particularly strong is the averaging effect of mergers in the years of heaviest merger activity, 1965–69. The coefficients on the interaction terms in the two cross-sections spanning these years are both significant and close to -3.

An even more pronounced averaging effect is apparent in the net-of-interest regressions. Six of the seven interaction term coefficients are negative and significant for this dependent variable. Only the 1970–72 cross section has a positive coefficient and it is insignificant. In this cross section, the coefficient on acquisition activity as a separate variable is also insignificant. The dependent variable in this cross section is profitability in the years 1973–75, the immediate post-oil-crisis years. Not surprisingly, mergers have little to do with changes in profitability between the end of the sixties upswing and the 1973–75 period.

The averaging effect of mergers on profitability makes their net effect dependent on the initial profit rate of a company.

$$\partial \Pi_{t+1}/\partial ACQ_t = c + d\Pi_{t-1}. \tag{8.6}$$

Substituting the mean values for c and d for the two cross sections 1965–67 and 1968–69 into (8.6) and solving for Π_{t-1}, we obtain a value of 0.219. The mean $\Pi G/K$ value for the 1962–64 and 1965–67 periods (see Table 8.3) is 0.10. Thus, for all firms earning roughly double the average return on assets over the 1962–67 period, mergers tended to reduce profitability; for all other companies, they tended to increase profitability. During the peak of the merger wave, mergers tended to have a positive net impact on profits plus interest divided by total assets for all but the most profitable companies.

The mean values of c and d for the six cross sections for which d is significant and for which profits net of interest is the dependent variable are 0.042 and -3.71, respectively. They imply a cutoff profit rate between mergers having a positive or negative impact on profitability of 0.011. This cutoff value must be compared with 0.0315, the mean of Π_t over the first six time periods in Table 8.3. Thus, for all companies with net-of-interest profit rates greater than one-third of the sample mean from 1947 through 1967, that is, for the preponderance of companies in the sample, mergers tended to reduce profitability; for companies with net profit over assets less than 0.011, mergers tended to increase the profit rate.

D.   The averaging effects of mergers: an example from the flat-glass industry

The flat-glass industry in the United States is dominated by two firms: Libby-Owens-Ford (L-O-F) and Pittsburgh Plate Glass (PPG). The 1972 *Moody's Industrial Manual* reported that 68 percent of L-O-F's sales were in flat glass. If all of these sales fell in SIC 3211, L-O-F would have a 1972 market share in flat glass of more than 30 percent. A *Dun's Review* article (September 1967, p. 86) lists PPG as the number one producer of flat glass. Thus, together PPG and L-O-F appear to have accounted for close to two-thirds of flat-glass production in the late sixties and early seventies. Each company appears to have tripled its market share since 1950.

But the benefits from this market dominance are apparent in only L-O-F's profit profile (Figure 8.1). L-O-F's profits lie consistently and substantially above the mean throughout the 1950–72 period. Of course, it might be that L-O-F is simply better than PPG at converting its market share into profits. Unfortunately, we do not have line-of-business profit rates to resolve this issue, although we do know that a greater percentage of PPG's 1972 profits came from glass products of all kinds than did its sales (*Moody's* 1975, p. 2200).

PPG's profit profile from 1950 through 1972 is precisely what one expects to observe for a company that begins with above-normal returns and engages in substantial merger activity, if mergers have an averaging effect on profitability. Even in 1950, PPG was a diversified manufacturer producing industrial chemicals, paints, and many other products besides flat glass. In total, it operated in nine two-digit SIC industries in 1950. In contrast, L-O-F had more than 95 percent of its sales in glass products. L-O-F's profits in the early fifties must reflect largely its returns in glass products, of which flat glass should have been a major part. If PPG's flat-glass operations were equally profitable in the early fifties, then its much lower, but still above-average, returns in these years already reflect the averaging effect of its greater diversification.

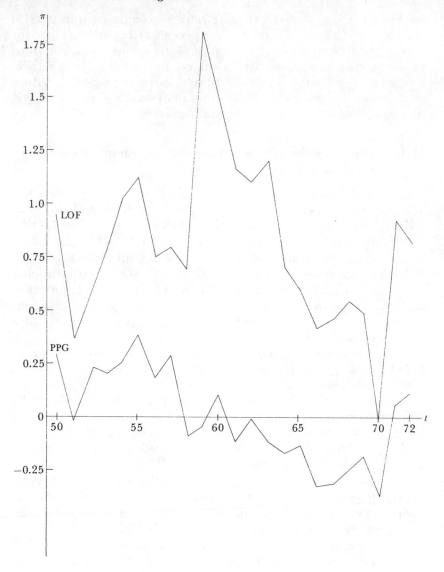

Figure 8.1 Profit profiles of two leading flat-glass manufacturers, 1950–72. Key: LOF = Libby-Owens-Ford, PPG = Pittsburgh Plate Glass.

In the intervening years, PPG continued to emphasize diversification through both internal expansion and mergers. The 1968 and 1975 *Moody's* record 20 domestic and international mergers through 1972, whereas L-O-F remained relatively concentrated in glass products. Thus, in 1971–72, L-O-F's profits were as in 1950 some 75 to 85 percent above the average firm's profits, whereas PPG's had fallen from a level of some 20–35 percent above average in the early fifties to only slightly more than the normal return on capital. Given that its market share in flat glass increased threefold and that it surpassed L-O-F's market share in the late sixties, only two explanations for PPG's decline in profitability are possible. Either it is not able to translate market share into profits as well as L-O-F, or its returns in the other markets in which it sells bring its profits from flat glass down to those of the average manufacturing company.

PPG did not enjoy market positions in most of its other markets as it did in flat glass. *Dun's Review* (September 1967) placed PPG second or third in the paint industry with sales only half those of industry leader Sherwin-Williams, "a distant second" to Owens-Corning Fiberglass in fiberglass, and characterized its chemicals' division at that time as "just an also ran," with the exception of chlorine production, where it was tied with Dow for the industry lead.

These figures and rankings suggest the PPG's market share would be much closer to the mean market share for all firms, 0.07, than would L-O-F's mean market share, for which flat glass is a much larger factor, just as PPG's profits lie closer to the sample mean than do L-O-F's. Thus, the evidence seems most consistent with the hypothesis that PPG's decline in profitability between the early fifties and early seventies came about as a result of its diversification into areas of lower relative profitability.

E. Summary and conclusions

Mergers can have two distinct effects on company returns on total assets. They may raise or lower the profits of the merging firms from what they would have been in the absence of the merger; they can have an averaging effect when companies with different ratios of profits to assets combine. The latter effect can be compounded by reevaluations of company assets at the time of the mergers.

There is considerable evidence in the results in this chapter of an averaging effect of mergers. Over the 23-year period, 1950–72, that is the only effect of mergers we were able to identify. On the average, the projected profit rates of companies appear to come 25 percent closer to the sample mean as a result of the averaging effect of mergers than would otherwise be the case. Had the surviving companies from 1950 made no acquisitions between 1950 and 1972, we estimate that roughly 50 percent of the differences in profitability that existed in 1950–52 would have persisted over time. Mergers reduced the observed tendency of profits to persist to 38.5 percent of their original value.

Over the entire 23-year period, acquisition activity had, if anything, a slight negative synergistic effect beyond the averaging effect of mergers. But somewhat stronger evidence was found in some of the individual cross-sectional results for a positive synergistic effect. Perhaps the difference in the results with respect to synergy between the individual cross sections and the entire 23-year cross section lies in the fact that it takes several years for the negative consequences of mergers to work themselves out (see Mueller 1980a, Chapters 9, 10). Thus, the 23-year time span 1950–72 may have been long enough to capture the full impact of most of the mergers on long-run profitability, whereas the lags in the individual cross sections were not.

Be that as it may, the results from the individual cross sections do provide consistent evidence of the averaging effect of mergers, thereby confirming the conclusions reached for the entire time span.

The results of this chapter cast considerable doubt on the validity of concluding that mergers have a positive synergistic effect by observing that the returns on capital of companies, which are initially below average, rise to the average following considerable merger activity, as, for example, Weston and Mansinghka (1971) do. All that may be at work is the simple arithmetic of averaging. The results of this chapter further strengthen the conclusion reached in Chapter 2 that there exist persistent differences in profitability across firms. They also suggest that these differences are tied to the markets that companies operate in and their relative strength in these markets. For if success and failure were tied only to the management of the firm or its organization, then when an above-average-profits firm acquired a lower profit company, it would transform the latter to the acquiring firm's higher performance level. Similarly, below-normal-profit acquiring firms would bring down the profitability of their acquisitions. The importance of averaging in our results suggests that profitability is tied somehow to a firm's assets in given markets and not to the firm itself.

Beyond these general results regarding persistent profitability, the results of this chapter are reassuring in that they suggest that the findings regarding the effects of market share, concentration, and product differentiation underlying the basic model used throughout much of this book hold up after allowing for the impact of mergers on profitability.

CHAPTER 9

Mergers and market share

The previous chapter indicates that mergers may not have much of an impact on the profitability of the two merging companies other than through the averaging effect of combining companies with different profit rates. These results, in turn, are consistent with those that find mergers do not have much of a positive effect on either corporate efficiency or market power.

The FTC market share data for 1950 and 1972 allow us to examine another effect of mergers, their effect on market share. We focus specifically on the effects of mergers on the market shares of the acquired companies. We begin by analyzing the expected effects of mergers using the firm approach model of Chapter 4. After discussing the data and methodology, we turn to the empirical results. Conclusions follow.

A.   The effects of changes in efficiency, product quality, and the degree of cooperation on market share

1.   Conglomerate mergers

The number of hypotheses about the causes and effects of conglomerate mergers has grown so much over the years that even a mere listing of all candidates would take an inordinate amount of space (see Steiner 1975; Mueller 1980a, Chapter 2). Considerable time can be saved by grouping existing theories into those implying changes in internal efficiency and those implying changes in market power. We assume that any improvement in efficiency eventually translates into lower costs of production. We depict changes in market power as changes in the degree of cooperation or collusion among the firms in an industry. Although changes in the degree of cooperation seem more likely to follow horizontal mergers, John Scott (1982) has recently presented evidence suggesting that conglomerate mergers can lead to enhanced collusion, when the acquiring company and several of the incumbent companies have contact with one another in several industries. Moreover, claims that a given conglomerate acquisition would have a "chilling" effect or an exhilarating effect on the degree of cooperation in an industry have often appeared in the case literature. Thus, allowing for possible anticompetitive effects from conglomerate as well as horizontal mergers seems warranted.

Given that we seek to examine the long-run effects of mergers, a third possible consequence must be considered. Its acquisition may change the actual or perceived characteristics of a firm's products. One of the leading hypotheses concerning conglomerate mergers sees them as improving the flow of capital by giving acquired firms access to more efficient internal capital markets (Weston, 1970; Williamson, 1970). The "deep pocket" doctrine, first put forward in Proctor and Gamble's acquisition of Clorox, also envisages greater expenditures, in this case for advertising, as a result of the acquired firm's having access to the greater resources of its acquirer. Should greater R&D or advertising follow a merger, changes in actual or perceived product characteristics are likely.

We thus need a model of the effects of mergers that allows for (1) changes in costs, (2) changes in product characteristics, and (3) changes in the degree of cooperation in the industry, and that is sufficiently tractable to relate changes in each parameter to market shares. These three goals can be accomplished with the firm-approach model set out in Chapter 4. Therefore, we assume that the acquired firm operates in a monopolistically competitive industry in which each firm i faces a linear demand schedule of the following form

$$p_i = a_i - bx_i - \sigma b \sum_{j \neq i}^{n} x_j, \qquad (9.1)$$

where p_i and x_i are price and quantity, respectively. A higher a_i implies a greater willingness by each buyer to pay for each unit of the product, and is treated as an index of perceived product quality. The parameter σ measures the degree of substitutability among the products in the industry, $0 \leq \sigma \leq 1$. If $\sigma = 1$, the products are perfect substitutes, an increase in any firm's output has the same impact on i's price. If $\sigma = 0$, each firm is effectively a monopolist. Marginal costs are allowed to differ across firms, and again for analytic convenience we assume a linear total cost function, $TC_i = c_i x_i$.

The degree of cooperation or collusion in an industry is again modeled as the weight, θ, each firm places on the profits of all other firms in the industry in its objective function. A $\theta = 1$ corresponds to perfect collusion, a $\theta = 0$ to Cournot quantity setting, a $\theta < 0$ to rivalrous competitive behavior. We again assume that a cooperative equilibrium exists in which all firms in the industry tacitly agree on the magnitude of θ. Each thus maximizes the objective function

$$0_i = \Pi_i + \theta \sum_{j \neq i}^{n} \Pi_j = x_i \left(a_i - bx_i - \sigma b \sum_{j \neq i} x_j \right) - c_i x_i$$

$$+ \theta \sum_{j \neq i} \left[x_j(a_j - bx_j - \sigma b \sum_{k \neq j} x_k) - c_j x_j \right], \quad (9.2)$$

which yields as a first order condition

$$x_i = \frac{a_i - c_i}{2b} - \frac{\sigma(1 + \theta)}{2} \sum_{j \neq i}^{n} x_j. \quad (9.3)$$

The first term in (9.3) plays an important role in the analysis and is defined as q_i, the quality-efficiency index for firm i. Increases in q_i imply either improvements in product quality or reductions in costs. If we call $\sigma(1 + \theta)/2$, r, and substitute into (9.3) along with each x_j, we get

$$x_i = q_i - r \left[\sum_{j \neq i} q_j - r(n-1)x_i - r(n-2) \sum_{j \neq i} x_j \right]. \quad (9.4)$$

Adding and subtracting rq_i and $r(n-2)x_i$ and rearranging, we obtain

$$x_i = (1 + r) q_i - rQ + r^2(n-2)X, \quad (9.5)$$

where

$$Q = \sum_i^n q_i, \qquad X = \sum_i^n x_i.$$

Summing (9.5) over all n firms in the industry and solving for industry output we obtain

$$X = \frac{Q}{nr - r + 1}, \quad (9.6)$$

which, upon substitution in (9.5), gives

$$x_i = \frac{q_i}{1 - r} - \frac{r Q}{(1 - r)(nr - r + 1)} = \frac{q_i}{1 - r} - \frac{rX}{1 - r}. \quad (9.7)$$

From (9.6) and (9.7) it is easy to show that an increase in the quality-efficiency index for any firm i results in an increase in both its output and the industry's output, holding the degree of cooperation θ, and the q_j for all other firms fixed, that is,

$$\frac{\partial X}{\partial q_i} > 0 , \qquad \frac{\partial x_i}{\partial q_i} > 0. \tag{9.8}$$

Over a long period of time, the sales of all firms in an industry expand. To allow for this growth, we look for the effects of a merger by examining firm market shares. Our assumption is that, in the absence of mergers, all firms in the industry would have grown at the same rate. Changes in market shares reflect changes in the relative quality-efficiency characteristics of the individual firms. From (9.6) and (9.7) we obtain for the ith firm's market share

$$m_i = x_i/X = \frac{q_i(nr-r+1)}{(1-r)Q} - \frac{r}{(1-r)} \tag{9.9}$$

$$\frac{\partial m_i}{\partial q_i} = \frac{nr-r+1}{(1-r)Q} - \frac{(nr-r+1)q_i}{(1-r)Q^2} = \frac{(Q-q_i)(nr-r+1)}{(1-r)Q^2} > 0. \tag{9.10}$$

An increase in the ith firm's quality-efficiency index following a merger increases its market share.

Equation (9.9) defines the ith firm's market share in quantity units. Our market share data are for revenues, however. It would be nice if we could derive the analogous condition to (9.10) for market shares measured in revenues, but we cannot. Obviously if price rises because quality has improved ($\Delta a_i > 0$), market share in revenue units rises also. Furthermore, if q_i increases because costs fall, but quality remains unchanged ($\Delta a_i = 0$, $\Delta c_i < 0$), revenue increases as the marginal revenue of the firm is positive for all relevant points along its demand schedule, if $c_i > 0$. But it is possible to construct cases in which both the demand schedule and the cost functions shift so that output expands but revenue falls ($\Delta(p_i - c_i) > 0$, $\Delta p_i < 0$, $\Delta c_i < 0$). That is, if the merger results in both a deterioration in product quality and a reduction in unit costs, the output of the firm may expand even though revenues fall. Despite this possibility, we employ an increase in market share as our criterion for deducing an improvement in the quality-efficiency index of an acquired firm. Mergers resulting in a significant worsening of quality characteristics, and more than offsetting cost and price reductions so that market share in physical units expands while market share in revenues decline, are likely to be rare. But the possibility remains a caveat to the analysis.

Up until now, we have assumed that the only effect of a merger is on the quality–efficiency index of the acquired firm. Two additional possibilities need to be explored. The first is that a change in q_i may affect some of the other q_j. It is unlikely that a conglomerate merger affects the costs of the other firms in an industry. But a change in q_i can come about because of a perceived change in the quality of i relative to j resulting in a simultaneous reduction in the q_j for some other firms. From (9.10) it is obvious that such an effect reinforces the positive effect of an increase in the acquired firm's quality–efficiency index on its market share.

Consider next a change in the degree of cooperation. Recalling that $r = \sigma(1+\theta)/2$, and taking the partial derivative of (9.9) with respect to θ, we have

$$\frac{\partial m_i}{\partial \theta} = \frac{\partial m_i}{\partial r}\frac{\partial r}{\partial \theta} = \frac{q_i(n-1)-Q}{(1-r)Q}$$

$$+ \frac{q_i(nr-r+1)-r}{(1-r)^2 Q}\frac{\sigma}{2} = \frac{q_i n - Q}{(1-r)^2 Q} \cdot \frac{\sigma}{2}. \quad (9.11)$$

Thus,

$$\frac{\partial m_i}{\partial \theta} \underset{<}{\overset{>}{=}} 0 \leftrightarrow q_i \underset{<}{\overset{>}{=}} \frac{Q}{n}. \quad (9.12)$$

A merger that increases the degree of cooperation in an industry increases the market shares of those companies having higher-than-average quality–efficiency indexes, and reduces the market shares of those with below-average q_i. Since m_i and q_i are themselves positively related, an increase in collusive activity should increase the market shares of the bigger firms and reduce those of the smaller companies. This result becomes intuitive when one recalls that θ is the weight placed on the other firms' profits in the industry. An increase in θ is an increase in the weight placed on the most profitable firms, that is, those with above-average quality–efficiency indexes.

Table 9.1 presents the four possible outcomes depending on the effect of the merger on θ, and the relationship between q_i and Q/n. Intuitively, the cases in quadrants 1 and 4 seem the most likely; that is, an acquisition of a relatively large firm increases the degree of cooperation, the acquisition of a small company reduces cooperation. Both cases imply an increase in the acquired firm's market share. Thus, when we observe market share increases following a merger, the possibility exists that we are observing changes in the degree of cooperation in the industry rather than improvements in quality or efficiency. Nevertheless, particularly for conglomerate mergers, changes in efficiency or quality seem so likely to outweigh changes in

Table 9.1. *Possible effects of changes in the degree of cooperation on market shares*

	$\Delta\theta > 0$	$\Delta\theta < 0$
$q_i > \dfrac{Q}{n}$	$\Delta m_i > 0$	$\Delta m_i < 0$
$q_i < \dfrac{Q}{n}$	$\Delta m_i < 0$	$\Delta m_i > 0$

the degree of cooperation that we decided to maintain our quality–efficiency–market share criterion. This possible source of bias must be kept in mind, however.

2. Horizontal mergers

In a horizontal merger, mutual interdependence in the industry must increase at least insofar as the outputs of the two merging firms are coordinated, as in perfect collusion, following the merger.[1] If j and k merged, we can write the objective function of the merged company as

$$0_m = \Pi_j + \Pi_k + \theta \sum_{i \neq j,k}^{n} \Pi_i. \tag{9.13}$$

If (9.13) is maximized with respect to x_j and x_k, and all other firms maximize their objective functions as before, industry output following the merger is

$$X = \frac{Q}{nr - r + 1} - \frac{\frac{\sigma}{2}(1 - \theta)}{nr - r - 1}(x_j + x_k). \tag{9.14}$$

The first term to the right of the equal sign is the output of the industry in the absence of the merger. If the products in the industry are partial substitutes ($\sigma > 0$) and collusion is not perfect ($\theta < 1$), industry output falls following a merger by a fraction of the merging companies' combined outputs.

The burden of reducing industry output falls entirely on the merged company. A glance at (9.7) reveals that the other firms in the industry expand output slightly in response to the reduction by the merged company. Since the merging companies' output declines as all other firms expand, its market share falls relative to the sum of the premerger market shares of the merging companies. Thus, when the only effect of a horizontal merger is to bring about perfect collusion between the two merging companies, the merger reduces the market share of the merging companies.

As with conglomerate mergers, increases in the quality–efficiency index of either participant in a horizontal merger tend to expand the market share of the merged company ceteris paribus. For the reasons just given, the ceteris paribus assumption definitely does not hold in a horizontal merger. Thus, the market share reducing effects of the increased cooperation between the merging firms and the market share increasing effects of an increase in q_j or q_k would tend to offset one another. Thus, for horizontal mergers, modest improvements in the quality–efficiency index of the merging firms may go undetected because of the reduction in output that perfect collusion between the merging firms brings about.

A traditional concern with horizontal mergers is that the reduction in the number of sellers enhances the degree of cooperation among the remaining firms; that is, θ increases. Returning to Table 9.1, we see that an increase in θ increases the market share of a firm with above-average q_i, reduces it for a firm with below-average q_i. When relatively large firms are involved in horizontal mergers, the two collusion effects tend to be offsetting. A rise in θ increases a large firm's market share, but the perfect collusion brought about between the two merging firms reduces their combined market share. When small firms join in a horizontal merger, their combined market share should definitely fall.

3.   Vertical acquisitions

In a vertical acquisition, both firms are in different industries and the effects of the merger on the acquired company can be studied as with a conglomerate merger; that is, we assume that all of the effects of vertical mergers on market shares are brought about either by efficiency–product quality increases or changes in the degree of cooperation. The FTC market share data were gathered on an establishment basis, and include intrafirm shipments, so the disappearance of acquired company shipments into intrafirm transfers following a vertical acquisition is not a problem.

4.   Summary

The model used to analyze the effects of mergers on market share is admittedly simple. The results of Chapter 6 suggest that little further insight will be gained by complicating the model to allow differences across companies in the slopes of the demand schedules or the degree of product differentiation. As it stands, the model gives rather clear predictions when mergers do not affect the degree of cooperation. When the only effect of a merger is to lower the acquired company's marginal costs or improve the quality of its products, its market share increases. When the only effect of a merger is to increase the degree of cooperation, a firm's market share could rise or fall following a merger. With respect to horizontal mergers, however, there is a greater likelihood of a fall in market share owing to the perfect collusion established between the merging companies. When the degree of cooperation and efficiency or product quality are changed, it becomes more difficult to predict the effects on market share. As it turns out, however, the nature of the results is such as to allow the drawing of fairly clear, and surprising, conclusions. Thus, we move on now to the empirical work and return to the various possible outcomes in the concluding section.

B.   Data and methodology

The sample of acquired firms consists of all companies that were (1) among the 1,000 largest of 1950, and (2) were acquired by a firm among the 1,000 largest in both 1950 and 1972. Any company meeting this criterion that was spun off or sold prior to 1973 was omitted from the sample. If a company A was acquired by B, which in turn was acquired by C, and A and C met the criterion, A was included in the sample. When only a division of a firm was acquired, this division was treated as the acquired firm. Using these criteria, we constructed a sample of 209 acquired and 123 acquiring companies. (Merging and control group companies are listed in Appendix 5.)

Whenever the five-digit product definition seemed too disaggregate, we aggregated upward until a more meaningful economic definition of the market was obtained, placing particular weight on substitution in production in defining the market (see Appendix 2 for the market definitions). Between 1950 and 1972, there were numerous changes in SIC product definitions. These changes required further combining and rearranging of product lines to match 1950 and 1972 markets. Fortunately, most industries that could not be compared had small 1950 sales, so that the percentage of 1950 sales that could not be matched to 1972 markets was only 5.8 percent, although in some cases the "match" was admittedly somewhat loose.

Given the changes in market boundaries and product definitions between 1950 and 1972, a firm's market share in 1972 in a given 1972 market might over- or understate what its market share would be in a truly comparable market. Overstatement can occur if a market is too broadly defined and the firm has sales in the erroneously included products, or because the market is too narrowly defined and a larger fraction of the market's sales are omitted than of the firm's. Understatement can occur when the errors run in the opposite direction. In general, we have an errors-in-observation problem and our estimated coefficients on market share variables will be biased toward zero. To control for these biases to some extent, we estimate the effects of mergers on market shares *relative* to a control group of companies whose 1950 and 1972 market shares are defined using the same market definitions as for the merger sample.

Firm i's market share is assumed to follow a simple first-order Markov process over time

$$m_{i\ t+1} = \alpha m_{it} + \mu_{it},$$

or

$$m_{i\ t+n} = \alpha^n m_{it} + \sum_{j=1}^{n-1} \alpha^j \mu_{i\ t+n-j}. \tag{9.15}$$

Assuming that the weighted sum or errors in (9.15) has the usual mean zero, constant variance property across firms, (9.15) can be estimated using the 1972 and 1950 market share data as

$$M_I = am_i + \epsilon_i, \tag{9.16}^*$$

where lowercase letters indicate 1950 values and uppercase letters stand for 1972. To test for the effects of mergers on market share, we test whether acquired companies have the same estimated $\hat{a}$ as a control group that is similar in size and industry composition to the acquired firms, but that was not acquired between 1950 and 1972. We do this by defining a dummy variable, $D = 1$ if the firm was acquired, and 0 if it is in the control group, and estimating (9.17) across the pooled sample:

$$M_I = am_i + bDm_i + \epsilon_i. \tag{9.17}$$

If mergers have no effect on market share, $\hat{b}$ should equal zero. We treat this prediction as the null hypothesis.

Two modifications are made to (9.17) in the empirical work. A constant, c, is added to allow for some "drift" in market shares because our industry definitions in 1950 and 1972 are not a perfect match.

Second-degree terms in m are added to allow for a regression-on-the-mean effect for larger market share firms.

For each company i acquired in a conglomerate merger, a weighted market share for 1950 was constructed using its 1950 sales in each market k, s_{ik} as weights

$$m_i = \left(\sum_k s_{ik} \cdot m_{ik}\right)/s_i, \tag{9.18}$$

where $s_i = \sum_k s_{ik}$ is i's total 1950 sales.

Firm i's market share in 1972 is computed over the K markets in 1972 that match the k markets in 1950 in which i had sales. In a conglomerate merger 1950 firm i has become 1972 acquiring firm I. Using I's 1972 sales in each market K as weights, we have

$$M_I^{72} = \left(\sum_K S_{IK} \cdot M_{IK}\right)/s_I, \tag{9.19}$$

where $S_I = \sum_K S_{IK}$ and the 72 superscript indicates that 1972 sales weights are used.

The use of 1972 sales as weights when computing 1972 market shares can in some cases give misleading results. Consider the following example. Firm i has 1950 sales of 100 in market 1 with a market share of .13 and 200 in market 2 with a market share of .10. Its weighted 1950 market share is then .11 = (.13 × 100 + .10 × 200)/300. In 1972, it has sales of 400 in market 1 with a market share of .12 and zero in market 2. If its 1972 sales are used as weights to calculate its 1972 market share, one records an increase in market share from .11 to .12 = (.12 × 400 + 0 × 0)/400, even though the firm lost market share in both markets. To guard against this bias, we also calculate 1972 market shares using 1950 sales weights:

$$M_I^{50} = \left(\sum_K s_{ik} \cdot M_{IK}\right)/s_i. \tag{9.20}$$

Although M_I^{72} in the previous example is .12, M_I^{50} is .04 = (.12 × 100 + 0 × 200)/300.

The use of these two measures of 1972 market shares allows us to test the Weston (1970) and Williamson (1970) hypothesis that conglomerate mergers improve efficiency by facilitating the redeployment of capital across divisions. Evidence in favor of this hypothesis would be a significantly better performance of companies acquired in conglomerate mergers relative to the control group, when 1972 market shares are calculated using 1972 sales weights (M_I^{72}), than when 1950 weights are used.

We define as horizontal those portions of a merger in which both the acquiring and acquired companies had 1950 sales in the same market.[2] For horizontal mergers the combined sales of the two companies in the k markets in which they both operated in 1950 are compared with the acquiring firm's sales in the K markets in 1972. Let q be the acquiring firm, d the acquired company. For horizontal mergers, we then define i's sales and market shares as

$$s_{ik} = s_{gk} + s_{dk}, \qquad m_{ik} = m_{gk} + m_{dk}, \tag{9.21}$$

and then compute 1950 market shares for the merging companies using (9.18).

To measure the effects of mergers on market shares, we selected two control groups of unacquired companies to compare with the conglomerate and horizontal merger samples. To be in a control group, a company must (1) be in the 1,000-largest lists in both 1950 and 1972, and (2) not have acquired a member of the 1950 list between 1950 and 1972. The FTC divided the 1950 1,000 largest into the 200 largest, 201–500 largest, and 501–1,000 largest. In forming the control groups, we chose companies at random from the three size categories in the same proportions as exist in the merger sample. The selection process was continued until enough firms were drawn so that the total sales by two-digit SIC for each control group roughly equaled those for the merger samples. There were so many companies acquired from the pulp and paper industry (SIC 26) that there were not enough firms left in the 1950 list to bring the sales of the conglomerate-merger control group up to the merger sample even when all possible candidates were included. With this exception, it was possible to select control group companies with sales roughly equal to the acquired firms' sales in 1950. A percentage breakdown of the two acquired firms' samples and their control groups is given in Table 9.2.

C.   The results

1.   Conglomerate mergers

All market shares must fall between zero and one and there is a heavy concentration of market shares below 0.1. The mean for the acquired

Table 9.2. *Percentage breakdown of sample companies' 1950 sales by two-digit industry*

Industry SIC code	Major industry group	Conglomerate merger sample	Conglomerate merger control group	Horizontal merger sample	Horizontal merger control group
20	Food & kindred products	.180	.203	.093	.095
21	Tobacco manufactures	.009	.009	0	0
22	Textile mill products	.063	.073	.242	.220
23	Apparel & related products	.007	.013	.012	.006
24	Lumber & wood products	.013	.016	.026	.019
25	Furniture & fixtures	.009	.015	.004	.002
26	Pulp & paper products	.134	.068	.128	.098
27	Printing & publishing	.006	.004	0	.001
28	Chemicals & related products	.147	.149	.019	.029
29	Petroleum & coal products	.008	.008	.128	.113
30	Rubber products	.004	.005	.007	.007
31	Leather & leather products	0	0	.013	.023
32	Stone, clay, & glass products	.020	.021	0	.001
33	Primary metal products	.062	.056	.113	.097
34	Fabricated metal products	.042	.062	.016	.035
35	Machinery, except electrical	.125	.128	.049	.046
36	Electrical machinery	.063	.072	.008	.017
37	Transportation equipment	.080	.128	.140	.188
38	Instruments & related products	.013	.015	0	.009
39	Miscellaneous manufactures	.014	.016	0	.001

firms was 0.067 in the conglomerate merger sample. This heavy concentration of observations near the origin raises the possibility that a few outliers swing the regression lines in one direction or another. To avoid this, we weighted all observations by 1950 sales. The sales-weighted equations also yield more meaningful economic estimates. A 10 percentage point increase in market share for a company with $300,000,000 in sales has greater economic significance than the same change for a firm with $30,000 in sales. All reported estimates are for sales-weighted regressions. Results of a similar qualitative nature were obtained from unweighted regressions, however.

The first two equations in Table 9.3 present results for the basic linear equation including a constant term to capture market share drift. (Closely analogous results to those reported were obtained when the intercepts were suppressed.) The coefficient on the m term indicates a high retention of market share even after 23 years has elapsed for companies in the top 1,000 in 1950, which were not acquired. The coefficient on the Dm term indicates that companies that were acquired between 1950 and 1972 retained a significantly smaller percentage of their 1950 market shares. For example, an unacquired firm retained 88.5 percent of its 1950 market share in 1972 using 1972 sales as weights, whereas an acquired firm retains but 18 percent of its 1950 market share.

The mergers in the sample took place throughout the period 1950–72.[3] It could be that the relative declines in market shares of the acquired companies took place before they were acquired, and that their postacquisition performance was no worse or even better than that of the control group. This observation would be consistent with the failing firm hypothesis (Dewey 1961), or with the hypothesis that takeovers occur to replace poor managers (Manne 1965). To test for this alternative possibility, D was redefined as $D = (73 - YR)/23$, where YR is year of acquisition, $YR = 50,72$. A merger occurring relatively early in the interval between 1950 and 1972 receives a heavier weight in the merger vector than a merger occurring late in the interval. Control group firms continue to have $D = 0$. If the decline in market shares preceded the acquisitions, this alternative weighting of observations in the Dm vector should reverse the sign, or at least raise the coefficient of this term.

But it lowers it still further. The coefficients on Dm are negative and *larger* in absolute value than when D is a 0,1 dummy. The relative deterioration in market shares for acquired companies is more severe the earlier they occur. Indeed, equation (3) [(4)] implies that a firm

Table 9.3. Conglomerate mergers

Equation	Dependent variable	c	m	Dm	Dm^2	D	n	$\bar{R}^2$
(1)	M^{50}	.009 2.34	.691 39.23	−.527 16.77		1,0	313	.922
(2)	M^{72}	.011 2.61	.885 45.02	−.705 20.09		1,0	313	.940
(3)	M^{50}	−.003 .78	.727 43.49	−.779 18.30		$\frac{73-YR}{23}$	313	.929
(4)	M^{72}	−.005 1.30	.933 49.24	−1.02 21.08		$\frac{73-YR}{23}$	313	.944
(5)	M^{50}	−.012 3.31	.750 37.84		−2.00 12.34	1,0	313	.901
(6)	M^{72}	−.017 3.97	.964 42.62		−2.77 14.93	1,0	313	.920
(7)	M^{50}	−.009 3.01	.753 45.35		−4.43 18.63	$\frac{73-YR}{23}$	313	.930
(8)	M^{72}	−.014 3.91	.968 52.16		−5.83 21.95	$\frac{73-YR}{23}$	313	.946

Note: t-values under coefficients. All variables and constant are weighted by 1950 sales.

acquired before 1956 (1952) is predicted to have a negative market share in 1972 when 1950 (1972) sales are used as weights.

It is impossible for a firm to have a negative market share, and the latter implication of equations (3) and (4) suggests nonlinearity. When both m^2 and Dm^2 were added to the equation, multicollinearity was present. The best-fit equation for $D = (73 - YR)/23$ was one in which a linear relationship between m and M is assumed for the control group firms, but a nonlinear relationship is assumed for the acquired firms (see equations [7] and [8]). The larger an acquired firm's 1950 market share was, the larger was the percentage loss in its market share between 1950 and 1972. The same equations are presented with D defined as a 0,1 dummy in equations (5) and (6). The nonlinear specification when D is zero or one is inferior, as judged by $\overline{R}^2$, to the linear. A comparison of equations (5) and (6) with (7) and (8) reveals again a lower coefficient on the D terms when D weights earlier acquisitions more heavily, however. The implication from equations (5)–(8) as from (1)–(4) is that the decline in market shares that acquired firms experience relative to the unacquired control group firms occurred after their acquisition.

Heteroscedasticity was present in both the sales weighted results reported and the unreported, unweighted results.[4] Efforts to remove heteroscedasticity by reweighting each observation did not yield a choice of weight that gave homoscedastic residuals for all obvious choices of scale variable. Although heteroscedasticity is troublesome, coefficients remain unbiased estimates of the true parameters, and inefficiency does not seem so serious a problem, given that we have 313 observations. Moreover, the key coefficients on the Dm and Dm^2 terms are 12 to 22 times their standard errors. Thus, a severalfold expansion of the standard errors is possible to allow for the downward bias in standard error estimate without overturning the conclusion that mergers have resulted in a relative deterioration in the acquired firms' market shares.

2.   *Horizontal mergers*

The first four equations in Table 9.4 reproduce results for the horizontal merger sample and its control group that parallel those for the conglomerate mergers reported in Table 9.3. The coefficient on m indicates that nonacquired companies in the industries in which horizontal mergers occurred were less successful at retaining their 1950 market shares through 1972, retaining little more than 50 percent. But they were considerably more successful than the firms en-

Table 9.4. *Horizontal mergers*
($n = 176$)

Equation	Dependent variable	c	m	Dm	m^2	Dm^2	D	$\bar{R}^2$
(1)	M^{50}	.024 9.57	.511 17.77	−.346 7.86			1,0	.832
(2)	M^{72}	.027 9.48	.547 16.94	−.403 8.15			1,0	.818
(3)	M^{50}	.024 9.83	.513 18.29	−.472 8.57			$\dfrac{73-YR}{23}$	.840
(4)	M^{72}	.027 9.80	.549 17.54	−.553 8.99			$\dfrac{73-YR}{23}$	.829
(5)	M^{50}	.015 4.65	.825 12.09	−.604 9.84	−.936 5.38	1.21 5.18	1,0	.862
(6)	M^{72}	.015 4.07	.962 12.92	−.710 10.59	−1.22 6.44	1.43 5.58	1,0	.859
(7)	M^{50}	.015 4.57	.826 12.44	−.784 10.46	−.931 5.49	1.52 5.22	$\dfrac{73-YR}{23}$	.869
(8)	M^{72}	.014 4.02	.966 13.51	−.932 11.55	−1.23 6.72	1.83 5.82	$\dfrac{73-YR}{23}$	.870

Note: t-values under coefficients. All variables anc constants are weighted by 1950 sales.

gaging in horizontal mergers. A comparison of equations (1) and (2) with (3) and (4) again reveals that placing heavier weight on earlier mergers worsens the relative performance of merging firms. A firm acquired in 1950 is projected to lose all of its market share by 1972 using 1972 sales weights to calculate M, all but 4 percent of its 1950 market share using 1950 sales weights. The earlier a merger occurred, the worse the relative loss of market share.

When m^2 and Dm^2 terms were added to the basic linear equation for the horizontal mergers' sample, multicollinearity did not appear to be a problem, although the two coefficients were of opposite signs. Equations (5) and (6) imply that the M-m curve for nonacquired companies is concave from below; the curve for merging firms is convex. The two curves cross at a 1950 market share of around .5. Only one pair of companies involved in a horizontal merger has their combined 1950 market share greater than .5. Thus, equations (5) and (6) predict a decline in market share for a pair of firms in a horizontal merger between 1950 and 1972 relative to a nonmerging firm with the same market share in 1950 as the combined market share of the merging firms, for every pair of merging companies save one.

The results for equations (7) and (8) parallel those for (5) and (6) except that D has been redefined once again to place heavier weight on the earlier observations. Both D-coefficients are larger in absolute value. Thus, this reweighting of observations exaggerates the curvature of each relationship. The convex curves in equations (7) and (8) lie beneath their respective curves in (5) and (6) for all 1950 market shares less than .56. For all mergers in the sample but one, the reweighted curves in (7) and (8) predict relatively lower market shares for merging firms than for nonmerging firms, the earlier the merger occurs.

D.   Biases and caveats

Before drawing conclusions, a few possible biases in the results must be reviewed. The most important of these is that we have data on only those acquired companies that were in the top 1,000 of 1950. If a company acquired two firms with sales in the same market, one in the 1950 1,000 largest, the other not, the 1972 market share reflects the contribution of both acquired firms, whereas we attribute all of the sales to the one acquired firm in our sample. The estimate of the merger's impact on the acquired firm's market share is biased upward, and this bias could be considerable. For example, St. Regis Paper acquired three firms from the 1950 1,000 largest list between 1950 and 1972; each is an observation in the sample. But the 1973 *Moody's Industrial Manual* lists some 53 companies as having been acquired by St. Regis between 1953 and 1972 alone, and most of these appear to be in the lumber and paper industries. Our comparison of 1950 and 1972 market shares ignoring these 50+ additional mergers must certainly overestimate any increase or underestimate any decline in St. Regis's market shares that occurred.

The most important biases are for firms such as St. Regis that made numerous acquisitions in the same industries. Numerous mergers in the same industry are more likely for horizontal mergers. Thus, the estimates for horizontal acquisitions are more likely to be biased in favor of finding a positive effect of mergers on market share than are the conglomerate mergers' estimates. It is important to recall that for horizontal mergers, 1950 market shares are defined as the *sum* of the acquiring and acquired firms' market shares. The nonlinear results in equations (5)–(8) of Table 9.4 imply that there was a smaller loss in market share for merging firms relative to the control group when the combined market share of the merging firms in 1950 was large. Large 1950 market shares in horizontal mergers tend to be due to the large market shares of the acquiring companies. The unrecorded acquisitions of these firms are also likely to be greater in number.

We define as conglomerate any acquisition, or part thereof, where the two firms did not sell in the same market in 1950. Often the acquiring firm had sales in a market neighboring the acquired company's markets, and made several acquisitions in these besides the one in our sample. In these market-extension conglomerate mergers, a considerable upward bias in our estimates of the beneficial effects of mergers on market shares is also possible. Nevertheless, the greater upward bias is probably in the horizontal merger results.

This bias in estimating the impact of mergers is offset to the extent that control group firms also made acquisitions during the period in the industries in which they were selling in 1950. Although they did, a comparison of the merger histories of the acquiring and control group companies reveals the former to be far more active in the market for corporate control. This finding is not surprising. Any company that was among the 1,000 largest in 1950 and made many acquisitions over the next 22 years is likely to have acquired at least one other company in the 1950 top 1,000, and thus is likely to appear in the merger sample. Whatever bias exists from not having data on premerger market shares of acquired firms not in the 1950 1,000 largest group leads toward an overestimate of the positive effects of mergers on market share.

An opposite bias could be introduced by our neglect of spin-offs. Although all acquisitions in which the acquiring firm sold the previously acquired company before 1973 were excluded from the sample, information allowing an adjustment for partial spin-offs was lacking. Although the control group firms also undertook unrecorded spin-offs, it is reasonable to assume that spin-offs of assets acquired through merger are more common than internally generated assets. If a bias from ignoring unreported spin-offs was significant, one would expect acquired firms to perform much better when their market shares are measured using 1972 sales as weights than when 1950 sales are used, since the 1972 sales weights allow for the spin-offs. But the deterioration in market shares for acquired firms is, if anything, greater when one uses 1972 sales as weights so that whatever bias exists is more than offset by other factors.

A bias in favor of a positive effect of mergers on market shares is introduced by omitting entirely all acquisitions in which full spin-offs subsequently occurred. Few firms buy a company, improve its performance, and then sell it. A spin-off of an acquired firm is, or at least was in the fifties and sixties, an admission of failure.

The matching of 1950 and 1972 markets is of varying degrees of accuracy. To the extent that these markets are not fully comparable, errors in observation are introduced in the market share data and regression coefficients are biased toward zero. The same market definitions have been used for the merging firms and the control group companies, so that this bias should be removed or reduced for the variables measuring the impact of the mergers, the D variables.

E.   Discussion

Only one other study has examined the effect of mergers on market shares. Lawrence Goldberg (1973) examined a sample of 44 companies acquired in the fifties and sixties and found no significant change in market shares or growth rates following the mergers. The longest time span following a merger in Goldberg's (1973, p. 146) sample was 11 years, the mean was 3½. The sample used in this chapter contains 209 acquired companies with an average postacquisition time period of 11 years and a maximum of 22. Moreover, Goldberg's sample was heavily concentrated in advertising-intensive industries whereas ours spans all manufacturing.

In one important dimension, Goldberg's data base was richer than ours, however. He was able to compute growth rates for the acquired firms in the years immediately preceding and following the mergers.

Our data observations are limited to two points in time, 1950 and 1972. Goldberg's data allowed him to test for a change in growth rate following the mergers. He found no significant change. We were forced to attempt to infer whether observed changes in market shares between 1950 and 1972 preceded or followed the mergers by re-weighting the sample observations by their point in time.

In a previous study of 133 mergers between 1962 and 1972, I found a significant decline in the growth rate of the acquiring companies in the five years following the mergers compared with both a matched control group sample, and their industries (Mueller, 1980a, pp. 289–91). These results are consistent with those of the present investigation. Taken together, Goldberg's study and the two by myself strongly imply that mergers in the United States in the fifties and sixties did not increase the market shares of acquired companies or their growth rates. The present study suggests a significant decline in market shares.

Two companies in the group that we examined in Chapter 5 were acquired prior to 1972. Sunshine Biscuit's profits declined in the two years immediately preceding its acquisition (see Figure 5.2), and this decline might signal internal problems or managerial failures that precipitated Sunshine's acquisition. But Sunshine's profits were above those of United Biscuit (Keebler) throughout the time period.

Continental Baking's market share rose from 5.8 in 1950 to 10.0 in 1963 (see Table 5.3). Neither its market share increase nor its profit profile suggests a company with management problems prior to its acquisition. Although we do not have figures on Continental's recent market share or profit rate, Continental was rumored to be up for sale by ITT in 1982 (*Forbes*, August 30, 1982, p. 49)

Few firms make an acquisition with the intention of selling it. Spin-offs are thus, perhaps, the most dramatic evidence of the deleterious effects of mergers. Table 9.5 contains four companies in the 1950 1,000 largest list for which both a purchase and a sale price could be found. Taking into account inflation and the normal growth in asset values that occurred in the years between purchase and sale, it is difficult to believe the operating efficiency of these companies improved following their acquisition. I expect the same is true of the nine other spin-offs for which no sales price is reported. Were it possible to calculate market shares for these companies in 1972 and include them in the sample, they would most certainly reinforce the negative findings of this chapter.

F. M. Scherer (1984a) has examined in depth 15 spin-offs of the late seventies and early eighties. Six of these were among the 1,000 largest of 1950. The first four companies in Table 9.6 were acquired

Table 9.5. *Purchase and sales prices of spin-offs of 1,000 largest acquisitions (thousands of dollars)*

Acquiring firm	Acquired firm	Year acquired	Year sold	Purchase price	Selling price
Murray (Wallace–Murray)	Easy Washer	1955, 1957	1963	9,400	770
National Sugar	Godchaux Sugar	1956	1961	14,000	9,600
Kennecott Copper	Okonite	1957	1966	31,300	31,700
Heublin	Theo Hamm	1965	1973	62,006	6,000

Source: Moody's Industrial Manual, 1973. Selling prices are in current values.

Table 9.6. Sales of spin-offs of 1950 1,000 largest companies
(millions of 1950 dollars)

Acquired company	Acquiring company	1950 sales	Year acquired	Sales in year prior to acquisition	Year of spin-off	Sales at spin-off
American Safety Razor (ASR)	Philip Morris	16.4	1960	27.3	1977	17.8
Harley-Davidson	AMF Corp.	14.4	1968	33.0	1981	107.7
Talon	Textron	34.2	1968	81.4	1981	53.9
Youngstown Sheet & Tube	Lykes	580.0	1969	628.0	1978	794.0
Electric Storage Battery (ESB)	Inco Ltd.	86.1	1974	291.0	1982–83	256.0
Marquette Cement	Gulf & Western	19.6	1976	68.8	1982	57.4

Sources: FTC (1972a), Scherer (1984a), *Moody's Industrials*, selected years.

prior to 1972, the last two afterward. Given the roughly 30-year time span from 1950 and eventual spin-off, I have converted all sales figures to 1950 dollars. The sales at spin-off figures are admittedly rough, since the spin-off firm may be involved in a somewhat different mix of activities than the firms acquired. But the figures give a reasonable picture of what was happening to each firm over time. All six companies, with the exception of Youngstown Sheet and Tube, enjoyed a rapid expansion in sales from 1950 up to the year of their acquisition. Four of the six experienced declines in sales following their acquisitions. The most spectacular exception appears to be Harley-Davidson. Although its sales only slightly more than doubled between 1950 and 1968, they more than tripled during the 12 years in which it was an AMF subsidiary. The market for motorcycles expanded even more rapidly than Harley-Davidson, however, so that by 1979 Harley had seen its share of the large cycle market (1,000 cc and above), the segment on which Harley concentrated its attention, decline from almost 100 percent to 40 percent in 1979 (Scherer 1984b, p. 14). It was this declining relative performance that precipitated AMF's decision to sell Harley.

The other company whose sales rose subsequent to its acquisition, Youngstown Sheet and Tube, also lost market share following its acquisition. Youngstown's share of total steel industry shipments declined from 4.4 percent in 1968 to 3.7 percent in 1977 (*Iron Age*, April 10, 1969, pp. 75–7; April 24, 1978, pp. 36–7). Thus, all six of the companies that were part of the 1950 1,000-largest list and that were among the spin-offs Scherer studied experienced either a loss in market share or a loss in total sales, or both.

Scherer chose his sample of spin-offs to gain knowledge of the causes of merger failure. He does not purport it to be a random draw from the merger population. Although some mergers are successful, the results of this chapter suggest that Scherer's 15 spin-offs and the 4 in Table 9.5 are far more representative of the population of all mergers than one might at first have suspected.

F.   Conclusions

Companies among the 1,000 largest manufacturers in 1950 that were acquired between 1950 and 1972 achieved smaller market shares than they would have had they performed as the industry- and size-matched control group did. Moreover, the earlier they were acquired, the greater the loss in market share. After a generation, the typical company acquired between 1950 and 1972 in a conglomerate merger has disappeared entirely.

The theoretical discussion of Section A suggests two explanations for this loss in market share: changes in the degree of cooperation, declines in efficiency or product quality. The results for the conglomerate acquisitions – relatively larger market share losses for acquired firms with larger initial market shares – are unlikely to come about due to changes in the degree of cooperation. A deterioration in efficiency or product quality is the most plausible cause of the loss of market shares by acquired companies in conglomerate mergers.

But the pattern of market share change following horizontal mergers is roughly consistent with that predicted from an increase in the degree of cooperation (Table 9.1). The market shares of firms with relatively small initial market shares are predicted to decline by a greater amount than are the market shares of the companies with relatively large initial market shares. The company with the largest initial market share is actually predicted to experience an increase in its market share following the horizontal merger. The model of Section A predicts increases for all companies with above-average market shares if the degree of cooperation increases. The results in Table 9.4 imply an increase for only the pair of merging firms in the horizontal merger sample with the highest combined market share. Thus, more is at work in the horizontal merger results than just a change in the degree of cooperation. The results seem to imply an increase in the degree of cooperation combined with a deterioration in efficiency or product quality.

These results would seem to require the rejection or at least reinterpretation of several leading hypotheses regarding mergers. No support was found for the hypothesis that mergers improve efficiency by consolidating the sales of the acquired companies on their most efficient product lines. The relative loss in market shares when 1972 sales are used as weights to calculate 1972 market shares are about the same or slightly greater than when M^{50} is the dependent variable. Acquired firms perform no better, if not worse, than nonacquired companies in those markets in which each chose to concentrate its sales.

Smiley (1976) and Mandelker (1974) found that acquired firms had below-average stock market performance prior to their acquisition. These below-average stock market returns may signal the declines in market shares we record following a company's acquisition. But if they do, and if it is bad management that precipitated the acquisitions, then the new management does not appear to have done much better than the old at improving company performance, as measured by comparing its market share to otherwise similar but nonacquired companies.

Donald Dewey (1961) expressed the view that mergers take place to rescue "falling firms" from bankruptcy. Firms acquired between 1950 and 1972 fell a long way relative to otherwise similar nonacquired firms. As in all merger studies, we can never truly test the counterfactual. Perhaps these companies would have suffered similar or even greater market share declines had they not been acquired. If we assume this interpretation is correct, our results imply an important modification to the "falling firm" hypothesis. At best, mergers cushion a company's fall; they do not alter its trajectory. Our results also offer an alternative to the falling-firm hypothesis, namely, that the acquired company's fall begins *after* its acquisition and that the acquisition causes the fall in market share.

The results reported in this chapter reinforce the impression obtained in the previous one that mergers did not improve the profitability of the merging companies by generating synergistic reductions in costs or improvements in product quality. Although the results in this chapter are for market share rather than profits, the link between firm market shares and profits that we have witnessed through the previous five chapters appears sufficiently strong that it is extremely unlikely that the mergers could have caused the reductions in market shares recorded here and somehow increased profitability. Indeed, if the results in this chapter raise any questions about the results of the previous chapter, it is perhaps why a more pronounced tendency for mergers to reduce profitability did not appear.

CHAPTER 10

The threads gathered and conclusions woven

In this chapter we pull together the various strands running through the preceding chapters, relate them to previous research on profitability, and draw policy implications. Section A combines the variables from the preceding chapters that have proven to be important determinants of long-run profits into a single model. In Section B some of the implications of the results for the structure-performance literature are drawn. Implications for future research and policy are discussed in Sections C and D.

A.   The complete model

In Chapter 6 we examined the effects of several firm-specific characteristics on projected profitability: advertising, patent intensity, risk, sales, diversification, and growth. Neither the firm's own advertising nor its patent intensity had a significant impact on its projected profitability. The covariance (β) measures of risk both had significant coefficients but of the wrong sign, if it is hypothesized that above-normal profits persist because of the existence of above-normal risks. We conjectured that reverse causality was involved. Firms with persistently high profits were perceived by the stock market to be less risky investments, that is, less subject to the systematic risks prevailing in the economy. Given the likelihood that reverse causality was involved in the β-α relationship, we did not include either β-type risk measure in the completed model. We did test to see whether the two-variance type measures of risk, whose coefficients did have the predicted positive coefficients, exhibited an enhanced explanatory power once the other significant exogenous variables uncovered throughout the study were included in the equation. They did not, and the results with σ_π and σ_α are not reported here.

Of the remaining variables added to the model in Chapter 6, only the log of the company's growth ($Ln(G)$) in sales had a significant coefficient and it is added to the completed model.

In Chapter 7 we explored the potential impact of several variables associated with the exercise of managerial discretion. Of these, only

209

Table 10.1. *Complete firm-effect model with industry dummies, best fit αs*

Variable	Industry name	Equation 1	2	3	4	5	6	7
CONST		-.040	-.160	-.155	-.128	-.106	-.232	-.223
		1.38	4.06	3.97	3.07	4.89	5.59	5.25
$(1-m)C_4^2$		-.583	-.696	-.695	-.665		-.389	-.316
		4.04	5.14	5.15	4.78		2.79	2.25
mA		.718	.693	.682	.707		.602	.575
		12.20	12.34	12.14	12.25		11.22	9.69
$mPat$		1.38	1.00	1.00	1.11		1.24	1.32
		5.44	4.13	4.18	4.15		5.28	5.26
π_{50}			.299					
			6.29					
$\pi_{50} \cdot GAQ$			-.079					
			1.23					
$\pi_{50}/(1+GAQ)$				.349	.330		.290	.277
				6.93	6.23		5.89	5.38
$Ln(G)$			.096	.094	.081		.093	.082
			5.84	5.82	4.75		6.03	5.07
MC^2					-.877			-.817
					2.82			2.91
I1202	Dairy products					-.179		
						1.42		
I1203	Canned and frozen fruits, vegetables					.396	.241	.341
						3.33	2.35	3.08
I1204	Flour and cereals					.239	.134	.144
						1.81	1.19	1.27

		2518	2188	2172
I206	Sugar and confectionery products	.292 / 3.78		
I208	Beer and distilled spirits	-.250 / 1.81	-.145 / 1.26	
I214	Tobacco	2.92 / 2.79		1.88 / 1.75
I235	Millinery, hats	3.40	3.54	3.60
I251	Furniture, wood and metal, mattresses	.363 / 1.86	.355 / 2.17	.363 / 2.27
I254	Wood and metal partitions	-2.43 / 1.32	-2.99 / 2.14	-3.00 / 2.20
I261	Wood pulp	1.76 / 1.66	1.12 / 1.24	1.18 / 1.34
I262	Paper and newsprint	-.636 / 2.43	-.649 / 2.95	-.622 / 2.88
I271	Newspapers	1.35 / 1.29	1.38 / 1.58	1.83 / 2.11
I275	Commercial printing, magazines	.505 / 2.88	.475 / 3.20	.540 / 3.70
I279	Photoengraving, electrotyping, typesetting	-12.4 / 1.75	-7.63 / 1.29	-9.47 / 1.62
I281	Inorganic chemicals		-.493 / 2.49	-.493 / 2.52
I283	Pharmaceuticals	1.40 / 5.81	1.11 / 5.51	1.14 / 5.77
I284	Soaps, detergents, polishes, toilet preparations	.688 / 4.27		.449 / 1.71

Table 10.1. (cont.)

| Variable | Industry name | | Equation | | | | | |
		1	2	3	4	5	6	7
I302	Rubber and plastics protective footwear						-2.46	-3.01
							1.67	2.11
I303	Reclaimed rubber						-19.8	
							1.85	
I307	Plastic products					.623	.338	.398
						2.52	1.60	1.91
I313	Nonrubber shoes and boots					14.7	12.6	22.2
						4.37	4.41	3.90
I317	Leather handbags, purses and personal leather							-23.7
								1.67
I323	Mirrors and other products made from purchased glass					3.00		
						1.23		
I324	Hydraulic cement					-.722	-.709	-.731
						2.45	2.85	3.00
I331	Steel mill products					-.216		
						2.33		
I333	Primary nonferrous metals						.359	.171
							1.58	1.30
I335	Nonferrous metals rolled and drawn							
I336	Nonferrous castings						2.69	2.67
							1.54	1.50
I342	Cutlery, razors, handtools					1.57	1.37	1.37
						3.76	3.94	4.03
I343	Plumbing and heating equipment						-1.47	
							1.32	

Code	Industry	(1)	(2)	(3)	(4)	(5)	(6)	(7)
1344	Fabricated structural metal products					−.411	−.444	−.394
						2.02	2.64	2.32
1349	Springs, valves and pipe fittings					.522		
						2.23		
1351	Turbine generators, gasoline and diesel engines					.759		
						2.90		
1354	Machine tools					.788	.436	.458
						4.23	2.73	2.91
1358	Laundry and refrigeration equipment					.572	.230	.206
						3.30	1.54	1.42
1362	Motors and generators, electrical equipment					.804	.580	.520
						2.49	2.14	1.95
1366	Telephone and communication equipment						−.357	−.356
							1.91	1.68
1367	Tubes and semiconductors						−.806	−.806
							2.21	2.25
1374	Locomotives and railroad equipment					−.527	−.296	−.300
						2.24	1.50	1.54
1381	Engineering and scientific equipment					−.153	−.120	
						1.45	1.37	
1384	Surgical and medical instruments					−1.04	−1.49	−1.79
						1.35	2.33	2.95
1386	Photographic and photocopying equipment					1.12		
						4.75		
n		551	551	551	504	551	551	504
$\bar{R}^2$		.278	.371	.375	.392	.291	.509	.540

the square of the fraction of outstanding shares held by management had a significant impact in the linear profit equation, and it is included here.

In Chapter 8 we observed a significant, averaging effect of mergers on profitability, and we allow for this effect in the completed model. Equation (1) presents once again the results of the basic model for comparison (see Table 10.1). Equation 2 has growth and the variables π_{50} and $\pi_{50} \cdot GAQ$ to adjust for the averaging effect of mergers. Both log growth and π_{50} are highly significant, but the averaging effect term is not. Equation 3 includes the π_{50} variables once again, but allows for the averaging effect of mergers by dividing π_{50} by $(1 + GAQ)$. This specification, as in Chapter 8, gives a slightly superior fit, as judged by $\overline{R}^2$. Equation (3) is the best firm-effect equation we can estimate over the full 551 observations. The key variables $(1 - m) C_4^2$, mA, and $mPat$ perform as they have throughout the study. The two variables $\mathrm{Ln}(G)$ and $\pi_{50}/(1 + GAQ)$ both capture characteristics of firms that are associated with persistent profit differences but do not translate into market share differences, or at least are not adequately captured by our projection of a firm's market share. The two variables are complementary. Growth is future oriented. Rapidly growing firms may have product differentiation and efficiency advantages that lead to projected future profitability growth that are not reflected in our projections of future market share. The firm's profitability in 1950–52 captures a past advantage that tends to persist and is not accounted for by growth and market share differences. The coefficient on $\pi_{50}/(1 + GAQ)$ implies that a firm earning profits double the mean in 1950–52 would, if it undertook no acquisitions, be projected to earn profits 35 percent above the average over and above those profits associated with market share, concentration, and growth differences. This difference from the mean is diluted directly in proportion to the amount of assets it acquired relative to its size. If at the time of acquisition the cumulative total of assets acquired equals the acquiring firm's premerger asset size $(GAQ = 1)$, then the projected difference in a firm's profits from the mean is reduced ceteris paribus by one half.

Equation (4) adds the MC^2 variable and forces us to throw out 47 observations for which managerial shareholdings could not be calculated. The performance of the other variables in the equation is not greatly different as between (4) and (3). The coefficient on MC^2 is negative and significant as before. The larger the fraction of shares management owns, the more immune it is from the threat of takeover and the greater the fraction of potential profits it can divert to uses more compatible with its own interest. The impact of the variables $(Ln(G))$, $\pi_{50}/(1 + GAQ)$, and MC^2 is largely additive. Each variable's coefficient is highly significant regardless of which of the other variables is included in the equation.

In Chapter 7, we also estimated a nonlinear version of the managerial discretion hypothesis, derived under the assumption that the effect of managerial discretion on reported profit is proportional to the projected profits predicted on the basis of market share and the other variables in the equation. In this variant of the managerial discretion hypothesis, both MC^2 and DIV, an index of diversification, were significant. Sales, $S72$, entered the equation with the wrong sign. We have reestimated this equation adding $Ln(G)$ and $\pi_{50}/(1 + GAQ)$ to the set of predictors of potential profitability, that is, we estimated

$$\alpha = \frac{b_5 + b_6(1 - m)C_4^2 + b_7 mA + b_8 mPat + b_9 Ln(G) + b_{10}\dfrac{\pi_{50}}{1 + GAQ}}{EXP(h_1 MC_i^2 + h_3 S72 + h_4 DIV)}.$$

The coefficient estimates and estimated t-values were as follows:

		Coefficient	t-value
h_1	MC^2	1.63	2.96
h_3	$S72$	.00015	0.49
h_4	DIV	−.614	3.04
b_5	Intercept	−.171	3.82
b_6	$(1-m)C_4^2$	−.718	4.46
b_7	mA	.953	7.15
b_8	$mPat$	1.03	3.24
b_9	$Ln(G)$	.094	5.24
b_{10}	$\pi_{50}(1 + GAQ)$	.404	6.37

All coefficients are of the predicted sign, including the size variable $S72$, which did not have a coefficient of the predicted sign in Chapter 7, although its coefficient is not significantly different from zero. All other coefficients in the equation are significantly different from zero at the 1 percent confidence level. Unlike the results of Chapter 7, the coefficients on the variables in the basic structural equation do not change very much from the linear version presented in Table 10.1. The significant coefficients on MC^2 and DIV reinforce the conclusion that managerial discretion leads to an absorption of potential profits into uses favored by management, and thus the underreporting of actual profits.

In Chapter 4 we drew the distinction between an industry model in which the key determinant of a firm's profitability is the identity

of the industries in which it sells, and the firm-effect model in which
the product and efficiency (dis)advantages of a firm determined its
profitability. Equation (5) reproduces the results for the industry-
effect model employing a stepwise regression in which all variables
are admitted for which the probability that their coefficients are not
significantly different from zero is .25. Twenty-nine percent of the
variation in profitability across firms can be explained by the 32 industries admitted into the equation via this procedure. This $\overline{R}^2$ might
reasonably be compared with the 37.5 percent of the variation in
profitability accounted for by the five firm-effect model variables in
(3). Equation (6) reports the results from a regression in which the
five firm-effect variables are forced into the equation and industry
intercepts are entered using the .25 probability criterion. All of the
firm-effect model coefficients remain significant at the 1 percent level
(two-tailed criterion), and 31 industries are entered into the equation.
The $\overline{R}^2$ is .51. When MC^2 is included, (7), 30 industries enter the
equation and the $\overline{R}^2$ climbs to .54.

The most noticeable effect of adding the separate industry intercepts to the firm-effect model is the reduction in the absolute value
and significance of the coefficient on $(1 - m)C_4^2$. In (7), the coefficient
is significant at only the 5 percent level. This effect indicates that some
of the industries with negative intercepts are highly concentrated. But
it does not tell us why this is so. What leads more concentrated industries to have lower profitability as a general rule, as implied by the
$(1 - m)C_4^2$ variable, and in the particular cases isolated by some of the
industry intercepts?

The list of industries included varies somewhat across the last three
equations in Table 10.1. This variability occurs mostly for those intercepts that would not be regarded as significant at normal confidence
intervals. It might be noted that when a criterion of .05 is used to
enter and delete industry intercepts, only 18 industries are entered
into the equation omitting MC^2 and containing 551 observations. The
$\overline{R}^2$ for this equation is .498, compared with the .509 of (6) in Table
10.1. Thus, attention should be focused on the dozen and a half
industries whose intercepts achieve t-values in excess of 2.0. This set
remains fairly stable across the three equations. Note also that there
is never a sign reversal for those industries that enter more than one
equation, and, for the most part, the coefficients tend to be of similar
magnitude across equations.

Although Chapter 4 depicted the industry- and firm-effect models
as alternatives, the results reported in Table 10.1 indicate that both
have something to contribute in explaining the profitability differ-

ences across firms. Both sets of variables result in a significant increase in explanatory power when added to the other set in the equation. Together they can explain over half the variation in long-run profitability across firms.

The explanatory powers of both the firm-effect and industry-effect models could undoubtedly be improved by a better specification of the individual variables. The key variables that distinguish the firm-effect model from its competitor are the market share–product differentiation interaction terms. We have used two, admittedly crude, indexes of product differentiation, industry advertising and patent intensity. Were we able to index the various dimensions of the abstruse product differentiation variable, the performance of the firm-effect model might be greatly improved.

By the same token, we have had to search for significant differences in profitability across industries using a three-digit industry breakdown. If we had enough observations to allow us to search at the four- and five-digit levels, more significant differences in industry profit levels might be observed, and the explanatory power of the industry-effect model enhanced. As always, larger samples and better-defined variables would improve our ability to describe what is happening. But a sample of 504 or 551 is large relative to most empirical studies of industrial organizations and an $\bar{R}^2$ greater than .5 compares favorably with other cross-sectional work. The results of this study allow us to draw more implications than just to describe the needs of further research.

B. Implications of the results for the structure-performance literature

To my knowledge, every study of the determinants of industry or firm profitability has been cross-sectional in nature. The closest the literature has come to a time-series analysis has been to include changes in a given variable between two cross-sections. This exclusive emphasis on cross-sectional analysis has left the literature vulnerable to attacks like those of Yale Brozen (1970, 1971) that the estimated relationships are unstable, and the profit differences observed transitory.

The present study begins to remedy this shortcoming in previous work by testing whether persistent differences in profitability exist across firms, and by using estimates of the permanent component of a firm's profitability as dependent variables in the cross-sectional structural equations. Thus, although the final equations are cross-sectional, the focus is upon explaining differences in the long-run profitability of firms.

The results resemble quite closely those of the newly emerging revisionist wisdom that finds market share to be a key variable in explaining differences in profitability across firms and concentration to be negatively related to firm profitability. Our reconfirmation of this finding is noteworthy, since our profit data are long run and drawn from the fifties and sixties, whereas most other recent studies use cross sections from the midseventies (e.g., Ravenscraft 1983; Martin 1982). More fundamentally, our results imply that knowledge of the characteristics (or at least of one characteristic) of the firm *as well as* knowledge of the industry to which it belongs is important when predicting its long-run profitability.

Our emphasis on the importance of the nature of the industry along with the success of the firm at winning market share should be kept in mind when viewing Richard Schmalensee's recent (1985), seemingly contradictory results. Schmalensee did an analysis of the variance in firm line of business profit rates and found that firm effects were totally insignificant, market share was statistically significant but of "negligible quantitative importance," and industry effects were highly significant and important quantitatively.

Part of the difference between Schmalensee's results and mine may be due to the time dimensions of the two studies. Foods, drugs, and other consumer nondurables have stable profit patterns over time that make them relatively more profitable in recessions, less so in booms. Consumer durables, capital goods, and intermediate goods such as steel, copper, and aluminum have profit profiles that vary directly with the cycle. Libby-Owens-Ford and PPG experienced profit peaks in 1950, 1955, 1960, and 1971–72, troughs in 1951, 1958, and 1970 (see Figure 8.1). L-O-F's profit profile exhibits greater cyclic variability than PPG's, consistent with its greater concentration of sales in flat glass. A short-run analysis of profit differences will pick up a lot of the cyclic variation in profitability that is industry related. Schmalensee uses but a single year's data, 1975. Thus, industry-related cyclic factors can be expected to be very significant in his study, but of minimal importance in mine. The long-run projections of profitability that we use average out industry-related cyclic perturbations, leaving the permanent rent components of each firm's profits to be explained. Firm market shares should, and apparently do, play a greater explanatory role in this long-run analysis. This point must be underlined when it is recalled that the OPEC price rise took perhaps its heaviest toll on corporate profits in 1975. Companies in energy- and capital-intensive industries had unusually low rates of return in 1975. (Schmalensee makes a similar observation; see also Martin 1982.) If industry effects are dominated by business cycle factors and firm effects by long-run factors, then my study should give maximum scope to observe firm effects, and Schmalensee's gives maximum scope to observe the effects of industry differences.

If we assume, nevertheless, that the difference between Schmalensee's results and mine is not purely due to the difference in the time dimension of the two studies, his results are complementary to mine, rather than contradictory, and actually help illuminate what aspects of efficiency the market share variable is capturing. Recall from Chapter 4 that market share and profitability are both directly related to what, in Chapter 9, I call a firm's quality-efficiency index,

$$q_i = \frac{a_i - c_i}{2b},$$

where a_i is the intercept of firm i's demand schedule with slope b common to all firms, and c_i is the height of i's horizontal marginal cost schedule. The firm's market share is related directly to the difference between the perceived quality of the product and cost of producing it. In the firm-approach model, it was the product of firm market share and the degree of industry product differentiation as measured by industry advertising and patent intensity that proved to be the two most important explanatory variables. Now q_i can differ from one firm to another *either* because the a_is differ, or the c_is differ. In an industry without any product differentiation, all firms must sell more or less the same quality products, and market share differences, if they are due to q_i differences, must be driven by cost differences. If we were to assume that Schmalensee's findings applied only to homogeneous product industries, then they might be interpreted as implying that cost differences across firms do not generate high market shares and profit rates as the firm-approach model suggests. Market share differences might then be the result of stochastic growth by a Gibrat-type process.

But the statistical performance of the industry advertising–market share and industry patenting–market share variables is too strong to be dismissed. Moreover, industry patent intensity is insignificant when introduced by itself, and industry advertising, although significant when introduced separately, is inferior to the market share–advertising interaction (see Mueller 1983, Chapter 4). Knowing how much of a differentiated product market a firm captures enables us to predict its profitability a great deal better than merely knowing it is in this market. These results suggest that it is the perceived quality differences in products, the a_is, that lead to market share and profitability differences across firms, and the greater the degree of product differentiation, the more important market share is in explaining profitability.

Thus, industry differences play an important role in our firm-approach model, and one assumes that the important industry differences that Schmalensee observes are in part differences in product differentiation. Recall, also, from Section A of this chapter that several industry dummies contributed to the explanation of firm-profitability differences, even in the presence of the market share–product differentiation variables. Our results thus imply that knowledge of a firm's pattern of industry participation, the degree of product differentiation of these industries, and its market share all contribute to the ability to predict its profitability.

Several of the findings of this study are also consistent with Schmalensee's zero firm-effect result. What Schmalensee found was that knowing that a firm is highly profitable in one market does not help one predict its profitability in another market. The firm-approach model of Chapter 4 relates a firm's quality-efficiency index within a given market to its share of that market and profitability in that market. It says nothing about generalized organizational efficiency. Only if the market shares of a firm tended to be correlated would the firm-approach model predict a correlation between a firm's profits across markets, and there is nothing in the firm-approach model that implies that intrafirm market shares should be correlated.

In Chapter 5 we discussed the example of Campbell Soup, which tried to enter the dry soup market, and failed to dislodge Lipton despite a more intensive advertising effort. This example illustrates Schmalensee's more general finding. Whatever it is that allows Campbell to dominate the wet soup market, it did not allow it to enter successfully the adjacent dry soup market. The results for mergers reported in Chapter 8 are also consistent with Schmalensee's zero, firm-effect finding. The dominant effect of mergers on profitability was an averaging effect. Strong evidence of synergy was not discerned. If a firm's profits in one market are independent of its profits in another, as Schmalensee's results imply, then mergers should have only an averaging effect on profitability.

If generalized organizational efficiency does not explain differences in firm profits, what does? Schmalensee's findings suggest that it is the composition of a firm's industry product mix. But we have presented enough examples in Chapter 5 to indicate that mere presence in an industry such as cereals or soups does not bring with it above-normal profitability. Indeed, one wonders whether it is the characteristics of the industry that make a firm profitable, or the characteristics of some firms that make the products of an industry profitable, or, more accurately, some products of some industries very profitable. There are but a handful of companies selling baby foods, for example, and thus the profitability of this industry and the profitability of Gerber must be closely related. For the past 20 years, presence in the computer industry has been persistently profitable for but one company. When one looks at an array of differentiated or potentially differentiated products, it is often not clear what characteristics of the products have allowed some firms to become and remain profitable for long periods of time. Why are soft drinks much more profitable than beer? Why are canned fruits and vegetables for babies more profitable than those sold for adult consumption? Why is selling razor blades very profitable and selling electric razors less so? We think the answers to these questions cannot be found without examining both the characteristics of the products sold and the companies that sell them.

The other main findings of this study indicate that the reported firm-level profit profiles of companies understate the tendency of the profits of a given firm in a given market to persist at above- or below-normal levels. Managerial discretion allows reported profits to be below potential profits. Mergers bring above- and below-normal returns back toward the sample average. Were one able to measure profit differences for a given firm in a given market over time, the evidence of persistent positive and negative returns would be greater.

To some it may seem quixotic to write of persistent profitability following a decade in which auto giants such as Ford and GM were driven into red ink, and a company such as International Harvestor, the company that started from McCormick's invention of the reaper and has been a dominant firm in the agricultural machinery industry for a century, is driven to near bankruptcy. The data on which this study rests are for the nonturbulent fifties and sixties, ending with 1972, the year before OPEC first sent economic shock waves through Western developed countries. Viewed from 1984, the fifties and sixties seem like one of those golden eras of prosperity under capitalism (the twenties were another) that occur all too infrequently. Perhaps the next golden era, when the results of this study will be particularly relevant, is a long way off. If so, then the analysis here can be viewed as an exercise in economic history: a study of what happened in a particular golden era, projections of what would have happened had the era not come to an end, and predictions of what might happen should a new golden era ever dawn.

The objective of the study has been to examine the speed with which the normal competitive process brings profit rates back to competitive levels, and the causes of any persistent deviations from normality. I do not think that the economic events that had such a devastating impact on profit-and-loss statements of so many companies in the seventies are what we typically have in mind when we think about the competitive process eroding above-normal profits. Thus, even our rather weak ability to predict the profitability of companies in 1980, as reported in Chapter 2, is not, to my mind, a serious challenge to our inferences as to how the competitive process works under normal economic conditions.

In addition to OPEC and inflation, the seventies brought a tremendous increase in foreign competition in U.S. markets. An important difference between the seventies and 1950–72 is the amount of import penetration. Our estimates of profit persistence and its causes may be inaccurate when applied to the seventies because they are based on a time period for which imports were a far less important factor in most markets.

The impact of imports is apparent in our data for some firms and industries, however. Several steel firms were among the group with long-run projected returns of less than half the average, and United States Steel was one of the two companies with a 1950 market share of more than .20 that was in this group (see Table 3.1). But it is certainly true that the full impact on long-run profitability from the intensification of foreign competition is not reflected in our data.

To the extent that a different picture would or does emerge in the seventies due to import penetration, the results we find for the 1950–72 period are of interest, by contrast, in showing how the forces of competition from within an economy work to erode long-run profitability. Presumably when Baumol, Panzer, and Willig (1982) speak of a contestable market, they do not have only the Japanese in mind as contestors. If the picture from the seventies is much different from that of the fifties and sixties, because of import competition, that would imply that entry by foreign firms is a much more potent force eroding market shares and profits than entry by other domestic firms. Indeed, one might speculate that American firms have suffered so badly from foreign competition in the seventies because they did not face much challenge to their market positions from other U.S. companies in the fifties and sixties.

An implication of the Baumol, Panzer, and Willig analysis is that the profits of a firm in a contestable market will be zero regardless of its share of this market. It appears that many markets did not contain sufficiently low entry barriers to be regarded as even approximately close to the definition of a contestable market. Beyond this rather obvious and perhaps not surprising inference, our results point out once again the importance of market definition and how subtle this concept is. Is breakfast cereals a contestable market? Scores of new cereals have been brought out in the last three decades by both members of the six leading cereals producers, and firms outside the industry. But the same six companies still dominate the industry and each relies heavily for its sales and profits on the products it was selling 30 years ago. The most important change in the industry has been the introduction of sugar-coated cereals, so that Sugar Frosted Flakes, for example, is now a leading brand along with Kellogg's Corn Flakes and Rice Krispies. Thus, the massive efforts to contest the market positions of the leading brands have not been very successful. But this may reflect the fact that there are different submarkets within the cereal market. A new sugar-coated oat cereal may not effectively impinge on an uncoated bran cereal's sales, although it may cut into other oat and other sugar-coated sales. Many brands in cereals seem able to maintain their market shares and profitability because the newcomers do not come "very close" to them in product characteristic space (Schmalensee 1978). The venerability of Corn Flakes, Rice Krispies, Cheerios, and Grape-Nuts also suggests considerable first-mover advantage in this market. When one looks at the list of highly profitable companies in Table 3.1, one sees that many of these are in markets, like cereals, in which entry into one part of the market is relatively free, but entry into that part of the market occupied by the company with persistent profits is very difficult.

C.   Implications for future research

The industrial organization literature has been dominated for more than a generation by an approach, bordering on a paradigm, that takes the industry as the focal point of analysis. The nature of the industry determines the shape of the cost function common to all companies, the height of the barrier behind which all firms in the industry are protected, the level of cooperation in which all companies participate. Differences among firms within an industry have been (implicitly) assumed to be irrelevant to the explanation of performance. The only major exception to this model has been the dominant firm model in which a dominant firm and competitive fringe operate within a given industry, and the dominant firm faces different demand and perhaps cost conditions. But, such a dominant firm industry structure is inherently unstable. In the long run, either the dominant firm loses its market dominance, if it does not have a cost advantage over the competitive fringe, or if it does it drives the fringe out (see Worcester 1957). Thus, to explain long-run equilibrium profits using the traditional industrial organization "paradigm," all one needed to look at was industry characteristics.

The present study adds to a growing literature suggesting that certain firm characteristics, like market share, may also be important. Moreover, it casts new light on why industry characteristics such as product differentiation may be positively related to profitability. Product differentiation does not automatically confer greater profitability on a company just because it is a member of an industry. In the firm-approach model, it offers the potential for greater profitability from *successful* product differentiation. Success, as measured by market share, is more profitable the more differentiated an industry's product structure.

The results of this book indicate that firm characteristics such as market share and growth add significantly to our ability to explain long-run differences in company returns. In developing and testing the firm-approach model, we have placed greater emphasis on firm-specific characteristics. But we do not wish to claim that it is only firm characteristics that matter. The industry intercepts bring about a significant improvement in explanatory power (see Table 10.1). The best model for explaining long-run differences in company profits combines industry and firm characteristics into its sets of explanatory variables.

The model used to explain company returns in this book, even in its most complete form in Table 10.1, must seem to many readers to be a rather "stripped down" version of what is now the standard structure-performance model, with its many exogenous and endogenous variables (Geroski 1982a; Martin 1982). There are two justifications for this simplicity. First, in wishing to emphasize the basic differences between the industry- and firm-approach models, we have chosen to focus upon admittedly extreme, polar versions of both models. *All* differences in firm profits are explained by *either* industry or firm characteristics. Moreover, a long-run equilibrium has been assumed so that variables often used to capture transitory characteristics, for example, the ratio of a firm's size to the minimum-efficient size in the industry, are inappropriate. But once the importance of firm and industry characteristics is recognized, one can begin to build back into the model the various other characteristics of firms and industries that are thought to be important.

The second reason we have chosen not to burden our equations with a host of industry characteristics is that the industry intercepts should effectively capture all of the influence of industry factors on firm profitability. If entry into a given industry is blockaded and profits for *all* firms in this industry are abnormally high, then the industry intercept term for that industry should capture that effect. Moreover, an intercept dummy can capture *all* forms of entry barriers in whatever combination that they occur, not just those that can be easily proxied by, say, advertising. Thus, the complete model estimated in this chapter does implicitly allow for entry and exit barriers, import penetration, growth in demand, and the other industry characteristics that previous research has found to be important, by its inclusion of industry intercepts. It implies that, over and above the combined effect of industry characteristics, there are significant differences in firm profits that are explained by firm characteristics.

The results in Table 10.1 also have an important bearing on the issue of the role of intangible capital stocks and accounting practice differences in explaining persistent differences in profitability across firms. If the returns to capital investment for all companies in a given industry follow a similar time pattern and all adopt similar depreciation schedules, then the accounting profits of all companies within the industry might systematically over- or underestimate true economic returns. Similarly, all companies in an industry may have comparable proportions of unmeasured intangible assets to total assets, thereby producing a systematic overestimate of returns on capital for all firms in the industry. Even if one treats all of the explanatory power of the industry dummies in Table 10.1 as if they were due to accounting profit definitional factors, a large amount of the variance in company returns beyond these factors can be explained by firm characteristics that should be unrelated to accounting phenomena.

The pharmaceutical industry receives a large positive and significant coefficient in both Tables 10.1 and 4.3. It is often asserted that pharmaceutical firm profits are overstated owing to the neglect of intangible capital. Under this interpretation, the large positive coefficient for the pharmaceutical industry would simply indicate the large fraction of pharmaceutical firm total capital made up by the intangible capital stocks of drug patents. Similarly, the group of companies with long-run projected profits 50 percent or more above the average is liberally populated by drug companies (Table 3.1). An examination of the 1950 market share figures for these companies in Table 3.1

reveals that most had surprisingly low market shares. The reason for this is that the 1950 market definitions in pharmaceuticals were so broad that the "true" market shares of these companies were grossly underestimated. The same would be true for 1972 even though the 1972 industry definitions for pharmaceuticals are narrower and more accurate than for 1950. The typical, highly profitable pharmaceutical company earns virtually all of its profits from a few drugs for which it has effective patent protection and for which it is the dominant seller, if not monopolist. Another role the industry intercepts play in the complete model is to indicate those "industries" for which existing four- and five-digit definitions are too broad, and thus market share and concentration figures are too low. Further refinement in the definition of industries would improve the performance of both the industry intercept terms, as a group, and the concentration and market share variables.

Although on the one hand this study has an advantage over previous studies in both the quality and quantity of data it employs, on the other hand considerable improvement in the quality of data is still possible. Our use of five-digit market share data where appropriate is a good case in point. Although superior to four-digit data in many cases, even more disaggregated data would be desirable in some instances, such as pharmaceuticals. A great effort was expended gathering the ownership of shares data, but as stressed in Chapter 7, only the data for management's shareholdings are probably reliable. R&D expenditures at the firm and disaggregate industry level would be superior to patent data, but these were not available for the 1950–72 period. This list could be extended. Given that it took some three years to assemble and clean this data set, it is difficult to urge that more effort be spent on data gathering, but the need is present. The usual qualification of caution because of uncertainty over data quality applies in various degrees of intensity to the results of this book.

The firm-approach model implies that profit rates among firms within an industry differ, depending on the relative quality of firm products and cost levels. The most plausible way to test for this relationship is to estimate a profit rate–market share equation for firms *within an industry*. Although we have market share data by industry, we do not have firm-level profits by industry. Thus, we have used weighted-average market shares and profits at the firm level. A preferable procedure would be to use line-of-business profit and sales data to estimate the relationship between profitability and market share within each industry, and then look across industries to see whether systematic differences exist between the slopes and intercepts of the industry profit rate–market share lines, and industry characteristics such as concentration and product differentiation. Initial efforts in this direction have been made,[1] but this line of research is still in its infancy.

We have made but minimal effort to allow for simultaneity among the variables employed. The simultaneous nature of the relationship between profit rate and market share has been stressed, however. Both are determined by the underlying demand and cost conditions of the firm. In effect, we have treated market share as a sufficient statistic for capturing a firm's quality-efficiency characteristics and used it in place of these unobservable factors (see also Donsimoni, Geroski, and Jacquemin 1984). Given the long-run orientation of this study, virtually any other firm-specific variable might legitimately be regarded as codetermined along with profits and market share – for example, advertising, R&D, merger activity, risk, diversification. Another book would be required to follow up each and every one of these possibilities. Some solace can be obtained from industry-level studies implying that single-equation results are not overturned once simultaneity is explicitly modeled. But the firm-approach model definitely needs to be generalized in this way.

Finally, some extensions of the long-run, time-series orientation of the study should be made. We have tested to see whether entry and exit drive firm profit rates to a common competitive level, but have not attempted to model entry and exit as such. In part, this omission is a natural consequence of or focus on firm characteristics rather than industries, in part a necessity of our having market share data at widely separated points in time. To construct an "entry" variable for each firm comparable to the other variables employed in this study, it would have been necessary to determine rates of entry into each of a company's markets, and then compute a weighted-average entry rate for each company. But too many markets changed definition between 1950 and 1972 to allow computation of this variable. Some interesting work on the entry issue exists (see, e.g., McGuckin 1972; Orr 1974; Duetsch 1975; Gorecki 1975), and more work addressing the persistence-of-profits question along with entry and exit barriers is warranted.

D.   Policy implications

The economic logic underlying U.S. antitrust policy presumes that managers maximize profits, and that firms compete by price. Given that managers seek maximum profit, the only social cost that firms can inflict upon society is the welfare loss from charging a price above competitive price. Thus the emphasis in the laws on monopolizing and attempts to monopolize.

During the fifties and sixties the growing conventional wisdom in industrial organization that entry barriers into industries are often high and that concentration facilitates collusion and higher prices led to an increasingly tough antitrust enforcement policy, particularly with respect to horizontal and vertical mergers, and some restrictive practices, such as tying arrangements.

The growing acceptance of the "new learning" in industrial organization, particularly among Reagan administration antitrust officials, has changed all of this. Entry barriers are presumed to be much lower, concentration is presumed to signal efficiency, vertical restraints and tying arrangements are presumed to be motivated to increase economic efficiency in the absence of direct evidence to the contrary.

The present study, although offering some support for the premises of the "new learning," also challenges the basic presumption of this school of thought, and of the antitrust laws more generally. Of central importance is the finding that some firms earn persistently above-normal profits, that some markets have the same leading firm or firms for a generation and more. As noted earlier, an important implication of contestable market theory is that the profits of all firms in a contestable market should be zero, or close to that figure. If many firms can enjoy persistently high profits, then many markets must not be contestable; that is, entry into these markets cannot be free. Similarly, the existence of companies with persistently below-normal profits suggests the existence of exit barriers. At least one of the premises of the "new learning" literature is patently false.

To the extent that it is firms that have persistently high profits and not industries, the possibility arises that it is some superior managerial talent or organizational efficiency that generates these persistent profits. If the talent of a particular manager or team of managers did account for a given firm's success (failure), one would expect that the market for managers would bid up (down) the salaries of these managers, and that the reported profits of the firm over a generation would converge to the norm. For reported profits to be persistently above or below the norm, they must be generated by some asset, for which either there is no market, or for which the firm need not pay rents, or the asset market value does not get included in the total assets of the firm. The importance of the market share–product differentiation interactions in the regression results, and the identities of the firms with persistently high profits as reported in Chapter 3, suggests that these profits stem from first-mover advantages in differentiated product markets, where buyers have some uncertainty over product quality (Schmalensee 1982). If this inference is generally valid, then the high-market-share-implies-greater-efficiency presumption of the new learning obtains a different interpretation than it usually receives, and there may be different policy implications than are implicit in the new-learning rhetoric.

The typical firm earning persistently high profits has a large market share in a differentiated product industry. If it is more efficient than its competitors, it is not because it produces the same product as they at lower costs, and sells it at lower prices. If anything, the price it charges probably exceeds that of its competitors for a product that is perceived to be superior along one or more product characteristic dimensions. Firms with high market shares tend to be more efficient than their competitors at developing their products, marketing them, and, perhaps most important of all, maintaining their image as a superior product. The successful firm is more efficient than its competitors in using nonprice modes of competition.

These implications of the results are important because of the orientation of the antitrust laws toward protecting competition by price. The beauty of price competition is that it is costless. Consumers who switch to firm A because A has cut its price enjoy the extra consumer's surplus from the lower price without there existing any offsetting social cost. But the gain in perceived consumer's surplus customers of A experience as a result of A's additional advertising must be weighed against these advertising costs. In a world of product differentiation the rents earned by the successful can generate substantial expenditures to maintain and transfer control over these rents. Rent-seeking expenditures are a necessary consequence of product differentiation, and the resources expended in rent seeking can easily exceed the social gains it generates (see Tullock 1967; Posner 1975; and other papers in Buchanan, Tollison, and Tullock 1980). In a world of nonprice competition, more competition can lower social welfare. There is no nonprice competition analogue to the invisible hand theorem.[2]

The antitrust laws, with their implicit assumption that all competition is price competition, derive their normative economic justification from the invisible hand theorem. The irrelevance of this theorem to the dominant mode of competition extant today makes the antitrust laws irrelevant for guiding the modern capitalist economy. So long as firms do not collude to set price, it matters not how high their prices are relative to costs, or how long they stay there, or how much resources are utilized in advertising and R&D to maintain them at that level.

If the results reported in this book have any implications for antitrust policy, then it is to point out the need for a new look at the basic premises underlying these laws, and perhaps the consideration of new antitrust statutes, laws that take into account the nonprice modes of competition that dominate capitalist competition.

Some years ago Oliver Williamson (1975, Chapter 11) proposed that a new antitrust law was needed that would challenge companies with dominant market positions over sustained periods of time. Boundary lines are always a bit arbitrary, but a market share of 50 percent for 25 years or more might be a reasonable set of numbers to consider. Firms meeting this criterion under the new statute would be subject to antitrust action, which might, if successful, involve self-suggested dissolution. Firms could offer an efficiency defense to protect their dominant positions; that is, a firm which could show that its products were cheaper or better than its competitors' would not face dissolution or other penalty.

Williamson's proposal is particularly relevant to the results of this study, first, because it addresses directly long-run market power and, second, because it could easily accommodate evidence of superiority based on product quality or other characteristics related to nonprice competition. Moreover, it would force Congress or the courts to come to grips with the first-mover advantages some firms enjoy in a world of product differentiation, in those cases in which a firm was not able to demonstrate that it was more efficient or that its product was superior to its competitors.

Chapter 7 presented evidence suggesting that managers use the discretion large shareholdings and diversification provide them to reduce the amount of corporate revenues reported as profits. In addition to increasing their own incomes, a plausible use of managerial discretion would be to increase the size of the firm, for size can yield both pecuniary and nonpecuniary advantages directly related to size and growth, *and* additional freedom from takeover and thus still more managerial discretion. Mergers are a natural vehicle for managers to increase their company's size and obtain the managerial advantages size and growth bring. Chapters 8 and 9 presented evidence consistent with the hypothesis that managers undertake mergers even when they will not increase the profits of the merging firms, or the efficiency of the acquired companies.

The antitrust laws make no allowance for managerial actions that lower social welfare without enhancing monopoly power. Implicitly the antitrust laws seem to accept the thesis of the market-for-corporate-control school, that management is constrained to maximize profits by the tight discipline of the market for corporate control. But the discipline of this market has not proven strong enough even to constrain managers from making unprofitable acquisitions, that is, from participating in the market for control itself.

Most mergers that have occurred in this country in the last 35 years have probably taken place with the expectation that they would neither substantially lessen competition nor improve economic efficiency. The results of Chapter 9 imply that they substantially weakened the efficiency of the firms acquired in conglomerate mergers. A similar implication can be drawn for horizontal mergers, although here the possibility does exist that the mergers increased market power. If, from results such as these, one felt that society would be better off with fewer mergers, either because there would be more independently controlled businesses in society, or because the loss in efficiency of the acquired firms would be prevented, then today's antitrust laws are not able to achieve this objective. As with an attack on persistent market power, new antimerger legislation is required to reduce significantly the number of mergers taking place in the United States.

Although there have been several proposals for new antimerger legislation in recent years, the one that would attack both the diversity of corporate control and the efficiency of merger issues most directly would be a flat ban on all acquisitions by, say, the 500 largest manufacturing corporations, subject to an efficiency defense (Broadley 1977, 1981; Mueller 1979). The largest corporations in other sectors could be covered by separate provisions for each sector. The major objection made against a merger ban with an efficiency defense is that an efficiency defense would be too difficult to sustain and would involve too large court costs.

But this need not be the case. In any merger that is likely to result in a substantial increase in efficiency, the acquiring firm's management must have made some sort of an analysis of the company it wishes to acquire, upon which it bases its acquisition decision. This analysis could be entered as evidence in court. More important, a company might enter evidence from its previous acquisitions that it had increased their market shares, improved their profitability, and so on. In an era of scientific management, it is difficult to believe that management does not keep track of the performance of the companies it acquires, and these data would seem to provide the most solid basis for judging an acquiring firm's likelihood of improving the performance of another firm. The evidence in Chapters 8 and 9 indicates that many firms would not be able to show that their past mergers had been successful, and thus would not be allowed to proceed with additional mergers, or would have to sustain a greater burden of proof that their next acquisition would differ from their previous ones. Thus, the number of mergers attempted and the number allowed would most likely be substantially smaller than today, once the usual period of postlegislative judicial probing had been completed, and the boundaries for approving a merger became known. Far fewer attempted mergers would mean far fewer mergers that might have to sustain an efficiencies defense in court, and the social objectives of maintaining diversity of control while preserving efficiency enhancing mergers would be accomplished.

A ban on mergers with an efficiencies defense would be a natural and desirable complement to antidominant firm legislation that would break up a company or force it to break itself up, if after a generation it still dominated a market, but could not demonstrate that it owed this position to superior efficiency or product quality. Both proposals share the view that all that transpires in the corporate economy that cannot be shown to lessen competition substantially need be presumed to increase efficiency. Both proposals would shift the burden of proof *in some situations* to management to show that economic efficiency will be maintained or enhanced, if its company is allowed to remain dominant in a market, or to acquire another firm. Instead of passively restraining anticompetitive behavior and hoping that greater efficiency ensues, the antitrust laws could require a demonstration that efficiency increases are likely to occur. Lest champions of laissez faire panic that these changes·would initiate a massive expansion of government intervention into the economy, I hasten to add that most normal economic activity would be unaffected by these changes. Although the number of markets with a dominant firm is greater than many believe, the majority of markets are not of this type. After a decade of "catching up," few cases should be brought under the dominant firm statute. Growth by internal expansion and mergers between small companies would not be affected by the merger ban. Although growth through merger would become a rare corporate strategy, those companies that were demonstrably good at improving the efficiency of other firms would be left to do so, and the rest would be forced to develop new products or improve existing ones if they wanted to grow. Together the two proposals would push companies seeking size to develop new products rather than standing pat with existing ones,

or merely acquiring ongoing enterprises. Given the performance of
the U.S. corporate economy in the seventies, it is difficult to imagine
why a little goading in the direction of greater efficiency and internal
growth would not be socially beneficial.

Appendix 1   Companies studied

This appendix lists the companies that were part of our study. The first three subsections list the 1,000 largest sample for 1950, divided into three groups, the 200 largest, 201–500 largest, and 501–1,000 largest. Column 2 of these three subsections indicates each firm's status as of 1972, where SR ≡ survived, AQ ≡ acquired through merger, LQ ≡ liquidated, PI ≡ privately held (i.e., the firm survived, but because of private control of the firm not enough information was available to include it in the sample), ID ≡ insufficient data to include in sample, NI ≡ no information as to what happened to the firm. Column 3 reports the same information for firms that is available in the 1980 *Moody's Industrial Manual*. If the firm was in our sample of 600 companies used to obtain original profit estimates, its rank in 1950–52 is presented in column 4. Column 5 lists either the company's current name, if the company survived, or, in parentheses, the name of the firm that acquired it and the year of acquisition.

Subsection D lists the names and 1950–52 profit ranks of companies in the 1972 1,000 largest sample that were not in the 1950 1,000 largest included in the study. Subsection E lists firms and 1950–52 profit ranks that were included in our study and that were in neither the 1950 nor the 1972 1,000 largest groups.

234

A. Largest 200 Companies	2	3	4	5
Admiral Corp.	SR	AQ	18	
Allegheny Ludlum Steel Corp.	SR	SR	418	ALLEGHENY LUDLUM IND.
Allied Chemical & Dye Corp.	SR	SR	225	ALLIED CHEMICAL
Allis-Chalmers Manufacturing Co.	SR	SR	395	
Aluminum Company of America	SR	SR	393	
American Can Co.	SR	SR	314	
American Cyanamid Co.	SR	SR	255	
American Home Products Corp.	SR	SR	138	
American Locomotive Co.	AQ			(RKO 1969)
American Radiator & Standard Sanitary Corp.	SR	SR	142	AMERICAN STANDARD
American Smelting & Refining Co.	SR	SR	159	
American Sugar Refining Co., The	SR	SR	496	AMSTAR
American Tobacco Co., The	SR	SR	468	AMERICAN BRANDS
American Viscose Corp.	AQ			(FMC 1963)
American Woolen Co.	AQ			(TEXTRON 1955)
Anaconda Copper Mining Co.	SR	AQ	471	
Anheuser Busch, Inc.	SR	SR	ID	
Archer-Daniels-Midland Co.	SR	SR	285	
Armco Steel Corp.	SR	SR	257	
Armour & Co.	SR	SR	572	
Armstrong Cork Co.	SR	SR	388	
Atlantic Refining Co., The (Pennsylvania)	SR	SR	292	
Avco Mfg. Corp.	SR	SR	427	
Babcock & Wilcox Co.	SR	AQ	348	
Baker & Co., Inc.	SR	SR	ID	
Baldwin Locomotive Works, The	AQ			
Beatrice Foods Co. (Delaware)	SR	SR	324	
Bemis Brothers Bag Co.	SR	SR	567	
Bendix Aviation Corp.	SR	SR	392	BENDIX CORP.
Bethlehem Steel Corp.	SR	SR	386	
Boeing Airplane Co.	SR	SR	424	
Borden Co., The	SR	SR	419	
Borg-Warner Corp.	SR	SR	169	
Briggs Manufacturing Co.	AQ			PANACON (CELOTEX 1972)
Budd Co., The	SR	SR	219	
Burlington Mills Corp.	SR	SR	441	BURLINGTON INDUSTRIES
California Packing Corp.	SR	AQ	467	DEL MONTE
Campbell Soup Co.	SR	SR	247	
Cannon Mills Co.	SR	SR	399	
Carnation Co.	SR	SR	277	
Case (J.I.) Co.	AQ			(TENNECO 1970)
Caterpillar Tractor Co.	SR	SR	246	
Celanese Corporation of America	SR	SR	366	
Champion Paper & Fibre Co.	AQ			(US PLYWOOD 1967)
Chrysler Corp.	SR	SR	198	
Cities Service Co.	SR	SR	442	

A. Largest 200 Companies	2	3	4	5
Coca-Cola Co., The	SR	SR	103	
Colgate-Palmolive-Peet Co.	SR	SR	359	
Colorado Fuel & Iron Corp.	SR	AQ	498	CF & I
Cone Mills Corp.	SR	SR	256	
Consolidated-Vultee Aircraft Corp.	SR	SR	598	GENERAL DYNAMICS
Container Corporation of America	SR	AQ	311	MARCOR
Continental Baking Co.	AQ			(ITT)
Continental Can Co., Inc.	SR	SR	489	
Continental Oil Co.	SR	SR	71	
Corn Products Refining Co.	SR	SR	183	
Corning Glass Works	SR	SR	136	
Crown Zellerbach Corp.	SR	SR	209	
Crucible Steel Company of America	AQ			(COLT INDUSTRIES)
Cudahy Packing Co., The	AQ			(GENERAL HOST 1971)
Curtis Publishing Co.	SR	SR	499	
Curtiss-Wright Corp.	SR	SR	524	
Dana Corp.	SR	SR	122	
Deere & Co.	SR	SR	173	
Douglas Aircraft Co., Inc.	SR	SR	155	
Dow Chemical Co.	SR	SR	412	
Dupont (E.I.) deNemours & Co.	SR	SR	69	DUPONT
Eastman Kodak Co.	SR	SR	197	
Eaton Manufacturing Co.	SR	SR	80	
Electric Auto-Lite Co.	AQ			(ELTRA CORP 1963)
Endicott Johnson Corp.	AQ			(McDONOUGH 1971)
Essex Wire Corp.	SR		ID	ESSEX INTERNATIONAL
Firestone Tire & Rubber Co.	SR	SR	274	
Ford Motor Co.	SR	SR	161	
General Electric Co.	SR	SR	152	
General Foods Corp.	SR	SR	337	
General Mills, Inc.	SR	SR	416	
General Motors Corp.	SR	SR	47	
General Tire & Rubber Co., The	SR	SR	270	
Glidden Co.	AQ			(SCM 1967)
Goodrich (B.F.) Co., The	SR	SR	188	
Goodyear Tire & Rubber Co.	SR	SR	443	
Gulf Oil Corp.	SR	SR	261	
Hearst Consolidated Publications, The	SR		ID	
Hercules Powder Company	SR	SR	151	
Hershey Chocolate Corp.	SR	SR	35	
Hormel (Geo. A.) & Co.	SR	SR	438	
Hudson Motor Car Co.	AQ			(AMERICAN MOTORS 1954)
Hygrade Food Products Corp.	SR	SR	469	
Inland Steel Co.	SR	SR	290	
International Business Machines Corp.	SR	SR	272	
International Harvester Co.	SR	SR	434	

A. Largest 200 Companies	2	3	4	5
Pittsburgh Plate Glass Co.	SR	SR	177	PPG
Pittsburgh Steel Co.	AQ			(WHEELING 1968)
Procter & Gamble Co., The	SR	SR	94	
Pullman, Inc.	SR	SR	521	
Pure Oil Co., The (Ohio)	AQ			(UNION OIL 1965)
Quaker Oats Co., The	SR	SR	288	
Radio Corporation of America	SR	SR	226	RCA
Ralston Purina Co.	SR	SR	260	
Rath Packing Co., The	SR	SR	528	
Remington Rand, Inc.	AQ			(SPERRY 1955)
Republic Steel Corp.	SR	SR	343	
Revere Copper & Brass, Inc.	SR	SR	181	
Reynolds Metals Co.	SR	SR	449	
Reynolds (R.J.) Tobacco Co.	SR	SR	431	
Richfield Oil Corp.	AQ			(ATLANTIC 1966)
St. Regis Paper Co.	SR	SR	334	
Schenley Industries, Inc.	AQ			(RAPID AMERICAN 1972)
Schlitz (Jos.) Brewing Co.	SR	SR	ID	
Scott Paper Co.	SR	SR	120	
Scovill Manufacturing Co.	SR	SR	497	
Seagram (Joseph E.) & Sons, Inc.	SR	SR	179	DISTILLERS CORP.
Sharon Steel Corp.	SR	SR	222	
Shell Oil Corp.	SR	SR	67	
Sherwin-Williams Co.	SR	SR	344	
Simmons Co.	SR	AQ	326	
Sinclair Oil Corp.	AQ			(ATLANTIC-RICHFIELD 1969)
Smith (A.O.) Corp.	SR	SR	387	
Socony-Vaccum Oil Co., Inc.	SR	SR	273	MOBIL OIL
Spencer Kellug & Sons	AQ			(TEXTRON 1960)
Sperry Corp., The	SR	SR	10	SPERRY RAND
Staley (A.E.) Manufacturing Co.	SR	SR	515	
Standard Brands, Inc.	SR	SR	422	
Standard Oil Co. of California	SR	SR	70	
Standard Oil Co. of Indiana	SR	SR	381	
Standard Oil Company (N.J.)	SR	SR	145	EXXON
Standard Oil Co., The (Ohio)	SR	SR	376	
Stevens (J.P.) & Co., Inc.	SR	SR	389	
Studebaker Corp., The	SR		ID	STUDEBAKER-WORTHINGTON
Sun Oil Co. (New Jersey)	SR	SR	146	SUN CO.
Swift & Co. (Illinois)	SR	SR	573	ESMARK
Sylvania Electric Products, Inc.	AQ			(GTE 1959)
Texas Co., The	SR	SR	147	TEXACO
Tide Water Associated Oil Co.	SR	SR	546	GETTY OIL
Time, Inc.	SR	SR	316	
Timken-Detroit Axle Co., The	AQ			(NORTH AMER. ROCK.)

A. Largest 200 Companies	2	3	4	5
Timken Roller Bearing Co.	SR	SR	129	TIMKIN
Union Bag & Paper Corp.	SR	SR	58	UNION CAMP CORP.
Union Carbide & Carbon Corp.	SR	SR	108	
Union Oil Co. of California	SR	SR	435	
United Aircraft Corp.	SR	SR	429	
United States Gypsum Co. (Illinois)	SR	SR	134	
United States Rubber Co.	SR	SR	426	UNIROYAL
United States Steel Corp.	SR	SR	486	
Wesson Oil & Snowdrift Co., Inc.	AQ			(HUNT FOOD 1959)
West Point Manufacturing Co.	SR	SR	63	WEST POINT PEPPERELL
West Virginia Pulp & Paper Co.	SR	SR	266	WESTVACO
Western Electric Co., Inc.	SR	SR	526	
Westinghouse Electric Corp.	SR	SR	391	
Weyerhaeuser Timber Co.	SR	SR	130	
Wheeling Steel Corp.	SR	SR	400	WHEELING-PITTSBURGH STEEL
Willys-Overland Motors, Inc.	AQ			(KAISER-FRASER 1952)
Wilson & Co., Inc.	AQ			(LTV)
Youngstown Sheet & Tube Co., The	SR	SR	394	
Zenith Radio Corp.	SR	SR	107	

B. Companies Ranked 201 to 500	2	3	4	5
Abbott Laboratories	SR	SR	115	
Brandon Corp. (Abney Mills)	SR		PI	
Acme Steel Co.	AQ			(INTERLAKE 1964)
Air Reduction Co., Inc.	SR	AQ	437	AIRCO
Allied Mills, Inc.	SR	AQ	322	
American Agricultural Che. Co.,The (Del)	AQ			(CONTINENTAL OIL 1963)
American Brake Shoe Co	AQ			(ILLINOIS CENTRAL)
American Car & Foundry Co.	SR	SR	531	ACF
American Chain & Cable Co. Inc.	SR	AQ	199	
American Enka Corp.	SR	SR	186	AKZONA
American Metal Co.,Ltd., The	SR	SR	398	AMAX
American Optical Co.	AQ			(WARNER LAMBERT 1967)
American Steel Foundries (New Jersey)	SR	SR	358	AMSTED
American Thread Co., Inc.	SR	SR	564	
American Zinc, Lead & Smelting Co.	SR	AQ	2	AZCON
Anchor Hocking Glass Corp.	SR	SR	217	
Arden Farms Co.	SR	SR	576	ARDEN-MAYFAIR
Armstrong Rubber Co., The	SR	SR	333	
Noblitt-Sparks Industries, Inc. (Arvin Ind.)	SR	SR	156	
Ashland Oil & Refining Co.	SR	SR	231	
Aurora Gasoline Co.	AQ			(ALLIED PRODUCTS)
Automatic Electric Co.	SR		PI	
Avondale Mills	SR	SR	476	
Bachmann Uxbridge Worsted Corp [3]	AQ			(AMERACE, ESNA 1957)

B. Companies Ranked 201 to 500

	2	3	4	5
Ballantine (P.) & Sons	AQ			(FALSTAFF 1972)
Barium Steel Corp	SR	SR	345	PHOENIX STEEL
Bates Manufacturing Co.	SR	LQ	491	
Beaunit Mills, Inc.	AQ			(EL PASO NATURAL GAS)
Beech-Nut Packing Co.	AQ			(SQUIBB 1968)
Bell Aircraft Corp.	AQ			(WHEELABRATOR-FRYE)
Berkshire Fine Spinning Associates,Inc.	SR	SR	535	BERKSHIRE-HATHAWAY
Best Foods, Inc. The	AQ			(CORN PRODUCTS 1958)
Bibb Manufacturing Co.	SR	SR	559	
Bigelow-Sanford Carpet Co.,Inc.	AQ			(SPERRY-HUTCHINSON)
Blaw-Knox Co.	AQ			(WHITE CONSOLIDATED,1968)
Blue Bell, Inc.	SR	SR	293	
Bohn Aluminum & Brass Corp.	AQ			(GULF & WESTERN)
Bridgeport Brass Co.	AQ			(NATIONAL DISTILLERS 1961)
Bristol-Myers Co.	SR	SR	307	
Brown Co.	SR	SR	240	
Brown Shoe Company, Inc.	SR	SR	306	BROWN GROUP
Brown & Williamson Tobacco Corp.	SR	SR	100	BRITISH AMER.TOBACCO
Bucyrus-Erie Co.	SR	SR	289	
Bulova Watch Co., Inc. (New York)	SR	SR	421	
Bunker Hill & Sullivan Mining & Concentrat.Co.	AQ			(GULF RESEARCH & CHEMICAL)
Burroughs Adding Machine Co.	SR	SR	547	BURROUGHS CORP.
Callaway Mills Co.	LQ			
Calumet & Hecla Consolidated Copper Co.	AQ			(UNIVERSAL OIL)
Carborundum Co. (Delaware)	SR	SR	174	
Carey (Philip) Manufacturing Co.	AQ			(GLEN ALDEN)
Carrier Corporation	SR	AQ	453	
Celotex Corp., The	AQ			(WALTER, JIM)
Central Soya Co.,Inc.	SR	SR	126	
Certain-teed Products Corp.	SR	SR	117	
Champion Spark Plug Co.	SR	SR	30	
Chase Bag Co.	SR		NI	
City Products Corp.	AQ			(HFC)
Clark Equipment Company	SR	SR	263	
Clinton Foods, Inc.	AQ			(STANDARD BRANDS 1956)
Cluett, Peabody & Co., Inc.	SR	SR	350	
Collins & Aikman Corp.	SR	SR	508	
Colorado Milling & Elevator Co.	AQ			(GREAT WESTERN UNITED 1962)
Combustion Engineering-Superheater,Inc.	SR	SR	383	
Commercial Solvents Corp.	SR	AQ	351	
Congoleum-Nairn, Inc.	AQ			(BATH INDUSTRIES 1968)
Consolidated Cigar Corp.	AQ			(GULF & WESTERN)
Consolidated Paper Co.	SR	SR	127	CONSOLIDATED PACKAGING
Consolidated Water Power & Paper Co.	SR	SR	248	CONSOLIDATED PAPERS
Crane Company	SR	SR	384	
Crowell-Collier Publishing Co.	AQ			

B. <u>Companies Ranked 201 to 500</u>

	2	3	4	5
Crown Cork & Seal Co.,Inc.	SR	SR	582	
Cummins Engine Co., Inc.	SR	SR	245	
Cuneo Press, Inc.	SR	SR	581	
Curtiss Candy Co.	AQ			(STANDARD BRANDS 1964)
Cutler-Hammer,Inc.	SR	AQ	105	
Dan River Mills,Inc.	SR	SR	503	
Detroit Steel Corporation	AQ			(CYCLOPS 1971)
Devoe & Raynolds Co., Inc.	AQ			(CELANESE 1964)
Diamond Alkali Co.	SR	SR	411	DIAMOND SHAMROCK
Diamond Match Co., The	SR	SR	320	DIAMOND INTERNATIONAL
Doehler-Jarvis Corp.	AQ			(NATIONAL LEAD 1952)
Donnelley (R.R.) & Sons Co.	SR	SR	456	
Dresser Industries, Inc.	SR	SR	354	
Dubuque Packing Co.	SR		NI	
Du Mont (Allen B.) Laboratories,Inc.	AQ			(FAIRCHILD CAMERA)
Eagle-Picher & Co.	SR	SR	342	
Eastern States Petroleum Co. Inc.	NI			
Electric Storage Battery Co., The	SR	AQ	533	ESB INC.
Electrolux Corp.	AQ			(CONSOLIDATED FOODS)
Elgin National Watch Co.	SR	SR	575	
Emerson Radio & Phonograph Corp.	AQ			(NATIONAL UNION ELECTRIC)
Erwin Mills, Inc.	AQ			(BURLINGTON INDUSTRIES 1962)
Fairbanks, Morse & Co.	AQ			(COLT INDUSTRIES)
Fairchild Engine & Airplane Corp.	SR	SR	509	FAIRCHILD HILLER
Fairmont Foods Co.	SR	SR	594	
Field Enterprises, Inc.	SR		NI	
Flintkote Co., The	SR	SR	301	
Florsheim Shoe Co., The	AQ			(INTERNATIONAL SHOE 1953)
Food Machinery & Chemical Corp.	SR	SR	160	FMC
Forstmann Woolen Co.	AQ			(J.P. STEVENS 1957)
Fruehauf Trailer Co.	SR	SR	402	FRUEHAUF CORP.
Fulton Bag and Cotton Mills	AQ			(ALLIED PRODUCTS)
Gair (Robert) Co., Inc.	AQ			(CONTINENTAL CAN 1956)
Gardner Board & Carton Co.	AQ			(DIAMOND MATCH 1957)
Gates Rubber Co.	SR		NI	
Gaylord Container Corp.	AQ			(CROWN ZELLERBACH 1955)
General American Transportation Corp.	SR	SR	539	GATX
General Aniline & Film Corp.	SR	SR	553	GAF
General Baking Co.	SR	SR	406	GENERAL HOST
General Cable Corp.	SR	SR	361	
General Shoe Corp.	SR	SR	190	GENESCO
Gerber Products Co.	SR	SR	172	
Gibson Refrigerator Co.	AQ			(WHITE CONSOLIDATED 1955)
Gillette Safety Razor Co. (Delaware)	SR	SR	3	GILLETTE CO.
Globe Oil & Refining Co.	AQ			(MID-WEST REFINING)
Globe-Union, Inc.	SR	AQ	243	

B. Companies Ranked 201 to 500   2   3   4   5

Godchaux Sugars, Inc.	AQ			(NATIONAL SUGAR 1956)
Golden State Co., Ltd.	AQ			(FOREMOST-McKESSON 1953)
Goodall-Sanford, Inc.	AQ			(BURLINGTON INDUSTRIES 1953)
National Battery (Gould-National Batteries)	SR	SR	297	GOULD INC.
Granite City Steel Co.	AQ			(NATIONAL STEEL 1971)
Graniteville Co.	SR	SR	341	
Great Northern Paper Co.	SR	SR	368	
Great Western Sugar Co., The	SR		459	GREAT WESTERN UNITED
Greenwood Mills, Inc.	SR		NI	
Grumman Aircraft Engineering Corp.	SR	SR	385	GRUMMAN CORP.
Hall (W.F.) Printing Co.	SR	AQ	340	
Handy & Harmon	SR	SR	462	
Harbison-Walker Refractories Co.	AQ			(DRESSER INDUSTRIES 1967)
Harnischfeger Corp.	SR		ID	
Hazel-Atlas Glass Co.	AQ			(CONTINENTAL CAN 1956)
Heinz (H.J.) Co.	SR	SR	538	
Hills Bros. Coffee Co.	AQ			
Hinde & Dauch Paper Co., The	AQ			(WESTVACO 1953)
Houdaille-Hershey Corp.	SR		ID	HOUDAILLE
Hughes Tool Co.	SR		ID	
Hunt Foods, Inc.	SR	SR	452	NORTON SIMON
Industrial Rayon Corp.	AQ			(MIDLAND-ROSS 1960)
Ingersoll-Rand Co.	SR	SR	27	
Interchemical Corp.	SR	AQ	439	INMONT
Interlake Iron Corp.	SR	SR	403	INTERLAKE INC.
International Milling Co.	SR	SR	460	INTERNATIONAL MULTI-FOODS
International Silver Co.	SR	SR	250	INSILCO
Interstate Bakeries Corp.	SR	AQ	187	INTERSTATE BRANDS
Joanna Western Mills Co.	SR			
Joslyn Mfg. & Supply Co.	SR	SR	319	
Joy Manufacturing Co.	SR	SR	305	
Juilliard (A.D.) & Co., Inc.	AQ			(UNITED MERCH. & MFG.1952)
Karagheusian (A.&M.), Inc.	AQ			(J.P. STEVENS 1963)
Kellogg Co.	SR	SR	16	
Kelsey-Hayes Wheel Co.	SR	AQ	204	KELSEY-HAYES
Kendall Co., The	SR	AQ	163	(COLGATE-PALMOLIVE 1972)
Keystone Steel & Wire Co.	SR	AQ	40	KEYSTONE CONSOLIDATED IND.
Kieckhefer Container Co.	AQ			(WEYERHAEUSER 1957)
Kohler Co.	SR		NI	
Kroehler Mfg. Co.	SR	SR	193	
Laclede Steel Co.	SR	SR	72	
Lees (James) & Sons Co.	AQ			(BURLINGTON INDUSTRIES 1960)
Lehigh Portland Cement Co.	SR	AQ	216	
Libby, McNeill & Libby	SR	AQ	552	
Liebmann Breweries, Inc.	SR		NI	
Lilly (Eli) & Co.	SR	SR	133	

Appendixes

B. Companies Ranked 201 to 500	2	3	4	5
Link-Belt Co.	AQ			(FMC 1967)
Lion Oil Co.	AQ			(MONSANTO 1954)
Lipton (Thomas J.), Inc.	SR		PI	
Lone Star Cement Corp.	SR	SR	148	LONE STAR INDUSTRIES
Long-Bell Lumber Co.	AQ			(INTERNATIONAL PAPER 1956)
Longview Fibre Co.	SR		ID	
Lowenstein (M.) & Sons, Inc.	SR	SR	258	
Luckens Steel Co.	SR	SR	401	
Mack Trucks, Inc.	AQ			(SIGNAL COMP.)
Magnavox Co., The	SR	AQ	88	
Mansfield Tire & Rubber Co., The	SR	SR	278	
Marathon Corp.	AQ			(AMERICAN CAN 1957)
Martin (Glenn L.) Co., The	SR	SR	601	MARTIN-MARIETTA
Masonite Corp.	SR	SR	192	
Massey-Harris Co.	SR	SR	139	MASSEY-FERGUSON
Mathieson Chemical Corp.	AQ			(OLIN)
Maytag Co., The	SR	SR	12	
McElwain (J.F.) Co. (major manufacturing subsidiary of Melville Shoe Corporation)	SR	SR	41	MELVILLE SHOE
McGraw Electric Co.	SR	SR	44	McGRAW-EDISON
McGraw-Hill Publishing Co., Inc.	SR	SR	282	
McLouth Steel Corp.	SR	SR	128	
Mengel Co., The	AQ			(MARCOR 1953)
Merck & Co., Inc.	SR	SR	215	
Mid-Continent Petroleum Corp.	AQ			(SUNRAY DX 1954)
Midland Steel Products Co., The	SR	SR	68	MIDLAND ROSS
Miller Brewing Co.	AQ			(PHILIP MORRIS 1969)
Minneapolis-Honeywell Regulator Co.	SR	SR	178	HONEYWELL INC.
Minneapolis-Moline Co.	SR		ID	DOLLY MADISON
Minnesota & Ontario Paper Co.	AQ			(BOISE-CASCADE)
Mohawk Carpet Mills, Inc.[1]	SR	SR	516	MOHASCO
Moore Business Forms, Inc.	SR		NI	MOORE CORP. LTD.
Motor Products Corp.	AQ			(WHITTAKER CORP.)
Motor Wheel Corp.	AQ			(GOODYEAR 1964)
Mount Vernon-Woodberry Mills, Inc.	AQ			(HOLLY)
Mrs. Tucker's Foods, Inc.	AQ			(ANDERSON-CLAYTON 1951)
Mullins Manufacturing Corp.	AQ			(AMERICAN STANDARD)
National Automotive Fibres, Inc.	SR	SR	218	CHRIS CRAFT
National Cash Register Co., The	SR	SR	318	NCR
National Container Corp.	AQ			(OWENS-ILLINOIS 1955)
National Cylinder Gas Co. (Delaware)	SR	AQ	207	CHEMETRON
National Gypsum Co.	SR	SR	279	
National Malleable & Steel Castings Co.	AQ			(MIDLAND ROSS 1964)
National Supply Company, The	AQ			(ARMCO STEEL 1958)
Nestle Co.	SR	SR	ID	
New Jersey Zinc Company	AQ			(GULF & WESTERN)
Newport News Shipbuilding & Dry Dock Co.	AQ			(TENNECO 1968)

B. <u>Companies Ranked 201 to 500</u>

	2	3	4	5
Newport Steel Corp.	AQ			(ACME STEEL 1956)
Northern Paper Mills	AQ			(AMERICAN CAN 1952)
Norton Co.	SR		ID	
Ohio Oil Co., The	AQ			(MARATHON OIL)
Oliver Corp., The	AQ	SR	ID	(WHITE MOTOR 1960)
Oneida, Ltd.	SR	SR	227	
Owens-Corning Fiberglas Corp.	SR	SR	237	
Oxford Paper Co.	AQ			(ETHYL 1967)
Pacolet Manufacturing Co.	AQ			(DEERING MILLIKEN)
Parke, Davis & Co.	AQ			(WARNER-LAMBERT 1970)
Penick & Ford, Ltd., Inc.	AQ			(R.J. REYNOLDS 1965)
Pepperell Mfg. Co.	AQ			(WEST POINT MFG. 1965)
Pepsi-Cola Co.	SR	SR	353	PEPSICO
Pfizer (Chas.) & Co., Inc.	SR	SR	110	
Publicker Industries, Inc.	SR	SR	574	
Purity Bakeries Corp. 2)	AQ			(AMERICAN BAKERIES 1953)
Raybestos-Manhattan, Inc.	SR	SR	189	
Rayonier, Inc.	AQ			(ITT)
Raytheon Manufacturing Company	SR	SR	577	
Reeves Brothers, Inc.	SR	SR	433	
Reeves Steel & Mfg. Co.	AQ			(UNIVERSAL CYCLOPS 1958)
Reichhold Chemicals, Inc.	SR	SR	593	
Reliance Manufacturing Co. (Illinois)	LQ			
Reo Motors, Inc.	AQ			(WHITE MOTOR 1957)
Republic Aviation Corp.	LQ			
Rexall Drug, Inc.	SR	SR	587	DART IND.
Rheem Manufacturing Co.	AQ			(CITY INVESTING)
Riegel Textile Corp. (Delaware)	SR	SR	478	
Robertshaw-Fulton Controls Co.	SR	SR	112	ROBERTSHAW CONTROLS
Rockwell Mfg. Co.	SR	AQ	104	
Roebling's (John A.) Sons Co.	AQ			(CF & I 1951)
Rohm & Haas Co.	SR	SR	213	
Royal Typewriter Co., Inc.	AQ			(LITTON INDUSTRIES)
Ruberoid Company, The	AQ			(GAF 1967)
Russell-Miller Milling Co.	AQ			(PEAVEY)
St. Joseph Lead Co. (New York)	SR	SR	31	ST. JOSEPH MINERAL
Savannah Sugar Refining Corp.	SR	SR	339	SAVANNAH FOODS
Schaefer (F.M.) Brewing Co.	SR		ID	
Seeger Refrigerator Co.	AQ			(WHIRLPOOL 1955)
Servel, Inc.	AQ			(GOULD 1966)
Sheller Manufacturing Corp.	SR	SR	26	SHELLER-GLOBE
Singer Manufacturing Co., The	SR	SR	504	
Skelly Oil Co.	SR	AQ	75	
Smith (Alexander) & Sons Carpet Co. 1)	AQ			(MOHASCO 1955)
Spartan Mills	SR		NI	
Springs Cotton Mill	SR		ID	SPRINGS MILLS

B. Companies Ranked 201 to 500

	2	3	4	5
Square D Co.	SR	SR	45	
Squibb (E.R.) & Sons	AQ			(MATHIESON 1952)
Standard Steel Spring Co.	AQ			(ROCKWELL SPRING & AXLE)
Stanley Works	SR	SR	251	
Stauffer Chemical Co.	SR	SR	548	
Sterling Drug, Inc.	SR	SR	176	
Stewart-Warner Corp.	SR	SR	405	
Stokely-Van Camp, Inc.	SR	SR	448	
Sunbeam Corp.	SR	SR	10	
Sunray Oil Corp.	AQ			(SUN OIL 1968)
Sunshine Biscuits, Inc.	AQ			(AMERICAN BRANDS 1966)
Sutherland Paper Co.	AQ			KALAMAZOO VEG.PARCH.(1959)
Swanson (C.A.) & Sons	AQ			(CAMPBELL SOUP 1954)
Tecumseh Products Co.	SR	SR	20	
Tennessee Corp.	AQ			(CITIES SERVICE 1963)
Textron, Inc.	SR	SR	591	
Thompson Products, Inc.	SR	SR	373	TRW
Times-Mirror Co.	SR	SR	556	
Tobin Packing Co., Inc.	SR	SR	451	
Todd Shipyards Corp.	SR	SR	537	
United Biscuit Co. of America	SR	SR	299	KEEBLER
United Engineering & Foundry Co.	AQ			(WEAN UNITED 1970)
United Merchants & Manufacturers, Inc.	SR	SR	300	
United Shoe Machinery Corp.	SR	AQ	472	USM
U.S. Industrial Chemicals, Inc.	AQ			(NATIONAL DISTILLERS 1962)
United States Pipe & Foundry Co.	AQ			(JIM WALTER 1969)
United States Plywood Corp.	SR	SR	182	CHAMPION INTERNATIONAL
Van Raalte Co., Inc.	AQ			(CLUETT PEABODY 1968)
Virginia-Carolina Chemical Corp.	AQ			(MOBIL OIL 1963)
Wagner Electric Corp.	SR	AQ	287	
Walker (Hiram) & Sons, Inc.	SR	SR	119	
Ward Baking Co.	SR	SR	295	WARD FOOD
Westinghouse Air Brake Co.	AQ			(AMERICAN STANDARD 1968)
Nineteen Hundred Corp. (Whirlpool Corp.)	SR	SR	85	
White Motor Co., The	SR	SR	502	
Wood (Alan) Steel Co.	SR		NI	
Worthington Pump & Machinery Corp.	SR		ID	STUDEBAKER-WORTHINGTON
Wrigley (Wm.), Jr. Co. (Delaware)	SR	SR	74	
Wyandotte Chemical Corp.	AQ			(BADISCHE-ANIL)
Wyman-Gordon Co.	SR		NI	
Yale & Towne Manufacturing Co., The	AQ			(EATON MFG. 1963)
Young (L.A.) Spring & Wire Corp.	SR		--	P. HARDEMAN INC.

C. Companies Ranked 501 to 1,000

	2	3	4	5
Addressograph-Multigraph Corp.	SR	SR	82	
Affiliated Gas Equip., Inc.	AQ			(CARRIER 1955)

C. Companies Ranked 501 to 1,000

	2	3	4	5
Alabama Mills, Inc.	AQ			(DAN RIVER 1955)
Allen-Bradley Co.	SR	NI		
Alpha Portland Cement Co.	SR	SR	208	ALPHA PORTLAND IND.
Alton Box Board Co.	SR	NI		
Aluminum Goods Mfg. Co.	SR	SR	160	MIRRO CORP.
Amalgamated Sugar Co.	SR	SR	369	
American Bakeries Company 2)	SR	SR	252	
American Bosch Corp.	SR	SR	541	AMBAC IND.
American Cast Iron Pipe Co.	SR	NI		
American Chicle Co.	AQ			(WARNER-LAMBERT 1962)
American Colortype Co. (New Jersey)	AQ			(RAPID AMERICAN)
American Crystal Sugar Co.	SR	AQ	532	
American Distilling Co., The	SR	SR	527	
American Hard Rubber Co.3)	SR	SR	562	AMERACE ESNA
American Hardware Corp., The	SR	SR	570	EMHART
American Hide & Leather Co.	SR	SR	9	TANDY
American Laundry Machinery Co.	AQ			(McGRAW-EDISON 1960)
American Liberty Oil Co.	SR	SR	66	AMERICAN PETROFINA
American Machine & Foundry Co.	SR	SR	484	AMF
American Maize Products Co.	SR	SR	480	
American Manufacturing Co.	SR	NI		
American-Marietta Co.	AQ			(MARTIN GLENN)
American Meter Co., Inc.	AQ			(GENERAL PRECISION 1967)
American Potash & Chemical Corp.	AQ			(KERR-McGEE)
American Safety Razor Corp.	AQ			(PHILIP MORRIS 1960)
American Seating Company	SR	SR	281	
American Ship Building Co., The	SR	SR	551	
American Snuff Co.	SR	SR	447	CONWOOD
American Stove Co.	SR	ID		MAGIC CHEF
American Window Glass Co.	SR	SR	460	AMERICAN ST. GOBAIN
American Yarn & Processing Co.	AQ			(RUDDICK)
Ames Worsted Co.	SR	ID		AMES TEXTILE
Anderson-Prichard Oil Corp.	LQ			
Apex Electrical Mfg. Co., The	AQ			(WHITE CONSOLIDATED 1956)
Arrow-Hart & Hegeman Electric Co.	SR	AQ	60	ARROW-HART
Art Metal Construction Co.	AQ			(WALTER HELLER)
Artistic Foundations, Ind.	NI			
Arvey Corp.	SR	NI		
Aspinook Corp.	AQ			(BARKER BROS)
Associated Spring Corp.	SR	ID		
Associated Plywood Mills, Inc.	AQ			(US PLYWOOD 1954)
ATF, Inc.	AQ			(SCHULEMBERGER)
Atlas Plywood Corp.	AQ			(CONSOLIDATED ELECTRIC)
Atlas Powder Co.	AQ			(IMPERIAL CHEMICAL 1971)
Autocar Co.	AQ			(WHITE MOTOR)
Ball Brothers Co.	SR	ID		BALL CORP.

C. Companies Ranked 501 to 1,000

	2	3	4	5
Bancroft (Joseph) & Sons Co.	AQ			(INDIAN HEAD 1961)
Barber-Colmon Co.	SR		NI	
Bassett Furniture Industries, Inc.	SR	SR	93	
Bath Iron Works Corp.	SR	AQ	488	BATH INDUSTRIES
Bausch & Lomb Optical Co.	SR	SR	563	
Bay Petroleum Corp.	AQ			(TEXAS GAS TRANS.)
Bayuk Cigars, Inc.	SR	SR	585	
Beacon Manufacturing Co.	AQ			(NATIONAL DIST. & CHEM. 1966)
Beech Aircraft Corp.	SR	AQ	542	
Bell Co., The	AQ			(PACIFIC COAST)
Bell & Howell Co.	SR	SR	365	
Beloit Iron Works	SR		NI	BELOIT CORP.
Berkshire Knitting Mills	AQ			(V.F. CORP.)
Bird & Son, Inc.	SR		NI	
Black & Decker Mfg. Co., The	SR	SR	178	
Black, Sivalls & Bryson, Inc.	AQ			(HUSTON OIL)
Blackstone Corp.	SR		NI	
Bliss, E.W., Co.	AQ			(GULF & WESTERN)
Blockson Chemical Co.	AQ			(OLIN 1955)
Blumenthal (Sidney) & Co., Inc.	AQ			(BURLINGTON INDUSTRIES)
Boston Woven Hose & Rubber Co.	AQ			(AMER. BILTRITE RUB.1957)
Botany Mills, Inc.	SR	NI	602	BOTANY INDUSTRIES
Cleveland Graphite Bronze Co., The	AQ			(GOULD 1969)
Cleveland Twist Drill Co.	AQ			(NATIONAL ACME 1967)
Cleveland Worsted Mills Co.	LQ			
Climax Molybdenum Co.	AQ			(AMERICAN METAL 1957)
Clow (James B.) & Sons	SR		ID	CLOW CORP.
Coleman Company, Inc. (Kansas)	SR	SR	123	
Columbia Broadcasting System, Inc.	SR	SR	485	
Columbia River Paper Co.	AQ			(BOISE CASCADE)
Columbian Carbon Co.	AQ			(CITY SERVICES 1962)
Conde Nast Publications, Inc.	AQ			(PATRIOT NAST)
Consolidated Chemical Industries, Inc.	AQ			(STAUFFER CHEMICAL 1951)
Continental-Diamond Fibre Co.	AQ			(BUDD 1955)
Continental Foundry & Machine Co.	LQ			
Continental Steel Corp.	SR	AQ	352	
Cook Paint & Varnish Co.	SR	PI	249	
Cooper-Bessemer Corp., The	SR	SR	235	
Coors (Adolph) Co.	SR	SR	NI	
Coos Bay Lumber Co.	AQ			(GEORGIA PACIFIC 1956)
Cornell Wood Products Co.	AQ			(ST. REGIS PAPER 1959)/
Cosden Petroleum Corp.	AQ			(AMERICAN PETROFINA 1963)
Creameries of America, Inc.	AQ			(BEATRICE FOODS 1952)
Crocker Burbank & Co., Assn.	AQ			(WEYERHAEUSER 1962)
Crompton & Knowles Loom Works	SR	SR	180	
Crossett Lumber Co.	AQ			(GEORGIA PACIFIC 1962)

C. Companies Ranked 501 to 1,000

	2	3	4	5
Crown Central Petroleum Corp.	SR	SR	469	
Cuban-American Sugar Co., The	LQ			
Darling & Co.	SR		NI	
Davison Chemical Corp.	AQ			(W.R. GRACE)
Dayton Malleable Iron Co.	SR	SR	430	
Dayton Rubber Co., The	SR	SR	347	DAYCO
De Laval Separator Co.	LQ			
Decca Records, Inc.	AQ			(M.C.A. 1966)
Deep Rock Oil Corp.	AQ			(NATIONAL INDUSTRIES)
Dennison Manufacturing Co.	SR	SR	114	
Detroit Harvester Co.	AQ			(WALTER KIDDE)
Detroit Steel Products Co.	AQ			(SPACE INDUSTRIES 1971)
Dewey & Almy Chemical Co.	AQ			(W.R. GRACE)
Diamond T Motor Car Co.	LQ			
Dierks Lumber & Coal Co.	AQ			(WEYERHAEUSER 1969)
Disston (Henry) & Sons	AQ			(H.K. PORTER 1962)
Dixie Cup Co.	AQ			(AMERICAN CAN 1957)
Dixie Mercerizing Co.	SR		NI	
Doniger (David D.) & Co. Inc.	NI			
Doubleday & Co., Inc.	SR		NI	
Doughnut Corp. of America	NI			
Draper Corp.	AQ			(NORTH AM. ROCKWELL)
Dunlop Tire & Rubber Corp.	SR		PI	
Duplan Corp.	SR	SR	555	
Duquesne Brewing Co. of Pittsburgh	AQ			(SCHMIDTS BREWING 1972)
Durez Plastics & Chemicals, Inc.	AQ			(OCCIDENTAL PETROL.)
Dwight Manufacturing Co.	AQ			(CONE MILLS 1951)
Eastern Corp.	AQ			(STANDARD PACKAGING)
Easy Washing Machine Corp.	AQ			(MURRAY 1955)
Eddy Paper Corp.	AQ			(WEYERHAEUSER 1957)
Edison (Thomas A.), Inc.	AQ			(McGRAW-EDISON 1957)
Ekco Products Co. (Illinois)	AQ			(AMER. HOME PRODUCTS 1965)
El Dorado Oil Works	AQ			(FOREMOST DAIRIES 1955)
Elliott Co.	AQ			(CARRIER 1957)
Emerson Electric Manufacturing Co.	SR	SR	321	
Emhart Manufacturing Co.	AQ			(AMER. HARD RUBBER 1964)
Emsco Derrick & Equipment Co.	AQ			(YOUNGSTOWN S & T. 1955)
B.V.D. Corp., The (Erlanger Mills Corp.)	LQ			
Evans Products Company	SR	SR	505	
Eversharp, Inc.	AQ			(WARNER-LAMBERT 1970)
Ex-Cell-O Corp.	SR	SR	205	
Fafnir Bearing Co.	AQ			(TEXTRON 1968)
Falstaff Brewing Corp.	SR	SR	118	
Falk Corp.	AQ			(SUNSTRAND)
Farrel-Birmingham Co., Inc.	AQ			(USM 1968)
Federal-Mogul Corp.	SR	SR	61	

C. <u>Companies Ranked 501 to 1,000</u>

	2	3	4	5
Federal Paper Board Co.	SR	SR	332	
Ferguson (Harry), Inc.	AQ			(MASSEY-HARRIS CO. 1953)
Ferro Corp.	SR	SR	356	
Firth Carpet Co.	AQ			(MOHASCO 1962)
Fisher Flouring Mills Co.	SR		NI	
Florence Stove Co.	SR	SR	440	ROPER GEO.
Flotill Products, Inc.	AQ			(OGDEN)
Flour Mills of America, Inc.	SR		NI	
Follansbee Steel Corp.	AQ			(UNION CHEM. & MAT.)
Foremost Dairies, Inc.	SR	SR	336	FOREMOST-McKESSON
Fort Wayne Corrugated Paper Co.	AQ			(CONTINENTAL CAN 1959)
Free Sewing Machine Co.	NI			
French Sardine Co. of Calif.	NI			
Froedtert Grain & Malting Co., Inc.	SR	AQ	230	SOLA BASIC
Fruit Growers Supply Co.	SR		NI	
Fry (Lloyd A.) Roofing Co.	SR		NI	
Fuller Brush Co.	AQ			(CONSOLIDATED FOODS)
Fuller (W.P.) & Co.	AQ			(NORTON SIMON)
Gardner-Denver Co.	SR	AQ	125	
Garlock Packing Co.	SR		ID	GARLOCK INC.
General Cigar Co.*	SR	SR	590	
General Fireproofing Co.	SR	SR	56	
General Portland Cement Co.	SR	SR	21	
General Precision Equipment Corp.	AQ			(SINGER 1968)
General Refractories Co.	SR	SR	196	
General Steel Castings Corp.	SR	SR	482	GENERAL STEEL INDUSTRIES
General Time Corp.	AQ			(TALLY INDUSTRIES)
Georgia-Pacific Plywood & Lumber Co.	SR	SR	194	
Gladding McBean & Co.	AQ			(INTERPACE 1962)
Glenmore Distilleries Co.	SR	SR	409	
Goebel Brewing Co.	AQ			(STROH's BREW.)
Gordon Baking Co.	AQ			(AMERICAN BRANDS 1956)
Gorham Mfg. Co.	AQ			(TEXTRON 1967)
Great Lakes Carbon Corp.	AQ			(KENNECOTT COPPER)
Greenbaum (J.) Tanning Co.	NI			
Green Giant Co.	SR	AQ	362	
Greif Brothers Cooperage Corp.	SR	AQ	408	
Griesedieck Western Brewery Co.#	AQ			(CARLING)
Grinnell Corp.	SR	AQ	210	
Gruen Watch Co.	SR	NI	317	GRUEN INDUSTRIES
Gulf States Paper Corp.	SR		ID	
Hall Brothers, Inc.	NI			
Hamilton Watch Co.	SR	SR	506	HMW
Hamm (Theo.) Brewing Co.	AQ			(HEUBLIN 1965)
Hammermill Paper Co.	SR	SR	455	
Hammond Lumber Co.	AQ			(GEORGIA PACIFIC 1956)

C. Companies Ranked 501 to 1,000

	2	3	4	5
Hanes (P.H.) Knitting Co.	SR		ID	
Harbor Plywood Corp.	AQ			(HUNT FOODS 1960)
Harley Davidson Motor Co.	AQ			(AMF 1969)
Harris-Seybold-Potter Co.	SR	SR	101	HARRIS INTERTYPE
Harshaw Chemical Co., The	AQ			(KEWANEE OIL 1966)
Hart, Schaffner & Marx	SR	SR	566	
Hathaway Manufacturing Co.	AQ			(BERKSHIRE-HATHAWAY 1955)
Heil Co.	SR		ID	
Heintz Mfg. Co.	AQ			(KELSEY-HAYES 1957)
Hercules Motors Corp.	AQ			(WHITE CONSOLIDATED 1960)
Hewitt-Robins, Inc.	AQ			(LITTON INDUSTRIES)
Heyden Chemical Corp.	AQ			(TENN. GAS TRANS.)
Heywood-Wakefield Co.	SR	NI	457	
Hines (Edward) Lumber Co.	SR	SR	51	
Hobart Manufacturing Co., The	SR	SR	214	
Hoe (R.) & Co., Inc.	SR	NI	150	
Hoffman-LaRoche, Inc.	SR	SR	PI	
Holeproof Hosiery Co.	AQ			(KAYSER-ROTH 1954)
Hollingsworth & Whitney Co.	AQ			(SCOTT PAPER 1953)
Holly Sugar Corp.	SR	SR	568	
Hooker Electrochemical Co.	AQ			(OCCIDENTAL PETROL.)
Hoover Co., The (Ohio)	SR	SR	291	
Howes Leather Co., Inc.	SR		ID	
Hubbard & Co.	AQ			(DYSON CORP.)
Huber (J.M.) Corp.	AQ			(A-T-O INC)
Hudson Pulp & Paper Corp.	SR	AQ	465	
Huron Portland Cement Co.	AQ			(NATIONAL GYPSUM 1959)
Ideal Cement Co.	SR		62	IDEAL BASIC INDUSTRIES
Imperial Paper & Color Corp.	AQ			(HERCULES 1960)
Imperial Sugar Co.	SR		NI	
Ingalls Iron Works Co., The	SR		NI	
Inland Container Corp.	SR		ID	
Inspiration Consolidated Copper Co.	SR	AQ	185	
International Latex Corp.	AQ			(GLEN ALDEN)
International Minerals & Chemical Corp.	SR	SR	284	
International Salt Co.	AQ	.		(AKZONA 1970)
I-T-E Circuit Breaker Co.	SR	AQ	377	I-T-E IMPERIAL
Jack & Heintz Precision Industries, Inc.	AQ			(LEAR-SIEGLER)
Jacobs (F.L.) Co.	SR	SR	600	
Jeffrey Mfg. Co.	SR		ID	
Jergens (Andrew) Co.	AQ			(AMERICAN BRANDS 1970)
Johnson (S.C.) & Son	AQ			
Kalamazoo Vegetable Parchment Co.	AQ			(GEORGIA PACIFIC 1967)
Kayser (Julius) & Co.	SR	AQ	540	KAYSER ROTH
Keasbey & Mattison Co.	AQ			(CERTAIN-TEED 1961)
Kendall Refining Company	AQ			(WITCO CHEMICAL 1966)

Appendixes

C. Companies Ranked 501 to 1,000

	2	3	4	5
King-Seeley Corp.	AQ			(HFC)
Koehring Co.	SR	SR	302	
Ladish Co.	SR		NI	
Lambert Co., The	SR	SR	536	WARNER-LAMBERT
Lamson & Sessions Co.	SR	SR	200	
Landers, Frary and Clark	AQ			(J.B. WILLIAMS)
Lavino (E.J.) & Co.	AQ			(INT. MIN. & CHEM. 1965)
Le Tourneau (R.G.), Inc.	SR		NI	
Lee (H.D.) Co., Inc.	AQ			(V.F. CORP. 1969)
Lee Rubber & Tire Corp.	SR		ID	LEE NATIONAL
Lennox Furnace Co., The	SR		NI	
Leviton Manufacturing Co., Inc.	SR		NI	
Lewin-Mathes Co.	AQ			(CERRO-deFASCO 1956)
Life Savers Corp.	AQ			(SQUIBB 1955)
Lily-Tulip Cup Corp.	AQ			(OWENS-ILLINOIS 1968)
Linen Thread Co., Inc.	AQ			(INDIAN HEAD 1959)
Lincoln Electric Co.	SR		NI	
Liquid Carbonic Corp., The	AQ			(GENERAL DYNAMICS)
Lock Joint Pipe Co.	AQ			(INTERPACE)
Lone Star Steel Co.	AQ			(NORTHWEST INDUSTRIES)
Lorraine Mfg. Co.	AQ			(GREAT AM. INDUSTRIES)
Lowe (Joe) Corp.	AQ			(CONS. FOODS 1964)
Lucky Lager Brewing Co.	SR		ID	LUCKY BREWING
Ludlow Manufacturing & Sales Co.	SR	SR	578	LUDLOW CORP.
M & M Wood Working Co.	SR		PI	
Magee Carpet Co.	SR			
Mallinckrodt Chemical Works	SR		ID	
Mallory (P.R.) & Co., Inc.	SR	AQ	221	
Manhattan Shirt Co., The	SR	SR	525	
Manitowoc Shipbuilding Co.	SR		NI	
Manning, Maxwell & Moore, Inc.	LQ			
Marion Power Shovel Co.	LQ			UNIVERSAL MARION
Marlin-Rockwell Corp.	AQ			(TRW 1963)
Marquette Cement Mfg. Co.	SR	AQ	191	
Mars, Inc.	SR		ID	
Masland (C.H.) & Sons	SR		ID	
Matthiessen & Hegeler Zinc Co.	SR		ID	
McCall Corp.	AQ			(NORTON SIMON 1968)
McCord Corp.	SR	AQ	39	
McCormick & Co.	SR	SR	212	
Mead Johnson & Co.	AQ			(BRISTOL MYERS 1967)
Medusa Portland Cement Co.	SR	SR	310	MEDUSA CORP.
Meredith Publishing Co.	SR	SR	64	
Mergenthaler Linotype Co.	SR	AQ	510	ELTRA
Mesta Machine Co.	SR	SR	97	
Metal & Thermit Corp.	AQ			(AMERICAN CAN 1962)

C. Companies Ranked 501 to 1,000

	2	3	4	5
Miehle Printing Press & Mfg. Co.	AQ			(NORTH AM. ROCKWELL)
Milprint, Inc.	AQ			(PHILIP MORRIS 1956)
Mississippi Cottonseed Products Co.	SR	NI		
Moloney Electric Co.	AQ			(COLT INDUSTRIES)
Monarch Mills	AQ			(DEERING MILLIKAN)
Moore (Benjamin) & Co.	SR	NI		
Mooresville Mills	AQ			(BURLINGTON IND. 1954)
Morton Salt Co.	AQ			(NORWICH 1969)
Mueller Brass Co.	SR	AQ	171	UV INDUSTRIES
Munsingwear, Inc.	SR	SR	414	
Murray Company of Texas, Inc.	AQ			(NORTH AM. AVIATION)
National Acme Co., The	SR	SR	232	ACME CLEVELAND
National Can Corp.	SR	SR	557	
National Coop. Refinery Association	SR	ID		(ASHLAND OIL)
National Electric Products Corp.	AQ			(McGRAW-EDISON 1958)
National Pressure Cooker Co.	SR	SR	331	NATIONAL PRESTO
National Screw & Manufacturing Co.	AQ			(MONOGRAM INDUSTRIES)
National-Standard Company	SR	SR	143	
Naumkeag Steam Cotton Co.	SR	AQ	596	INDIAN HEAD
Nekoosa-Edwards Paper Company	AQ			(GREAT NORTHERN PAPER 1970)
Neptune Meter Company	SR	AQ	81	NEPTUNE INTERNATIONAL
Nesco, Inc.	AQ			(N.Y. SHIPBUILDING 1954)
New York Air Brake Company, The	AQ			(GENERAL SIGNAL)
New York Shipbuilding Corporation	AQ			(MERRITT, CHAPMAN 1970)
Newport Industries, Inc.	AQ			(TENN. GAS TRANS.)
Nicholson File Co.	AQ			(COOPER INDUSTRIES 1971)
Niles-Bement-Pond Co.	AQ			(COLT INDUSTRIES)
Noma Electric Corp.	AQ			(SIRNAL CORP.)
Nopco Chemical Company, Inc.	AQ			(DIAMOND-SHAMROCK 1967)
Nordberg Mfg. Co.	AQ			(REXNORD 1970)
Northwest Engineering Co.	SR	SR	223	
Northwest Paper Co., The	AQ			(POTLATCH FORESTS 1964)
Northwestern Steel & Wire Co.	SR	SR	106	
Ohio Boxboard Co.	AQ			(CENTRAL FIBRE PROD.)
Ohio Brass Co., The	SR	AQ	14	
Ohio Crankshaft Co.	SR	AQ	487	PARK-OHIO
Ohio Match Company	AQ			(NORTON SIMON)
Ohio Rubber Co., The	AQ			(EAGLE PITCHER 1952)
Okonite Co.	AQ			(KENNECOTT COPPER 1957)
Oswego Falls Corporation	AQ			(PHILLIPS PETROLEUM 1964)
Otis Elevator Co. (New Jersey)	SR	AQ	102	
Outboard, Marine & Manufacturing Co.	SR	SR	111	
Pacific American Fisheries, Inc.	AQ			(UNITED PACIFIC 1966)
Pacific Car & Foundry Co.	SR	SR	428	PACCAR
Pacific Lumber Co.	SR	SR	137	
Parker Pen Co., The	SR	SR	118	

C. Companies Ranked 501 to 1,000

	2	3	4	5
Pasco Packing Co.	SR		ID	
Peerless Woolen Mills	AQ			(1952)
Pennsylvania-Dixie Cement Corp.	SR	SR	76	PENN-DIXIE INDUSTRIES
Pennsylvania Salt Manufacturing Co.	SR	SR	436	PENNWALT
Perfection Stove Co.	AQ			(WHITE CONSOLIDATED 1954)
Permanente Cement Co.	AQ			(KAISER CEMENT)
Peter Paul, Inc.	SR	AQ	239	
Petroleum Heat & Power Co.	LQ			
Pettibone Mulliken Corp.	SR	SR	454	PETTIBONE CORP.
Phillips-Jones Corp.	SR	SR	463	PHILLIPS-VanHEUSEN
Pittsburgh Coke & Chemical Co.	AQ			
Pittsburgh Forgings Co.	SR	AQ	149	
Pittsburgh Screw & Bolt Corp.	SR	SR	77	AMPCO-PITTSBURGH
Planters Nut & Chocolate Co.	AQ			(STANDARD BRANDS 1960)
Plymouth Cordage Co.	AQ			(EMHART 1960)
Pope & Talbot, Inc.	SR		ID	
Potlatch Forests, Inc.	SR	SR	275	POTLATCH CORP.
Powdrell & Alexander, Inc.	SR		PI	
Premier Petroleum Co.	NL			(SUN OIL)
Proctor & Schwartz, Inc.	AQ			(SCM 1966)
Publication Corp.	AQ			(CROWELL, COLLIER)
Puget Sound Pulp & Timber Co.	AQ			(GEORGIA PACIFIC 1963)
Quaker State Oil Refining Corp.	SR	SR	380	
Rahr Malting Co.	SR		NI	
Readers Digest Associates, Inc.	SR		NI	
Reed Roller Bit Co.	SR		238	REED TOOL
Reliance Electric & Engineering Co., The	SR	AQ	229	
Rhinelander Paper Co.	AQ			(ST. REGIS PAPER 1956)
Rice-Stix, Inc.	IQ			
Richardson Co.	SR	SR	364	
Richman Brothers Co.	AQ			(WOOLWORTH)
Riegel Paper Corp.	AQ			(FEDERAL PAPERBOARD 1972)
Robbins Mills, Inc.	AQ			(TEXTRON 1954)
Robertson (H.H.) Co.	SR	SR	83	
Rome Cable Corp.	AQ			(ALCOA 1959)
Ronson Art Metal Works, Inc.	SR	SR	253	RONSON CORP.
Royster (F.S.) Guano Co.	SR		ID	
Ruppert (Jacob)	AQ			(KRATTER CORP. 1962)
Russell, Burdsall & Ward Bolt & Nut Co.	SR		NI	
Saco-Lowell Shops (Maine)	AQ			(MAREMONT)
Sangamo Electric Co.	SR	AQ	262	
Savage Arms Corp.	AQ			(EMHART 1957)
Sayles Finishing Plants, Inc.	SR		NI	
Schweitzer (Peter J.), Inc.	AQ			(KIMBERLY-CLARK 1957)
Scullin Steel Company	LQ			
Seabrook Farms Co. (N.J.)	SR	AQ	554	

C. Companies Ranked 501 to 1,000

	2	3	4	5
Seiberling Rubber Co.	SR	SR	410	SEILON
Shamrock Oil & Gas Corp., The	AQ			(DIAMOND ALKALI 1967)
Sharp & Dohme, Inc. (Maryland)	AQ			(MERK 1953)
Sheaffer (W.A.) Pen Co.	AQ			(TEXTRON 1966)
Shellmar Products Corp.	AQ			(DIAMOND GARNER)
Shenango Furnace Co.	SR		NI	
Shuford Mills, Inc.	SR		NI	
Shwayder Bros., Inc.	NI			
Simonds Saw & Steel Co.	AQ			(WALLACE-MURRAY 1966)
Simpson Logging Co.	SR		NI	
S.K.F. Industries, Inc.	SR		PI	
Smith (L.C.) & Corona Typewriters, Inc.	SR	SR	390	SCM
Smith-Douglass Co., Inc.	AQ			(BORDEN 1964)
Smith, Kline & French Laboratories	SR	SR	15	SMITHKLINE
Sonoco Products Co.	SR	SR	158	
Sorg Paper Company	SR	SR	512	
Soundview Paper Company	AQ			(SCOTT PAPER 1950)
South Penn Oil Co.	SR	SR	78	PENNZOIL
Southern Advance Bag & Paper Co., Inc.	AQ			(CONTINENTAL CAN 1954)
Southland Paper Mills, Inc.	SR	AQ	50	
Southwestern Portland Cement Co.	AQ			(SOUTHDOWN)
Spalding (A.G.) & Brothers, Inc.	AQ			(QUESTOR 1969)
Standard-Coosa-Thatcher Co.	SR	SR	313	
Standard Lime & Stone Co.	NI			
Standard Railway Equipment Mfg. Co.	SR	AQ	33	STANRAY
Standard Screw Co.	SR	SR	269	STANADYNE
Stanley Home Products, Inc.	SR	SR	32	
St. Joe Paper Co.	SR		NI	
St. Paul & Tacoma Lumber Co.	AQ			(ST. REGIS PAPER '56)
Stetson (John B.) Co.	SR	AQ	500	
Stromberg-Carlson Co.	AQ			(GENERAL DYNAMICS)
Sun Chemical Corp.	SR	SR	372	
Superior Steel Corp.	AQ			(COPPERWELD STEEL 1956)
Surface Combustion Corp.	AQ			(MIDLAND-ROSS 1956)
Swisher (Jno. H.) & Son, Inc.	AQ			(AMERICAN MAIZE 1966)
Talon, Inc.	AQ			(TEXTRON 1968)
Taylor Forge & Pipe Works	AQ			(GULF & WESTERN)
Tennessee Products & Chemical Corp.	AQ			(MERRITT, CHAPMAN)
Textile Machine Works	NI			
Textiles-Incorporated	SR	SR	73	
Thatcher Glass Manufacturing Co.	AQ			(REXALL DRUG 1966)
Thermoid Co.	AQ			(H.K. PORTER)
Thew Shovel Co.	AQ			(KOEHRING 1964)
Thomaston Mills	SR	SR	19	
Thor Corp.	AQ			(SCM 1967)
Toledo Scale Co.	AQ			(RELIANCE ELECTRIC 1967)

C. Companies Ranked 501 to 1,000

	2	3	4	5
Torrington Co., The	AQ			(Ingersoll-Rand 1969)
Trailmobile Co.	AQ			(PULLMAN 1951)
Trane Company	SR	SR	116	
Triangle Conduit & Cable Co.	SR		ID	TRIANGLE INDUSTRIES
Trico Products Corp.	SR	SR	164	
True Temper Corp.	AQ			(ALLEGHENY LUDLUM 1967)
Twin Coach Co.	AQ			(WHEELABATON)
Underwood Corp.	AQ			(OLIVETTI)
United Carbon Co.	AQ			(ASHLAND OIL 1963)
United Carr Fastener Corp.	AQ			(TRW 1968)
United Drill & Tool Corp.	AQ			(TRW 1968)
United Elastic Corp.	AQ			(J.P. STEVENS 1968)
United States Envelope Co.	AQ			(WESTVACO 1960)
United States Hoffman Machinery Corp.	NI			
United States Playing Card Co.	AQ			(DIAMOND INTERNATIONAL 1968)
U.S. Printing & Lithograph Co., The	AQ			(DIAMOND INTERNATIONAL 1959)
United States Radiator Corp.	AQ			(NATIONAL U.S. RADIATOR 1954)
United States Tobacco Co.	SR	SR	327	
Universal-Cyclops Steel Corp.	SR	SR	121	CYCLOPS CORP.
Upjohn Co., The	SR	SR	599	
Utah-Idaho Sugar Co.	SR	SR	580	U & I INC.
Utica & Mohawk Cotton Mills, Inc.	AQ			(J.P. STEVENS 1952)
Van Norman Co.	AQ			(GULF & WESTERN)
Vanadium Corp. of America	AQ			(FOOTE MINERAL)
Verney Corp.	AQ			(GLEN ALDEN)
Vick Chemical Co.	SR	SR	154	RICHARDSON-MERRILL
Victor Chemical Works	AQ			(STAUFFER-CHEMICAL 1959)
Visking Corp.	AQ			(UNION CARBIDE 1955)
Waldorf Paper Products Co.	AQ			(HOERNER-WALD 1966)
Walworth Co.	AQ			(INTERNATIONAL UTILITIES 1972)
Wanskuck Co.	SR		ID	
Warner & Swasey Co., The	SR	AQ	232	
Warren (S.D.) Co.	AQ			(SCOTT PAPER 1967)
Washburn Wire Co.	SR	NI	328	
Waukesha Motor Co.	AQ			(BANGOR PUNTA)
Weatherhead Co., The	SR	AQ	473	
Welch Grape Juice Co.	SR		ID	
Werthan Bag Corp.	SR		NI	
Western Printing & Lithographing Co.	SR	AQ	206	WESTERN PUBLISHING
White Sewing Machine Corp.	SR	SR	507	WHITE CONSOLIDATED
Whitin Machine Works	AQ			(WHITE CONSOL. 1965)
Whitman (William) Co., Inc.	LQ			(GULF OIL 1960)
Wilshire Oil Co.	AQ			
Wiscassett Mills Co.	SR		NI	
Wood (Gar) Industries, Inc.	AQ			(SARGENT IND. 1970)
Wood (John) Mfg. Co., Inc.	AQ			(MOLSON IND.)

C. <u>Companies Ranked 501 to 1,000</u>   2 3   4   5

Woodside Mills		AQ	(DAN RIVER 1956)
Woodward Iron Co.		AQ	(MEAD 1968)
Wurlitzer (Rudolph) Co.	SR SR 558		
York Corp.		AQ	(BORG-WARNER 1956)

---

* Through an error in the company's report General Cigar Co. was considered
to have manufacturing shipments too small to be included among the 1,000
largest manufacturing companies. Subsequently the tabulations on the cigar
industry were amended to include it.

\# Through an error in the company's report Griesedieck Western Brewery Co.
was considered to be among the companies ranked 201 to 500. The tabulations
on the beer industry are based on the company's amended report.

1) Smith acquired Mohawk Carpet in 1955, but Mohawk is regarded as surviving
   to avoid dropping observation.

2) American Bakeries acquired by Purity in 1953, but American regarded as surviving
   to avoid losing observation.

3) Bachmann Uxbridge acquired American Hard Rubber in 1957. Name changed to
   Amerace, Amerace sold Bachman Uxbridge in 1960.

D. Companies in 1000 largest of 1972 but not in 1000 largest 1950, and in
   sample of 603.

Name	Profit Rank 1950-1952	Name	Profit Rank 1950-1952
Air Products & Chemicals	475	Faberge	211
Allied Products	203	Fairchild Camera & Instrument	561
Amcord	99	Fairchild Industries	509
American Biltrite	474	Fansteel	363
Ametek	233	Fedders	89
Anderson, Clayton	404	Foster Wheeler Corp.	565
Armada Corporation	8	Central Foundry	259
Atlantic Steel	571	Culbro	590
Avon Products	59	General Dynamics	597
Bangor Punta	423	General Instrument Corp.	544
Beckman Instruments	325	General Signal	375
Beech Aircraft	542	Grace, W.R. & Co.	549
Belden Corp.	170	Grolier, Inc.	514
Belding Hemingway	470	Grumman Corp.	385
Bliss & Laughlin Industries	501	Gulf & Western Industries	141

D. Companies in 1000 largest of 1972 but not in 1000 largest 1950, and in

sample of 603.

Name	Profit Rank 1950-1952	Name	Profit Rank 1950-1952
Boeing	424	National Union Electric Corp.	367
Boise Cascade	335	Northrop Corp.	323
Briggs & Stratton	22	Noxell Corp.	7
Carling Brewing Co.	309	Ogden Corp.	595
Cerro Corp.	338	Oxford Industries	479
Cessna Aircraft	519	Parker-Hannifin Corp.	513
Chesebrough-Pond's Inc.	90	Pitney-Bowes, Inc.	357
Collins Radio Co.	483	Polaroid	65
Colt Industries	598	Porter, H.K. Co.	355
CBS	485	Purex Corp.	308
Consolidated Foods	530	Purolator, Inc.	79
Cont. Copper & Steel Ind.	543	Ranco, Inc.	25
Copeland Corp.	91	Rapid-American Corp.	517
Copper Range	420	Rockwell International Corp.	52
Curtis-Wright Corp.	524	Rohr Industries	167
Diebold	445	Royal Crown Cola	36
Dr. Pepper	330	Rubbermaid, Inc.	5
Ethyl	407	Schering-Plough Corp.	296
Halliburton Co.	49	Searle, G.D. & Co.	4
Hammond Corp.	12	Signal Companies	589
Heileman, G. Brewing Co.	29	Signode Corp.	236
Helena Rubinstein	255	Skil Corp.	46
Helme Products	360	Sprague Electric Co.	23
Hercules Incorporated	151	Standard Pressed Steel	86
Heublein Corp.	520	Stone Container Corp.	43
Interpace	279	Sucrest Corporation	545
Kaiser Cement & Gypsum	24	Sundstrand Corp.	254
Kerr-McGee Corp.	417	Tenneco	224
Kidde, Walter & Co.	493	Thiokol Corp.	511
LTV	588	Thomas & Betts Corp.	53
Lehigh Valley Industries	584	Trans Union Corp.	477
Lockheed Aircraft Corp.	518	UMC Industries	397
Marathon Oil	28	United Technologies Corp.	429
Maremont Corp.	241	United Brands Co.	57
Martin Marietta	601	V.F. Corp.	312
Masco Corp.	34	Victor Comptometer Corp.	124
McDonnell Douglas Corp.	155	Walter, Jim Corp.	444
Miles Laboratories	96	Whittaker Corp.	1
Mohawk Rubber Co.	201	Wickes Corp.	166
Monroe Auto Equipment Co.	446	Witco Chemical Corp.	349
Morton-Norwich Products	132	Xerox Corp.	464
Nalco Chemical Co.	55		

E.   Companies in 603 firm sample but in neither the 1,000 largest sample of
      1950 nor the 1,000 largest sample for 1972.

Name	Profit Rank 1950–1952
Adams-Mills	415
Bond Clothing	523
British Petroleum	267
Baldwin	492
Freepont Minerals	42
Foote	195
Giant Portland Cement	95
Giddings Lewis	490
Hazeltine	294
Helene Curtis	466
Howmet	168
Leesona	579
Mississippi Portland Cement	280
Moly Corp.	315
Monarch Machine	286
Pittston	583
Tootsie Roll	98
Standard Kollsman	6
Starrett	432

Appendix 2   Industry categories

What follows is a list of the names of the industry categories used in this study to determine market shares and the weights used to define industry variables such as advertising intensity and concentration. The 1950 industry names are presented first. *New SIC* is the number Carl Schwinn assigned to the industry or industries listed to the right with their appropriate SIC (old SIC) numbers. These are followed by the 1972 industry list with the Weiss C4, where available. Where not available, we constructed a C4 from the census (national-level) figures.

NEW SIC	CENSUS VALUE* OF SHIPMENTS	OLD SIC	DESCRIPTION
19110	999999**	19110	GUNS AND MOUNTS - 20 MM AND ABOVE--THE CODE 999999 INDICATES THAT THE CPR SAMPLE TOTAL WAS USED IN PLACE OF THE CENSUS VALUE OF SHIPMENTS
19210	999999	19210	AMMUNITION - 20 MM AND ABOVE
19290	999999	19290	BOMBS - DEPTH CHARGES - MINES - TORPEDOES
19310	999999	19311 19312	COMBAT TANKS AND PARTS RECOVERY TANKS AND PARTS
19410	999999	19411	BOMB SHACKLES AND GUNSIGHT REFLECTORS
19510	999999	19512	SMALL ARMS UNDER 20 MM (EXCEPT MACHINE GUNS)
19610	999999	19610	AMMUNITION UNDER 20 MM
20110	61893	20111 20114 20133	FRESH MEATS (MADE IN ESTABLISHMENTS PRIMARILY ENGAGED IN OWN SLAUGHTERING) HIDES, BONES AND INEDIBLE MEATS (MADE IN ESTABLISHMENTS PRIMARILY ENGAGED IN OWN SLAUGHTERING PREPARED MEAT PRODUCTS FOR HUMAN CONSUMPTION-INCLUDING LARD (MADE PRIMARILY FROM PURCHASED MEATS)
		20151	POULTRY AND SMALL GAME (KILLED & DRESSED IN THIS ESTABLISHMENT)
20210	849342	20210 20930	BUTTER (CHURNED IN THIS PLANT) MARGARINE
20220	394449	20221	NATURAL CHEESE
20230	623931	20231 20232 20233	DRIED MILK, DRIED BUTTERMILK, ETC. CANNED MILK BULK EVAPORATED AND CONDENSED MILK (WHOLE MILK, SKIM MILK, BUTTERMILK, AND WHEY)
20240	641840	20234 20240	ICE CREAM MIX AND ICE MILK MIX ICE CREAM AND ICES
20250	231759	20252	PROCESS CHEESE (MADE FROM PURCHASED NATURAL CHEESE)
20251	50004	20251	SPECIAL DAIRY PRODUCTS (MALTED MILK POWDER, ETC.)
20260	2377858	20262 20263	BOTTLED FRESH MILK AND CREAM BULK FRESH MILK AND CREAM
20310	223246	20311	CANNED FISH AND OTHER SEA FOOD
20331	417139	20331	CANNED FRUITS
20332	782861	20332	CANNED VEGETABLES AND SPECIALTIES
20334	180192	20334	CANNED FRUIT JUICES

* The value of shipments is in 1,000's.

** 999999 indicates that Census values were not available and the CPR sample total was used as the population total.

NEW SIC	CENSUS VALUE OF SHIPMENTS	OLD SIC	DESCRIPTION
20335	59528	20335	CANNED VEGETABLE JUICES
20336	118839	20336	CANNED BABY FOODS
20337	265659	20337	CANNED SOUPS AND POULTRY PRODUCTS
20338	155773	20338	JAMS, JELLIES, AND PRESERVES
20339	16457	20339	OTHER CANNED OR PRESERVED PRODUCTS
20340	109703	20341	DRIED FRUITS
		20342	DEHYDRATED VEGETABLES AND SOUP MIX
20351	109418	20351	CATSUP AND OTHER TOMATO SAUCES
20352	114441	20352	PICKLES AND OTHER PICKLED PRODUCTS
20353	28284	20353	MUSTARD AND OTHER MEAT SAUCES, EXCEPT TOMATO
20354	175060	20354	SALAD DRESSINGS-INCLUDING MAYONNAISE
20371	62180	20371	FROZEN PACKAGED FISH
20372	141616	20372	FROZEN FRUITS AND JUICES
20373	111453	20373	FROZEN VEGETABLES
20410	1712224	20411	WHEAT FLOUR-PLAIN
		20412	WHEAT BRAN, SHORTS, AND MIDDLINGS
		20413	CORN MEAL
		20414	OTHER GRAIN, MILL PRODUCTS, INCLUDE RYE FLOUR, HOMINY GRITS, ETC.
		20415	BLENDED AND PREPARED FLOUR MADE IN FLOUR MILLS
20420	2263172	20421	PREPARED ANIMAL FEEDS, EXCLUDE DOG AND CAT FOOD
		20422	DOG AND CAT FOOD (PREPARED)
		20423	ALFALFA MEAL AND MINERAL MIXTURES
20430	254383	20430	CEREAL BREAKFAST FOODS
20440	241557	20441	MILLED RICE AND BYPRODUCTS
20510	2685091	20510	BREAD, ROLLS, CAKES, PIES AND PASTRIES
20520	604641	20520	BISCUITS, CRACKERS AND PRETZELS
20610	1112462	20611	RAW CANE SUGAR

NEW SIC	CENSUS VALUE OF SHIPMENTS	OLD SIC	DESCRIPTION
20710	880445	20612	OTHER CANE SUGAR MILL PRODUCTS AND BYPRODUCTS
		20621	REFINED CANE SUGAR (EXCLUDE EXCISE TAXES)
		20622	OTHER CANE SUGAR REFINERY PRODUCTS AND BYPRODUCTS
		20631	REFINED BEET SUGAR (EXCLUDED EXCISE TAXES)
		20632	OTHER BEET SUGAR FACTORY PRODUCTS AND BYPRODUCTS
20720	364770	20711	CONFECTIONERY, EXCEPT SOLID CHOCOLATE BARS
		20715	SALTED, ROASTED, AND BLANCHED NUTS
		20718	PEANUTS AND PEANUT HULLS
20730	132172	20721	CHOCOLATE COATINGS
		20722	REPORT TOTAL OF FOLLOWING: CHOCOLATE, COCOA, SOLID CHOCOLATE BARS
		20730	CHEWING GUM AND CHEWING-GUM BASE
20810	830590	20810	BOTTLED SOFT DRINKS AND CARBONATED WATERS
20820	1469481	20821	BEER, ALE, AND OTHER MALT LIQUORS, EXCLUDE EXCISE TAXES
		20822	BREWERS GRAINS AND OTHER BREWERY PRODUCTS
20830	206759	20831	MALT
		20832	MALT BYPRODUCTS
20840	170900	20841	REPORT THE TOTAL OF THE FOLLOWING: WINES, BRANDY
20850	971751	20851	DISTILLED LIQUORS, EXCEPT BRANDY (REPORT RAW VALUE OR COST OF PRODUCTION)
		20852	DISTILLERS GRAINS
		20853	BOTTLED LIQUORS (SHIPPED FROM RECTIFYING PLANTS OR TAX-PAID BOTTLING HOUSES)-EXCLUDE EXCISE TAXES
20900	223145	20901	EGGS (LIQUID, FROZEN AND DRIED)
20910	81280	20911	BAKING POWDER
		20912	YEAST
20920	598177	20921	SHORTENING AND SALAD OILS
20940	405107	20941	WET CORN-MILLING PRODUCTS
20950	341931	20951	FLAVORING, EXTRACTS, EMULSIONS AND OTHER LIQUID FLAVORS: EXCLUDE BEVERAGE BASES (20952) AND SYNTHETIC FLAVORING MATERIAL
		20952	BEVERAGE BASES
		20953	FLAVORING SIRUPS AND CONCENTRATES
20960	16737	20960	VINEGAR AND CIDER
20970	150973	20970	MANUFACTURED ICE

NEW SIC	CENSUS VALUE OF SHIPMENTS	OLD SIC	DESCRIPTION
20980	118586	20980	MACARONI AND NOODLE PRODUCTS (NOT CANNED)
20991	98721	20991	DESSERTS, READY-TO-MIX, EXCEPT ICE-CREAM MIX (CODE 20234)
20992	116314	20992	POTATO CHIPS
20993	83872	20993	SWEETENING SIRUP AND MOLASSES
20994	490543	20994	FOOD PREPARATIONS NOT ELSEWHERE CLASSIFIED
20996	1263295	20996	ROASTED COFFEE
21110	1326351	21110	CIGARETTES, EXCLUDE EXCISE TAXES
21210	314409	21210	CIGARS, EXCLUDE EXCISE TAXES
21310	174142	21310	TOBACCO: CHEWING AND SMOKING AND SNUFF, EXCLUDE EXCISE TAXES
21410	1024505	21410	TOBACCO, STEMMED AND/OR REDRIED
		21510	TOBACCO, PACKED ONLY
22110	105821	22110	NOILS AND WASTE -- WOOL TOPS
22120	1293519	22120	YARNS SPUN ON WOOLEN AND WORSTED SYSTEMS, EXCLUDE CARPET YARN (22712)
		22220	THROWN YARNS
		22240	YARNS SPUN ON COTTON SYSTEM
22130	5922747	22130	WOOLEN AND WORSTED FABRICS--OVER 12 INCHES IN WIDTH
		22330	COTTON FABRICS, INCLUDE ALL COTTON, RAYON, NYLON TIRE CORD AND TIRE FABRIC OVER 12 INCHES IN WIDTH
		2234C	RAYON AND RELATED FABRICS
22230	206786	22231	THREAD FOR USE IN THE HOME
		22232	THREAD FOR INDUSTRIAL USE
22410	276453	2241	ELASTIC COTTON FABRICS
		22411	COTTON NARROW FABRICS (51% OR MORE COTTON)
		22413	RAYON NARROW FABRICS (51% OR MORE RAYON)
		22415	NARROW FABRICS OTHER THAN COTTON OR RAYON
			COVERED RUBBER THREAD
22510	652587	22511	FINISHED FULL-FASHIONED HOSIERY--KNIT IN THIS PLANT
		22513	FULL-FASHIONED HOSIERY SHIPPED IN THE GREIGE
22520	383705	22523	MENS FINISHED SEAMLESS HOSIERY, INCLUDE BUNDLE GOODS AND ATHLETIC AND CREW SOCKS
		22524	SEAMLESS HOSIERY SHIPPED IN THE GREIGE
		22529	FINISHED SEAMLESS HOSIERY, INCLUDING ANKLETS, NOT ELSEWHERE CLASSIFIED

NEW SIC	CENSUS VALUE OF SHIPMENTS	OLD SIC	DESCRIPTION
22530	444181	22531	KNIT OUTERWEAR MADE IN KNITTING MILLS
22540	656756	22541	KNIT UNDERWEAR AND NIGHTWEAR MADE IN KNITTING MILLS
22550	100015	22551	KNIT GLOVES AND MITTENS MADE IN KNITTING MILLS
		23811	DRESS AND SEMI-DRESS GLOVES AND MITTENS. FABRIC AND COMBINATION FABRIC AND. LEATHER. FROM FABRIC MADE ELSEWHERE
22560	328702	22561	KNIT FABRICS
22590	12123	22590	OTHER KNITTING MILL PRODUCTS NOT ELSEWHERE SPECIFIED
22710	667287	22711	WOOL CARPETS AND RUGS
		22730	CARPETS, RUGS AND MATS FROM FIBER, EXCEPT WOOL
22740	241818	22741	LINOLEUM
		22742	ASPHALTED FELT-BASE FLOOR AND WALL COVERING
		22743	PLASTIC FLOOR COVERING
22810	352488	22810	FUR-FELT HATS AND HAT BODIES
		23510	MILLINERY (TRIMMED HATS)
22830	21882	22830	STRAW HATS
22910	96319	22911	FELT GOODS EXCEPT WOVEN FELTS (CODE 22130) AND HATS
22920	58757	22920	LACE GOODS (LEVERS LACES. BOBBINET. NATTINGHAM LACE. BARMEN LACE. ETC.)
22930	128548	22930	PADDINGS AND UPHOLSTERY FILLING
22940	128548	22940	PROCESSED WASTE AND RECOVERED FIBERS
22950	246212	22951	PYROXYLIN-COATED FABRICS
		22952	RESIN-COATED FABRICS
		22953	UNSUPPORTED FILMS
		22954	OTHER IMPREGNATED AND COATED FABRICS (OILCLOTH, ETC.)
22970	55938	22971	LINEN GOODS
		22972	JUTE GOODS EXCEPT JUTE FELT (22911) AND JUTE CORDAGE AND TWINE (22982)
22980	189788	22981	HARD FIBER CORDAGE AND TWINE
		22982	SOFT FIBER CORDAGE AND TWINE EXCEPT COTTON
		22983	COTTON CORDAGE AND TWINE
22990	60037	22990	OTHER TEXTILE GOODS NOT ELSEWHERE SPECIFIED
		22994	OTHER TEXTILE. N.E.C.
23110	1021469	23111	SUITS. COATS AND OVERCOATS; MENS AND BOYS

NEW SIC	CENSUS VALUE OF SHIPMENTS	OLD SIC	DESCRIPTION
23210	573858	23211	SHIRTS EXCEPT WORK SHIRTS (23280) AND NIGHTWEAR MADE OF WOVEN FABRIC -- MENS AND BOYS
23220	202541	23221	KNIT UNDERWEAR AND NIGHTWEAR MADE FROM FABRIC KNIT ELSEWHERE AND WOVEN UNDERWEAR--MENS AND BOYS
23230	107876	23230	NECKWEAR - MENS AND BOYS
23250	3524880	23250	CLOTH HATS AND CAPS - MENS AND BOYS
23270	294458	23270	SEPARATE TROUSERS - MENS AND BOYS
23280	110893	23280	WORK SHIRTS
23290	847346	23291	MENS AND BOYS WORK, SPORT, AND OTHER APPAREL NOT LISTED ABOVE (INCLUDE KNIT SHIRTS, SWEATERS, BATHINGSUITS, AND TRUNKS MADE FROM FABRIC KNIT ELSEWHERE; WORK PANTS; OVERALLS; ONE-PIECE WORK SUITS; JACKETS, AND OTHER HEAVY OUTERWEAR; OILED FABRIC GARMENTS; WASHABLE SERVICE APPAREL; BOYS' WASH SUITS; ETC.)
23310	257737	23310	BLOUSES AND WAISTS - WOMENS AND MISSES
23340	359741	23341	DRESSES SOLD AT A DOZEN-PRICE APRONS, UNIFORMS AND OTHER WASHABLE SERVICE APPAREL - WOMENS AND MISSES
23350	815510	23351	SUITS, JACKETS AND COATS EXCEPT FUR COATS--WOMENS AND MISSES
23350	150028	23364	SKIRTS - WOMENS AND MISSES
23390	121094	23391	WOMENS AND MISSES OUTERWEAR NOT LISTED ABOVE (INCLUDE KNIT JACKETS, SWEATERS, SHIRTS, PULLOVERS, AND BATHING SUITS MADE FROM FABRIC KNIT ELSEWHERE; OVERALLS AND COVERALLS; PLEYSUITS AND SHORT; SLACKS AND SLACK SUITS; WOVEN BATHING SUITS; ETC.)
23410	377148	23410	WOMENS, CHILDRENS AND INFANTS WOVEN UNDERWEAR AND NIGHTWEAR AND KNIT UNDERWEAR AND NIGHTWEAR MADE FROM FABRIC KNIT ELSEWHERE, INCLUDING NEGLIGEES AND BEDJACKETS
23420	331165	23422	CORSETS, GIRDLES, ROLL-ONS AND GARTER BELTS
23690	254210	23694	CHILDREN AND INFANTS OUTERWEAR NOT LISTED ABOVE (INCLUDING KNIT SHIRTS, SWEATERS, JERSEYS, AND BATHING SUITS MADE FROM FABRIC KNIT ELSEWHERE; BUNTINGS; CREEPERS, ROMPERS, AND BABY BOYS' WASH SUITS; OVERALLS AND COVERALLS; SUNSUITS AND SHORTS; WOVEN BATHING SUITS; ETC.
23820	68761	23821	WORK GLOVES AND MITTENS, FABRIC AND COMBINATION FABRIC-AND-LEATHER, FROM FABRIC MADE ELSEWHERE

265

NEW SIC	CENSUS VALUE OF SHIPMENTS	OLD SIC	DESCRIPTION
23830	15886	23830	SUSPENDERS, GARTERS, HOSE SUPPORTERS AND RELATED PRODUCTS
23840	100722	23841	ROBES AND DRESSING GOWNS
		23842	BREAKFAST COATS, BRUNCH COATS, HOUSE COATS AND LOUNGING PAJAMAS
23850	11940	23850	REPORT THE TOTAL OF THE FOLLOWING CATAGORIES: RAINWEAR AND OTHER FINISHED WATERPROOF OUTER GARMENTS MADE FROM PURCHASED RUBBERIZED FABRICS; WATERPROOF AND WATER-REPELLENT RAINCOATS, AND OTHER WATERPROOF OUTER GARMENTS. (INCLUDE 23111 AND 23291).
23860	42309	23860	LEATHER AND SHEEP-LINED CLOTHING
23880	42850	23880	HANDKERCHIEFS
23910	135163	23910	CURTAINS AND DRAPERIES - EXCEPT LACE (22920)
23920	740158	23921	BEDSPREADS AND BED SETS
		23922	SHEETS AND PILLOWCASES
		23923	TOWELS AND WASHCLOTHS
		23929	OTHER HOUSE FURNISHINGS (SHOWER BATH CURTAINS, TABLECLOTHS, NAPKINS, COMFORTERS, ETC.)
23930	313072	23930	TEXTILE BAGS EXCEPT LAUNDRY AND WARDROBE BAGS (23929)
23940	102916	23940	CANVAS PRODUCTS
23950	29240	23950	PLEATING, STITCHING AND TUCKING FOR THE TRADE
23960	181793	23960	TRIMMINGS, STAMPED ART GOODS AND ART NEEDLEWORK
23990	191348	23990	FABRICATED TEXTILE PRODUCTS N.E.C.
24110	618076	24110	LOGS, BOLTS, PULPWOOD, ETC.
24210	3177535	24210	ROUGH LUMBER AND SAWED TIES
		24211	HARDWOOD FURNITURE DIMENSION
		24212	HARDWOOD DIMENSION OTHER THAN FURNITURE
		24213	SOFTWOOD CUT-STOCK (PREDIMENSIONED TO SPECIFIC INDUSTRIAL USES IN FURTHER FABRICATION, I.E., DOOR, WINDOW FURNITURE, ETC., STOCK)
		24214	DRESSED LUMBER EXCLUDING FLOORING
		24215	SOFTWOOD FLOORING
		24216	HARDWOOD FLOORING
		24219	LATH; PICKETS
		24290	SPECIAL PRODUCTS SAWMILLS N.E.C. (FUELWOOD, WOOD CHIPS, PRESTO-LOGS)
24220	91089	24221	HARDWOOD VENEER
		24222	SOFTWOOD VENEER
24230	32804	24230	SHINGLES AND SHAKES

NEW SIC	CENSUS VALUE OF SHIPMENTS	OLD SIC	DESCRIPTION
24240	44194	24240	COOPERAGE STOCK (STAVES, HEADING AND HOOPS FOR TIGHT OR SLACK COOPERAGE)
24250	9117	24250	EXCELSIOR PRODUCTS
24310	811861	24311	SASH OTHER THAN STORM SASH
		24312	WINDOW AND DOOR FRAMES
		24313	DOORS--GENERAL CONSTRUCTION INTERIOR AND EXTERIOR
		24314	CABINET WORK (TO BE BUILT-IN - KITCHEN CABINETS, BROOM CLOSETS, MEDICINE CABINETS, VEGETABLE BINS), MANTELS, CHINA CASES, ETC.
		24315	STAIR WORK, INCLUDING BALUSTERS, BRACKETS, CROOKS, NEWELS, RAILS, TREADS, RISERS, STAIRS, ETC.
		24316	EXTERIOR MILLWORK: PORCH COLUMNS, RAILS AND NEWELS, TRELLISES, OUTSIDE BLINDS
		24317	MILLWORK PRODUCTS NOT ELSEWHERE CLASSIFIED
24320	443336	24321	HARDWOOD PLYWOOD
		24322	SOFTWOOD PLYWOOD - INTERIOR GRADE
		24323	SOFTWOOD PLYWOOD - EXTERIOR GRADE
		24324	PLYWOOD-INCLUDE FANCY AND FIGURED SOFTWOOD PLYWOOD AND CONTAINER SOFTWOOD PLYWOOD NOT ELSEWHERE CLASSIFIED
		24325	NONWOOD FACE PLYWOOD
24330	154045	24332	PREFABRICATED DWELLINGS
24410	31947	24410	FRUIT AND VEGETABLE BASKETS
24430	8733	24430	CIGAR BOXES -- WOODEN AND PART WOODEN
24440	362987	24442	WIREBOUND BOXES FOR INDUSTRIAL AND OTHER USES
		24443	NON-WIREWOUND BOXES FOR FRUITS AND VEGETABLES
		24444	NON-WIREBOUND BOXES FOR INDUSTRIAL AND OTHER USES
		24445	COMBINATION WOOD AND FIBER BOXES
		24448	BOX SHOOK: FRUIT, VEGETABLE, INDUSTRIAL (MADE FROM PURCHASED LUMBER)
24450	98833	24451	SLACK COOPERAGE (BARRELS, KEGS ETC.)
		24453	TIGHT COOPERAGE (BARRELS, KEGS ETC.)
24910	293113	24910	WOOD OWNED AND TREATED FOR SALE
24920	11177	24920	LASTS AND RELATED PRODUCTS - LASTS FOR BOOTS AND SHOES - LAST SOLE PATTERNS - SHOE TREES AND STRETCHERS
24991	35791	24991	HANDLES, WOOD (HAND-TOOL HANDLES AND OTHER HANDLES)
24992	56432	24992	FURNITURE PARTS, TEXTILE MACHINERY TURNINGS AND VEHICLE STOCK
24993	17272	24993	LADDERS, WOOD

NEW SIC	CENSUS VALUE OF SHIPMENTS	OLD SIC	DESCRIPTION
24999	198209	24999	UNKNOWN
25110	2072999	25110	WOOD HOUSEHOLD FURNITURE EXCEPT UPHOLSTERED. INCLUDE LIVING ROOM, DINING, BEDROOM (EXCLUDE MATTRESSES AND BEDSPRING)
		25120	HOUSEHOLD FURNITURE, UPHOLSTERED - INCLUDE LIVING ROOM SUITES, SOFAS, DAVENPORTS, SETTEES, LOVE SEATS, CHAIRS, ROCKERS, OTTOMANS, ETC.
		25140	METAL HOUSEHOLD FURNITURE, EXCEPT UPHOLSTERED - INCLUDE LIVING ROOM, DINING ROOM, BEDROOM, KITCHEN INFANTS, CHILDRENS, PORCH AND LAWN FURNITURE, ETC.
25150	300867	25150	MATTRESSES AND BEDSPRINGS--INCLUDE HOLLYWOOD BEDS-BED SPRINGS (BOX, COIL AND FLAT)
25210	209166	25212	DESKS - WOODEN OFFICE FURNITURE
		25213	CABINETS AND CASES - WOODEN OFFICE FURNITURE
		25219	OFFICE FURNITURE - INCLUDE TABLES AND STANDS ETC., NOT ELSEWHERE CLASSIFIED - WOODEN OFFICE FURNITURE
		25221	CHAIRS, STOOLS, COUCHES ETC. - METAL OFFICE FURNITURE
		25222	DESKS - METAL OFFICE FURNITURE
		25223	CABINETS AND CASES - METAL OFFICE FURNITURE
		25229	METAL OFFICE FURNITURE N.E.C.
25310	9090	25310	PUBLIC-BUILDING FURNITURE - SCHOOLS, CHURCHES, THEATERS, AUDITORIUMS (DESKS, PEWS, GANGED CHAIRS, SEATS FOR PUBLIC CONVEYANCES
25320	58681	25320	REPORT THE TOTAL OF THE FOLLOWING CATEGORIES: PROFESSIONAL FURNITURE - INCLUDE BEDS, CABINETS, DESKS, CASES, ETC. FOR USE IN HOSPITALS, LABORATORIES, DOCTORS' AND DENTISTS' OFFICES; BEAUTY AND BARBER SHOP FURNITURE AND EQUIPMENT. DOCTORS-DENTISTS OFFICICES; BEAUTY AND BARBER SHOP FURNITURE AND EQUIPMENT
25410	200703	25411	PARTITIONS, SHELVING AND LOCKERS
		25412	CASES, CABINETS, COUNTERS AND OTHER FIXTURES
25610	151755	25611	WOOD SCREEN DOORS AND WINDOW SCREENS
		25612	METAL SCREEN DOORS AND WINDOW SCREENS
		25613	WOOD STORM SASH AND WOOD COMBINATION SCREEN AND STORM SASH AND DOORS
		25614	METAL STORM SASH AND METAL COMBINATION SCREEN AND STORM SASH AND DOORS
25620	59138	25620	WINDOW SHADES AND ACCESSORIES
25910	33087	25910	RESTAURANT FURNITURE - INCLUDE CHAIRS AND STOOLS, TABLES, BOOTHS, ETC.
25990	12215	25990	FURNITURE AND FIXTURES, N.E.C.
26110	1027476	26111	BLEACHED SULPHITE WOOD PULP
		26112	UNBLEACHED SULPHITE WOOD PULP
		26113	BLEACHED SULPHATE WOOD PULP. INCLUDE SEMIBLEACHED
		26114	UNBLEACHED SULPHATE WOOD PULP

NEW SIC	CENSUS VALUE OF SHIPMENTS	OLD SIC	DESCRIPTION
		26115	SODA WOOD PULP
		26116	GROUND-WOOD PULP
		26117	MISCELLANEOUS WOOD PULP - INCLUDE SEMICHEMICAL, CHEMFIBER, DEFIBRATED, EXPLODED ASPLUND FIBER AND SCREENINGS
		26118	PULP OTHER THAN WOOD - INCLUDE ONLY PULP MADE FOR SALE, - MADE OF COTTON, COTTON LINTERS, RAG STRAW, AND SIMILAR FIBERS
		26119	MISCELLANEOUS PULP PRODUCTS-INCLUDE TALL OIL (CRUDE AND REFINED) ROAD-BINDING MATERIAL ETC.
26120	2924927	26120	NEWSPRINT AND GROUND-WOOD PAPER
		26121	BOOK AND FINE PAPER
		26122	COARSE PAPER
		26123	SPECIAL INDUSTRIAL AND ABSORBENT PAPER
		26124	SANITARY AND TISSUE PAPER
		26125	CONTAINER BOARD
		26126	BENDING BOARD
		26127	NONBENDING BOARD
		26129	OTHER PAPER AND PAPERBOARD MILL PRODUCTS - INCLUDE TUBE STOCK, MATCH SPLINT STOCK LINER FOR GYPSUM AND PLASTERBOARD, STOCK FOR LAMINATED WALLBOARD, ETC.
26130	275397	26131	BUILDING BOARD - INCLUDE SHEATHING BOARD, INSULATING AND NON-INSULATING WALLBOARD, ETC.
		26132	BUILDING PAPER AND BUILDING BOARD MILL PRODUCTS - INCLUDING FLEXIBLE FIBER INSULATION, ETC. N.E.C.
26411	85672	264-1	COATED PAPER FOR PRINTING (OFF PAPER MACHINE)
26412	179660	264 2	WAXED AND WAX LAMINATED PAPER
26413	57414	26413	GLAZED AND FANCY PAPERS - INCLUDE CASEIN AND SIMILARLY COATED PAPERS, SPECIAL METALLIC AND PYROXYL IN COATED EMBOSSED LEATHERETTE, PLAIN AND COATED
26414	87134	26414	GUMMED PAPER - INCLUDE ROLLS, FLATS AND CLOTH BACK PAPER
26415	43307	26415	OTHER COATED PAPER N.E.C.
26510	145303	26510	ENVELOPES, ALL TYPES - EXCEPT BOXED STATIONERY (26991)
26610	487422	26611	GROCERY AND VARIETY BAGS
		26612	SPECIALTY PAPER BAGS (GLASSINE, CELLOPHANE, GREASE, PROOFED, WAXED AND FOIL-BACKED)
		26613	PAPER BAGS - INCLUDE WARDROBE, MOTHPROOF, SHOPPING AND TWISTED PAPER N.E.C.
		26614	SHIPPING SACKS, SINGLE, DOUBLE AND MULTIWALL
26710	1640418	26711	SHIPPING CONTAINERS, SOLID FIBER AND CORRUGATED
		26712	FOLDING BOXES AND CARTONS
		26713	SET-UP BOXES
		26714	PAPERBOARD BOXES - INCLUDE VULCANIZED, TOTE BOXES, ETC. N.E.C.
26740	97946	26740	FIBER CANS, TUBES, DRUMS, ETC.

NEW SIC	CENSUS VALUE OF SHIPMENTS	OLD SIC	DESCRIPTION
26910	166117	26911 26912 26913	FILING ACCESSORIES (FILE FOLDERS, GUIDE CARDS-ETC.) CARDS. DIE-CUT AND DESIGNED (NOT PRINTED) MISCELLANEOUS DIE-CUT PRODUCTS N.E.C.
26930	41815	26930	WALLPAPER - INCLUDE DESIGNING, PRINTING AND EMBOSSING
26940	31622	26940	PULP GOODS - PRESSED AND MOLDED, EXCEPT STATUARY (32981)
26991	72480	26991	STATIONERY-TABLETS AND RELATED PRODUCTS
26992	187093	26992	WRAPPING PRODUCTS - EXCEPT COATED, OILED AND WAXED. INCLUDE CORRUGATED PAPER IN ROLLS. WATER-PROOF CREPED AND LINED
26993	231232	26993	SANITARY FOOD CONTAINERS - INCLUDE MILK BOTTLES. CUPS, ICE-CREAM PAILS, ETC.
26994	293584	26994	SANITARY HEALTH PRODUCTS - INCLUDE TOILET PAPER, DIAPERS, FACIAL TISSUES, TABLE NAPKINS. TOILET SEAT COVERS, ETC.
26996	311951	26996	CONVERTED PAPER AND BOARD PRODUCTS - INCLUDE GAMES, TOYS, NOVELTIES, PLAYING CARDS, LAMINATED WALL BOARD, ETC., N.E.C.
27110	2375109	27111 27112	RECEIPTS FROM SUBSCRIPTIONS AND SALES RECEIPTS FROM ADVERTISING (NET AFTER DEDUCTING AD AGENCY COMMISSION AND CASH DISCOUNT)
27210	1118546	27211 27212	RECEIPTS FROM SUBSCRIPTIONS AND SALES RECEIPTS FROM ADVERTISING (NET AFTER DEDUCTING AD AGENCY COMMISSION AND CASH DISCOUNT)
27310	619369	27311	BOOKS AND PAMPHLETS (REPORT TOTAL SALES OF ALL ORIGINAL AND REPRINT BOOKS AND PAMPHLETS PUBLISHED BY YOU)
27320	131792	27321	BOOK AND PAMPHLET PRINTING AND COMPLETE BOOK MANUFACTURING (REPORT TOTAL RECEIPTS FROM PRINTING AND LITHOGRAPHING BOOKS AND PAMPHLETS, INCLUDING COMPLETE BOOK MANUFACTURING)
27410	169617	27410	MISCELLANEOUS PUBLISHING (INCLUDE RECEIPTS FROM PUBLISHING SUCH PRODUCTS AS MAPS, ATLASES. SHEET MUSIC. DIRECTORIES. AND OTHER MISCELLANEOUS PUBLICATIONS NOT LISTED ABOVE)
27510	2299235	27511 27611	LETTERPRESS AND GRAVURE PRINTING-INCLUDE RECEIPTS FOR GENERAL COMMERCIAL AND SPECIALIZED PRINTING EXCEPT BOOK PRINTING (27321) AND PRINTING GREETING CARDS (27711) LITHOGRAPHING EXCEPT RECEIPTS FROM LITHOGRAPHING BOOKS AND PAMPHLETS (27321) AND GREETING CARDS (27711)
27710	126303	27711	GREETING CARDS - INCLUDE SALES OF GREETING CARDS AS WELL AS RECEIPTS FROM PRINTING OR LITHOGRAPHING GREETING CARDS
27810	113109	27811	BOOKBINDING - INCLUDE RECEIPTS FOR EDITION, TRADE, JOB, LIBRARY BOOKBINDING
27820	82539	27821	BLANKBOOKS AND PAPER RULING - INCLUDE SALES BOOKS, ACCOUNT BOOKS, COMPOSITION BOOKS, ALBUMS. CHECK BOOKS, INVENTORY AND SIMILAR BOOKS, AND RECEIPTS FROM PAPER RULING

NEW SIC	CENSUS VALUE OF SHIPMENTS	OLD SIC	DESCRIPTION
27830	59933	27830	LOOSE-LEAF BINDERS AND DEVICES - INCLUDE FORMS, FILLERS AND BINDERS
27910	102934	27910	TYPESETTING-MACHINE AND HAND - INCLUDE ADVERTISING TYPOGRAPHY
27920	59733	27921	ENGRAVING (STEEL, COPPERPLATE, ETC.) AND PLATE PRINTING
27930	146464	27930	PHOTOENGRAVING
27940	70994	27941	ELECTROTYPING AND STEREOTYPING
28120	260000	2812C	CHLORINE AND ALKALIES
28190	1092229	2819C	REPORT THE TOTAL OF SULPHURIC ACID, INDUSTRIAL INORGANIC CHEMICALS N.E.C.
28210	78247	2821C	CYCLIC (COAL TAR) CRUDES
28230	894200	2823	CELLULOSE PLASTICS MATERIALS
		2823?	SYNTHETIC RESINS-EXCLUDE RESINS FOR PROTECTIVE COATINGS (28234)
		2823?	VULCANIZED FIBER
		2823?	PLASTICS AND RESIN MATERIALS OTHER THAN SPECIFIED ABOVE - INCLUDE PROTEIN BASE PLASTICS, RESINS FOR PROTECTIVE COATINGS AND CELLOPHANE
28240	301454	2824D	SYNTHETIC (CHEMICAL) RUBBERS
28250	1098524	28251	RAYON YARN, ACETATE PROCESS
		28252	RAYON YARN, VISCOSE AND CUPRAMMONIUM PROCESSES
		28254	SYNTHETIC FIBERS OTHER THAN RAYON
		28255	CELLULOSE PRODUCTS OTHER THAN RAYON (SAUSAGE CASINGS, CAPS, BANDS, SPONGES) - TRANSPARENT WRAPPING MATERIALS ARE INCLUDED IN PLASTICS MATERIAL ABOVE
28260	134752	28260	EXPLOSIVES - INCLUDE SAFETY FUSES AND BLASTING AND DETONATING CAPS
26291	174592	28231	SYNTHETIC ORGANIC CHEMICALS N.E.C.
28292	77908	28232	ETHYL ALCOHOL (INDUSTRIAL) - EXCLUDE SYNTHETIC ALCOHOL (28291)
28293	49388	28293	ORGANIC CHEM. (NON-SYNTHETIC)-EXCLUDE 28610 28620 28920 28870
23294	52936	28294	INTERMEDIATES, DYES, COLOR LAKES AND TONERS
28310	69171	28510	BIOLOGICAL PRODUCTS
28320	10225	28320	BOTANICAL PRODUCTS (DERIVED FROM GRADING, GRINDING AND MILLING BOTANICAL DRUGS AND HERBS) EXCLUDE PREPARATIONS (28341, 28342, 28343, AND 28344)
28331	327313	28331	DRUGS OF ANIMAL ORIGIN - UNCOMPOUNDED (BULK)

271

NEW SIC	CENSUS VALUE OF SHIPMENTS	OLD SIC	DESCRIPTION
28341	1196987	28332	INORGANIC AND ORGANIC MEDICINALS (BULK) INCLUDE ANTIBIOTICS, ALKALOIDS, BULK VITAMINS
28341	1196987	28341	ETHICAL PREPARATIONS FOR HUMAN USE (PRODUCTS ADVERTISED OR OTHERWISE PROMOTED TO OR PRESCRIBED BY THE MEDICAL PROFESSION)
28342	24394	28342	ETHICAL PREPARATIONS FOR VETERINARY USE (PRODUCTS ADVERTISED OR OTHERWISE PROMOTED TO OR PRESCRIBED BY THE MEDICAL PROFESSION)
28344	28513	28344	PROPRIETARY PREPARATIONS FOR VETERINARY USE (PRODUCTS ADVERTISED OR OTHERWISE PROMOTED TO THE GENERAL PUBLIC)
28413	69714	28413	GLYCERIN
28415	619717	28415	SOAPS, EXCEPT SPECIALTY SOAPS - INCLUDE CLEANSERS CONTAINING ABRASIVES AND WASHING POWDERS
28416	35939	28416	SPECIALTY SOAPS - INCLUDE MECHANICS HAND SOAPS, MEDICATED SOAPS, SHAVING SOAPS
28421	19556	28421	SYNTHETIC ORGANIC DETERGENTS - INCLUDE COMBINATIONS OF SYNTHETIC ORGANIC DETERGENTS WITH SOAP OR WITH ALKALINE DETERGENTS
28422	273657	28422	ALKALINE DETERGENTS
28423	64046	28423	SPECIALTY DETERGENTS - INCLUDE WINDOW GLASS CLEANERS, WALL PAPER, WINDOW SHADE, PAINT CLEANERS ETC.
28424	159608	28424	POLISHING PREPARATIONS AND RELATED PRODUCTS - INCLUDE BLACKINGS, STAINS, DRESSINGS, POLISHING CLOTHS, ETC.
28430	55381	28430	SULFONATE OILS AND FATS AND ASSISTANTS
28510	1289930	28511 28512 28513	OIL AND WATER PAINTS AND STAINS VARNISHES, LACQUERS, ENAMELS, JAPANS, DOPES AND THINNERS - EXCLUDE TURPENTINE (28620 28630) PAINT PRODUCT N.E.C. (INCLUDE VINYL COATINGS-PIGMENT DISPERSONS-BLEACHED SHELLAC ETC.)
28520	346892	28520	INORGANIC COLOR PIGMENTS
28530	36046	28530	WHITING, PUTTY, WOOD FILLERS, AND ALLIED PAINT PRODUCTS
28610	13882	28610	HARDWOOD DISTILLATION PRODUCTS
28620	61237	28620	SOFTWOOD DISTILLATION PRODUCTS
28630	29277	28630	GUM NAVAL STORE
28650	15201	28650	REPORT TOTAL OF - NATURAL DYEING MATERIALS; NATURAL TANNING MATERIALS
28710	658776	28711 28712	MIXED FERTILIZERS-COMPLETE AND INCOMPLETE FERTILIZER MATERIALS OF ORGANIC ORIGIN

NEW SIC	CENSUS VALUE OF SHIPMENTS	OLD SIC	DESCRIPTION
28810	465669	28713	SUPERPHOSPHATE
28820	1116515	28810	COTTON OIL MILL PRODUCTS
		28820	LINSEED OIL MILL PRODUCTS
		28830	SOYBEAN OIL MILL PRODUCTS
		28840	VEGETABLE OIL MILL PRODUCTS, OTHER THAN SPECIFIED ABOVE - INCLUDE PEANUT, COCONUT, CASTOR. HYDROGENATED VEGETABLE
		28850	MARINE ANIMAL OIL MILL PRODUCTS - EXCLUDE VITAMIN OILS (28332)
28860	365944	28861	GREASE AND TALLOW
		28862	FEED AND FERTILIZER BYPRODUCTS - INCLUDE TANKAGE, MEAT SCRAPS AND BONEMEAL
28870	51628	28870	FATTY ACIDS
28890	28447	28891	RAW AND ACIDULATED SOAP STOCK AND FOOTS (ALL TYPES)
		28892	STEARIN AND OTHER ANIMAL OIL MILL PRODUCTS OTHER THAN FATTY ACIDS
28910	145868	28910	PRINTING INK
28920	26550	28920	ESSENTIAL OILS
28931	50600	2893	PERFUMES-TOILET WATERS AND COLOGNES--INCLUDE COMPOUND PERFUME BASES AND CONCRETES
28932	128707	28931	HAIR PREPARATIONS - INCLUDE SHAMPOOS, TONICS, PERMANENT WAVE SOLUTIONS AND KITS
28933	87330	28933	DENTIFRICES
28934	263741	28934	COSMETICS AND TOILET PREPARATIONS - EXCLUDE PERFUMES, TOILET WATERS, COLOGNES, HAIR PREPARATIONS AND DENTIFRICES
28941	55953	289-1	GLUE (VEGETABLE AND ANIMAL ONLY)
28942	32300	28912	GELATIN - EXCLUDE READY-TO-MIX DESSERTS (20991)
28950	89385	28951, 28952	CARBON BLACK - CHANNEL (CONTACT) BLACK AND FURNACE BLACK INCLUDING THERMAL BLACKS-LAMP AND BONE BLACK ONLY
28960	142410	28960	COMPRESSED AND LIQUEFIED GASES (ACETYLENE-CARBON DIOXIDE-ELEMENTAL ETC.)
28970	185468	28970	AGRICULTURAL INSECTICIDE AND FUNGICIDE PREPARATIONS.
28980	57313	28980	SALT (SODIUM CHLORIDE--EDIBLE)
28991	41780	28991	HOUSEHOLD INSECTICIDES AND REPELLENTS - INCLUDE LIVESTOCK SPRAYS, ANIMAL DIPS, RODENT POISONS AND MOTH CONTROL AGENTS
28992	20104	28992	WEED KILLERS

NEW SIC	CENSUS VALUE OF SHIPMENTS	OLD SIC	DESCRIPTION
30210	137418	30210	RUBBER FOOTWEAR - INCLUDE BOOTS, ARCTICS, GAITERS, RUBBERS, ETC.
30310	53269	30310	RECLAIMED RUBBER
30991	67052	30991	CAMELBACK AND TIRE REPAIR MATERIALS
30992	123084	30992	RUBBER AND PLASTIC HEELS AND SOLES - INCLUDE SOLING SLABS AND TOPLIFT SHEETS
30993	894113	30993	MECHANICAL RUBBER OR PLASTIC GOODS
30994	48021	30994	DRUGGIST AND MEDICAL SUNDRIES - INCLUDE WATER BOTTLES, ICE BAGES AND CAPS, ETC.
30995	264869	30995	RUBBER PRODUCTS N.E.C.
31110	879549	31111	CATTLE HIDE AND KIP SIDE LEATHERS
		31112	CALF AND WHLE KIP LEATHERS
		31113	SHEEP AND LAMB LEATHERS
		31114	LEATHERS OTHER THAN CATTLE, CALF AND SHEEP
31210	57738	31211	INDUSTRIAL LEATHER BELTING
		31212	LEATHER PACKINGS, OIL AND GREASE RETAINERS, AND WASHERS
		31213	TEXTILE LEATHERS, AND OTHER INDUSTRIAL LEATHER PRODUCTS
31310	248640	31311	BOOT AND SHOE CUT STOCK
		31312	PLATFORMS, HEELS, HEEL BLOCKS, AND OTHER BOOT AND SHOE FINDINGS - EXCEPT CUT STOCK
31410	1680435	31411	MEN'S YOUTH'S, AND BOYS' SHOES, EXCEPT ATHLETIC SHOES, PLAYSHOES AND MEN'S WORK SHOES
		31412	MEN'S WORK SHOES
		31413	WOMEN'S MISSES', AND CHILDREN'S SHOES - EXCEPT ATHLETIC SHOES
		31414	INFANTS' AND BABIES' SHOES
		31415	ATHLETIC SHOES
		31416	PLAYSHOES
31420	82612	31420	SLIPPERS FOR HOUSEWEAR
31610	129447	31610	SUITCASES, BRIEFCASES, BAGS TRUNKS, AND OTHER LUGGAGE - INCLUDE NON-LEATHER
31710	169321	31710	WOMEN'S HANDBAGS AND PURSES - INCLUDE NON-LEATHER
31720	46040	31720	LEATHER BILLFOLDS, WALLETS, KEY CASES, AND OTHER SMALLER LEATHER GOODS
31990	44195	31990	MISCELLANEOUS LEATHER GOODS OTHERS THAN SADDLERY, HARNESS, AND WHIPS
32110	235119	32112	SHEET (WINDOW) GLASS
		32113	PLATE GLASS
		32114	FLAT GLASS OTHER THAN LAMINATED, SHEET AND PLATE

NEW SIC	OLD SIC	CENSUS VALUE OF SHIPMENTS	DESCRIPTION
28993	28993	385166	REPORT TOTAL OF THE FOLLOWING CATEGORIES: ADHESIVES OR CEMENT (IF RUBBER OR ASBESTOS, SPECIFY); STAMP PAD INKS AND WRITING INKS; SIZES; CHEMICAL SPECIALTIES, AUTOMOTIVE CHEMICALS, NON-PERSONAL DEODORANTS, DISINFECTANTS, CHEMICAL FOUNDRY SUPPLIES, METAL TREATING COMPOUNDS, ROSIN AND OTHER SIZES, FRIT, ETC.; CHEMICAL SPECIALTIES, N.E.C. - INCLUDE AUTOMOTIVE CHEMICAL FOUNDRY SUPPLIES, CATALYTIC AGENTS - EXCLUDE THOSE PRODUCTS REPORTED AS OTHER FURNISHED PETROLEUM PRODUCTS.
29110	29110	4732042	GASOLINE - INCLUDE AVIATION, AUTOMOTIVE, AND ALL OTHER FINISHED GASOLINES
29111	29111	433324	KEROSENE
29112	29112	1410129	DISTILLATE FUEL OIL
29113	29113	758381	RESIDUAL FUEL OIL
29115	29115	65722	LUBRICATING-OIL BASE STOCKS - INCLUDE LIGHT, MEDIUM, HEAVY NEUTRAL AND RESIDUAL STOCKS
29116	29116	121947	LUBRICATING GREASES MADE IN PETROLEUM REFINERIES
29117	29117	148068	ASPHALT
29118	29118	98134	UNFINISHED OILS - INCLUDE CRACKING STOCK, UNFINISHED PETROLEUM OILS, EXCLUDE LUBRICATING-OIL BASE STOCKS NATURAL GAS AND CYCLE CONDENSATES
29119	29119	200478	PETROLATUM, PETROLEUM COKE, ROAD OIL, STILL GAS SOLD, AND OTHER FINISHED PETROLEUM PRODUCTS
29320	29321 29322 29323	1278958	COKE, SCREENING AND BREEZE-MADE IN BYPRODUCT OVENS COKE-OVEN GAS OTHER COKE-OVEN PRODUCTS
29510	29510	84345	PAVING MIXTURES AND BLOCKS
29520	29521 29522	423995	ASPHALT AND TAR ROOFING-SIDINGS AND FELTS ASPHALT AND TAR ROOF COATINGS-CEMENTS AND PITCHES
29910	29911	34470	FUEL BRIQUETS
29920	29924 29925 29926 29927	787594	LUBRICATING OILS LUBRICATING OIL BASE STOCKS LUBRICATING GREASES BLENDED AND COMPOUNDED PETROLEUM PRODUCTS OTHER THAN LUBRICATING OILS AND GREASES
29990	29990	15710	PRODUCTS OF PETROLEUM AND COAL N.E.C
30110	30110	1602269	TIRES AND INNER TUBES

275

NEW SIC	CENSUS VALUE OF SHIPMENTS	OLD SIC	DESCRIPTION
32210	472418	32210	GLASS CONTAINERS
32290	324696	32290	PRESSED AND BLOWN GLASS AND GLASSWARE - EXCEPT GLASS CONTAINERS
32311	189242	32311	LAMINATED GLASS
32312	60872	32312	MIRRORS
32313	122501	32313	GLASS PRODUCTS OTHER THAN LAMINATED GLASS AND MIRRORS
32410	604011	32413	HYDRAULIC CEMENT - INCLUDE COST OF SHIPPING CONTAINERS
32510	201804	32510	CLAY BRICK AND HOLLOW TILE
32530	61579	32530	CLAY FLOOR AND WALL TILE - EXCEPT QUARRY TILE
32540	53402	32540	CLAY SEWER PIPE
32550	126686	32550	CLAY REFRACTORIES
32590	38185	32590	STRUCTURAL CLAY PRODUCTS OTHER THAN BRICK, HOLLOW TILE, FLOOR AND WALL TILE, SEWER PIPE AND CLAY REFRACTORIES - INCLUDE DRAIN TILE, QUARRY TILE, ETC. (SPECIFY KIND)
32610	532931	32610 34311 34312	VITREOUS AND SEMIVITREOUS PLUMBING FIXTURES METAL PLUMBING FIXTURES PLUMBING FIXTURE FITTINGS AND TRIM (BRASS GOODS)
32620	113569	32620 32630	VITREOUS-CHINA TABLE AND KITCHEN ARTICLES FINE EARTHENWARE (WHITEWARE) TABLE AND KITCHEN ARTICLES
32640	74640	32640	PORCELAIN AND STEATITE ELECTRICAL SUPPLIES
32691	30711	32691	ART, DECORATIVE, AND NOVELTY POTTERY WARE
32692	20482	32692	POTTERY PRODUCTS N.E.C.
32710	563470	32711 32712 32713	CONCRETE BLOCK AND BRICK CONCRETE PIPE PRECAST CONCRETE PRODUCTS OTHER THAN CONCRETE BLOCK, BRICK AND PIPE
32720	206390	32720	GYPSUM PRODUCTS
32740	84613	32741	LIME - INCLUDE COST OF SHIPPING CONTAINERS
32750	115664	32750	MINERAL WOOL (FROM ROCK, SLAG, AND GLASS)

NEW SIC	CENSUS VALUE OF SHIPMENTS	OLD SIC	DESCRIPTION
32810	109875	32813	CUT-LIMESTONE AND LIMESTONE PRODUCTS MADE IN PLANTS NOT OPERATED IN CONJUNCTION WITH MINES OR QUARRIES
32910	324713	32911 32912 32913	NONMETALLIC ABRASIVES METAL ABRASIVES BUFFING AND POLISHING WHEELS AND LAPS
32922	22088	32922	ASBESTOS TEXTILES
32923	76239	32923	ASBESTOS FRICTION MATERIALS
32924	66803	32924	ASPHALT FLOOR TILE
32925	66433	32925	ASBESTOS-CEMENT SHINGLES AND CLAPBOARD
32926	23179	32926	ASBESTOS-CEMENT FLAT AND CORRUGATED SHEETS AND WALLBOARD
32927	21943	32927	ASBESTOS-CEMENT PRODUCTS N.E.C. - INCLUDE PIPE, CONDUIT AND DUCTS
32930	161789	32931 32932 32933	ASBESTOS INSULATIONS GASKETS, ALL TYPES OF MATERIAL PACKING - EXCLUDE LEATHER (31212) RUBBER (30993) AND METAL
32950	122106	32951 32952	LIGHTWEIGHT AGGREGATE - EXCLUDE VERMICULITE MINERALS AND EARTHS, GROUND OR OTHERWISE TREATED, MADE IN PLANTS NOT OTHERWISE OPERATED IN CONJUNCTION WITH MINE
32960	2554	32960	SAND-LIME BRICK, BLOCK, AND TILE
32970	111971	32970	NONCLAY REFRACTORIES
32990	52065	32992	SHEET MICA PRODUCTS, EXCEPT RADIO PARTS
33110	2477678	33112 33113	PIG IRON BLAST-FURNACE PRODUCTS OTHER THAN PIG IRON AND FERRO-ALLOYS AND OTHER ADDITIVES
33120	94744	33120	STEEL INGOTS
33121	529786	33121	SEMIFINISHED STEEL SHAPES AND FORMS - INCLUDE BLOOMS, BILLETS, TUBE ROUNDS SKELP, WIRE RODS ETC.
33122	525000	33122	STEEL PLATES
33123	1505644	33123	HOT-ROLLED SHEET AND STRIP
33124	716555	33124	TIN, TERNEPLATE, AND BLACKPLATE
33125	329447	33125	STRUCTURAL SHAPES AND PILING

NEW SIC	OLD SIC	CENSUS VALUE OF SHIPMENTS	DESCRIPTION
33126	33126	993157	HOT-ROLLED BARS AND BAR SHAPES - INCLUDE CONCRETE REINFORCING BARS TOOL STEEL BARS ETC.
33128	33128	2125770	VALUE OF ALL STEEL MILL PRODUCTS TRANSFERRED TO OTHER PLANTS OF YOUR COMPANY INCLUDE VALUE INGOTS, BARS PLATES ETC.
33129	33129	324533	STEEL MILL SHAPES AND FORMS, N.E.C.
33130	33131	345956	ELECTRIC FURNACE FERROALLOYS AND OTHER ADDITIVES
33210	33210	1422520	GRAY IRON CASTINGS
33220	33220	213420	MALLEABLE IRON CASTINGS
33230	33230	474610	STEEL CASTINGS (CARBON, ALLOY AND STAINLESS)
33310	33311 33312	690963	REFINED UNALLOYED COPPER PRODUCED FROM ORE COPPER SMELTER PRODUCTS - INCLUDE BLISTER AND ANODE COPPER, MATTE, SPEISS, FLUE DUST, RESIDUES ETC.
33320	33321	213773	LEAD SMELTER PRODUCTS - INCLUDE BASE BULLION, MATTE, SPEISS ETC.
33330	33331	259667	ZINC RESIDUES AND OTHER MISCELLANEOUS ZINC SMELTER PRODUCTS
33411	33411	128350	COPPER BASE ALLOY INGOTS PRODUCED FOR SALE OR INTERPLANT TRANSFER
33412	33412	160098	LEAD AND TIN-BASE ALLOY INGOTS PRODUCED FOR SALES OR INTERPLANT TRANSFER
33413	33413	40026	ZINC-BASE ALLOY INGOTS PRODUCED FOR SALE OR INTERPLANT TRANSFER
33414	33414	247143	REFINED UNALLOYED ALUMINUM AND ALUMINUM BASE ALLOYS PRODUCED FROM SCRAP, AND ALUMINUM-BASED ALLOY INGOTS
33415	33415	123238	PRECIOUS METAL BASE ALLOY INGOTS PRODUCED FOR SALE OR INTERPLANT TRANSFER
33418	33418	999999	NONFERROUS METALS (OTHER THAN COPPER, LEAD, ZINC, ALUMINUM AND PRECIOUS METALS) PRODUCE FROM SCRAP
33440	33448	999999	UNKNOWN. ONE FIRM: PHELPS DODGE. VALUE OF SHIP. 27694
33517	33517	1044288	ROLLED, DRAWN, AND EXTRUDED COPPER AND COPPER BASE ALLOY MILL PRODUCTS OTHER THAN COPPER BASE ALLOY INGOTS
33526	33526	329634	ALUMINUM PLATE, SHEET, AND STRIP
33527	33527	193780	ROLLED, DRAWN AND EXTRUDED ALUMINUM MILL PRODUCTS OTHER THAN ALUMINUM BASE ALLOY INGOTS ETC.

278

NEW SIC	CENSUS VALUE OF SHIPMENTS	OLD SIC	DESCRIPTION
33597	10716	33597	ROLLED, DRAWN AND EXTRUDED MAGNESIUM MILL PRODUCTS
33598	105750	33598	ROLLED, DRAWN AND EXTRUDED NONFERROUS METAL MILL PRODUCTS OTHER THAN LEAD, TIN, ZINC AND PRECIOUS METAL BASE ALLOY INGOTS; AND ROLLED, DRAWN, AND EXTRUDED MAGNESIUM MILL PRODUCTS
33610	726810	33610	NONFERROUS CASTINGS (INCLUDING DIE CASTINGS)
33910	666925	33911 33912 33913	DROP, UPSET AND PRESS STEEL FORGINGS (ONLY CLOSED DIE) PRESS AND HAMMER STEEL FORGINGS (ONLY OPEN DIE) WROUGHT IRON FORGINGS
33920	683579	33921 33925 33926 33927 33928 33929	NAILS, SPIKES, AND BRADS PRODUCED FROM WIRE DRAWN IN THIS ESTABLISHMENT ALUMINUM WIRE DRAWN FROM PURCHASED RODS OR BARS COPPER WIRE DRAWN FROM PURCHASED RODS OR BARS STEEL WIRE DRAWN FROM PURCHASED RODS OR BARS - SHIPPED TO OTHER COMPANIES INTERPLANT TRANSFERS OF STEEL WIRE DRAWN FROM PURCHASED RODS OR BARS WIRE OTHER THAN ALUMINUM, COPPER, AND STEEL, DRAWN FROM PURCHASED RODS OR BARS
33930	1303083	33937 33938	STEEL PIPE AND TUBES MADE FROM PURCHASED MATERIALS INTERPLANT TRANSFERS OF STEEL PIPE MADE FROM PURCHASED MATERIAL
33993	1286098	33993 33997	COLD-ROLLED SHEET AND STRIP MADE FROM PURCHASED HOT-ROLLED MATERIAL COLD-ROLLED AND COLD-FINISHED STEEL BARS AND BAR SHAPES MADE FROM PURCHASED HOT-ROLLED MATERIALS
33994	52928	33994	NONFERROUS FORGINGS
33935	38260	33995	METAL POWDERS
33996	265272	33996	COLD-FINISHED BARS AND BARS SHAPES MADE FROM PURCHASED HOT-ROLLED MATERIALS
34110	1061419	3411 34113 34114	METAL CANS FLUID MILK SHIPPING CONTAINERS TINWARE OTHER THAN METAL CANS AND FLUID MILL SHIPPING CONTAINERS
34211	111328	34211	CUTLERY, SCISSORS, SHEARS TRIMMERS, AND SNIPS
34212	69895	34212	SAFETY RAZORS AND BLADES
34220	63321	34220	EDGE TOOLS
34230	254479	34231 34232	MECHANICS' HAND SERVICE TOOLS HAND TOOLS OTHER THAN CUTLERY, SCISSORS, SHEARS, TRIMMERS, AND SNIPS, EDGE TOOLS, ETC.
34240	27110	34240	FILES, RASPS AND FILE ACCESSORIES
34250	66241	34250	HAND SAWS, SAW BLADES AND SAW ACCESSORIES

279

NEW SIC	CENSUS VALUE OF SHIPMENTS	OLD SIC	DESCRIPTION
34291	384912	34291	TRANSPORTATION EQUIPMENT HARDWARE
34292	52271	34292	FURNITURE AND CABINET HARDWARE
34293	19199	34293	VACUUM BOTTLES AND JUGS
34295	243324	34295	BUILDERS' HARDWARE
34296	154427	34296	HARDWARE N.E.C.
34320	64433	34320	OIL BURNERS
34390	205484	34390	WARM AIR FURNACES AND PARTS
34391	81112	34391	CAST IRON HEATING BOILERS
		34392	CAST IRON RADIATORS AND CONVECTORS
34393	21729	34393	STEEL AND NONFERROUS CONVECTORS
34394	125687	34394	WATER HEATERS, EXCEPT ELECTRIC
34395	88248	34395	DOMESTIC HEATING STOVES (SPACE HEATERS)
34396	276934	34396	DOMESTIC COOKING STOVES, RANGES AND APPLIANCES - EXCEPT ELECTRIC
34397	33486	34397	COMMERCIAL COOKING AND FOOD WARMING EQUIPMENT, EXCEPT ELECTRIC
34398	55794	34398	STEEL HEATING BOILERS (15 PSI AND UNDER OR EQUIVALENT)
34399	53790	34399	COOKING AND HEATING EQUIP. N.E.C. - EXCEPT ELECTRIC (35671,36191,36212,36214,36215)
34410	1104104	34413	ORNAMENTAL METAL WORK - INCLUDE STAIRS, RAILINGS, FIRE ESCAPES, STEEL GRATINGS, ETC.
		34414	PREFABRICATED AND PORTABLE METAL BUILDINGS AND PARTS
		34415	MISCELLANEOUS METAL BUILDING MATERIALS - INCLUDE EXPANDED METAL LATH, CORNER BEADS, FABRICATED CONCRETE REINFORCING BARS, ETC.
		34416	FABRICATED STRUCTURAL IRON AND STEEL - EXCLUDE RECEIPTS FROM ERECTION OR INSTALLATION
34420	390088	34421	METAL DOORS AND METAL FRAMES
		34422	METAL WINDOW SASH AND FRAMES
		34423	METAL MOLDING AND TRIM, AND STORE FRONTS
34431	243620	34431	METAL TANKS, COMPLETE AT FACTORY
34432	173926	34432	FABRICATED STEEL PLATE (CUT, PUNCHED, OR SHAPED FOR ASSEMBLY ON JOB)
34433	140451	34433	POWER BOILERS, PARTS AND ATTACHMENTS (OVER 15 PSI STEAM WORKING PRESSURE)
34434	85419	34434	GAS CYLINDERS, SMOKE STACKS AND OTHER STACKS (IRON AND STEEL) AND OTHER PLATE STEEL

NEW SIC	CENSUS VALUE OF SHIPMENTS	OLD SIC	DESCRIPTION
			FABRICATING
34440	561380	34440	SHEET-METAL PRODUCTS
34610	77868	34611	VITREOUS-ENAMELED COOKING AND KITCHEN UTENSILS - INCLUDE HOUSEHOLD, HOSPITAL AND COMMERCIAL
		34612	VITREOUS-ENAMELED PRODUCTS OTHER THAN VITREOUS-ENAMELED HOSPITAL AND COMMERCIAL COOKING AND KITCHEN UTENSILS
34630	1752129	34631	JOB STAMPINGS - EXCEPT AUTOMOTIVE
		34633	PAILS (EXCEPT SHIPPING CONTAINERS), ASH CANS AND GARBAGE CANS
		34634	METAL HOME CANNING CLOSURES
		34635	METAL COMMERCIAL CLOSURES - EXCEPT CROWNS
		34636	CROWNS
		34637	PERFORATED METAL END PRODUCTS AND OTHER STAMPED AND PRESSED METAL END PRODUCTS
		34638	JOB STAMPINGS - AUTOMOTIVE
		34639	STAMPED AND SPUN COOKING AND KITCHEN UTENSILS (HOUSEHOLD, HOSPITAL AND COMMERCIAL) EXCLUDE VITREOUS ENAMELED
34650	32963	34650	ENAMELING, JAPANNING, AND LACQUERING
34660	28472	34660	GALVANIZING AND OTHER HOT-DIP COATING
34670	23657	34670	ENGRAVING ON METAL
34680	235021	34680	ELECTROPLATING, PLATING, AND POLISHING
34710	589319	34711	INCANDESCENT LIGHTING FIXTURES - EXCEPT SPECIALTIES LISTED SEPARATELY BELOW
		34712	INCANDESCENT PORTABLE LAMPS
		34714	INCANDESCENT VEHICULAR LIGHTING EQUIPMENT
		34714	INCANDESCENT HAND PORTABLE LIGHTING EQUIPMENT
		34715	FLUORESCENT LIGHTING EQUIPMENT (FIXTURES AND PORTABLE LAMPS) AND PARTS
		34716	NONELECTRIC LIGHTING EQUIPMENT
		34718	INCANDESCENT STREET AND HIGHWAY LIGHTING EQUIPMENT
		34719	SPECIALIZED INCANDESCENT LIGHTING EQUIPMENT SUCH AS SEARCHLIGHTS, FLOODLIGHTS, MARINE CHANNEL, AVIATION GROUND TYPE, RAILWAY ROUTE ETC. (OTHER THAN PORTABLE LAMPS, VEHICULAR LIGHTING EQUIPMENT, AND STREET AND HIGHWAY LIGHTING EQUIPMENT, INCANDESCENT)
34892	190236	34892	WIRE ROPE, AND CABLE - EXCEPT INSULATED MADE FROM PURCHASED WIRE
34893	111246	34893	FENCING AND FENCE GATES - INCLUDE CHAIN LINK, FIELD, ETC. MADE FROM PURCHASED WIRE
34894	135072	34894	WIRE CLOTH AND WOVEN WIRE PRODUCTS MADE FROM PURCHASED WIRE
34895	321254	34895	WIRE SPRINGS MADE FROM PURCHASED WIRE
34896	252628	34896	WIRE PRODUCTS N.E.C. SUCH AS BARBED WIRE, WELDED WIRE FABRIC, GARMENT HANGERS, PAPER CLIPS MADE FROM PURCHASED

NEW SIC	CENSUS VALUE OF SHIPMENTS	OLD SIC	DESCRIPTION
34911	218011	34911	METAL AMMUNITION BOXES AND CHESTS
34912	43818	34912	STEEL SHIPPING PACKAGES, KEGS, AND PAILS (1 TO 12 GALLONS)-EXCLUDE BEER BARRELS
34913	7501	34913	STEEL AND ALUMINUM BEER BARRELS
34914	135661	34914	STEEL SHIPPING BARRELS AND DRUMS (OVER 12 GALLON CAP.) EXCLUDE BEER BARRELS
34930	105608	34930	STEEL SPRINGS, EXCEPT WIRE
34940	643688	34941	BOLTS, NUTS, SCREWS, WASHERS, RIVETS, AND OTHER INDUSTRIAL FASTENERS - STANDARD TYPE ONLY
		34942	SPECIALS - PRODUCTS OTHER THAN STANDARD TYPE FASTENERS - MADE ON THE SAME TYPE OF MACHINES (HEADERS, THREADERS ETC.)
34950	324124	34950	SCREW-MACHINE PRODUCTS
34960	37968	34960	COLLAPSIBLE TUBES
34970	99454	34970	FOIL AND LEAF
34990	117848	34990	FABRICATED METAL PRODUCTS N.E.C.
35110	266195	35111	STEAM AND HYDRAULIC TURBINES; STEAM ENGINES; PARTS FOR STEAM ENGINES, TURBINES AND HYDRAULIC TURBINES
		35112	STEAM AND HYDRAULIC TURBINE GENERATOR-SET UNITS
35191	147449	35191	GASOLINE ENGINES - EXCLUDE OUTBOARD, AIRCRAFT, AUTOMOBILE, TRUCK AND BUS
35192	167386	35192	DIESEL ENGINES - EXCEPT TRUCK AND BUS
35193	33943	35193	GAS ENGINES
35194	164557	35194	PARTS AND ATTACHMENTS FOR INTERNAL COMBUSTION ENGINES - EXCEPT AIRCRAFT, AUTOMOBILE, TRUCK, AND BUS
35195	41037	35195	OUTBOARD MOTORS
35199	48777	35199	INTERNAL COMBUSTION ENGINES N.E.C.
35211	367507	35211	WHEEL-TYPE TRACTORS - INCLUDE PARTS AND ATTACHMENTS FOR REPLACEMENT AND REPAIR
35212	190756	35212	TRACK-LAYING TYPE TRACTORS - INCLUDE PARTS AND ATTACHMENTS FOR REPLACEMENT AND REPAIR
35213	28404	35213	GARDEN TRACTORS - INCLUDE PARTS AND ATTACHMENTS FOR REPLACEMENT AND REPAIR
35214	59798	35214	TRACTOR PARTS AND ATTACHMENTS, SHIPPED TO OTHER PLANTS PRODUCING TRACTORS

NEW SIC	OLD SIC	CENSUS VALUE OF SHIPMENTS	DESCRIPTION
35221	35221	663581	FARM MACHINES AND EQUIPMENT (EXCEPT TRACTORS)
35222	35222	173439	PARTS AND ATTACHMENTS FOR FARM MACHINES AND EQUIPMENT. SHIPPED TO OTHER PLANTS PRODUCING FARM EQUIPMENT.
35227	35227	99924	LAWN MOWERS
35311	35311	113548	CRANES, HOISTS, WINCHES, AND DERRICKS - EXCEPT (35631,35312,35320)
35312	35312	222580	POWER CRANES, DRAGLINES, AND SHOVELS; PARTS AND FRONT END ATTACHMENTS FOR POWER CRANES, DRAG LINES AND SHOVELS
35313	35313	53840	MIXERS, PAVERS, AND RELATED EQUIPMENT
35314	35314	102545	SPECIALIZED MINING MACHINERY AND EQUIPMENT
35315	35315	71120	CRUSHING, PULVERIZING, AND SCREENING MACHINERY
35317	35317	216422	EXCAVATING AND ROAD-CONSTRUCTION AND MAINTENANCE MACHINERY-EXCEPT POWER CRANES, DRAGLINES AND SHOVELS
35319	35319	131536	CONSTRUCTION, MINING, AND SIMILAR MACHINERY N.E.C
35320	3532C	333048	OIL-FIELD MACHINERY AND TOOLS
35411	3541	315743	MACHINE TOOLS. EXCLUDE HOMESHOP TYPE
35418	3541B	18539	MACHINE TOOLS DESIGNED PRIMARILY FOR HOME WORKSHOPS, GAARAGES AND SERVICE SHOPS, EXCEPT POWER-DRIVEN HAND TOOLS
35419	35413	12594	REBUILT MACHINE TOOLS
35421	35421	142731	ROLLING MILL MACHINERY
35422	35422	91050	METALWORKING PRESSES - EXCEPT FORGING
35423	3542.3	112668	POWER-DRIVEN HAND TOOLS - INCLUDE PARTS, ATTACHMENTS AND ACCESSORIES
35425	35425	24319	ACETYLENE WELDING AND CUTTING APPARATUS
35426	35426	144097	METALWORKING MACHINERY N.E.C
35431	35431	454632	JIGS, FIXTURES, FORMING, STAMPING, AND PIERCING PUNCHES AND DIES, DIE SETS AND SUBPRESSES
35432	35432	262629	SMALL CUTTING TOOLS FOR MACHINE TOOLS AND METAL-WORKING MACHINERY

NEW SIC	OLD SIC	CENSUS VALUE OF SHIPMENTS	DESCRIPTION
35433	35433	43333	PRECISION MEASURING TOOLS
35434	35434	75229	METALWORKING ACCESSORIES N.E.C.
35511	35511	70614	DAIRY AND MILK PRODUCTS PLANT MACHINERY AND EQUIPMENT
35512	35512	48765	BAKERY MACHINERY AND EQUIPMENT
35513	35513	42683	BOTTLING MACHINERY - EXCEPT DAIRY
35514	35514	124041	FOOD-PRODUCTS MACHINERY N.E.C.
35520	35520	428880	TEXTILE MACHINERY
35530	35531	137347	WOODWORKING MACHINERY-OTHER THAN THAT DESIGNED PRIMARILY FOR HOME WORKSHOPS, GARAGES, AND SERVICE SHOPS
	35538		WOODWORKING MACHINERY DESIGNED PRIMARILY FOR HOME WORKSHOPS, GARAGES AND SERVICE SHOPS-EXCEPT POWER-DRIVEN HAND TOOLS (35423)
35540	35540	114994	PAPER-INDUSTRIES MACHINERY
35550	35550	200682	PRINTING-TRADES MACHINERY AND EQUIPMENT
35591	35591	64131	CHEMICAL MANUFACTURING INDUSTRIES MACHINERY AND EQUIPMENT
35592	35592	117844	FOUNDRY MACHINERY AND EQUIPMENT-INCLUDE FOUNDRY PATTERNS AND MOLDS
35593	35593	52740	PLASTICS-WORKING MACHINERY AND EQUIPMENT
35594	35594	45649	RUBBER-WORKING MACHINERY AND EQUIPMENT
35595	35595	25698	PETROLEUM REFINERY MACHINERY AND EQUIPMENT
35599	35599	254010	SPECIAL INDUSTRY MACHINERY AND EQUIPMENT N.E.C.
35611	35611	257252	INDUSTRIAL PUMPS-INCLUDE ROTARY, CENTRIFUGAL, RECIPROCATING, TURBINE ETC.
35612	35612	60204	DOMESTIC WATER SYSTEMS
35613	35613	113129	AIR COMPRESSORS
35614	35614	140199	PUMPS, GAS COMPRESSORS, AND PUMPING EQUIPMENT N.E.C. - INCLUDE PARTS AND ATTACHMENTS FOR PUMPS AND COMPRESSORS
35620	35620	102195	ELEVATORS AND MOVING STAIRWAYS
35630	35631	240696	OVERHEAD TRAVELING CRANES AND MONORAIL SYSTEMS
	35635		CONVEYORS AND CONVEYING EQUIPMENT- INCLUDE UNDERGROUND MINE CONVEYORS

NEW SIC	CENSUS VALUE OF SHIPMENTS	OLD SIC	DESCRIPTION
35640	120785	35640	INDUSTRIAL FANS AND BLOWERS
35650	166259	35650	INDUSTRIAL TRUCKS, TRACTORS, TRAILERS, AND STACKERS
35660	463833	35661 35662 35663	PLAIN BEARINGS AND BUSHINGS SPEED REDUCERS, GEARS, AND INDUSTRIAL HIGH SPEED DRIVES MECHANICAL POWER-TRANSMISSION EQUIPMENT N.E.C.
35671	19779	35671	ELECTRIC INDUSTRIAL FURNACES AND OVENS
35672	33717	35672	FUEL-FIRES INDUSTRIAL FURNACES AND OVENS
35673	18410	35673	PARTS AND ATTACHMENTS FOR INDUSTRIAL FURNACES AND OVENS
35630	19153	3568C	MECHANICAL STOKERS
35690	327745	3569- 3569-	HEAT EXCHANGERS UNKNOWN
35710	349670	3571m	COMPUTING MACHINES
35720	130410	35720	TYPEWRITERS
35760	53274	3576D	SCALES AND BALANCES
35791	23586	3579I	AUTOMATIC MERCHANDISING MACHINES-EXCLUDE REFRIGERATED
35792	49355	3579I	AMUSEMENT AND OTHER COIN-OPERATED MACHINES
35793	133111	3579I	OFFICE AND STORE MACHINES, N.E.C - INCLUDE TIME-RECORDING CLOCKS
35810	532084	35811 35812	HOUSEHOLD MECHANICAL WASHING MACHINES HOUSEHOLD LAUNDRY EQUIPMENT, N.E.C. SUCH AS WRINGERS DRIERS AND IRONERS
35820	77441	35820	COMMERCIAL LAUNDRY, DRY-CLEANING AND PRESSING MACHINES
35830	170636	35830	SEWING MACHINES
35840	167260	35841	HOUSEHOLD VACUUM CLEANERS - INCLUDE ATTACHMENTS AND CLEANING TOOLS
35851	925131	35151	HOUSEHOLD MECHANICAL REFRIGERATORS - INCLUDE ELECTRIC AND GAS
35852	132469	35352	HOME AND FARM FREEZERS
35853	231034	35353	UNITARY COMMERCIAL REFRIGERATION EQUIPMENT

NEW SIC	CENSUS VALUE OF SHIPMENTS	OLD SIC	DESCRIPTION
35854	80886	35854	COMPRESSORS AND COMPRESSOR UNITS
35855	106189	35855	CONDENSING UNITS
35856	425589	35856	REFRIGERATION MACHINERY AND AIR CONDITIONING EQUIPMENT N.E.C.
35860	121793	35860	MEASURING AND DISPENSING PUMPS
35890	151852	35890	SERVICE-INDUSTRY AND HOUSEHOLD MACHINES, N.E.C.
35910	711778	35911	VALVES AND FITTINGS FOR PIPING SYSTEMS - EXCLUDE PLUMBING AND HEATING VALVES
		35912	PLUMBING AND HEATING VALVES AND SPECIALTIES - EXCLUDE PLUMBING FIXTURE FITTINGS AND TRIM (34312)
		35913	VALVES AND FITTINGS - EXCLUDE PLUMBING FIXTURE FITTINGS AND TRIM (34312), N.E.C.
35920	154623	35920	FABRICATED PIPE MADE FROM PURCHASED PIPE
35930	450495	35930	BALL AND ROLLER BEARINGS AND COMPONENTS
35990	627114	35990	MACHINE SHOP PRODUCTS
		35994	UNKNOWN
36110	491959	36111	CURRENT-CARRYING WIRING DEVICES
		36112	NONCURRENT-CARRYING WIRING DEVICES AND SUPPLIES
		36113	POLE LINE AND TRANSMISSION HARDWARE
36120	100554	36120	CARBON AND GRAPHITE PRODUCTS
36130	149800	36131	INTEGRATING INSTRUMENTS, ELECTRICAL
		36132	TEST EQUIPMENT FOR TESTING ELECTRICAL, RADIO AND COMMUNICATION CIRCUITS AND MOTORS
		36133	ELECTRICAL MEASURING INSTRUMENT N.E.C.
36140	888136	36141	FRACTIONAL HORSEPOWER MOTORS
		36142	INTEGRAL HORSEPOWER MOTORS AND GENERATORS-OTHER THAN FOR LAND TRANSPORTATION EQUIPMENT
		36143	PRIME MOVER GENERATOR SETS-OTHER THAN STEAM OR HYDRAULIC TURBINE
		36144	MOTOR-GENERATOR SETS AND OTHER ROTATING EQUIPMENT
		36145	MOTORS, GENERATORS, AND CONTROL APPARATUS (INCLUDING PARTS) FOR TRANSPORTATION EQUIPMENT
		36146	PARTS AND SUPPLIES FOR MOTORS, GENERATORS, AND MOTOR-GENERATOR SETS-EXCLUDE THOSE FOR LAND TRANSPORTATION EQUIPMENT
36151	83891	36151	SPECIALTY TRANFORMERS
36152	278041	36152	POWER AND DISTRIBUTION TRANSFORMERS
36153	43548	36153	TRANSFORMER PARTS AND SUPPLIES, POWER REGULATORS, BOOSTERS, AND REACTORS
36161	331736	36161	SWITCHGEAR AND SWITCHBOARD APPARATUS

NEW SIC	CENSUS VALUE OF SHIPMENTS	OLD SIC	DESCRIPTION
36162	200489	36162	INDUSTRIAL ELECTRICAL CONTROL EQUIPMENT-EXCEPT RAILWAY AND MOTOR VEHICLE CONTROLLERS(36145)
36163	168795	36163	DOMESTIC AUTOMATIC CONTROLS
36170	109825	36171 36172 36173	ARC WELDING MACHINES, COMPONENTS, AND ACCESSORIES-EXCEPT ELECTRODES ARC WELDING ELECTRODES RESISTANCE WELDERS, PARTS, COMPONENTS, ACCESSORIES AND ELECTRODES
36191	11337	36191	HIGH FREQUENCY INDUCTION AND DI-ELECTRIC HEATING APPARATUS
36192	33101	36192	CAPACITORS FOR INDUSTRIAL USE-POWER CAPACITORS, FLUORESCENT LAMP BALAST CAPACITORS, ETC. EXCLUDE (36614)
36193	57868	36-93	ELECTRICAL EQUIPMENT FOR INDUSTRIAL USE, N.E.C.
36211	60402	36211	ELECTRIC FANS, EXCEPT INDUSTRIAL TYPE-INCLUDE DESK, WALL BRACKET, HIGH PEDESTAL ETC.
36212	63522	36212	HOUSEHOLD WATER HEATERS, ELECTRIC (PERMANENT INSTALLATION TYPES ONLY)
36213	306004	36213	TOTAL OF DRY SHAVERS; SMALL HOUSEHOLD ELECTRIC APPLIANCES, INCLUDE IRONS, TOASTERS, FOOD MIXERS, ETC. - EXCLUDE
36214	218478	36214	HOUSEHOLD RANGES, ELECTRIC
36215	16639	36215	COMMERCIAL COOKING AND FOOD WARMING EQUIPMENT, ELECTRIC
36217	85000	36217	PARTS AND ACCESSORIES FOR ELECTRIC APPLIANCES
36310	879915	36317	INSULATED WIRE AND CABLE MADE FROM PURCHASED WIRE (PURCHASED WIRE INCLUDES WIRE TRANSFERRED FROM OTHER ESTABLISHMENTS OF SAME COMPANY AS WELL AS WERE PURCHASED FROM OTHER COMPANIES)
36410	486964	36410	ELECTRICAL EQUIPMENT FOR INTERNAL COMBUSTION ENGINES INCLUDING BATTERY-CHARGING GENERATORS, CRANKING MOTORS,ETC.
36510	243157	36511	ELECTRIC LAMPS (BULBS)
36512	1687073	36612	HOUSEHOLD RADIO RECEIVERS, TELEVISION SETS, RADIO-PHONOGRAPHS, PHONOGRAPHS, AND RECORD PLAYERS
36613	268611	36613	COMMERCIAL RADIO COMMUNICATIONS, RADIO NAVIGATION AIDS, AND RADIO AND TELEVISION BROADCAST EQUIPMENT
36614	23309	36164 36614	FUSES AND FUSE EQUIPMENT, UNDER 2300 VOLTS ELECTRONIC TYPE COMPONENTS FOR WIRE, RADIO, TELEVISION, AND PHONOGRAPH EQUIPMENT, INDUST. CONTROLS AND SPECIAL ELECTRONIC APPLICATIONS SUCH AS RADAR, INDUSTRIAL HEATING, ETC.
36615	46597	36615	RECORDERS, AMPLIFIERS, AUDIO EQUIPMENT AND RECORDING MAGNETIC TAPES AND WIRE

NEW SIC	CENSUS VALUE OF SHIPMENTS	OLD SIC	DESCRIPTION
36622	85172	36622	TOTAL OF TRANSMITTING TYPE TUBES - EXCLUDE X-RAY AND INDUSTRIAL TYPE TUBES; X-RAY EQUIPMENT AND X-RAY AND INDUSTRIAL TYPE TUBES
36623	197732	36623	RADIO RECEIVING-TYPE TUBES-EXCLUDE CATHODE RAY
36624	102870	36624	CATHODE RAY TUBES (TELEVISION RECEIVER TYPE)
36630	93852	36631 36632	PHONOGRAPH RECORDS RECORDING BLANKS (DISC AND CYLINDER)
36640	449546	36640	TELEPHONE AND TELEGRAPH EQUIPMENT
36690	86296	36690	COMMUNICATION EQUIPMENT N.E.C.
36910	318546	36911 36912 36913	STORAGE BATTERIES, S.L.I. TYPE STORAGE BATTERIES, OTHER THAN S.L.I. TYPE PARTS AND SUPPLIES FOR STORAGE BATTERIES
36920	95491	36920	PRIMARY BATTERIES (DRY AND WET)
36932	48244	36932	ELECTRO-THERAPEUTIC APPARATUS
36990	114905	36991 36992	ELECTRIC LAMP COMPONENTS, INCANDESCENT PRODUCTS AND COILS ELECTRICAL HEARING AIDS
37150	229685	37150	TRUCK TRAILERS AND PARTS-INCLUDE FULL AND SEMITRAILERS
37160	176853	37160	AUTOMOBILE TRAILERS AND PARTS
37171	9415476	37171	PASSENGER CARS, KNOCKED DOWN OR ASSEMBLED
37172	1843489	37172	TRUCK TRACTORS, TRUCK CHASSIS, AND TRUCKS PRODUCED FROM CHASSIS MADE IN THIS ESTABLISHMENT KNOCKED DOWN OR ASSEMBLED
37173	72632	37173	MOTOR COACHES (EXCEPT 37423) PRODUCED FROM CHASSIS MADE IN THIS ESTABLISHMENT
37174	999999	37174	TOTAL OF 37120 AND 37122
37175	999999	37175	TOTAL OF 37140 AND 37141
37176	18541	37176	FIRE-DEPARTMENT VEHICLES PRODUCED FROM CHASSIS MADE IN THIS ESTABLISHMENT
37177	999999	37177	AMPHIBIAN COMBAT VEHICLE OR CARRIER ASSEMBLY
37178	999999	37178	MOTOR CARRIAGE (FOR ARTILLERY PIECES) ASSEMBLY
37211	1813927	37211	COMPLETE AIRCRAFT, MILITARY TYPE

288

NEW SIC	CENSUS VALUE OF SHIPMENTS	OLD SIC	DESCRIPTION
37214	88043	37214	MODIFICATIONS CONVERSIONS AND OVERHAUL OF PREVIOUSLY DELIVERED AIRCRAFT
37220	447211	37221	AIRCRAFT ENGINES - EXCEPT PARTS
		37222	AIRCRAFT ENGINE PARTS
		37223	RECEIPTS FOR RESEARCH AND DEVELOPMENT WORK ON AIRCRAFT ENGINES
37230	50468	37231	RECEIPTS FOR RESEARCH AND DEVELOPMENT WORK ON AIRCRAFT PROPELLERS
		37232	AIRCRAFT PROPELLERS AND PARTS
37290	1351635	37291	AIRCRAFT PARTS AND AUXILIARY EQUIPMENT N.E.C.
		37292	AIRCRAFT PARTS AND AUXILIARY EQUIPMENT N.E.C.
37310	566349	37315	SELF-PROPELLED SHIPS (VESSELS OVER 65 FT. IN LENGHT)
		37316	SHIP REPAIR (ON VESSELS OVER 65 FT. IN LENGTH)
		37317	NON-PROPELLED SHIPS (VESSELS OVER 65 FT. IN LENGTH) NON-MILITARY
		37318	SELF-PROPELLED SHIPS (VESSELS OVER 65 FT. IN LENGTH) NON-MILITARY
		37319	SHIP REPAIR (ON VESSELS OVER 65 FT. IN LENGTH) NON-MILITARY
37320	130371	37323	BOATS (VESSELS 65 FT. IN LENGTH AND LESS)
		37324	BOAT REPAIR (ON VESSELS 65 FT. IN LENGTH AND LESS)
		37325	BOATS (VESSELS 65 FT. IN LENGTH AND LESS) NON-MILITARY
		37326	BOAT REPAIR (ON VESSELS 65 FT IN LENGTH AND LESS) NON-MILITARY
37410	731000	37411	LOCOMOTIVES (NEW) RAILROAD ROAD SERVICE TYPE INCLUDE COMBINATION LINE AND SWITCHING
		37412	LOCOMOTIVES (NEW) SWITCHING TYPE
		37413	LOCOMOTIVES (NEW) INDUSTRIAL AND MINING TYPE
		37414	PARTS FOR LOCOMOTIVES- INCLUDE TENDERS, FOR SALE SEPARATELY
		37415	REBUILT-LOCOMOTIVES
37420	483447	37421	PASSENGER TRAIN CARS (NEW)
		37422	FREIGHT TRAIN CARS (NEW)
		37423	STREET, RAPID TRANSIT, AND INTER-URBAN CARS; TROLLEY BUSSES; SELF-PROPELLED CARS
		37424	PARTS AND ACCESSORIES FOR RAILROAD AND STREET CARS
		37425	REBUILD PASSENGER AND FREIGHT TRAIN CARS
37511	20509	37511	MOTORCYCLES, MOTORBIKES, MOTOR-SCOOTERS AND PARTS
37512	85704	37512	BICYCLES AND PARTS
37990	33821	37990	TRANSPORTATION EQUIPMENT N.E.C.
38111	180570	38111	AIRCRAFT FLIGHT INSTRUMENTS AND AUTOMATIC PILOTS
38113	76716	38113	LABRATORY AND SCIENTIFIC INSTRUMENTS EXCLUDE SURGICAL, MEDICAL, AND DENTAL
38211	37333	38211	AIRCRAFT AND NAUTICAL INSTRUMENTS-EXCLUDE FLIGHT INSTRUMENTS (38111)
38212	92147	38212	INTEGRATING METERS, NONELECTRICAL TYPE

NEW SIC	CENSUS VALUE OF SHIPMENTS	OLD SIC	DESCRIPTION
38213	216567	38213	INDUSTRIAL PROCESS INSTRUMENTS INCLUDE INDICATING, RECORDING AND CONTROLLING INSTRUMENTS
38214	80145	38214	MOTOR-VEHICLE INSTRUMENTS
38310	51254	38311	OPTICAL INSTRUMENTS AND LENSES
		38312	GUN FIRE-CONTROL EQUIPMENT
38410	44042	38410	SURGICAL AND MEDICAL INSTRUMENTS
38423	62375	38423	SANITARY NAPKINS AND TAMPONS
38424	216688	38424	SURGICAL AND ORTHOPEDIC APPLIANCES AND SUPPLIES
38430	70239	38430	DENTAL INSTRUMENTS, EQUIPMENT AND SUPPLIES
38510	110843	38510	OPHTHALMIC GOODS INCLUDING EYEGLASS FRAMES AND FITTINGS AND SUN OR GLARE GLASSES
38612	102769	38612	STILL PICTURE EQUIPMENT EXCEPT FILM
38613	195586	38613	FILM
38614	82308	38614	PHOTOGRAPHIC (SENSITIZED) PAPER
38615	12951	38615	PREPARED PHOTOGRAPHIC CHEMICALS INCLUDE DEVELOPERS, FIXERS AND TONERS
38616	44797	38616	35 MM MOTION PICTURE CAMERAS AND PROJECTORS
38617	44079	38617	MOTION PICTURE EQUIPMENT N.E.C. EXCEPT FILM
38710	307488	38711	CLOCKS INCLUDE ELECTRIC CLOCKS, CLOCK MOVEMENTS, AND TIMING MECHANISMS, NOT FOR TIMEPIECE USE, BUT EXCLUDE TIME
		38712	WATCHES WITH DOMESTIC MOVEMENTS JEWELED LEVER ESCAPEMENT TYPE
		38713	WATCHES WITH DOMESTIC MOVEMENTS PIN LEVEL ESCAPEMENT TYPE
		38714	WATCHES WITH IMPORTED MOVEMENTS
		38715	CLOCK AND WATCH PARTS EXCEPT WATCH CASES SOLD TO OTHER COMPANIES
		38716	INTERPLANT TRANSFERS OF WATCH AND CLOCK MOVEMENTS AND PARTS
39110	234484	39110	JEWELRY, MADE OF PRECIOUS METAL
39120	77838	39120	JEWELERS' FINDINGS AND MATERIALS
39140	239289	39142	SILVERWARE AND PLATED WARE
39310	63953	39310	PIANOS
39320	25613	39320	ORGANS

290

NEW SIC	CENSUS VALUE OF SHIPMENTS	OLD SIC	DESCRIPTION
39390	33670	39390	MUSICAL INSTRUMENTS AND PARTS - EXCLUDE PIANOS AND ORGANS
39410	277835	39410	GAMES AND TOYS, EXCEPT DOLLS AND CHILDREN'S VEHICLES
39420	92656	39420	DOLLS AND STUFFED TOY ANIMALS
39430	73937	39430	CHILDREN'S VEHICLES (BABY CARRIAGES, WALKERS, STROLLERS, ETC.)
39490	240916	39490	SPORTING AND ATHLETIC GOODS
39510	116520	39510	PENS, MECHANICAL PENCILS, AND PEN POINTS
39520	49212	39520	LEAD PENCILS AND CRAYONS
39530	27274	39530	HAND STAMPS, STENCILS, AND BRANDS
39540	17713	39540	ARTISTS' MATERIALS
39550	57500	39550	CARBON PAPER AND INKED RIBBONS
39630	61777	39630	BUTTONS AND PARTS
39640	189550	39640	NEEDLES, PINS, HOOKS AND EYES, AND SIMILAR NOTIONS
33711	468334	39711	MOLDED PLASTIC PRODUCTS
39712	85438	39712	LAMINATED PLASTIC SHEETS-RODS-TUBES
39713	251644	39713	FABRICATED PLASTIC PRODUCTS, OTHER THAN MOLDED PRODUCTS INCLUDING SEMIMANUFACTURED FORMS
39811	31665	39811	BROOMS
39812	55522	39812	PAINT BRUSHES
39813	98260	39813	BRUSHES N.E.C. SUCH AS TOILET, INDUSTRIAL, MAINTENANCE
39820	37193	39820	CORK PRODUCTS
39830	58597	39830	MATCHES
39840	19715	39840	CANDLES
39850	12562	39850	FIREWORKS AND PYROTECHNICS-INCLUDE FIREWORKS, FLARES, RAILROAD TORPEDOES, AND FUSES
39860	35086	39860	JEWELRY CASES AND INSTRUMENT CASES

291

NEW SIC	CENSUS VALUE OF SHIPMENTS	OLD SIC	DESCRIPTION
39930	229764	39930	SIGNS AND ADVERTISING DISPLAYS
39960	14179	39960	TOBACCO PIPES AND CIGARETTE HOLDERS
39970	26855	39970	SODA-FOUNTAIN AND BEER-DISPENSING EQUIPMENT
39990	199168	39992	HAND FIRE EXTINGUISHERS AND PARTS
		39999	UNKNOWN

NEW SIC	4-FIRM CR WEISS	CENSUS VALUE OF SHIPMENTS	OLD SIC	DESCRIPTION
20110	0.000 *	289924**	20110	MISCELLANEOUS BYPRODUCTS OF MEATPACKING PLANTS
			20111	BEEF, NOT CANNED OR MADE INTO SAUSAGE
			20111	OTHER MEATPACKING PLANT PRODUCTS, EXCEPT SAUSAGE CASINGS
			20112	VEAL, NOT CANNED OR MADE INTO SAUSAGE
			20113	LAMB AND MUTTON, NOT CANNED OR MADE INTO SAUSAGE
			20114	PORK, FRESH AND FROZEN
			20115	LARD
			20116	PORK, PROCESSED, MADE IN MEATPACKING PLANTS
			20117	SAUSAGE AND SIMILAR PRODUCTS, MADE IN MEATPACKING PLANTS
			20118	CANNED MEATS CONTAINING 20 PERCENT OR MORE MEAT (EXECPT DOG AND CAT FOOD)
			20119	HIDES, SKINS, AND PELTS
			20130	SAUSAGES AND OTHER PREPARED MEATS, N.S.K.
			20136	PORK, PROCESSED CURED, NOT MADE IN MEATPACKING PLANTS
			20137	SAUSAGE AND SIMILAR PRODUCTS, NOT MADE IN MEATPACKING PLANTS
			20138	CANNED MEATS CONTAINING 20 PERCENT OR MORE MEAT (EXCEPT D AND C FOOD) NOT MADE IN MEATPACKING PLANTS
			20139	NATURAL SAUSAGE CASINGS
			20161	YOUNG CHICKENS (USUALLY UNDER 20 WEEKS OF AGE), INCLUDING BROILERS, FRYERS, ROASTERS AND CAPONS
			20162	HENS AND/OR FOWL
			20163	TURKEYS
			20164	OTHER POULTRY AND SMALL GAME
			20171	PROCESSED POULTRY, EXCEPT SOUPS
20170	0.360	1567	20172	LIQUID, DRIED, AND FROZEN EGGS
20210	0.370	7911	20210	CREAMERY BUTTER
20221	0.360	14000	20221	NATURAL CHEESE, EXCEPT COTTAGE CHEESE
20222	0.600	11340	20222	PROCESS CHEESE AND RELATED PRODUCTS
20230	0.328	17062	20231	DRY MILK PRODUCTS
			20232	CANNED MILK PRODUCTS (CONSUMER TYPE CANS)
			20233	CONCENTRATED MILK, SHIPPED IN BULK
			20234	ICE CREAM MIX AND ICE MILK MIX
20240	0.620	15194	20240	ICE CREAM AND ICES
20260	0.529	76627	20260	FLUID MILK AND RELATED PRODUCTS, N.S.K.
			20261	BULK FLUID MILK AND CREAM
			20262	PACKAGED FLUID MILK AND RELATED PRODUCTS
			20263	COTTAGE CHEESE (INCLUDING BAKERS' CHEESE, POT CHEESE, AND FARMERS' CHEESE)
			20264	BUTTERMILK, CHOCOLATE DRINK, AND OTHER FLAVORED MILK PRODUCTS
20321	0.950	3467	20321	CANNED BABY FOODS
20322	0.640	9774	20322	SOUPS AND OTHER CANNED SPECIALTIES AND CANNED

* Weiss' adjusted concentration ratio was not applicable to the industry classification adopted here.
** Hundred thousands.

NEW SIC	4-FIRM CR WEISS	CENSUS VALUE OF SHIPMENTS	OLD SIC	DESCRIPTION
				SPECIALTIES, N.S.K. (INCLUDES 20324 AND 20320)
20323	0.500	3058	20323	CANNED DRY BEANS
20330	0.171	39229	20330	CANNED FRUITS AND VEGETABLES, N.S.K.
			20331	CANNED FRUITS (EXCEPT BABY FOODS)
			20332	CANNED VEGETABLES (EXCEPT HOMINY AND MUSHROOMS)
			20333	CANNED HOMINY AND MUSHROOMS
			20334	CANNED FRUITS JUICES, NECTARS, AND CONCENTRATES
			20335	CANNED VEGETABLE JUICES
			20336	CATSUP AND OTHER TOMATO SAUCES
			20338	JAMS, JELLIES, AND PRESERVES
20340	0.295	6256	20340	DEHYDRATED FRUITS, VEGETABLES AND SOUP MIXES, N.S.K.
			20341	DRIED FRUITS AND VEGETABLES, EXCEPT SOUP MIXES
			20342	SOUP MIXES, DRIED
20350	0.000	753	20350	PICKLES, SAUCES, AND SALAD DRESSINGS, N.S.K.
20352	0.380	3625	20352	PICKLES AND OTHER PICKLED PRODUCTS
20353	0.500	1513	20353	MEAT SAUCES (EXCEPT TOMATO)
20354	0.520	5760	20354	MAYONNAISE, SALAD DRESSINGS, AND SANDWICH SPREADS
20370	0.263	16487	20371	FROZEN FRUITS, JUICES, AND ADES
			20372	FROZEN VEGETABLES
20380	0.357	17426	20380	OTHER FROZEN SPECIALTIES, N.S.K. (INCLUDES 20370, FROZEN FRUITS AND VEGETABLES, N.S.K.)
			20381	FROZEN PIES AND OTHER FROZEN BAKED GOODS
			20382	FROZEN DINNERS, BEEF, PORK, POULTRY PIES, AND NATIONALITY FOOD, ETC.
			20383	OTHER FROZEN SPECIALTIES
20410	0.000	30267	20411	WHEAT FLOUR, EXCEPT FLOUR MIXES
			20412	WHEAT MILL PRODUCTS OTHER THAN FLOUR
			20413	CORN MILL PRODUCTS
			20415	FLOUR MIXES AND REFRIGERATED DOUGHS MADE IN FLOUR MILLS
			20416	OTHER GRAIN MILL PRODUCTS
			20455	FLOUR MIXES AND REFRIGERATED DOUGHS NOT MADE IN MILLS
20430	0.836	9346	20430	CEREAL BREAKFAST FOODS
20440	0.417	6713	20440	MILLED RICE AND BYPRODUCTS
20460	0.617	7866	20460	WET CORN MILLING

NEW SIC CR WEISS	4-FIRM CR WEISS	CENSUS VALUE OF SHIPMENTS	OLD SIC	DESCRIPTION
20470	0.491	14511	20471	DOG AND CAT FOOD
			20472	OTHER PET AND SPECIALTY FEED
20480	0.330	46582	20480	PREPARED FEEDS, N.E.C., N.S.K.
			20481	EGG-TYPE FEED, INCLUDING STARTER-GROWER AND LAYER-BREEDER
			20482	BROILER FEED
			20483	TURKEY FEED
			20484	DAIRY CATTLE FEED
			20485	SWINE FEED
			20486	BEEF CATTLE FEED
			20487	HORSE AND MULE FEED
			20488	OTHER POULTRY AND LIVESTOCK FEED
			20489	OTHER PREPARED ANIMAL FEEDS
20510	0.428	51808	20510	BREAD, CAKE, AND RELATED PRODUCTS, N.S.K.
			20511	BREAD, WHITE, WHEAT, AND RYE
			20512	ROLLS, BREAD-TYPE, INCLUDING BROWN AND SERVE, STUFFING AND CRUMBS
			20513	SWEET YEAST GOODS
			20514	SOFT CAKES
			20515	PIES
			20516	PASTRIES
			20517	DOUGHNUTS (CAKE TYPE)
20520	0.573	17133	20521	CRACKERS AND PRETZELS
			20522	COOKIES AND ICE CREAM CONES
20610	0.000	30529	20610	SUGAR CANE MILL PRODUCTS AND BYPRODUCTS
			20620	REFINED CANE SUGAR AND BYPRODUCTS
			20630	REFINED BEET SUGAR AND BYPRODUCTS
20650	0.311	23348	20650	CONFECTIONERY PRODUCTS, N.S.K.
			20651	BAR GOODS (EXCEPT SOLID CHOCOLATE BARS)
			20652	5 CENT AND 10 CENT SPECIALTIES
			20653	PACKAGE GOODS (EXCEPT SOLID CHOCOLATE)
			20654	BULK GOODS (EXCEPT SOLID CHOCOLATE)
			20655	PENNY GOODS
			20657	CHOCOLATE-TYPE CONFECTIONERY MADE FROM PURCHASED CHOCOLATE (SEE ALSO 20662)
			20658	SALTED NUTS AND OTHER CONFECTIONERY-TYPE PRODUCTS
20660	0.000	7240	20661	CHOCOLATE COATINGS
			20662	CONFECTIONERY-TYPE CHOCOLATE AND COCOA PRODUCTS, MADE FROM COCOA BEANS GROUND IN THE SAME ESTABLISHMENT (SEE ALSO 20657)
			20668	OTHER CHOCOLATE AND COCOA PRODUCTS MADE FROM PURCHASED CHOCOLATE AND SALTED NUTS
			20998	CHOCOLATE AND COCOA PRODUCTS, EXCEPT CONFECTIONERY (MADE FROM PURCHASED CHOCOLATE AND COCOA)
20670	0.830	3848	20670	CHEWING GUM AND CHEWING GUM BASE

NEW SIC	4-FIRM CR WEISS	CENSUS VALUE OF SHIPMENTS	OLD SIC	DESCRIPTION
20740	0.370	43033	20741	COTTONSEED OIL, CRUDE
			20742	COTTONSEED OIL, ONCE REFINED
			20743	COTTON LINTERS
			20744	COTTONSEED CAKE, MEAL, AND OTHER BYPRODUCTS
			20751	SOYBEAN OIL
			20752	SOYBEAN CAKE, MEAL, AND OTHER BYPRODUCTS
			20760	VEGETABLE OIL MILL PRODUCTS, N.E.C., N.S.K.
			20761	LINSEED OIL
			20762	VEGETABLE OILS (OTHER THAN COTTONSEED, SOYBEAN, AND LINSEED)
			20763	OTHER VEGETABLE OIL MILL PRODUCTS, EXCEPT COTTONSEED AND SOYBEAN
			20770	ANIMAL AND MARINE FATS AND OILS, N.S.K.
			20771	GREASE AND INEDIBLE TALLOW
			20772	MEAT MEAL AND TANKAGE
			20773	ANIMAL AND MARINE OIL PRODUCTS, INCLUDING FOOTS
20790	0.373	22745	20791	SHORTENING AND COOKING OILS
			20792	MARGARINE
20820	0.662	40387	20821	CANNED BEER AND ALE
			20822	BOTTLED BEER AND ALE
			20823	BEER AND ALE IN BARRELS AND KEGS
			20824	ALL OTHER MALT BEVERAGES AND BREWING BYPRODUCTS
20830	0.480	2128	20830	MALT AND MALT BYPRODUCTS
20840	0.388	8510	20840	WINES, BRANDY, AND BRANDY SPIRITS
20850	0.358	15572	20851	DISTILLED LIQUORS, EXCEPT BRANDY
			20853	BOTTLED LIQUORS, EXCEPT BRANDY
20860	0.650	48072	20860	BOTTLED AND CANNED SOFT DRINKS
20870	0.614	14529	20870	FLAVORING EXTRACTS AND SIRUPS, N.S.K.
			20871	FLAVORING EXTRACTS, EMULSIONS, AND OTHER LIQUID FLAVORS
			20872	LIQUID BEVERAGE BASES, NOT FOR USE BY SOFT DRINK BOTTLERS
			20873	FLAVORING SIRUPS FOR USE BY SOFT DRINK BOTTLERS
			20874	OTHER FLAVORING AGENTS (EXCEPT CHOCOLATE SIRUPS)
20910	0.260	5183	20910	CANNED AND CURED SEAFOOD, INCLUDING SOUP (EXCEPT FROZEN)
20920	0.134	10168	20922	FRESH PACKAGED FISH AND OTHER SEAFOOD
			20923	FROZEN PACKAGED FISH, EXCLUDING SHELLFISH
			20924	FROZEN PACKAGED SHELLFISH AND OTHER SEAFOOD, INCLUDING SOUP
20950	0.612	21634	20951	ROASTED COFFEE, WHOLE BEAN OR GROUND
			20952	CONCENTRATED COFFEE
20970	0.860	1057	20970	MANUFACTURED ICE

NEW SIC	4-FIRM CR WEISS	CENSUS VALUE OF SHIPMENTS	OLD SIC	DESCRIPTION
20980	0.331	3552	20980	MACARONI, SPAGHETTI, AND NOODLES
20990	0.000	3477	20990	MISCELLANEOUS FOODS, N.S.K.
20991	0.800	2672	20991	DESSERTS (READY-TO-MIX)
20992	0.490	10421	20992	CHIPS, (POTATO, CORN, ETC.)
20993	0.530	1673	20993	SWEETENING SIRUPS AND MOLASSES
20994	0.890	826	20994	BAKING POWDER AND YEAST
20995	0.790	3598	20995	TEA IN CONSUMER PACKAGES
20996	0.480	806	20996	VINEGAR AND CIDER
20999	0.240	13589	20999	OTHER FOOD PREPARATIONS, N.E.C.
21110	0.840	35894	21110	CIGARETTES
21210	0.535	3573	21210	CIGARS
21310	0.551	2575	21310	CHEWING AND SMOKING TOBACCO AND SNUFF
21410	0.556	13358	21411	TOBACCO, REDRIED
			21412	TOBACCO, STEMMED
22110	0.233	62888	22110	OTHER FABRICATED COTTON TEXTILE PRODUCTS
			22111	GRAY GOODS: COTTON DUCK AND ALLIED FABRICS
			22112	GRAY GOODS: COTTON SHEETING AND ALLIED FABRICS
			22113	GRAY GOODS: COTTON PRINT CLOTH YARN FABRICS
			22114	GRAY GOODS: COTTON COLORED YARN FABRICS, TOWELING AND DISHCLOTH FABRICS AND NAPPED COTTON FABRICS, INCLUDING BLANKETING
			22115	GRAY GOODS: FINE COTTON GOODS
			22116	GRAY GOODS: OTHER BROADWOVEN COTTON FABRICS AND SPECIALTIES
			22117	FINISHED COTTON BROADWOVEN FABRICS MADE IN WEAVING MILLS
			22118	COTTON SHEETS AND PILLOWCASES MADE IN WEAVING MILLS
			22119	COTTON SHEETS AND PILLOWCASES MADE IN WEAVING MILLS, MANMADE
22210	0.249	62888	22210	WEAVING MILLS, MANMADE FIBER AND SILK, N.S.K.
			22211	GRAY GOODS: 100 PERCENT FILAMENT RAYON AND/OR ACETATE FABRICS, INCLUDING COMBINATIONS CHIEFLY RAYON AND/OR ACETATE
			22212	GRAY GOODS: 100 PERCENT FILAMENT FABRICS, EXCEPT RAYON AND/OR ACETATE
			22213	GRAY GOODS: 100 PERCENT SPUN RAYON AND/OR ACETATE FABRICS INCLUDING BLENDS
			22214	GRAY GOODS: 100 PERCENT SPUN POLYESTER BLENDS WITH COTTON
			22215	GRAY GOODS: ALL OTHER 100 PERCENT SPUN NONCELLULOSIC FABRICS

NEW SIC	4-FIRM CR WEISS	CENSUS VALUE OF SHIPMENTS	OLD SIC	DESCRIPTION
			22216	GRAY GOODS: COMBINATIONS OF FILAMENT AND SPUN YARN FABRICS, CHIEFLY MANMADE FIBERS
			22217	GRAY GOODS: BLANKETING, SILK, PAPER, AND OTHER SPECIALTY MANMADE FIBER FABRICS
			22218	FINISHED MANMADE FIBER AND SILK BROADWOVEN FABRICS, MADE IN WEAVING MILLS
			22219	FABRICATED MANMADE FIBER AND SILK TEXTILE PRODUCTS (MADE IN WEAVING MILLS). (SEE ALSO 22118 AND 23928.)
22310	0.307	4407	22311	FINISHED WOOL YARN, TOPS OR RAW STOCK, NOT COMBED OR SPUN AT SAME ESTABLISHMENT
			22312	WOOL FABRICS (GRAY GOODS)
			22313	FINISHED WOOL APPAREL FABRICS
			22314	FINISHED WOOL NONAPPAREL FABRICS AND FELTS
			22319	WOOL AND CHIEFLY WOOL BLANKETS
22410	0.172	5215	22411	WOVEN NARROW FABRICS
			22414	BRAIDED NARROW FABRICS
			22415	COVERED RUBBER THREAD
22510	0.337	8990	22511	WOMEN'S FINISHED FULL-FASHIONED STOCKINGS
			22513	WOMEN'S FINISHED SEAMLESS HOSIERY, FULL-LENGTH AND KNEE-LENGTH
			22514	WOMEN'S FULL-FASHIONED HOSIERY SHIPPED IN THE GREIGE
			22515	WOMEN'S SEAMLESS FULL-LENGTH AND KNEE-LENGTH HOSIERY SHIPPED IN THE GREIGE
22520	0.207	5880	22522	MEN'S FINISHED SEAMLESS HOSIERY
			22523	ALL OTHER FINISHED SEAMLESS HOSIERY
			22524	SEAMLESS HOSIERY (EXCEPT WOMEN'S FULL-LENGTH AND KNEE-LENGTH) SHIPPED IN THE GREIGE
22530	0.117	15711	22531	SWEATERS, KNIT JACKETS, AND JERSEYS (MADE FROM YARNS OR FABRICS KNIT IN THE SAME ESTABLISHMENT). (SEE ALSO 23292, 23393, AND 23690.)
			22532	KNIT OUTERWEAR SPORT SHIRTS (MADE FROM YARNS OR FABRICS KNIT IN THE SAME ESTABLISHMENT). (SEE ALSO 23212, 23312 AND 23612.)
			22533	ALL OTHER KNIT OUTERWEAR PRODUCTS (MADE FROM YARNS OR FABRICS KNIT IN THE SAME ESTABLISHMENT). (SEE ALSO 23292, 23393 AND 2369.)
			22539	CONTRACT AND COMMISSION RECEIPTS FOR KNITTING AND/OR DYEING KNIT OUTERWEAR PRODUCTS
22540	0.438	4815	22541	MEN'S AND BOYS' KNIT UNDERWEAR AND NIGHTWEAR (MADE FROM YARNS OR FABRICS KNIT IN THE SAME ESTABLISHMENT). (SEE ALSO 23215 AND 23221.)
			22542	WOMEN'S AND CHILDREN'S KNIT UNDERWEAR
			22543	WOMEN'S AND CHILDREN'S KNIT NIGHTWEAR
22570	0.192	27702	22571	GREIGE GOODS, EXCEPT HOSIERY
			22572	UNDERWEAR AND NIGHTWEAR FINISHED FABRIC
			22573	OUTERWEAR FINISHED FABRIC
			22574	HIGH PILE FINISHED FABRIC
			22576	ALL OTHER CIRCULAR KNIT FINISHED FABRIC
			22579	CONTRACT AND COMMISSION RECEIPTS FOR KNITTING AND/OR DYEING CIRCULAR KNIT FABRIC

NEW SIC CR WEISS	4-FIRM CR WEISS	CENSUS VALUE OF SHIPMENTS	OLD SIC	DESCRIPTION
22580	0.250	9286	22580	WARP KNIT FABRIC MILLS, N.S.K.
			22581	GREIGE GOODS, EXCEPT HOSIERY
			22582	UNDERWEAR AND NIGHTWEAR FINISHED FABRIC
			22583	OUTERWEAR FINISHED FABRIC
			22584	ALL OTHER FINISHED WARP KNIT FABRIC
			22589	CONTRACT AND COMMISSION RECEIPTS FOR KNITTING AND/OR DYEING WARP KNIT FABRIC
22590	0.400	850	22590	KNIT GLOVES AND KNIT PRODUCTS, N.E.C., MADE FROM YARNS OR FABRICS KNIT IN THE SAME ESTABLISHMENT. (SEE ALSO 23811 AND 23812).
22610	0.388	11513	22617	FINISHED COTTON BROADWOVEN FABRICS NOT MADE IN WEAVING MILLS
			22619	COMMISSION FINISHING OF COTTON BROADWOVEN FABRICS
22620	0.352	17907	22628	MANMADE FIBER AND SILK BROADWOVEN FABRIC FINISHING, NOT FINISHED IN WEAVING MILLS
			22629	COMMISSION FINISHING OF MANMADE FIBER AND SILK BROADWOVEN FABRICS
22690	0.340	5228	22690	FINISHED YARN, RAW STOCK AND NARROW FABRICS, EXCEPT KNIT AND WOOL (NOT SPUN, THROWN, WOVEN, OR BRAIDED IN SAME ESTABLISHMENT). (SEE ALSO 22811, 22812, AND 22814.)
22710	0.540	2025	22710	WOVEN CARPETS AND RUGS
22720	0.210	26258	22720	TUFTED CARPETS AND RUGS
22790	0.318	1165	22790	CARPETS, RUGS, AND MATS, N.E.C.
22810	0.197	28593	22810	YARN MILLS, EXCEPT WOOL, N.S.K.
			22811	CARDED COTTON YARNS. (SEE ALSO PRODUCT CLASS 22690.)
			22812	COMBED COTTON YARNS. (SEE ALSO PRODUCT CLASS 22690.)
			22813	RAYON AND/OR ACETATE SPUN YARNS. (SEE ALSO PRODUCT CLASS 22690.)
			22814	SPUN NONCELLULOSIC FIBER AND SILK YARNS. (SEE ALSO PRODUCT CLASS 22690.)
22820	0.318	17488	22822	REWOUND, PLIED, ETC., YARNS, OTHER THAN WOOL (NOT SPUN OR THROWN AT SAME ESTABLISHMENT)
			22823	THROWN FILAMENT YARNS, EXCEPT TEXTURED
			22824	TEXTURED, CRIMPED, OR BULKED FILAMENT YARNS
			22829	COMMISSION THROWING, PLYING, ETC. OF YARNS
22830	0.294	2227	22831	WOOL YARNS, EXCEPT YARNS, INCLUDING YARNS SPUN AND FINISHED AT SAME ESTABLISHMENT
			22832	WOOL YARNS, CARPET
22840	0.561	3403	22841	FINISHED THREAD FOR USE IN THE HOME
			22842	FINISHED THREAD FOR INDUSTREAL OR MANUFACTURES' USE
			22843	UNFINISHED THREAD

NEW SIC	4-FIRM CR WEISS	CENSUS VALUE OF SHIPMENTS	OLD SIC	DESCRIPTION
22910	0.497	1308	22910	PRESSED, PUNCHED, OR NEEDLED FELTS, EXCEPT HATS
22920	0.200	398	22920	LACE AND NET GOODS
22930	0.238	1543	22930	PADDINGS AND UPHOLSTERY FILLING
22940	0.454	1242	22940	PROCESSED TEXTILE WASTE
22950	0.306	8086	22951 22952 22953	PYROXYLIN-COATED FABRICS VINYL COATED FABRICS OTHER COATED FABRICS
22960	0.797	6208	22960	TIRE CORD AND TIRE FABRICS
22970	0.426	5176	22971 22972	NONWOVEN FABRICS FABRICATED NONWOVEN PRODUCTS
22980	0.235	1747	22981 22982 22983	HARD FIBER CORDAGE AND TWINE SOFT FIBER CORDAGE AND TWINE (EXCEPT COTTON) COTTON CORDAGE AND TWINE
22990	0.000	1334	22990	TEXTILE GOODS, N.S.K.
22992	0.680	210	22992	JUTE GOODS (EXCEPT JUTE FELTS,CORDAGE OR TWINE) AND LINEN GOODS
22993	0.920	600	22993	SCOURING AND COMBING MILL PRODUCT
23110	0.181	22308	23111 23112 23113 23119	MEN'S SUITS MEN'S OVERCOATS AND TOPCOATS MEN'S TAILORED DRESS AND SPORT COATS AND JACKETS CONTRACT AND COMMISSION WORK ON MEN'S AND BOYS' SUITS AND COATS
23210	0.176	19629	23212 23214 23215 23219	MEN'S AND BOYS' KNIT OUTERWEAR SPORT SHIRTS, MADE FROM PURCHASED KNIT FABRICS. (SEE ALSO 22532.) MEN'S AND BOYS' DRESS AND SPORT SHIRTS EXCEPT KNIT OUTERWEAR SPORT SHIRTS MEN'S AND BOYS' NIGHTWEAR, MADE OF WOVEN OR PURCHASED KNIT FABRICS. (SEE ALSO 22541.) CONTRACT AND COMMISSION WORK ON MEN'S AND BOYS' SHIRTS (EXCEPT WORK) AND NIGHTWEAR
23220	0.485	2323	23221	MEN'S AND BOYS' UNDERWEAR, MADE FROM WOVEN OR PURCHASED KNIT FABRICS. (SEE ALSO 22541.)
23230	0.250	2793	23230	MEN'S, YOUTHS', AND BOYS' NECKWEAR
23270	0.242	17759	23271	MEN'S AND BOYS' SEPARATE DRESS AND SPORT TROUSERS DRESS SHORTS

NEW SIC CR WEISS	4-FIRM CR WEISS	CENSUS VALUE OF SHIPMENTS	OLD SIC	DESCRIPTION
23280	0.377	16248	23279	CONTRACT AND COMMISSION WORK ON MEN'S AND BOYS' SEPARATE DRESS AND SPORT TROUSERS
23290	0.140	7465	23281	MEN'S AND BOYS' WORK SHIRTS
			23282	MEN'S AND BOYS' WORK CLOTHING (EXCEPT SHIRTS) AND WASHABLE SERVICE APPAREL
			23289	CONTRACT AND COMMISSION WORK ON MEN'S AND BOYS' WORK CLOTHING
23310	0.086	12788	23291	MEN'S AND BOYS' HEAVY OUTERWEAR COATS AND JACKETS, NONTAILORED
			23292	MEN'S AND BOYS' OUTERWEAR, N.E.C., MADE FROM WOVEN OR PURCHASED KNIT FABRICS. (SEE ALSO 22531 AND 22533.)
			23312	WOMEN'S, MISSES', AND JUNIORS' KNIT OUTERWEAR SPORT SHIRTS, MADE FROM PURCHASED KNIT FABRICS. (SEE ALSO 22532.)
			23317	WOMEN'S, MISSES', AND JUNIORS' BLOUSES AND SHIRTS, EXCEPT KNIT OUTERWEAR SPORT SHIRTS
			23319	CONTRACT AND COMMISSION WORK ON WOMEN'S, MISSES', AND JUNIORS' BLOUSES AND SHIRTS
23350	0.089	35362	23350	WOMEN'S AND MISSES' DRESSES, N.S.K.
			23351	WOMEN'S, MISSES', AND JUNIORS' DRESSES SOLD AT A UNIT PRICE
			23353	WOMEN'S, MISSES', AND JUNIORS' DRESSES SOLD AT A DOZEN PRICE
			23359	CONTRACT AND COMMISSION WORK ON WOMEN'S, MISSES', AND JUNIORS' DRESSES
23370	0.058	17255	23371	WOMEN'S, MISSES', AND JUNIORS' COATS (EXCEPT FUR AND LEATHER)
			23372	WOMEN'S, MISSES', AND JUNIORS' SUITS
			23374	WOMEN'S, MISSES', AND JUNIORS' SKIRTS AND JACKETS
			23379	CONTRACT AND COMMISSION WORK ON WOMEN'S, MISSES', AND JUNIORS SUITS, COATS, AND SKIRTS
23390	0.133	16481	23390	WOMEN'S AND MISSES' OUTERWEAR, N.E.C., N.S.K.
			23392	WOMEN'S, MISSES', AND JUNIORS' WASHABLE SERVICE APPAREL
			23393	WOMEN'S, MISSES', AND JUNIORS' OUTERWEAR, N.E.C. (SEE ALSO 22531 AND 22533.)
			23399	CONTRACT AND COMMISSION WORK ON WOMEN'S, MISSES', AND JUNIORS' OUTERWEAR, N.E.C.
23410	0.138	12887	23412	WOMEN'S AND CHILDREN'S UNDERWEAR
			23413	WOMEN'S AND CHILDREN'S NIGHTWEAR
			23419	CONTRACT AND COMMISSION WORK ON WOMEN'S AND CHILDREN'S UNDERWEAR AND NIGHTWEAR
23420	0.328	6795	23421	BRASSIERES
			23422	CORSETS, GIRDLES, COMBINATIONS, AND ACCESSORIES
23510	0.149	587	23510	MILLINERY
23520	0.214	1475	23521	HATS AND HAT BODIES (EXCEPT CLOTH AND MILLINERY)
			23522	CLOTH HATS AND CAPS
23610	0.120	6547	23610	CHILDREN'S AND INFANTS' DRESSES, BLOUSES AND SHIRTS, EXCEPT KNIT SPORT SHIRTS
			23612	CHILDREN'S AND INFANTS' KNIT SPORT SHIRTS, MADE FROM PURCHASED KNIT FABRICS.

NEW SIC	4-FIRM CR WEISS	CENSUS VALUE OF SHIPMENTS	OLD SIC	DESCRIPTION
			23619	(SEE ALSO 22532.) CONTRACT AND COMMISSION WORK ON CHILDREN'S AND INFANTS' DRESSES, BLOUSES, AND SHIRTS
23630	0.153	1725	23630	CHILDREN'S AND INFANTS' COATS, SUITS, SNOWSUITS, AND COAT-AND-LEGING SETS
23690	0.127	6231	23690	CHILDREN'S AND INFANTS' OUTERWEAR, N.E.C.; MADE FROM WOVEN OR PURCHASED KNIT FABRIC. (SEE ALSO 22531 AND 22533.)
			23699	CONTRACT AND COMMISSION WORK ON CHILDREN'S AND INFANTS' OUTERWEAR, N.E.C.
23710	0.067	2136	23710	FUR GOODS
23810	0.319	1717	23811	DRESS GLOVES AND MITTENS, MADE FROM WOVEN OR PURCHASED KNIT FABRICS. (SEE ALSO 22590.)
			23812	WORK GLOVES AND MITTENS, MADE FROM WOVEN OR PURCHASED KNIT FABIRCS. (SEE ALSO 22590.)
23840	0.228	1696	23840	ROBES AND DRESSING GOWNS, EXCEPT CHILDREN'S
23850	0.242	3216	23850	RAINCOATS AND OTHER WATERPROOF OUTERGARMENTS
23860	0.100	1735	23860	LEATHER AND SHEEP LINED CLOTHING
23870	0.196	2341	23871 23872	LEATHER BELTS (FOR SALE SEPARATELY) BELTS, OTHER THAN LEATHER
23890	0.215	1232	23890	APPAREL, N.E.C.
23910	0.280	6262	23910	CURTAINS AND DRAPERIES, EXCEPT LACE
23920	0.222	14423	23920 23926 23928 23929	OTHER HOUSEFURNISHINGS BEDSPREADS AND BEDSETS, NOT MADE IN WEAVING MILLS. (SEE ALSO 22110.) SHEETS AND PILLOWCASES, NOT MADE IN WEAVING MILLS TOWELS AND WASHCLOTHS NOT MADE IN WEAVING MILLS
23930	0.239	2315	23930	TEXTILE BAGS, EXCEPT LAUNDRY, WARDROBE, AND SHOE
23940	0.204	2721	23940	CANVAS PRODUCTS
23950	0.190	2618	23951	EMBROIDERIES (EXCEPT SCHIFFLI MACHINE PRODUCTS), STAMPED ART GOODS, AND ART NEEDLEWORK
23961	0.520	942	23961	MEN'S AND BOYS' SUIT AND COAT FINDINGS, HATTERS' FUR, AND OTHER HAT AND CAP MATERIAL
23962	0.000	8231	23962 23963	AUTOMOBILE AND FURNITURE TRIMMINGS OTHER TRIMMINGS AND FINDINGS

302

NEW SIC	4-FIRM CR WEISS	CENSUS VALUE OF SHIPMENTS	OLD SIC	DESCRIPTION
23970	0.199	991	23970	SCHIFFLI MACHINE EMBROIDERIES
23990	0.212	7339	23990	FABRICATED TEXTILE PRODUCTS, N.E.C.
24110	0.266	26014	24110	LOGS, BOLTS, AND PULPWOOD
			24119	RECEIPTS FOR CONTRACT LOGGING
24210	C.140	60476	24210	SAWMILL AND PLANING MILL PRODUCTS, N.S.K.
			24211	HARDWOOD LUMBER, ROUGH AND DRESSED
			24212	SOFTWOOD LUMBER, ROUGH AND DRESSED
			24215	WOOD CHIPS
			24217	SOFTWOOD CUT STOCK
			24218	SOFTWOOD FLOORING AND OTHER GENERAL SAWMILL AND PLANING MILL PRODUCTS
			24219	CONTRACT OR CUSTOM SAWING OF LOGS OWNED BY OTHERS
24260	0.104	5715	24261	HARDWOOD FLOORING
			24262	HARDWOOD DIMENSION STOCK, FURNITURE PARTS, AND VEHICLE STOCK
			24266	WOOD FRAMES FOR HOUSEHOLD FURNITURE
24290	0.174	1757	24290	SHINGLES, COOPERAGE STOCK, AND EXCELSIOR
24310	0.089	22297	24310	MILLWORK PRODUCTS, N.S.K.
			24311	WINDOW UNITS, WOOD
			24312	WOOD WINDOW SASH, INCLUDING COMBINATION SCREEN AND STORM SASH, EXCLUDING WINDOW SCREENS AND WINDOW UNITS
			24313	WOOD WINDOW AND DOOR FRAMES
			24314	DOORS, WOOD, INTERIOR AND EXTERIOR (INCLUDING THOSE SHIPPED WITH GLAZED SECTIONS AND DOORS SHIPPED IN DOOR UNITS)
			24315	OTHER WOOD DOORS, INCLUDING GARAGE, SCREEN, STORM, AND COMBINATION SCREEN AND STORM, AND LOUVRE
			24316	WOOD MOULDINGS, EXCEPT PREFINISHED MOULDINGS, MADE FROM PURCHASED MOULDINGS
			24317	PREFINISHED WOOD MOULDINGS, MADE FROM PURCHASED MOULDINGS
			24318	OTHER MILLWORK PRODUCTS, INCLUDING WINDOW SCREENS AND ARCHITECTURAL MILLWORK
24340	0.117	8584	24341	WOOD KITCHEN CABINETS, STOCK LINE
			24342	WOOD KITCHEN CABINETS, CUSTOM
			24343	VANITIES AND OTHER CABINETWORK
24350	0.198	8732	24350	HARDWOOD VENEER AND PLYWOOD, N.S.K.
			24351	HARDWOOD PLYWOOD
			24352	PREFINISHED HARDWOOD PLYWOOD, MADE FROM PURCHASED PLYWOOD
			24353	OTHER HARDWOOD PLYWOOD-TYPE PRODUCTS
			24354	HARDWOOD VENEER
24360	0.359	19417	24361	SOFTWOOD PLYWOOD, INTERIOR TYPE
			24362	SOFTWOOD PLYWOOD, EXTERIOR TYPE

NEW SIC	4-FIRM CR WEISS	CENSUS VALUE OF SHIPMENTS	OLD SIC	DESCRIPTION
24390	0.470	4555	24363 24364	OTHER SOFTWOOD PLYWOOD-TYPE PRODUCTS SOFTWOOD VENEER
24410	0.228	2328	24390	STRUCTURAL WOOD PRODUCTS
24480	0.060	2874	24411 24412	NAILED OR LOCK-CORNER WOODEN BOXES BOX SHOOK FOR FRUITS, VEGETABLES, AND INDUSTRIAL USES
24490	0.218	2189	24480	PALLETS AND SKIDS
24510	0.270	31909	24491 24493 24495	WIREBOUND BOXES MADE FROM LUMBER VENEER, AND PLYWOOD VENEER AND PLYWOOD CONTAINERS, EXCEPT BOXES AND CRATES SLACK AND TIGHT COOPERAGE
24510	0.270	31909	24510 24511 24512	MOBILE HOMES, N.S.K. MOBILE HOMES (35 FEET OR MORE IN LENGTH) MOBILE BUILDINGS, NONRESIDENTIAL (35 FEET OR MORE IN LENGTH)
24520	0.470	10019	24520 24521	PREFABRICATED WOOD BUILDINGS, N.S.K. PREFABRICATED WOOD BUILDINGS, COMPONENTS FOR STATIONARY BUILDINGS (NOT SOLD AS COMPLETE UNITS)
			24522 24523	PRECUT PACKAGES FOR STATIONARY BUILDINGS (SOLD AS COMPLETE UNITS) STATIONARY BUILDINGS SOLD AS COMPLETE UNITS AND SHIPPED IN PANEL FORM (TWO-DIMENSIONAL)
			24524	STATIONARY BUILDINGS SHIPPED IN THREE-DIMENSIONAL ASSEMBLIES
24910	0.350	4613	24911 24919	WOOD OWNED AND TREATED BY SAME ESTABLISHMENT CONTRACT WOOD PRESERVING
24920	0.447	2928	24920	PARTICLEBOARD
24991	0.370	1730	24991	MIRROR AND PICTURE FRAMES
24994	0.630	181	24994	CORK PRODUCTS
24995	0.170	7016	24995	WOOD PRODUCTS, N.E.C.
24996	0.530	2585	24996	FABRICATED HARDBOARD PRODUCTS, MADE FROM HARDBOARD PRODUCED AT THE SAME ESTABLISHMENT
25110	0.202	27168	25110 25112	WOOD HOUSEHOLD FURNITURE, N.S.K. WOOD LIVING ROOM, LIBRARY, SUNROOM, AND HALL FURNITURE, EXCEPT SEWING MACHINE CABINETS
			25113 25115 25116 25117	WOOD DINING ROOM AND KITCHEN FURNITURE, EXCEPT CABINETS WOOD BEDROOM FURNITURE INFANTS' AND CHILDREN'S WOOD FURNITURE WOOD OUTDOOR FURNITURE AND UNPAINTED WOOD FURNITURE

NEW SIC	4-FIRM CR WEISS	CENSUS VALUE OF SHIPMENTS	OLD SIC	DESCRIPTION
25120	0.287	19905	25120	UPHOLSTERED WOOD HOUSEHOLD FURNITURE
25140	0.289	8593	25141	METAL HOUSEHOLD, DINING, AND BREAKFAST FURNITURE
			25142	METAL KITCHEN FURNITURE
			25143	METAL PORCH, LAWN, AND OUTDOOR FURNITURE
			25144	OTHER METAL HOUSEHOLD FURNITURE
25150	0.356	10796	25151	INNERSPRING MATTRESSES, OTHER THAN CRIB SIZE
			25152	OTHER MATTRESSES, INCLUDING CRIB MATTRESSES
			25153	BEDSPRINGS
			25154	CONVERTIBLE SOFAS
			25155	JACKKNIFE SOFA BEDS AND CHAIR BEDS
			25156	STUDIO COUCHES
25170	0.325	2930	25170	WOOD TELEVISION, RADIO, STEREO, AND SEWING MACHINE CABINETS
25190	0.134	1903	25190	HOUSEHOLD FURNITURE, N.E.C.
25210	0.220	10404	25210	WOOD OFFICE FURNITURE
25220	0.441	10404	25220	METAL OFFICE FURNITURE, N.S.K.
			25221	METAL OFFICE SEATING, INCLUDING UPHOLSTERED
			25222	DESKS
			25223	CABINETS AND CASES
			25224	OTHER METAL OFFICE FURNITURE, INCLUDING TABLES, STANDS, ETC.
25310	0.172	4968	25311	SCHOOL FURNITURE, EXCEPT STONE AND CONCRETE
			25312	PUBLIC BUILDING AND RELATED FURNITURE, EXCEPT SCHOOL FURNITURE
25410	0.048	14853	25410	WOOD PARTITIONS AND FIXTURES, N.S.K.
			25411	WOOD PARTITIONS, SHELVING, AND LOCKERS
			25412	PLASTIC LAMINATED FIXTURE TO*S
			25413	WOOD FIXTURES FOR STORES, BANKS, OFFICES, AND OTHER MISCELLANEOUS FIXTURES
25420	0.125	14853	25420	METAL PARTITIONS AND FIXTURES, N.S.K.
			25421	METAL PARTITIONS
			25422	METAL SHELVING AND LOCKERS
			25423	METAL STORAGE RACKS AND ACCESSORIES
			25424	METAL FIXTURES FOR STORES, BANKS, OFFICES AND MISCELLANEOUS FIXTURES
25910	0.460	3113	25911	WINDOW SHADES AND ACCESSORIES
			25912	VENETIAN BLINDS
25990	0.115	3799	25990	FURNITURE AND FIXTURES, N.E.C.
26110	0.259	11324	26111	SPECIAL ALPHA AND DISSOLVING WOODPULP

NEW SIC	4-FIRM CR WEISS	CENSUS VALUE OF SHIPMENTS	OLD SIC	DESCRIPTION
			26112	OTHER PULP (INCLUDING WOOD) AND PULPMILL BYPRODUCTS, EXCEPT TALL OIL
26210	0.209	61822	26210	TISSUE PAPER AND OTHER MACHINE-CREPED PAPER
			26211	NEWSPRINT
			26212	GROUNDWOOD PAPER, UNCOATED
			26213	COATED PRINTING AND CONVERTING PAPER
			26214	BOOK PAPER, UNCOATED
			26215	BLEACHED BRISTOLS (EXCLUDING COTTON FIBER INDEX AND BOGUS)
			26216	WRITING AND RELATED PAPERS
			26217	UNBLEACHED KRAFT PACKAGING AND INDUSTRIAL CONVERTING PAPER
			26218	PACKAGING AND INDUSTRIAL CONVERTING PAPER EXCEPT UNBLEACHED KRAFT
			26219	SPECIAL INDUSTRIAL PAPER
26310	0.260	36574	26310	PAPERBOARD MILL PRODUCTS, N.S.K.
			26311	UNBLEACHED KRAFT PACKAGING AND INDUSTRIAL CONVERTING PAPERBOARD
			26312	BLEACHED PACKAGING AND INDUSTRIAL CONVERTING PAPERBOARD
			26313	SEMICHEMICAL PAPERBOARD
			26314	COMBINATION FURNISH PAPERBOARD
			26318	WET MACHINE BOARD
26410	0.000	513	26410	PAPER COATING AND GLAZING, N.S.K.
26411	0.560	1118	26411	PRINTING PAPER COATED AT ESTABLISHMENTS OTHER THAN WHERE THE PAPER WAS PRODUCED
26412	0.430	1532	26412	OILED, WAXED, AND WAX-LAMINATED PAPER, PLAIN OR PRINTED
26413	0.300	1392	26413	GUMMED PRODUCTS
26414	0.590	5745	26414	PRESSURE SENSITIVE TAPE
26417	0.350	3569	26417	LAMINATED OR COATED ROLLS AND SHEETS, FOR PACKAGING USES, EXCEPT WAXED
26418	0.400	2636	26418	OTHER COATED AND PROCESSED PAPER, EXCEPT FOR PACKAGING USES AND EXCEPT WAXED
26420	0.270	5872	26420	ENVELOPES, ALL TYPES AND MATERIALS (EXCLUDING STATIONERY ENVELOPES)
26430	0.210	18294	26431	GROCERS' AND VARIETY BAGS (PAPER), AND WARDROBE,SHOPPING AND OTHER BAGS
			26432	SPECIALTY BAGS AND LINERS
			26433	SHIPPING SACKS AND MULTIWALL BAGS
26450	0.370	6459	26450	DIE-CUT PAPER AND BOARD, N.S.K.
			26451	OFFICE SUPPLIES (FILING ACCESSORIES) AND MISCELLANEOUS PRODUCTS
			26452	PASTED, LINED, LAMINATED, OR SURFACE-COATED PAPERBOARD
26461	1.000	213	26461	BITUMINOUS FIBER PIPE, SEWER, AND DRAINAGE, CONDUIT AND FITTINGS-MOLDED PULP OR PAPIER-MACHE

NEW SIC	4-FIRM CR WEISS	CENSUS VALUE OF SHIPMENTS	OLD SIC	DESCRIPTION
26462	0.880	1363	26462	OTHER PRESSED AND MOLDED PULP GOODS
26471	0.910	2811	26471	SANITARY NAPKINS AND TAMPONS
26472	0.700	16927	26472	SANITARY TISSUE HEALTH PRODUCTS
26480	0.260	4215	26480 26481 26482	STATIONERY PRODUCTS, N.S.K. STATIONERY TABLETS AND RELATED PRODUCTS
26492	0.520	1812	26492	WRAPPING PRODUCTS (GIFT WRAP, ETC.)
26493	0.490	830	26493	WALLPAPER
26495	0.150	3910	26495	OTHER CONVERTED PAPER AND BOARD PRODUCTS
26510	0.420	13721	26510	BENDING PAPERBOARD PACKAGING AND PACKAGING COMPONENTS, INCLUDING DIE-CUT, NONFOLDED PACKAGING ITEMS, FOR PRODUCTS EXCEPT LIQUID, MOIST, OILY, OR PERISHABLE FOODS
26520	0.310	3426	26520	SETUP PAPERBOARD BOXES
26530	0.310	41969	26530	CORRUGATED AND SOLID FIBER BOXES, INCLUDING PALLETS
26540	0.000	147	26540	SANITARY FOOD CONTAINERS, N.S.K.
26541	0.790	3315	26541	MILK AND OTHER BEVERAGE CARTONS
26542	0.770	4437	26542	CUPS AND LIQUID-TIGHT CONTAINERS
26543	0.280	5915	26543	OTHER SANITARY FOOD CONTAINERS, BOARDS, AND TRAYS
26550	0.520	6200	26551 26552	PAPERBOARD FIBER DRUMS WITH METAL, WOOD OR PAPERBOARD ENDS FIBER CANS, TUBES, AND SIMILAR FIBER PRODUCTS
26610	0.466	4019	26611 26612	INSULATING BOARD CONSTRUCTION PAPER
27110	0.679	79084	27111 27112 27113 27114	DAILY AND SUNDAY NEWSPAPERS, RECEIPTS FROM SUBSCRIPTIONS AND SALES DAILY AND SUNDAY NEWSPAPERS, RECEIPTS FROM ADVERTISING WEEKLY AND OTHER NEWSPAPERS, RECEIPTS FROM SUBSCRIPTIONS AND SALES WEEKLY AND OTHER NEWSPAPERS, RECEIPTS FROM ADVERTISING
27211	0.380	759	27211 27212	FARM PERIODICALS, RECEIPTS FROM SUBSCRIPTIONS AND SALES FARM PERIODICALS, RECEIPTS FROM ADVERTISING
27213	0.280	910	27213	SPECIALIZED BUSINESS AND PROFESSIONAL PERIODICALS, RECEIPTS FROM SUBSCRIPTIONS AND SALES

NEW SIC CR WEISS	4-FIRM CR WEISS	CENSUS VALUE OF SHIPMENTS	OLD SIC	DESCRIPTION
			27214	SPECIALIZED BUSINESS AND PROFESSIONAL PERIODICALS, RECEIPTS FROM ADVERTISING
27215	0.380	17285	27215	GENERAL PERIODICALS, RECEIPTS FROM SUBSCRIPTIONS AND SALES
			27216	GENERAL PERIODICALS, RECEIPTS FROM ADVERTISING
27217	0.280	2821	27217	OTHER PERIODICALS, EXCEPT SHOPPING NEWS, DIRECTORIES, OR CATALOGS, N.E.C.
27311	0.330	8096	27311	TEXT BOOKS, INCLUDING TEACHERS' EDITIONS
27313	0.390	4030	27313	TECHNICAL, SCIENTIFIC, AND PROFESSIONAL BOOKS
27314	0.360	1312	27314	RELIGIOUS BOOKS
27315	0.290	10067	27315	GENERAL BOOKS (TRADE, ETC.)
27317	0.710	2353	27317	GENERAL REFERENCE BOOKS
27318	0.540	1254	27318	OTHER BOOKS (EXCLUDING PAMPHLETS)
27319	0.620	487	27319	PAMPHLETS
27320	0.190	10499	27321	BOOKS, PRINTING ONLY, LITHOGRAPHIC
			27322	BOOKS, PRINTING AND BINDING, LITHOGRAPHIC
			27323	PAMPHLETS, WORKBOOKS, STANDARDIZED AND OBJECTIVE TESTS, PRINTING ONLY, LITHOGRAPHIC
			27324	PAMPHLETS, WORKBOOKS STANDARDIZED AND OBJECTIVE TESTS, PRINTING AND BINDING, LITHOGRAPHIC
			27326	BOOKS, PRINTING AND BINDING, OTHER THAN LITHOGRAPHIC
27410	0.524	10583	27411	CATALOGS AND DIRECTORIES, PUBLISHING
			27412	BUSINESS SERVICE PUBLICATIONS
			27413	OTHER MISCELLANEOUS PUBLISHING
27510	0.179	83251	27510	COMMERCIAL PRINTING, LETTERPRESS, N.S.K.
			27511	MAGAZINE AND PERIODICAL PRINTING (LETTERPRESS)
			27512	LABELS AND WRAPPERS PRINTING (LETTERPRESS)
			27513	CATALOGS AND DIRECTORIES PRINTING (LETTERPRESS)
			27514	FINANCIAL AND LEGAL PRINTING (LETTERPRESS)
			27515	ADVERTISING PRINTING (LETTERPRESS)
			27516	OTHER GENERAL JOB PRINTING (LETTERPRESS)
			27519	SCREEN PROCESS PRINTING, EXCEPT TEXTILES
			27520	COMMERCIAL PRINTING, LITHOGRAPHIC, N.S.K.
			27521	MAGAZINE AND PERIODICAL PRINTING (LITHOGRAPHIC)
			27522	LABELS AND WRAPPERS PRINTING (LITHOGRAPHIC)
			27523	CATALOGS AND DIRECTORS PRINTING (LITHOGRAPHIC)
			27524	FINANCIAL AND LEGAL PRINTING (LITHOGRAPHIC)
			27525	ADVERTISING PRINTING (LITHOGRAPHIC)

NEW SIC	4-FIRM CR WEISS	CENSUS VALUE OF SHIPMENTS	OLD SIC	DESCRIPTION
27530	0.230	2050	27526	OTHER GENERAL JOB PRINTING (LITHOGRAPHIC)
27540	0.368	7951	27530	ENGRAVING AND PLATE PRINTING (EXCEPT PHOTOENGRAVING)
			27540	COMMERCIAL PRINTING, GRAVURE, N S.K.
			27541	PUBLICATION PRINTING, GRAVURE
			27542	LABELS, WRAPPERS AND WRAP PRINTING, GRAVURE
			27543	ADVERTISING PRINTING, GRAVURE
			27544	OTHER COMMERCIAL PRINTING, GRAVURE
			27545	GRAVURE PLATES AND CYLINDERS
27610	0.430	13819	27610	MANIFOLD BUSINESS FORMS, N.S.K.
			27612	UNIT-SET FORMS
			27613	SALES AND OTHER MANIFOLD BOOKS
			27615	CUSTOM CONTINUOUS FORMS WITH OR WITHOUT CARBON, MARGINALLY PUNCHED OR NOT MARGINALLY PUNCHED
			27617	STOCK CONTINUOUS FORMS
27710	0.636	5835	27711	GREETING CARDS, PUBLISHERS' SALES
			27712	GREETING CARDS, PRINTED FOR PUBLICATION BY OTHERS
27820	0.354	5662	27821	BLANKBOOK MAKING
			27822	LOOSELEAF BINDERS AND DEVICES
27890	0.110	3692	27891	EDITION, LIBRARY, AND OTHER HARD COVER BOOKBINDING
			27892	OTHER BOOK AND PAMPHLET BINDING AND RELATED BINDING WORK
27910	0.320	5087	27910	TYPESETTING
27930	0.380	2213	27930	PHOTOENGRAVING PLATES MADE FOR OTHERS
27940	0.630	355	27940	ELECTROTYPING AND STEREOTYPING DUPLICATE PLATES MADE FOR OTHERS
27950	0.170	2630	27951	LITHOGRAPHIC PLATES
			27952	LITHOGRAPHIC SERVICES
28121	0.460	2102	28121	CHLORINE COMPRESSED OR LIQUEFIED
28122	0.000	1476	28122	SODIUM CARBONATE (SODA ASH)
28123	0.550	4109	28123	SODIUM HYDROXIDE (CAUSTIC SODA)
28124	0.710	337	28124	OTHER ALKALIES
28130	0.747	6591	28132	ACETYLENE
			28133	CARBON DIOXIDE
			28134	ELEMENTAL GASES AND COMPRESSED AND LIQUEFIED GASES, N.E.C.

NEW SIC	4-FIRM CR WEISS	CENSUS VALUE OF SHIPMENTS	OLD SIC	DESCRIPTION
28160	0.466	7562	28161 28162 28163	TITANIUM PIGMENTS OTHER WHITE OPAQUE PIGMENTS CHROME COLORS AND OTHER INORGANIC PIGMENTS
28190	0.000	225	28190	INDUSTRIAL INORGANIC CHEMICALS, N.S.K.
28193	0.550	2454	28193	SULFURIC ACID
28194	0.560	1604	28194	INORGANIC ACIDS, EXCEPT NITRIC, SULFURIC, AND PHOSPHORIC
28195	0.990	3886	28195	ALUMINUM OXIDE
28196	0.710	1755	28196	OTHER ALUMINUM COMPOUNDS
28197	0.510	5031	28197	POTASSIUM AND SODIUM COMPOUNDS (EXCEPT BLEACHES, ALKALIES, AND ALUMS)
28198	0.380	1728	28198	CHEMICAL CATALYTIC PREPARATIONS
28199	0.270	13346	28199	OTHER INORGANIC CHEMICALS, N.E.C.
28210	0.246	44864	28210 28213 28214	PLASTICS MATERIALS AND RESINS, N.S.K. THERMOPLASTIC RESINS AND PLASTICS MATERIALS THERMOSETTING RESINS AND PLASTICS MATERIALS
28220	0.512	12886	28220	SYNTHETIC RUBBER (VULCANIZABLE ELASTOMERS)
28230	0.000	36337	28231 28232 28240 28241 28242	ACETATE YARN RAYON YARN, VISCOSE AND CUPRAMMONIUM PROCESSES ORGANIC FIBERS, NONCELLULOSIC, N.S.K. POLYAMIDE FIBERS, NYLON, EXCEPT NONTEXTILE MONOFILAMENT OTHER NONCELLULOSIC SYNTHETIC ORGANIC FIBERS
28311	0.670	1259	28311	BLOOD AND BLOOD DERIVATIVES, FOR HUMAN USE
28312	0.840	705	28312	VACCINES AND ANTIGENS, FOR HUMAN USE
28313	0.690	183	28313	ANTITOXINS, TOXOIDS AND TOXINS FOR IMMUNIZATION, AND THERAPEUTIC IMMUNE SERUMS, FOR HUMAN USE
28314	0.540	1925	28314	DIAGNOSTIC SUBSTANCES AND OTHER BIOLOGICS, FOR HUMAN USE
28315	0.440	741	28315	BIOLOGICAL PREPARATIONS FOR VETERINARY USE
28330	0.490	7935	28331 28332	SYNTHETIC ORGANIC MEDICINAL CHEMICALS, IN BULK OTHER MEDICINAL CHEMICALS AND BOTANICAL PRODUCTS, IN BULK, N.E.C.

NEW SIC	4-FIRM CR WEISS	CENSUS VALUE OF SHIPMENTS	OLD SIC	DESCRIPTION
28340	0.000	866	28340	PHARMACEUTICAL PREPARATIONS, N.S.K.
28341	0.480	6154	28341	PHARMACEUTICAL PREPARATIONS AFFECTING NEOPLASMS, ENDOCRINE SYSTEMS AND METABOLIC DISEASES, FOR HUMAN USE
28342	0.430	16381	28342	PHARMACEUTICAL PREPARATIONS ACTING ON THE CENTRAL NERVOUS SYSTEM AND THE SENSE ORGANS, FOR HUMAN USE
28343	0.570	3831	28343	PHARMACEUTICAL PREPARATIONS ACTING ON THE CARDIOVASCULAR SYSTEM, FOR HUMAN USE
28344	0.480	5799	28344	PHARMACEUTICAL PREPARATIONS ACTING ON THE RESPIRATORY SYSTEM, FOR HUMAN USE
28345	0.350	7640	28345	PHARMACEUTICAL PREPARATIONS ACTING ON THE DIGESTIVE OR THE GENITO-URINARY SYSTEMS, FOR HUMAN USE
28346	0.350	3485	28346	PHARMACEUTICAL PREPARATIONS ACTING ON THE SKIN, FOR HUMAN USE
28347	0.270	6905	28347	VITAMIN, NUTRIENT, AND HEMATINIC PREPARATIONS, FOR HUMAN USE
28348	0.450	9490	28348	PHARMACEUTICAL PREPARATIONS AFFECTING PARASITIC AND INFECTIVE DISEASES, FOR HUMAN USE
28349	0.390	2403	28349	PHARMACEUTICAL PREPARATIONS FOR VETERINARY USE
28410	0.000	1030	28410	SOAP AND OTHER DETERGENTS, N.S.K.
28411	0.310	6525	28411	SOAP AND DETERGENTS, NON-HOUSE-HOLD
28412	0.840	16339	28412	HOUSEHOLD DETERGENTS
28413	0.720	4120	28413	SOAPS, EXCEPT SPECIALTY CLEANERS, HOUSEHOLD
28414	0.750	504	28414	GLYCERINE, NATURAL
28420	0.000	2090	28420	POLISHES AND SANITATION GOODS, N.S.K.
28422	0.750	2335	28422	HOUSEHOLD BLEACHES
28423	0.360	8989	28423	SPECIALTY CLEANING AND SANITATION PRODUCTS
28424	0.470	3918	28424	POLISHING PREPARATIONS AND RELATED PRODUCTS
28430	0.186	5807	28430	SURFACE ACTIVE AND FINISHING AGENTS
28441	0.570	2507	28441	SHAVING PREPARATIONS
28442	0.480	6770	28442	PERFUMES, TOILET WATER, AND COLOGNES

NEW SIC	4-FIRM CR WEISS	CENSUS VALUE OF SHIPMENTS	OLD SIC	DESCRIPTION
28443	0.460	10651	28443	HAIR PREPARATIONS (INCLUDING SHAMPOOS)
28444	0.790	4846	28444	DENTIFRICES, INCLUDING MOUTHWASHES, GARGLES, AND RINSES
28445	0.450	16736	28445	OTHER COSMETICS AND TOILET PREPARATIONS
28510	0.220	35202	28510	PAINTS AND ALLIED PRODUCTS, N.S.K.
			28511	EXTERIOR OIL-TYPE TRADE SALES PAINT PRODUCTS
			28512	EXTERIOR WATER-TYPE TRADE SALES PAINT PRODUCTS, INCLUDING TINTING BASES
			28513	INTERIOR OIL-TYPE TRADE SALES PAINT PRODUCTS
			28514	INTERIOR WATER-TYPE TRADE SALES PAINT PRODUCTS, INCLUDING TINTING BASES
			28515	TRADE SALES LACQUERS
			28516	INDUSTRIAL PRODUCT FINISHES, EXCEPT LACQUERS
			28517	INDUSTRIAL LACQUERS, INCLUDING ACRYLICS
			28518	PUTTY AND ALLIED PRODUCTS
			28519	MISCELLANEOUS PAINT PRODUCTS
28610	0.458	3008	28611	SOFTWOOD DISTILLATION PRODUCTS
			28612	OTHER GUM AND WOOD CHEMICALS
28650	0.300	23324	28651	CYCLIC INTERMEDIATES
			28652	SYNTHETIC ORGANIC DYES
			28653	SYNTHETIC ORGANIC PIGMENTS, LAKES, AND TONERS
			28655	CYCLIC (COAL TAR) CRUDES
28690	0.000	729	28690	INDUSTRIAL ORGANIC CHEMICALS, N.E.C., N.S.K.
28691	0.310	4650	28691	MISCELLANEOUS CYCLIC CHEMICAL PRODUCTS
28692	0.470	54352	28692	MISCELLANEOUS ACYCLIC CHEMICALS AND CHEMICAL PRODUCTS EXCLUDING UREA
28693	0.380	7230	28693	SYNTHETIC ORGANIC CHEMICALS, N.E.C., EXCEPT BULK SURFACE ACTIVE AGENTS
28694	0.570	4893	28694	PESTICIDES AND OTHER ORGANIC CHEMICALS (NOT FORMULATIONS)
28695	0.280	2803	28695	ETHYL ALCOHOL AND OTHER INDUSTRIAL ORGANIC CHEMICALS N.E.C.
28730	0.236	9373	28730	NITROGENOUS FERTILIZERS, N.S.K.
			28731	SYNTHETIC AMMONIA, NITRIC ACID, AND AMMONIUM COMPOUNDS
			28732	UREA
			28733	FERTILIZER MATERIALS OF ORGANIC ORIGIN
28740	0.246	10525	28741	PHOSPHORIC ACID
			28742	SUPERPHOSPHATE AND OTHER PHOSPHATIC FERTILIZER MATERIALS
			28743	MIXED FERTILIZERS, PRODUCED FROM ONE OR MORE MATERIALS, MADE IN SAME PLANT
28752	0.024	6519	28752	FERTILIZERS, MIXING ONLY. (SEE PRODUCT CLASS 28743.)

NEW SIC	4-FIRM CR WEISS	CENSUS VALUE OF SHIPMENTS	OLD SIC	DESCRIPTION
28791	0.480	3876	28791	INSECTICIDAL PREPARATIONS (FORMULATIONS) PRIMARILY FOR AGRICULTURAL, GARDEN, AND HEALTH SERVICE USE
28792	0.770	4320	28792	HERBICIDAL PREPARATIONS (FORMULATIONS) PRIMARILY FOR AGRICULTURAL, GARDEN, AND HEALTH SERVICE USE
28793	0.490	856	28793	AGRICULTURAL CHEMICALS, N.E.C.
28794	0.520	1068	28794	HOUSEHOLD INSECTICIDES AND REPELLANTS, INCLUDING INDUSTRIAL EXTERMINANTS
28910	0.158	9543	28910	ADHESIVES AND SEALANTS, N.S.K.
			28913	NATURAL BASE GLUES AND ADHESIVES
			28914	SYNTHETIC RESIN AND RUBBER ADHESIVES, INCLUDING ALL TYPES OF BONDING AND LAMINATING ADHESIVES
			28915	CAULKING COMPOUNDS AND SEALANTS
28920	0.676	2376	28921	EXPLOSIVES
28930	0.368	4980	28930	PRINTING INKS, N.S.K.
			28931	LETTERPRESS INKS (BLACK AND COLOR)
			28932	LITHOGRAPHIC AND OFFSET INKS (BLACK AND COLOR)
			28933	GRAVURE INKS
			28934	FLEXOGRAPHIC INKS
			28935	PRINTING INKS, N.E.C.
28950	0.739	2271	28950	CARBON BLACK (CHANNEL AND FURNACE PROCESS ONLY)
28990	0.000	2298	28990	CHEMICAL PREPARATIONS, N.E.C., N.S.K.
28991	0.700	1339	28991	SALT
28992	0.500	1553	28992	FATTY ACIDS
28994	0.760	682	28994	GELATIN, EXCEPT READY-TO-EAT DESSERTS
28995	0.160	16410	28995	ESSENTIAL OILS, FIREWORKS, AND PYROTECHNICS, SIZES, AND CHEMICAL PREPARATIONS, N.E.C
29110	0.503	254148	29110	OTHER FINISHED PETROLEUM PRODUCTS, INCLUDING WAXES
			29111	GASOLINE
			29112	JET FUEL
			29113	KEROSENE
			29114	DISTILLATE FUEL OIL
			29115	RESIDUAL FUEL OIL
			29116	LIQUEFIED REFINERY GASES (FEED STOCK AND OTHER USES
			29117	LUBRICATING OILS AND GREASES, MADE IN REFINERIES
			29118	UNFINISHED OILS AND LUBRICATING OIL BASE STOCK
			29119	ASPHALT
			29920	LUBRICATING OILS AND GREASES MADE FROM PURCHASED MATERIALS

NEW SIC	4-FIRM CR WEISS	CENSUS VALUE OF SHIPMENTS	OLD SIC	DESCRIPTION
29510	0.326	8934	29510	PAVING MIXTURES AND BLOCKS
29520	0.477	9022	29521	ASPHALT AND TAR SATURATED FELTS AND BOARDS FOR NONBUILDING USE
			29522	ROOFING ASPHALTS AND PITCHES, COATINGS, AND CEMENTS
			29523	ASPHALT AND TAR ROOFING AND SIDING PRODUCTS
29990	0.668	1392	29990	PETROLEUM AND COAL PRODUCTS, N.E.C.
30110	0.664	48984	30111	PASSENGER CAR AND MOTORCYCLE PNEUMATIC TIRES (CASINGS)
			30112	TRUCKS AND BUS (AND OFF-THE-HIGHWAY) PNEUMATIC TIRES
			30113	OTHER PNEUMATIC TIRES AND SOLID TIRES
			30114	ALL INNER TUBES
			30115	TREAD RUBBER, TIRE SUNDRIES, AND REPAIR MATERIALS
30210	0.343	4939	30211	RUBBER AND PLASTICS PROTECTIVE FOOTWEAR
			30212	RUBBER AND PLASTICS SHOES, SLIPPERS, OTHER FOOTWEAR, N.E.C.
30310	0.729	520	30310	RECLAIMED RUBBER
30410	0.461	8860	30411	RUBBER AND PLASTICS BELT AND BELTING, FLAT
			30412	RUBBER AND PLASTICS BELT AND BELTING, OTHER THAN FLAT
			30413	RUBBER AND PLASTICS HOSE, HORIZONTAL REINFORCED
			30414	RUBBER AND PLASTICS HOSE, CONTINUOUS MOLDED NONHYDRAULIC EXCEPT GARDEN
			30415	RUBBER AND PLASTICS GARDEN HOSE
			30416	ALL OTHER RUBBER AND PLASTICS HOSE
30690	0.000	1407	30690	FABRICATED RUBBER PRODUCTS, N.E.C., N.S.K.
30693	0.530	3501	30693	SPONGE AND FOAM RUBBER GOODS
30694	0.470	984	30694	RUBBER FLOOR AND WALL COVERING
30695	0.190	11444	30695	MECHANICAL RUBBER GOODS, N.E.C.
30696	0.570	1545	30696	RUBBER HEELS AND SOLES
30697	0.440	1168	30697	DRUGGIST AND MEDICAL SUNDRIES
30698	0.220	5338	30698	OTHER RUBBER GOODS, N.E.C.
30790	0.000	23438	30790	CONSUMER AND COMMERCIAL PLASTICS PRODUCTS, N.E.C., AND MISCELLANEOUS PLASTICS PRODUCTS, N.S.K.
30791	0.180	20688	30791	UNSUPPORTED PLASTICS FILM, SHEETS, RODS, AND TUBES
30792	0.250	8782	30792	FOAMED PLASTICS PRODUCTS

314

NEW SIC	4-FIRM CR WEISS	CENSUS VALUE OF SHIPMENTS	OLD SIC	DESCRIPTION
30793	0.370	5681	30793	LAMINATED SHEETS, RODS, AND TUBES
30794	0.200	12714	30794	PACKAGING AND SHIPPING CONTAINERS
30795	0.090	18195	30795	INDUSTRIAL PLASTICS PRODUCTS, EXCEPT BELTING, PACKING AND SEALS
30796	0.230	11148	30796	CONSTRUCTION PLASTICS PRODUCTS
30797	0.420	3773	30797	PLASTICS DINNERWARE, TABLEWARE, AND KITCHENWARE
30798	0.780	4293	30798	REGENERATED CELLULOSIC PRODUCTS, EXCEPT RAYON
30799	0.320	2272	30799	CUSTOM COMPOUNDED PURCHASED RESINS
31110	0.147	10264	31111	FINISHED CATTLE HIDE AND KIP SIDE LEATHERS
			31112	FINISHED CALF AND WHOLE KIP LEATHERS
			31113	FINISHED SHEEP AND LAMB LEATHERS
			31114	OTHER FINISHED LEATHERS, N.E.C.
			31115	ROUGH, RUSSET, AND CRUST LEATHER (NOT FINISHED IN THIS ESTABLISHMENT)
			31119	CONTRACT AND COMMISSION RECEIPTS FOR TANNING AND FINISHING LEATHER OWNED BY OTHERS
31310	0.729	1961	31310	BOOT AND SHOE CUT STOCK AND FINDINGS
31420	0.354	1594	31420	HOUSE SLIPPERS
31430	0.300	11813	31431	MEN'S DRESS SHOES
			31432	MEN'S CASUAL SHOES
			31433	MEN'S WORK SHOES
			31434	MEN'S DRESS AND CASUAL BOOTS, EXCEPT WORK
31440	0.267	13055	31440	WOMEN'S FOOTWEAR, EXCEPT ATHLETIC, N.S.K.
			31441	WOMEN'S SHOES, FLATS
			31442	WOMEN'S SHOES, LOW HEEL
			31443	WOMEN'S SHOES, MEDIUM HEEL
			31444	WOMEN'S SHOES, HIGH HEEL
			31445	WOMEN'S BOOTS
31490	0.198	4757	31491	YOUTHS' AND BOYS' SHOES
			31492	MISSES' AND CHILDREN'S SHOES
			31493	INFANTS' AND BABIES' SHOES
			31494	ALL OTHER FOOTWEAR, EXCEPT RUBBER AND SLIPPERS
31510	0.250	799	31510	DRESS AND WORK GLOVES AND MITTENS, ALL LEATHER
31610	0.306	3219	31610	SUITCASES, BRIEFCASES, BAGS, AND MUSICAL INSTRUMENT CASES

NEW SIC	4-FIRM CR WEISS	CENSUS VALUE OF SHIPMENTS	OLD SIC	DESCRIPTION
31710	0.105	3444	31710	WOMEN'S AND CHILDREN'S HANDBAGS AND PURSES
31720	0.300	2318	31720	PERSONAL LEATHER GOODS, EXCEPT HANDBAGS AND PURSES
31990	0.124	1460	31990	SADDLERY, HARNESS AND WHIPS, AND OTHER LEATHER PRODUCTS, N.E.C.
32110	0.752	12471	32111	SHEET (WINDOW) GLASS
			32112	PLATE AND FLOAT GLASS
			32113	LAMINATED GLASS MADE FROM GLASS PRODUCED IN SAME ESTABLISHMENT
			32114	OTHER FLAT GLASS MADE FROM GLASS PRODUCED IN THE SAME ESTABLISHMENT
			32313	LAMINATED GLASS MADE OF PURCHASED GLASS
32210	0.557	20852	32210	GLASS CONTAINERS
32291	0.740	4329	32291	TABLE, KITCHEN, ART, AND NOVELTY GLASSWARE (HANDMADE AND MACHINE-MADE)
32292	0.830	3946	32292	LIGHTING AND ELECTRONIC GLASSWARE
32293	0.950	2535	32293	GLASS FIBER (TEXTILE TYPE FIBER)
32294	0.800	1666	32294	OTHER PRESSED AND BLOWN GLASSWARE
32315	0.240	2545	32315	MIRRORS
32316	0.400	6258	32316	OTHER GLASS PRODUCTS MADE OF PURCHASED GLASS
32410	0.696	17700	32410	CEMENT, HYDRAULIC (INCLUDING COST OF SHIPPING CONTAINERS)
32510	0.375	4713	32511	BRICK, EXCEPT CERAMIC GLAZED AND REFRACTORY
			32512	GLAZED BRICK AND STRUCTURAL HOLLOW TILE
32530	0.380	1579	32530	CLAY FLOOR AND WALL TILE, INCLUDING QUARRY TILE
32550	0.475	3022	32550	CLAY REFRACTORIES
32590	0.386	1693	32590	STRUCTURAL CLAY PRODUCTS, N.E.C., N.S.K.
			32591	VITRIFIED CLAY SEWER PIPE AND FITTINGS
			32592	STRUCTURAL CLAY PRODUCTS, N.E.C.
32610	0.368	5640	32610	VITREOUS AND SEMIVITREOUS PLUMBING FIXTURES, ACCESSORIES, AND FITTINGS
			34310	METAL PLUMBING FIXTURES
32620	0.339	819	32620	VITREOUS CHINA AND PORCELAIN TABLE AND KITCHEN ARTICLES (FELDSPAR AND BONE)
32630	0.226	580	32630	EARTHENWARE (SEMIVITREOUS) TABLE AND KITCHEN ARTICLES

NEW SIC	4-FIRM CR WEISS	CENSUS VALUE OF SHIPMENTS	OLD SIC	DESCRIPTION
32640	0.408	2590	32640	PORCELAIN, STEATITE, AND OTHER CERAMIC ELECTRICAL PRODUCTS
32690	0.102	1469	32690	POTTERY PRODUCTS, N.E.C., INCLUDING CHINA DECORATING FOR THE TRADE
32710	0.319	7957	32710	CONCRETE BLOCK AND BRICK
32720	0.448	18647	32720	CONCRETE PRODUCTS, N.E.C., N.S.K.
			32721	CONCRETE PIPE
			32722	PRECAST CONCRETE PRODUCTS
			32723	PRESTRESSED CONCRETE PRODUCTS
32730	0.510	35788	32730	READY-MIXED CONCRETE
32740	0.353	2378	32740	LIME (INCLUDING COST OF SHIPPING CONTAINERS)
32750	0.789	5831	32750	GYPSUM PRODUCTS, N.S.K.
			32751	GYPSUM BUILDING MATERIALS
			32752	OTHER GYPSUM PRODUCTS
32810	0.424	2868	32811	CUT GRANITE AND GRANITE PRODUCTS
			32812	CUT LIMESTONE AND LIMESTONE PRODUCTS
			32813	CUT MARBLE AND OTHER CUT STONE PRODUCTS
32910	0.466	8923	32911	NONMETALLIC ARTIFICAL (SYNTHETIC) SIZED GRAINS, AND FLOUR ABRASIVES (INCLUDING GRADED PRODUCTS ONLY)
			32912	NONMETALLIC BONDED ABRASIVE PRODUCTS, INCLUDING DIAMOND ABRASIVES
			32913	NONMETALLIC COATED ABRASIVE PRODUCTS AND BUFFING WHEELS, POLISHING WHEELS AND LAPS
			32914	METAL ABRASIVES, INCLUDING SCOURING PADS
32920	0.720	7426	32922	ASBESTOS FRICTION MATERIALS
			32924	ASBESTOS-CEMENT SHINGLES AND CLAPBOARD
			32925	ASPHALT FLOOR TILE
			32926	VINYL ASBESTOS FLOOR TILE
			32927	ASBESTOS TEXTILES, ASBESTOS INSULATION, AND OTHER ASBESTOS-CEMENT PRODUCTS
32930	0.214	7147	32930	GASKETS, PACKING AND SEALING DEVICES, N.S.K.
			32932	GASKETS, ALL TYPES
			32933	PACKING AND SEALING DEVICES
32950	0.243	3915	32950	MINERALS AND EARTHS, GROUND OR OTHERWISE TREATED
32960	0.721	7386	32961	MINERAL WOOL FOR STRUCTURAL INSULATION
			32962	MINERAL WOOL FOR INDUSTRIAL AND EQUIPMENT INSULATION
32970	0.402	3721	32970	NONCLAY REFRACTORIES, EXCEPT DEAD-BURNED MAGNESIA
3299C	0.268	1697	32990	OTHER NONMETALLIC MINERAL PRODUCTS, N.E.C.

317

NEW SIC	4-FIRM CR WEISS	CENSUS VALUE OF SHIPMENTS	OLD SIC	DESCRIPTION
33120	0.000	2899	33120	OTHER STEEL MILL PRODUCTS, EXCEPT WIRE PRODUCTS
33121	0.560	14973	33121	COKE OVEN AND BLAST FURNACE PRODUCTS, INCLUDING FERROLLOYS. (SEE ALSO PRODUCT GROUP 3313-.)
33122	0.580	25029	33122	STEEL INGOT AND SEMIFINISHED SHAPES
33123	0.540	67401	33123	HOT-ROLLED SHEET AND STRIP, INCLUDING TIN-MILL PRODUCTS
33124	0.590	56128	33124	HOT-ROLLED BARS AND BAR SHAPES, PLATES, STRUCTURAL SHAPES, AND PILING
33125	0.350	7263	33125 33155	STEEL WIRE MADE IN STEEL MILLS STEEL WIRE NOT MADE IN STEEL MILLS
33126	0.360	27655	33126 33176	STEEL PIPE AND TUBES MADE IN STEEL MILLS STEEL PIPE AND TUBES NOT MADE IN STEEL MILLS
33127	0.350	40379	33127 33167	COLD-ROLLED STEEL SHEET AND STRIP MADE IN STEEL MILLS COLD-ROLLED STEEL SHEET AND STRIP NOT MADE IN STEEL MILLS
33128	0.410	8276	33128 33168	COLD-FINISHED STEEL BARS AND BAR SHAPES MADE IN STEEL MILLS COLD-FINISHED STEEL BARS AND BAR SHAPES NOT MADE IN STEEL MILLS
33129	0.390	5245	33129 34629	PRESS AND HAMMER STEEL FORGINGS MADE IN STEEL WORKS PRESS AND HAMMER STEEL FORGINGS MADE IN STEEL FORGINGS AND OTHER INDUSTRIES
33130	0.672	5523	33131 33132 33133 33134	FERROMANGANESE FERROCHROME. FERROSILICON OTHER FERROALLOYS PRODUCED IN ELECTRIC FURNACES
33150	0.000	495	33150	STEEL WIRE AND RELATED PRODUCTS, N.S.K.
33151	0.000	3666	33151 34961	NONINSULATED FERROUS WIRE ROPE, CABLE AND STRAND MADE IN 3212, 3315 NONINSULATED FERROUS WIRE ROPE, CABLE AND STRAND MADE IN 3496
33152	0.440	2485	33152	STEEL NAILS AND SPIKES
33156	0.300	2456	33156 34966	FENCING AND FENCE GATES MADE IN 3312, 3315 FENCING AND FENCE GATES MADE IN 3496
33157	0.000	1289	33157 34964	FERROUS WIRE CLOTH AND OTHER WOVEN FERROUS WIRE PRODUCTS MADE IN 3312, 3315 FERROUS WIRE CLOTH AND OTHER WOVEN FERROUS WIRE PRODUCTS MADE IN 3496
33159	0.260	8475	33159 34969	OTHER FABRICATED WIRE PRODUCTS MADE IN 3312, 3315 OTHER FABRICATED WIRE PRODUCTS MADE IN 3496

NEW SIC	4-FIRM CR WEISS	CENSUS VALUE OF SHIPMENTS	OLD SIC	DESCRIPTION
33210	0.457	40338	33210	GRAY IRON FOUNDRIES, N.S.K.
			33215	DUCTILE IRON CASTINGS
			33216	MOLDS FOR HEAVY STEEL INGOTS
			33217	CAST IRON PRESSURE PIPE AND FITTINGS (EXCEPT DUCTILE)
			33218	CAST IRON SOIL PIPE AND FITTINGS
			33219	OTHER GRAY IRON CASTINGS (EXCEPT DUCTILE)
33220	0.506	4848	33221	STANDARD MALLEABLE CASTINGS
			33222	PEARLITIC MALLEABLE CASTINGS
33240	0.526	2377	33240	STEEL INVESTMENT CASTINGS
33250	0.210	10503	33250	STEEL CASTINGS, N.E.C., N.S.K.
			33252	CARBON STEEL CASTINGS
			33254	HIGH ALLOY STEEL CASTINGS (EXCEPT INVESTMENT)
			33255	OTHER ALLOY STEEL CASTINGS
33310	0.680	28471	33310	PRIMARY COPPER, N.S.K.
			33311	COPPER SMELTER PRODUCTS
			33312	REFINED COPPER MADE BY PRIMARY COPPER REFINERS
			33412	REFINED COPPER MADE BY SECONDARY REFINERS AND OTHER INDUSTRIES
33320	0.000	5082	33321	LEAD SMELTER PRODUCTS (USING CPR SAMPLE AS UNIVERSE)
			33323	REFINED LEAD MADE BY PRIMARY LEAD REFINERS (USING CPR SAMPLE AS UNIVERSE)
			33413	REFINED LEAD MADE BY SECONDARY REFINERS (USING CPR SAMPLE AS UNIVERSE)
33330	0.000	4469	33331	ZINC RESIDUES AND OTHER ZINC SMELTER PRODUCTS
			33334	REFINED ZINC MADE BY PRIMARY ZINC REFINERS
			33414	SECONDARY ZINC (PIG, INGOT, S-OT, ETC.)
33340	0.000	22906	33347	ALUMINUM INGOT MADE IN PRIMARY ALUMINUM INDUSTRY AND OTHER PRIMARY NONFERROUS INDUSTRIES
			33348	ALUMINUM EXTRUSION BILLET MADE IN PRIMARY ALUMINUM INDUSTRY AND OTHER PRIMARY NONFERROUS INDUSTRIES
			33417	ALUMINUM INGOT MADE IN SECONDARY NONFERROUS METALS INDUSTRY AND ALL OTHER INDUSTRIES
			33418	ALUMINUM EXTRUSION BILLET MADE IN SECONDARY NONFERROUS METALS
			33553	ALUMINUM INGOT MADE ALUMINUM ROLLING AND DRAWING MILLS
			33554	ALUMINUM EXTRUSION BILLET MADE IN ALUMINUM ROLLING AND DRAWING MILLS
33395	0.670	5274	33395	PRECIOUS METALS
			33415	PRECIOUS METALS
33397	0.560	5773	33397	OTHER PRIMARY NONFERROUS METALS, INCLUDING MAGNESIUM
			33416	OTHER PRIMARY NONFERROUS METALS, INCLUDING MAGNESIUM
33410	0.230	1714	33410	SECONDARY NONFERROUS METALS, N.S.K.

NEW SIC CR WEISS	4-FIRM CR WEISS	CENSUS VALUE OF SHIPMENTS	OLD SIC	DESCRIPTION
33510	0.493	28250	33510	COPPER ROLLING AND DRAWING, N.S.K.
			33511	COPPER AND COPPER-BASE ALLOY WIRE (BARE AND TINNED) FOR PURPOSES OTHER THAN ELECTRICAL TRANSMISSION
			33513	COPPER AND COPPER-BASE ALLOY ROD, BAR, AND SHAPES
			33514	COPPER AND COPPER-BASE ALLOY SHEET, STRIP, AND PLATE
			33515	COPPER AND COPPER-BASE ALLOY PIPE AND TUBE
33530	0.699	22380	33531	ALUMINUM PLATE
			33532	ALUMINUM SHEET
			33533	PLAIN ALUMINUM FOIL
			33534	ALUMINUM WELDED TUBE
33540	0.358	10264	33540	ALUMINUM EXTRUDED PRODUCTS, N.S.K.
			33541	EXTRUDED ALUMINUM, ROD, BAR, AND OTHER EXTRUDED SHAPES
			33542	ALUMINUM EXTRUDED AND DRAWN TUBE
33552	0.870	3030	33552	ROLLED ALUMINUM ROD, BAR (INCLUDING CONTINUOUS CAST) AND STRUCTURAL SHAPES
33560	0.000	450	33560	NONFERROUS ROLLING AND DRAWING, N.E.C., N.S.K.
33561	0.850	2704	33561	NICKEL AND NICKEL-BASE ALLOY MILL SHAPES (INCLUDING MONEL)
33562	0.770	1111	33562	TITANIUM MILL SHAPES
33563	0.880	3640	33563	PRECIOUS METAL MILL SHAPES
33569	0.370	2851	33569	ALL OTHER NONFERROUS METAL MILL SHAPES (MADE IN INDUSTRY 3356). (SEE ALSO PRODUCT CLASS 33573.)
33570	0.000	44381	33551	ALUMINUM AND ALUMINUM-BASED ALLOY WIRE MADE IN ALUMINUM ROLLING MILLS
			33570	NONFERROUS WIREDRAWING AND INSULATING, N.S.K.
			33571	ALUMINUM AND ALUMINUM-BASED ALLOY WIRE MADE IN NONFERROUS WIREDRAWING PLANTS AND INDUSTRIES
			33572	COPPER AND COPPER-BASE ALLOY WIRE (INCLUDING STRAND AND CABLE), BARE AND TINNED FOR ELECTRICAL TRANSMISSION
			33573	OTHER BARE NONFERROUS METAL WIRE. MADE IN NONFERROUS WIREDRAWING PLANTS. (SEE PRODUCT CLASS 33569.)
			33574	COMMUNICATION WIRE AND CABLE
			33575	NONFERROUS WIRE CLOTH AND OTHER WOVEN WIRE PRODUCTS MADE IN NONFERROUS WIREDRAWING PLANTS
			33576	APPLIANCE WIRE AND CORD AND FLEXIBLE CORD SETS MADE IN NONFERROUS WIREDRAWING AND INSULATION
			33577	MAGNET WIRE
			33578	POWER WIRE AND CABLE
			33579	OTHER INSULATED WIRE AND CABLE, N.E.C.
			34965	NONFERROUS WIRE CLOTH AND OTHER WOVEN WIRE PRODUCTS MADE BY OTHER THAN NONFERROUS WIRE

NEW SIC	4-FIRM CR WEISS	CENSUS VALUE OF SHIPMENTS	OLD SIC	DESCRIPTION
33610	0.412	11723	36996	APPLIANCE WIRE AND CORD AND FLEXIBLE CORD SETS MADE IN ELECTRICAL EQUIPMENT AND SUPPLIES N.S.K.,
				ALUMINUM FOUNDRIES, N.S.K.
			33610	ALUMINUM AND ALUMINUM-BASE ALLOY CASTINGS
			33611	OTHER ALUMINUM AND ALUMINUM-BASE ALLOY CASTINGS
			33612	
33620	0.136	4629	33620	COPPER AND COPPER-BASE ALLOY CASTINGS
33690	0.234	6035		ZINC AND ZINC-BASE ALLOY CASTINGS
			33691	MAGNESIUM AND MAGNESIUM-BASE ALLOY CASTINGS
			33692	OTHER NONFERROUS CASTINGS (EXCLUDING ZINC AND MAGNESIUM)
			33693	
33980	0.000	4541	33980	HEAT TREATING OF METAL FOR THE TRADE
33991	0.310	3227	33991	METAL POWDERS AND PASTE
33992	0.290	938	33992	OTHER PRIMARY METAL PRODUCTS, INCLUDING NONFERROUS NAILS, BRADS, SPIKES, AND STAPLES
34110	0.658	42244	34111	STEEL CANS AND TINWARE END PRODUCTS, (INCLUDES 34112, ALUMINUM CANS)
34120	0.359	5094	34121	STEEL PAILS (12-GALLON CAPACITY AND UNDER)
			34122	STEEL SHIPPING BARRELS AND DRUMS (OVER 12-GALLON CAPACITY)
			34123	ALL OTHER METAL BARRELS
34211	0.290	1833	34211	CUTLERY, SCISSORS, SHEARS, TRIMMERS, AND SNIPS
34212	0.970	2072	34212	RAZOR BLADES AND RAZORS, EXCEPT ELECTRIC
34230	0.000	780	34230	HAND AND EDGE TOOLS, N.E.C., N.S.K.
34231	0.330	6012	34231	MECHANICS'HAND SERVICE TOOLS
34232	0.330	1601	34232	EDGE TOOLS, HAND OPERATED
34233	0.480	2747	34233	FILES, RASPS, AND FILE ACCESSORIES AND OTHER HANDTOOLS
34250	0.351	2018	34250	HANDSAWS, SAW BLADES, AND SAW ACCESSORIES
34292	0.380	2050	34292	FURNITURE HARDWARE
34293	0.930	854	34293	VACUUM AND INSULATED BOTTLES, JUGS, AND CHESTS
34294	0.290	9283	34294	BUILDERS' HARDWARE
34296	0.000	11803	34296	MOTOR VEHICLE HARDWARE

NEW SIC	4-FIRM CR WEISS	CENSUS VALUE OF SHIPMENTS	OLD SIC	DESCRIPTION
34297	0.270	1756	34297	OTHER TRANSPORTATION EQUIPMENT HARDWARE, EXCEPT MOTOR VEHICLE HARDWARE
34298	0.230	3939	34298	OTHER HARDWARE, N.E.C.
34320	0.230	6766	34320	PLUMBING FIXTURE FITTINGS AND TRIM (BRASS GOODS)
34330	0.160	673	34330	HEATING EQUIPMENT, EXCEPT ELECTRIC, N.S.K.
34333	0.490	1525	34333	CAST-IRON HEATING BOILERS, RADIATORS, AND CONVECTORS, EXCEPT PARTS
34334	0.480	700	34334	DOMESTIC HEATING STOVES (EXCEPT ELECTRIC), EXCEPT PARTS
34335	0.450	687	34335	STEEL HEATING BOILERS (15 P.S.I. AND UNDER), EXCEPT PARTS
34337	0.250	5655	34337	OTHER HEATING EQUIPMENT, EXCEPT ELECTRIC
34410	0.417	33059	34410	FABRICATED STRUCTURAL METAL, N.S.K.
			34411	FABRICATED STRUCTURAL METAL FOR BUILDINGS
			34412	FABRICATED STRUCTURAL METAL FOR BRIDGES
			34413	OTHER FABRICATED STRUCTURAL METAL
34420	0.110	19029	34420	METAL DOORS, SASH, AND TRIM, N.S.K.
			34421	METAL DOORS AND FRAMES (EXCEPT STORM DOORS)
			34422	METAL WINDOW SASH AND FRAMES (EXCEPT STORM SASH)
			34423	METAL MOLDING AND TRIM AND STORE FRONTS
			34424	METAL COMBINATION SCREEN AND STORM SASH AND DOORS
			34425	METAL WINDOW AND DOOR SCREENS (EXCEPT COMBINATION), AND METAL WEATHERSTRIP
34430	0.270	1984	34430	FABRICATED PLATEWORK (BOILER SHOPS), N.S.K.
34431	0.310	4471	34431	HEAT EXCHANGERS AND STEAM CONDENSERS
34432	0.170	6173	34432	FABRICATED STEEL PLATE, INCLUDING STACKS AND WELDMENTS
34433	0.830	7282	34433	STEEL POWER BOILERS, PARTS, AND ATTACHMENTS (OVER 15 P.S.I. STEAM WORKING PRESSURE)
34434	0.540	935	34434	GAS CYLINDERS
34435	0.340	1747	34435	METAL TANKS, COMPLETE AT FACTORY (STANDARD LINE, PRESSURE)
34437	0.130	2551	34437	METAL TANKS, COMPLETE AT FACTORY (STANDARD LINE, NON-PRESSURE)
34438	0.220	3821	34438	METAL TANKS AND VESSELS, CUSTOM FABRICATED AT THE FACTORY
34439	0.580	3693	34439	METAL TANKS AND VESSELS, CUSTOM FABRICATED AND FIELD ERECTED

NEW SIC	4-FIRM CR WEISS	CENSUS VALUE OF SHIPMENTS	OLD SIC	DESCRIPTION
34440	0.240	26507	34440	SHEET METALWORK, N.S.K.
			34442	CULVERTS, FLUMES, AND IRRIGATION PIPES
			34444	METAL ROOFING AND ROOF DRAINAGE EQUIPMENT
			34445	METAL FLOORING AND SIDING
			34446	OTHER SHEET METALWORK
34460	0.108	5894	34460	ARCHITECTURAL AND ORNAMENTAL METALWORK (EXCEPT CURTAIN WALL AND OTHER EXTERIOR PANELS)
34480	0.310	5788	34481	PREFABRICATED METAL INDUSTRIAL AND COMMERCIAL BUILDINGS
			34482	OTHER PREFABRICATED AND PORTABLE METAL BUILDINGS AND PARTS
34490	0.456	9946	34490	MISCELLANEOUS METALWORK, N.S.K.
			34494	FABRICATED CONCRETE REINFORCING BAR AND BAR JOISTS
			34495	OTHER MISCELLANEOUS METAL BUILDING MATERIALS AND CURTAIN WALL
34510	0.140	10831	34510	SCREW MACHINE PRODUCTS, N.S.K.
			34511	AUTOMOTIVE SCREW MACHINE PRODUCTS
			34512	OTHER SCREW MACHINE PRODUCTS
34520	0.150	19884	34520	BOLTS, NUTS, RIVETS, AND WASHERS, N.S.K.
			34524	EXTERNALLY THREADED FASTENERS, EXCEPT AIRCRAFT
			34525	INTERNALLY THREADED FASTENERS, EXCEPT AIRCRAFT
			34526	NONTHREADED FASTENERS, EXCEPT AIRCRAFT
			34527	AIRCRAFT AEROSPACE FASTENERS
			34528	OTHER FORMED PARTS
34620	0.297	18387	34620	IRON AND STEEL FORGINGS, N.S.K.
			34621	DROP, UPSET AND PRESS STEEL FORGINGS (CLOSED DIE)
34630	0.486	2808	34630	NONFERROUS FORGINGS, N.S.K.
			34631	ALUMINUM AND ALUMINUM-BASE ALLOY FORGINGS
			34632	OTHER NONFERROUS FORGINGS (EXCEPT ALUMINUM)
34650	0.696	51558	34650	JOB STAMPINGS, AUTOMOTIVE
34660	0.476	3394	34661	METAL COMMERCIAL CLOSURES AND METAL HOME CANNING CLOSURES (EXCEPT CROWNS)
			34662	METAL CROWNS
34690	0.000	3540	34690	METAL STAMPINGS, N.E.C., N.S.K.
34692	0.110	12831	34692	JOB STAMPINGS, EXCEPT AUTOMOTIVE
34694	0.560	2050	34694	STAMPED AND SPUN UTENSILS, COOKING AND KITCHEN, ALUMINUM
34695	0.510	1844	34695	STAMPED AND SPUN UTENSILS, COOKING AND KITCHEN, EXCEPT ALUMINUM
34699	0.090	5884	34699	OTHER STAMPED AND PRESSED METAL END PRODUCTS

NEW SIC	4-FIRM CR WEISS	CENSUS VALUE OF SHIPMENTS	OLD SIC	DESCRIPTION
34710	0.240	9934	34710	ELECTROPLATING, PLATING, AND POLISHING
34790	0.150	6820	34790	COATING, ENGRAVING, AND ALLIED SERVICES, N.E.C.
34820	0.847	4226	34820	SMALL ARMS AMMUNITION, 30MM. AND UNDER (OR 1.18 INCHES AND UNDER)
34830	0.388	13032	34830	AMMUNITION, EXCEPT FOR SMALL ARMS, N.E.C., N.S.K.
			34831	ARTILLERY AMMUNITION OVER 30 MM. (OR OVER 1.18 INCHES'). (INCLUDES 34832, RECEIPTS FOR AMMUNITION LOADING AND ASSEMBLY OVER 30 MM.)
			34833	AMMUNITION, EXCEPT FOR SMALL ARMS, N.E.C.
34840	0.440	3341	34841	MACHINE GUNS, 30MM. AND UNDER (OR 1.18 INCHES AND UNDER)
			34842	SMALL ARMS, 30MM. AND UNDER (OR 1.18 INCHES AND UNDER)
34890	0.398	4549	34891	GUNS, HOWITZERS MORTARS, AND RELATED EQUIPMENT, OVER 33 MM. (OR OVER 1.18 INCHES)
			34892	ORDNANCE AND ACCESSORIES, N.E.C.
34930	0.358	3618	34930	STEEL SPRINGS, EXCEPT WIRE, N.S.K.
			34931	HOT FORMED SPRINGS
			34932	COLD FORMED SPRINGS
34940	0.105	24047	34940	VALVES AND PIPE FITTINGS, N.S.K.
			34941	AUTOMATIC REGULATING AND CONTROL VALVES
			34942	VALVES FOR POWER TRANSFER (PNEUMATIC AND HYDRAULIC)
			34943	OTHER METAL VALVES FOR PIPING SYSTEMS AND EQUIPMENT
			34944	PLUMBING AND HEATING VALVES AND SPECIALITIES (EXCEPT PLUMBERS' BRASS GOODS)
			34945	METAL FITTINGS, FLANGES, AND UNIONS FOR PIPING SYSTEMS
			34946	FITTINGS AND ASSEMBLIES FOR TUBING AND HOSE (EXCEPT PLUMBERS' BRASS GOODS)
34950	0.240	5661	34952	PRECISION MECHANICAL SPRINGS
			34953	OTHER WIRE SPRINGS
34960	0.318	1902	34960	MISCELLANEOUS FABRICATED WIRE PRODUCTS, N.S.K.
34970	0.381	5118	34970	METAL FOIL AND LEAF, N.S.K.
			34971	CONVERTED UNMOUNTED ALUMINUM FOIL PACKAGING PRODUCTS, NOT LAMINATED TO OTHER MATERIALS
			34972	LAMINATED ALUMINUM FOIL ROLL AND SHEETS FOR FLEXIBLE PACKAGING USES
			34973	CONVERTED ALUMINUM FOIL FOR NONPACKAGING APPLICATIONS AND FOIL AND LEAF
34980	0.190	6705	34980	FABRICATED PIPE AND FITTINGS
34990	0.000	3782	34990	FABRICATED METAL PRODUCTS, N.E.C., N.S.K.
34991	0.890	1462	34991	SAFES AND VAULTS

324

NEW SIC	4-FIRM CR WEISS	CENSUS VALUE OF SHIPMENTS	OLD SIC	DESCRIPTION
34992	0.700	491	34992	COLLAPSIBLE TUBES
34993	0.850	1678	34993	FLAT METAL STRAPPING
34994	0.180	13905	34994	ALL OTHER FABRICATED METAL PRODUCTS, EXCEPT FLAT
35110	0.774	20797	35110 35111 35112	TURBINES AND TURBINE GENERATOR SETS, N.S.K. STEAM, GAS, AND HYDRAULIC TURBINE GENERATOR SET UNITS AND PARTS STEAM, GAS, AND HYDRAULIC TURBINES AND PARTS
35191	0.910	3268	35191	GASOLINE ENGINES, UNDER 11 HORSEPOWER, EXCEPT AIRCRAFT, AUTOMOBILE, TRUCK, BUS, AND TANK
35192	0.590	1640	35192	GASOLINE ENGINES, 11 HORSEPOWER AND OVER, EXCEPT AIRCRAFT, AUTOMOBILE, TRUCK, BUS, AND TANK
35193	0.800	6040	35193	DIESEL ENGINES, EXCEPT FOR TRUCKS AND BUSES
35194	0.960	6346	35194	DIESEL ENGINES FOR TRUCKS AND BUSES
35195	0.850	4259	35195	OUTBOARD MOTORS AND TANK AND CONVERTED INTERNAL COMBUSTION ENGINES (INCLUDES 35197)
35196	0.770	352	35196	GAS ENGINES (EXCEPT GAS TURBINES)
35199	0.510	11449	35199	PARTS AND ACCESSORIES FOR INTERNAL COMBUSTION ENGINES
35230	0.000	2046	35230	FARM MACHINERY AND EQUIPMENT, N.S.K.
35231	0.810	12152	35231	WHEEL TRACTORS AND ATTACHMENTS (EXCEPT CONTRACTORS' OFF-HIGHWAY TYPE, GARDEN TRACTORS, AND MOTOR TILLERS)
35232	0.270	1578	35232	FARM DAIRY MACHINES, SPRAYERS, AND DUSTERS, FARM ELEVATORS, AND FARM BLOWERS
35233	0.430	1720	35233	PLANTING, SEEDING, AND FERTILIZING MACHINERY
35234	0.360	1918	35234	HARROWS, ROLLERS, PULVERIZERS, STALK CUTTERS, AND SIMILAR EQUIPMENT
35235	0.710	5804	35235	HARVESTING MACHINERY
35236	0.820	1841	35236	HAYING MACHINERY
35237	0.700	854	35237	PLOWS AND LISTERS
35238	0.150	6108	35238	ALL OTHER FARM MACHINERY AND EQUIPMENT
35239	0.510	7414	35239	PARTS FOR FARM MACHINERY AND EQUIPMENT, SOLD SEPARATELY
35240	0.274	11434	35242	GARDEN TRACTORS AND MOTOR TILLERS

NEW SIC	4-FIRM CR WEISS	CENSUS VALUE OF SHIPMENTS	OLD SIC	DESCRIPTION
35310	0.000	1177	35247 35249	LAWNMOWERS AND SNOW BLOWERS PARTS FOR LAWN AND GARDEN EQUIPMENT, FOR SALE SEPARATELY
35311	0.760	2515	35310	CONSTRUCTION MACHINERY, N.S.K.
35312	0.910	5640	35311	CONTRACTORS' OFF-HIGHWAY WHEEL TRACTORS, EXCEPT
35313	0.700	8657	35312	TRACKLAYING TYPE TRACTORS, EXCEPT PARTS AND ATTACHMENTS
35314	0.430	9142	35313	PARTS AND ATTACHMENTS FOR TRACKLAYING TYPE TRACTORS, CONTRACTORS' OFF-HIGHWAY WHEEL TRACTORS, AND TRACTOR SHOVEL LOADERS
35316	0.390	2520	35314	POWER CRANES (INCLUDING LOCOMOTIVE AND FULL-CIRCLE REVOLVING WITH BOOMS), DRAGLINES, SHOVELS AND PARTS
35317	0.750	8107	35316	MIXERS, PAVERS, AND RELATED EQUIPMENT, EXCLUDING PARTS
35318	0.480	9648	35317	TRACTOR SHOVEL LOADERS, EXCLUDING PARTS AND ATTACHMENTS
35319	0.220	9130	35318	SCRAPERS, GRADERS, ROLLERS, AND OFF-HIGHWAY TRUCKS, TRAILERS, AND WAGONS (EXCLUDING PARTS)
35320	0.332	7298	35319	OTHER CONSTRUCTION MACHINERY AND EQUIPMENT, INCLUDING PARTS
35331	0.560	3482	35321 35322 35323 35324	UNDERGROUND MINING AND MINERAL BENEFICIATION MACHINERY AND EQUIPMENT CRUSHING, PULVERIZING, AND SCREENING MACHINERY ALL OTHER MINING MACHINERY AND EQUIPMENT PARTS AND ATTACHMENTS FOR MINING MACHINERY AND EQUIPMENT
35332	0.500	870	35331	ROTARY OILFIELD AND GASFIELD DRILLING MACHINERY AND EQUIPMENT
35333	0.400	3765	35332	OTHER OILFIELD AND GASFIELD DRILLING MACHINERY AND EQUIPMENT
35334	0.370	1136	35333	OILFIELD AND GASFIELD PRODUCTION MACHINERY AND EQUIPMENT (EXCEPT PUMPS)
35340	0.515	4122	35334	OTHER OILFIELD AND GASFIELD MACHINERY AND TOOLS (EXCEPT PUMPS), INCLUDING WATER WELL
35350	0.188	8256	35340	ELEVATORS AND MOVING STAIRWAYS
35360	0.205	4460	35351 35352	CONVEYORS AND CONVEYING EQUIPMENT (EXCEPT HOISTS AND FARM ELEVATORS) PARTS, ATTACHMENTS, AND ACCESSORIES FOR CONVEYORS AND CONVEYING EQUIPMENT
			35360 35361 35362	HOISTS, CRANES, AND MONORAILS, N.S.K. HOISTS OVERHEAD TRAVELING CRANES AND MONORAIL SYSTEMS

NEW SIC	4-FIRM CR WEISS	CENSUS VALUE OF SHIPMENTS	OLD SIC	DESCRIPTION
35370	0.445	10048	35370 35371 35372	INDUSTRIAL TRUCKS AND TRACTORS, N.S.K. INDUSTRIAL TRUCKS AND TRACTORS PARTS AND ATTACHMENTS FOR INDUSTRIAL TRUCKS AND TRACTORS, AND MISCELLANEOUS MATERIALS HANDLING EQUIPMENT
35411	0.430	587	35411	BORING MACHINES
35412	0.330	737	35412	DRILLING MACHINES
35413	0.790	567	35413	GEAR CUTTING AND FINISHING MACHINES
35414	0.400	1686	35414	GRINDING AND POLISHING MACHINES (EXCLUDING GEAR TOOTH GRINDING, HONING, LAPPING, POLISHING, AND BUFFING MACHINES)
35415	0.380	1976	35415	LATHES
35416	0.620	866	35416	MILLING MACHINES
35418	0.260	3031	35418	OTHER MACHINE TOOLS (INCLUDING THOSE PRIMARILY DESIGNED FOR HOME WORKSHOPS, LABORATORIES, ETC.)
35419	0.280	2421	35419	PARTS FOR METAL-CUTTING TYPE MACHINE TOOLS, SOLD SEPARATELY, AND REBUILT MACHINE TOOLS
35420	0.304	6701	35420 35421 35422 35423 35424	MACHINE TOOLS, METAL-FORMING, N.S.K. PUNCHING, SHEARING, BENDING, AND FORMING MACHINES PRESSES, INCLUDING FORGING PRESSES OTHER METAL-FORMING MACHINE TOOLS, INCLUDING FORGING MACHINES PARTS FOR METAL-FORMING MACHINE TOOLS AND REBUILT METAL-FORMING MACHINERY
35440	0.098	27135	35440 35441 35442	SPECIAL DIES, TOOLS, JIGS AND FIXTURES, N.S.K. SPECIAL DIES AND TOOLS, DIE SETS, JIGS, AND FIXTURES INDUSTRIAL MOLDS
35450	0.000	999	35450	MACHINE TOOL ACCESSORIES, N.S.K.
35451	0.230	7380	35451	SMALL CUTTING TOOLS FOR MACHINE TOOLS AND METALWORKING MACHINERY
35452	0.520	947	35452	PRECISION MEASURING TOOLS
35453	0.170	2188	35453	OTHER ATTACHMENTS AND ACCESSORIES FOR MACHINE TOOLS AND METAL-WORKING MACHINERY
35460	0.379	6229	35460 35461 35462	POWER-DRIVEN HANDTOOLS, N.S.K. POWER-DRIVEN HANDTOOLS, ELECTRIC POWER-DRIVEN HANDTOOLS, PNEUMATIC AND POWDER ACTUATED
35470	0.717	2479	35470	ROLLING MILL MACHINERY, N.S.K.

NEW SIC	4-FIRM CR WEISS	CENSUS VALUE OF SHIPMENTS	OLD SIC	DESCRIPTION
35493	0.630	937	35471	HOT ROLLING MILL MACHINERY, EXCEPT TUBE ROLLING
			35472	COLD ROLLING MILL MACHINERY
			35473	OTHER ROLLING MILL MACHINERY, INCLUDING TUBE MILL MACHINERY
35494	0.430	1111	35493	WELDING AND CUTTING APPARATUS, EXCEPT ELECTRIC
35495	0.240	1545	35494	AUTOMOTIVE MAINTENANCE EQUIPMENT
35511	0.570	574	35495	OTHER METALWORKING MACHINERY
35512	0.330	1850	35511	DAIRY AND MILK PRODUCTS PLANT MACHINERY AND EQUIPMENT, EXCEPT BOTTLING AND PACKAGING MACHINERY
35513	0.230	2962	35512	COMMERCIAL FOOD PRODUCTS MACHINERY, EXCEPT WRAPPING MACHINES
35514	0.310	2321	35513	OTHER INDUSTRIAL FOOD PRODUCTS MACHINERY (EXCEPT PACKING AND BOTTLING MACHINERY) AND PARTS AND ATTACHMENTS
35520	0.159	7381	35514	PACKING, PACKAGING, AND BOTTLING MACHINERY FOR INDUSTRIAL FOOD PRODUCTS
35531	0.390	3725	35521	TEXTILE MACHINERY
			35522	PARTS AND ATTACHMENTS FOR TEXTILE MACHINERY
35532	0.900	515	35531	WOODWORKING MACHINERY (EXCEPT HOME WORKSHOP), INCLUDING PARTS AND ATTACHMENTS
35540	0.259	3814	35532	WOODWORKING MACHINERY FOR HOME WORKSHOP (EXCEPT POWERDRIVEN HANDTOOLS), INCLUDING PARTS AND ATTACHMENTS
35550	0.000	493	35540	PAPER INDUSTRIES MACHINERY AND PARTS AND ATTACHMENTS
35551	0.710	1560	35550	PRINTING TRADES MACHINERY, N.S.K.
35552	0.510	902	35551	PRINTING PRESSES, LITHOGRAPHIC
35553	0.720	1041	35552	PRINTING PRESSES, OTHER THAN LITHOGRAPHIC
35554	0.750	335	35553	TYPESETTING MACHINERY AND EQUIPMENT
35555	0.260	3035	35554	BINDERY EQUIPMENT
35590	0.000	1695	35555	OTHER PRINTING TRADES MACHINERY AND EQUIPMENT AND PARTS AND ATTACHMENTS FOR ALL PRINTING TRADES MACHINERY AND EQUIPMENT
35591	0.290	2125	35590	SPECIAL INDUSTRY MACHINERY, N.E.C., N.S.K.
			35591	CHEMICAL MANUFACTURING INDUSTRIES MACHINERY AND EQUIPMENT AND PARTS

NEW SIC	4-FIRM CR WEISS	CENSUS VALUE OF SHIPMENTS	OLD SIC	DESCRIPTION
35592	0.560	1323	35592	FOUNDRY MACHINERY AND EQUIPMENT, EXCLUDING PATTERNS AND MOLDS
35593	0.310	4341	35593	PLASTICS-WORKING MACHINERY AND EQUIPMENT, EXCLUDING PATTERNS AND MOLDS
35594	0.530	1373	35594	RUBBER-WORKING MACHINERY AND EQUIPMENT, EXCLUDING TIRE MOLDS
35595	0.260	12814	35595	OTHER SPECIAL INDUSTRY MACHINERY AND EQUIPMENT
35610	0.000	754	35610	PUMPS AND PUMPING EQUIPMENT, N.S.K.
35611	0.220	6119	35611	INDUSTRIAL PUMPS, EXCEPT HYDRAULIC FLUID POWER PUMPS
35612	0.440	2616	35612	HYDRAULIC FLUID POWER PUMPS
356-3	0.410	1511	35613	DOMESTIC WATER SYSTEMS AND PUMPS, INCLUDING PUMP JACKS AND CYLINDERS
35615	0.260	1864	35615	PUMPS AND PUMPING EQUIPMENT, N.E.C.
35616	0.210	3465	35616	PARTS AND ATTACHMENTS FOR PUMPS AND PUMPING EQUIPMENT
35620	0.619	14187	35621 35622 35623 35624 35629	BALL BEARINGS, COMPLETE / TAPER (EXCEPT THRUST) ROLLER BEARINGS, COMPLETE / OTHER ROLLER BEARINGS, COMPLETE / MOUNTED BEARINGS / PARTS AND COMPONENTS FOR BALL AND ROLLER BEARINGS, INCLUDING BALLS AND ROLLERS, SOLD SEPARATELY
35630	0.384	7227	35631 35632	AIR AND GAS COMPRESSORS AND VACUUM PUMPS / PARTS AND ATTACHMENTS FOR AIR AND GAS COMPRESSORS, EXCEPT REFRIGERATION EQUIPMENT
35640	0.153	6820	35640 35643 35644 35645 35646	BLOWERS AND FANS, N.S.K. / CENTRIFUGAL FANS AND BLOWERS / PROPELLER FANS AND ACCESSORIES, AXIAL FANS, AND POWER ROOF VENTILATORS / DUST COLLECTION AND OTHER AIR PURIFICATION EQUIPMENT FOR HEATING, VENTILATING AND AIR-CONDITIONING SYSTEMS / DUST COLLECTION AND OTHER AIR PURIFICATION EQUIPMENT FOR INDUSTRIAL GAS CLEANING SYSTEMS
35650	0.060	2344	35650	INDUSTRIAL PATTERNS, EXCEPT SHOE PATTERNS
35660	0.243	5930	35660	SPEED CHANGERS, INDUSTRIAL HIGH-SPEED DRIVES, AND GEARS (INCLUDES 35680, POWER TRANSMISSION EQUIPMENT, N.E.C., N.S.K.)
35670	0.000	294	35670	INDUSTRIAL FURNACES AND OVENS, N.S.K.
35671	0.440	675	35671	ELECTRIC INDUSTRIAL FURNACES AND OVENS, METAL PROCESSING

NEW SIC	4-FIRM CR WEISS	CENSUS VALUE OF SHIPMENTS	OLD SIC	DESCRIPTION
35672	0.430	972	35672	FUEL-FIRED INDUSTRIAL FURNACES AND OVENS, METAL PROCESSING
35673	0.400	1470	35673	HIGH FREQUENCY INDUCTION AND DIELECTRIC HEATING EQUIPMENT AND PARTS, ATTACHMENTS, AND COMPONENTS
35680	0.309	9750	35681 35683	PLAIN BEARINGS AND BUSHINGS; OTHER MECHANICAL POWER TRANSMISSION EQUIPMENT, EXCEPT SPEED CHANGERS, DRIVES, AND GEARS
35690	0.000	1445	35690	GENERAL INDUSTRIAL MACHINERY, N.E.C., N.S.K.
35691	0.250	1774	35691	PACKING AND PACKAGING MACHINERY, N.E.C.
35692	0.290	2754	35692	FILTERS AND STRAINERS
35699	0.120	5355	35699	ALL OTHER GENERAL INDUSTRIAL MACHINERY, N.E.C.
35731	0.750	18843	35731	ELECTRONIC COMPUTING EQUIPMENT (EXCEPT PARTS AND ATTACHMENTS)
35732	0.520	27453	35732	PERIPHERAL EQUIPMENT FOR ELECTRONIC COMPUTERS
35733	0.630	14032	35733	PARTS AND ATTACHMENTS FOR ELECTRONIC COMPUTING EQUIPMENT
35740	0.495	6942	35742 35745	ELECTRONIC CALCULATING MACHINES; PARTS AND ATTACHMENTS FOR ADDING, CALCULATING, ACCOUNTING MACHINES AND CASH REGISTERS (INCLUDES 35741, ADDING AND CALCULATING MACHINES EXCEPT ELECTRONIC; AND 35743 ACCOUNTING MACHINES AND CASH REGISTERS.)
35760	0.512	1821	35760	SCALES AND BALANCES, EXCEPT LABORATORY
35790	0.000	180	35790	OFFICE MACHINES, N.E.C., N.S.K.
35793	0.870	836	35793	DUPLICATION MACHINES
35795	0.770	1286	35795	MAILING, LETTER HANDLING, AND ADDRESSING MACHINES
35796	0.390	2547	35796	ALL OTHER OFFICE MACHINES, N.E.C. (INCLUDES 35794, DICTATING, TRANSCRIBING, AND RECORDING MACHINES.)
35798	0.840	5620	35798	PARTS AND ATTACHMENTS FOR ADDRESSING, DICTATING, DUPLICATING, AND OTHER OFFICE STORE MACHINES, N.E.C. (INCLUDES 357200, TYPEWRITERS, INCLUDED CODED MEDIA, PARTS AND ATTACHMENTS.)
35810	0.492	3063	35811 35812	AUTOMATIC MERCHANDISING MACHINES; COIN-OPERATED MECHANISMS AND PARTS FOR AUTOMATIC MERCHANDISING MACHINES
35820	0.402	1853	35820	COMMERCIAL LAUNDRY EQUIPMENT

NEW SIC	4-FIRM CR WEISS	CENSUS VALUE OF SHIPMENTS	OLD SIC	DESCRIPTION
35851	0.450	16805	35851	HEAT TRANSFER EQUIPMENT, EXCEPT ROOM AND UNITARY AIRCONDITIONERS AND DEHUMIDIFIERS
35852	0.480	10706	35852	UNITARY AIR-CONDITIONERS
35853	0.290	4823	35853	COMMERCIAL REFRIGERATION EQUIPMENT
35854	0.720	10654	35854	COMPRESSORS AND COMPRESSOR UNITS, ALL REFRIGERANTS
35855	0.480	1468	35855	CONDENSING UNITS, ALL REFRIGERANTS
35856	0.540	6796	35856	ROOM AIR-CONDITIONERS AND DEHUMIDIFIERS
35857	0.440	5703	35857	OTHER REFRIGERATION AND AIR-CONDITIONING EQUIPMENT, INCLUDING SODA FOUNTAIN AND BEER DISPENSING EQUIPMENT
35858	0.340	3842	35858	WARM AIR FURNACES (EXCEPT FLOOR AND WALL) AND PARTS AND ATTACHMENTS
35860	0.371	1834	35860	MEASURING AND DISPENSING PUMPS
35890	0.000	882	35890	SERVICE INDUSTRY MACHINES, N.E.C., N.S.K.
35891	0.270	2170	35891	COMMERCIAL COOKING AND FOOD WARMING EQUIPMENT
35892	0.180	4965	35892	SERVICE INDUSTRY MACHINES AND PARTS
35893	0.490	627	35893	COMMERCIAL AND INDUSTRIAL VACUUM CLEANERS, INCLUDING PARTS AND ATTACHMENTS
35920	0.704	7919	35920 35921 35922 35923	CARBURETORS, PISTONS, RINGS, AND VALVES, N.S.K. CARBURETORS, NEW AND REBUILT PISTONS AND PISTON RINGS VALVES, INTAKE AND EXHAUST
35990	0.000	13058	35990	MACHINERY, EXCEPT ELECTRICAL, N.E.C., N.S.K.
35992	0.270	1892	35992	PNEUMATIC AND HYDRAULIC CYLINDERS
35994	0.120	4425	35994	MISCELLANEOUS MACHINERY PRODUCTS
35995	0.030	14258	35995	RECEIPTS FOR MACHINE SHOP JOB WORK
36120	0.000	249	36120	TRANSFORMERS, N.S.K.
36122	0.670	9139	36122	POWER AND DISTRIBUTION TRANSFORMERS, EXCEPT PARTS
36124	0.960	1606	36124	FLUORESCENT LAMP BALLASTS
36125	0.530	2253	36125	SPECIALTY TRANSFORMERS (EXCEPT FLUORESCENT LAMPBALLASTS)

NEW SIC	4-FIRM CR WEISS	CENSUS VALUE OF SHIPMENTS	OLD SIC	DESCRIPTION
36127	0.800	1114	36127	POWER REGULATORS, BOOSTERS, REACTORS, OTHER TRANSFORMERS, AND TRANSFORMER PARTS
36131	0.550	5971	36131	SWITCHGEAR, EXCEPT DUCTS AND RELAYS
36132	0.860	1827	36132	POWER CIRCUIT BREAKERS, ALL VOLTAGES
36133	0.600	5390	36133	LOW VOLTAGE PANELBOARDS AND DISTRIBUTION BOARDS AND OTHER SWITCHING AND INTERRUPTING DEVICES 750 VOLTS AND UNDER
36134	0.830	997	36134	FUSES AND FUSE EQUIPMENT, UNDER 2,300 VOLTS (EXCEPT POWER DISTRIBUTION CUT-OUTS)
36135	0.720	2830	36135	MOLDED CASE CIRCUIT BREAKERS, 750 VOLTS AND UNDER
36136	0.670	657	36136	DUCT, INCLUDING PLUG-IN UNITS AND ACCESSORIES, 750 VOLTS AND UNDER
36137	0.400	2234	36137	RELAYS, CONTROL CIRCUIT
36210	0.000	364	36210	MOTORS AND GENERATORS, N.S.K.
36211	0.470	11377	36211	FRACTIONAL HORSEPOWER MOTORS
36212	0.590	5677	36212	INTEGRAL HORSEPOWER MOTORS AND GENERATORS, EXCEPT FOR LAND TRANSPORTATION EQUIPMENT
36213	0.790	1063	36213	LAND TRANSPORTATION MOTORS, GENERATORS, AND CONTROL EQUIPMENT AND PARTS
36214	0.590	2473	36214	PRIME MOVER GENERATOR SETS, EXCEPT STEAM OR HYDRAULIC TURBINE
36217	0.770	2288	36217	MOTOR-GENERATOR SETS AND OTHER ROTATING EQUIPMENT, INCLUDING HERMETICS (FRACTIONAL)
36218	0.760	1229	36218	MOTOR-GENERATOR SETS AND OTHER ROTATING EQUIPMENT, INCLUDING HERMETICS (INTEGRAL)
36219	0.390	1886	36219	PARTS AND SUPPLIES FOR MOTORS, GENERATORS, AND MOTORGENERATOR SETS, EXCEPT FOR LAND TRANSPORTATION EQUIPMENT
36220	0.384	12456	36220	GENERAL INDUSTRY POWER CIRCUIT DEVICES AND CONTROLS AND PARTS
36230	0.374	5700	36231 36232 36233	ARC WELDING MACHINES, COMPONENTS, AND ACCESSORIES, EXCEPT ELECTRODES ARC WELDING ELECTRODES, METAL RESISTANCE WELDERS, COMPONENTS, ACCESSORIES, AND ELECTRODES
36240	0.720	3359	36240 36241 36249	CARBON AND GRAPHITE PRODUCTS, N.S.K. ELECTRODES ALL OTHER CARBON AND GRAPHITE PRODUCTS
36291	0.780	1124	36291	CAPACITORS FOR INDUSTRIAL USE, EXCEPT FOR ELECTRONIC APPLICATIONS

NEW SIC	4-FIRM CR WEISS	CENSUS VALUE OF SHIPMENTS	OLD SIC	DESCRIPTION
36292	0.410	1526	36292	RECTIFYING APPARATUS
36293	0.320	1459	36293	OTHER ELECTRICAL EQUIPMENT FOR INDUSTRIAL USE
36310	0.441	10270	36311	ELECTRIC HOUSEHOLD RANGES AND OVENS AND SURFACE COOKING UNIT EQUIPMENT AND PARTS, EXCEPT SMALL APPLIANCES
			36312	HOUSEHOLD OVENS AND RANGES, EQUIPMENT AND PARTS, EXCEPT ELECTRIC
36320	0.690	14194	36320	HOUSEHOLD REFRIGERATORS AND FREEZERS, N.S.K.
			36321	HOUSEHOLD REFRIGERATORS, INCLUDING COMBINATION REFRIGERATOR-FREEZERS
			36322	HOME AND FARM FREEZERS
36330	0.749	12899	36331	HOUSEHOLD MECHANICAL WASHING MACHINES, DRYERS, AND WASHER-DRYER COMBINATIONS
			36333	OTHER HOUSEHOLD LAUNDRY EQUIPMENT AND PARTS
36340	0.000	554	36340	ELECTRIC HOUSEWARES AND FANS, N.S.K.
36341	0.520	1277	36341	ELECTRIC FANS, EXCEPT INDUSTRIAL TYPE
36342	0.940	643	36342	ELECTRIC RAZORS AND DRY SHAVERS
36343	0.420	11216	36343	OTHER SMALL HOUSEHOLD ELECTRIC APPLIANCES
36344	0.510	790	36344	PARTS AND ATTACHMENTS FOR SMALL ELECTRIC APPLIANCES
36350	0.653	4392	36350	HOUSEHOLD VACUUM CLEANERS, INCLUDING PARTS AND ATTACHMENTS
36360	0.298	1521	36360	SEWING MACHINES AND PARTS, EXCLUDING CASES AND CABINETS SOLD SEPARATELY
36391	0.620	1199	36391	HOUSEHOLD WATER HEATERS, ELECTRIC
36392	0.670	1795	36392	HOUSEHOLD WATER HEATERS, EXCEPT ELECTRIC
36394	0.710	4179	36394	DISHWASHING MACHINES AND FOOD WASTE DISPOSERS
36399	0.500	864	36399	OTHER HOUSEHOLD APPLIANCES AND PARTS
36410	0.814	10691	36410	ELECTRIC LAMPS (BULBS ONLY), INCLUDING SEALED BEAM LAMPS
36430	0.251	12068	36430	CURRENT-CARRYING WIRING DEVICES, INCLUDING LIGHTNING RODS
36441	0.530	2223	36441	POLE, LINE, AND TRANSMISSION HARDWARE
36442	0.290	3937	36442	ELECTRICAL CONDUIT AND CONDUIT FITTINGS
36443	0.340	1959	36443	OTHER NONCURRENT-CARRYING WIRING DEVICES AND SUPPLIES

NEW SIC	4-FIRM CR WEISS	CENSUS VALUE OF SHIPMENTS	OLD SIC	DESCRIPTION
36450	0.243	7461	36450 / 36451 / 36457	RESIDENTIAL LIGHTING FIXTURES, N.S.K. / RESIDENTIAL TYPE ELECTRIC FIXTURES, EXCEPT PORTABLE / PORTABLE RESIDENTIAL TYPE LIGHTING FIXTURES AND PARTS AND ACCESSORIES FOR RESIDENTIAL LIGHTING FIXTURES
36460	0.236	7018	36462 / 36463	COMMERCIAL AND INSTITUTIONAL-TYPE ELECTRIC LIGHTING FIXTURES / INDUSTRIAL-TYPE ELECTRIC LIGHTING FIXTURES AND PARTS
36470	0.612	3581	36470	VEHICULAR LIGHTING EQUIPMENT
36485	0.360	3165	36485	OUTDOOR LIGHTING EQUIPMENT
36489	0.350	1647	36489	OTHER ELECTRIC AND NONELECTRIC LIGHTING EQUIPMENT AND PARTS AND ACCESSORIES
36510	0.000	839	36510	RADIOS AND TV RECEIVING SETS, N.S.K.
36511	0.570	7545	36511	HOUSEHOLD AND AUTOMOBILE RADIOS, AND RADIO-PHONOGRAPH COMBINATIONS
36512	0.660	21487	36512	HOUSEHOLD TELEVISION RECEIVERS, INCLUDING TELEVISION COMBINATIONS
36514	0.360	3734	36514	RECORDERS, PHONOGRAPHS, AND RADIO AND TELEVISION CHASSIS
36515	0.260	2492	36515	SPEAKER SYSTEMS, MICROPHONES, HOME-TYPE ELECTRONIC KITS, AND COMMERCIAL SOUND EQUIPMENT, INCLUDING PUBLIC ADDRESS SYSTEMS
36520	0.458	5373	36520	PHONOGRAPH RECORDS, RECORD BLANKS, AND PRERECORDED TAPES
36610	0.858	39739	36611 / 36612	TELEPHONE SWITCHING AND SWITCHBOARD EQUIPMENT / OTHER TELEPHONE AND TELEGRAPH (WIRE) APPARATUS, EQUIPMENT, AND COMPONENTS
36620	0.000	2072	36620	RADIO, TV COMMUNICATION EQUIPMENT, N.S.K.
36621	0.400	15548	36621	COMMERCIAL, INDUSTRIAL, AND MILITARY COMMUNICATION EQUIPMENT, EXCEPT TELEPHONE COMMUNICATION EQUIPMENT
36622	0.420	4297	36622	RADIO AND TELEVISION BROADCAST EQUIPMENT AND CLOSED
36623	0.240	3362	36623	INTERCOMMUNICATION EQUIPMENT (EXCEPT TELEPHONE AND TELEGRAPH) AND ELECTRIC ALARM AND SIGNAL SYSTEMS AND DEVICES
36624	0.460	10739	36624	ELECTRONIC NAVIGATIONAL AIDS (EXCEPT MISSILE-BORNE AND SPACE VEHICLE-BORNE EQUIPMENT)
36625	0.380	22640	36625	ELECTRONIC SEARCH AND DETECTION APPARATUS, INCLUDING RADAR, INFRARED AND SONAR
36626	0.270	14600	36626	ELECTRONIC MILITARY, INDUSTRIAL AND COMMERCIAL EQUIPMENT, N.E.C.

NEW SIC	4-FIRM CR WEISS	CENSUS VALUE OF SHIPMENTS	OLD SIC	DESCRIPTION
36527	0.820	1247	36627	SPACE SATELLITE-BORNE COMMUNICATIONS SYSTEMS (COMPLETE PACKAGE)
36628	0.520	7778	36628	MISSLE-BORNE NAVIGATION AND GUIDANCE SYSTEMS AND EQUIPMENT
36629	0.580	1483	36629	MICROWAVE AND MOBILE TELEPHONE COMMUNICATION EQUIPMENT
36710	0.700	1896	36710	RECEIVING TYPE ELECTRON TUBES. EXCEPT CATHODE RAY
36720	0.820	6336	36720	CATHODE RAY PICTURE TUBES, INCLUDING REBUILT
36730	0.500	3662	36730	TRANSMITTAL, INDUSTRIAL, AND SPECIAL PURPOSE ELECTRON TUBES (EXCEPT X-RAY)
36740	0.448	23608	36740 36741 36742 36743 36749	SEMICONDUCTORS AND RELATED DEVICES, N.S.K. INTEGRATED MICROCIRCUITS (SEMICONDUCTOR NETWORKS) TRANSISTORS DIODES AND RECTIFIERS OTHER SEMICONDUCTOR DEVICES
35750	0.335	4544	36750	CAPACITORS FOR ELECTRONIC APPLICATIONS
36760	0.385	4381	36760	RESISTORS FOR ELECTRONIC APPLICATIONS
36770	0.136	3853	36770	COILS, TRANSFORMERS, REACTORS, AND CHOKES FOR ELECTRONIC APPLICATIONS
36780	0.463	5236	36780	ELECTRONIC CONNECTORS
36790	0.319	32098	36790	ELECTRONIC COMPONENTS, N.E.C.
36910	0.570	9527	36911 36912	STORAGE BATTERIES, STARTING, LIGHTING, AND IGNITION (SLI) TYPE STORAGE BATTERIES. OTHER THAN SLI TYPE. INCLUDING PARTS FOR STORAGE BATTERIES, ALL TYPES
36920	0.853	3167	36920	PRIMARY BATTERIES. DRY AND WET
36930	0.432	3830	36930	X-RAY EQUIPMENT. INCLUDING X-RAY TUBES AND ELECTROTHERAPEUTIC APPARATUS
36940	0.000	448	36940	ENGINE ELECTRICAL EQUIPMENT. N.S.K.
36941	0.430	1128	36941	IGNITION HARNESS AND CABLE SETS
36942	0.800	3821	36942	BATTERY CHARGING GENERATORS
36943	0.880	3137	36943	CRANKING MOTORS
36944	0.990	2903	36944	SPARK PLUGS

NEW SIC	4-FIRM CR WEISS	CENSUS VALUE OF SHIPMENTS	OLD SIC	DESCRIPTION
36945	0.630	4118	36945	OTHER COMPLETE ELECTRICAL EQUIPMENT FOR INTERNAL COMBUSTION ENGINES
36946	0.620	2255	36946	COMPONENTS AND PARTS FOR ENGINE ELECTRICAL EQUIPMENT
36990	0.260	1472	36990	ELECTRICAL EQUIPMENT AND SUPPLIES, N.E.C., N.S.K.
36992	0.440	3320	36992	LAMP BULB COMPONENTS AND OTHER ELECTRICAL PRODUCTS
37110	0.000	270	37110	MOTOR VEHICLES AND CAR BODIES, N.S.K.
37111	0.990	292462	37111	PASSENGER CARS, KNOCKED DOWN OR ASSEMBLED, AND CHASSIS FOR SALE SEPARATELY
37112	0.840	95661	37112	TRUCK TRACTORS, TRUCK CHASSIS AND TRUCKS (CHASSIS OF OWN MANUFACTURE)
37113	0.800	2409	37113	BUSES (EXCEPT TROLLEY BUSES) AND FIRE DEPARTMENT VEHICLES, (CHASSIS OF OWN MANUFACTURE)
37115	0.960	19657	37115	PASSENGER CAR BODIES (INCLUDES 37114, COMBAT VEHICLES AND TACTICAL VEHICLES. EXCEPT TANKS)
37130	0.188	14440	37130 37131 37132	TRUCK AND BUS BODIES, N.S.K. TRUCK, BUS, AND OTHER VEHICLE BODIES, EXCEPT KITS AND REBUILT PARTS COMPLETE VEHICLES, EXCEPT PASSENGER CARS, PRODUCED ON PURCHASED CHASSIS
37140	0.562	194170	37141 37143	PARTS AND ACCESSORIES FOR MOTOR VEHICLES, EXCLUDING KITS AND REBUILT PARTS REBUILT ENGINES AND PARTS FOR MOTOR VEHICLES. EXCEPT CARBURETORS
37150	0.460	10790	37151 37152	TRUCK TRAILERS AND CHASSIS (16,000 POUNDS PER AXLE OR OVER) TRUCK TRAILERS AND CHASSIS (LESS THAN 10,000 POUNDS PER AXLE)
37211	0.740	28029	37211	COMPLETE AIRCRAFT, MILITARY TYPE
37212	0.740	4742	37212	COMPLETE AIRCRAFT, PERSONAL AND UTILITY TYPE
37213	0.970	27873	37213	COMPLETE AIRCRAFT, COMMERCIAL TRANSPORT TYPE
37214	0.630	3739	37214	MODIFICATIONS, CONVERSIONS, AND OVERHAUL OF PREVIOUSLY ACCEPTED AIRCRAFT
37216	0.770	10671	37216	OTHER AERONAUTICAL SERVICES ON AIRCRAFT
37240	0.715	30697	37241 37242 37243 37244	AIRCRAFT ENGINES FOR U.S. MILITARY CUSTOMERS AIRCRAFT ENGINES FOR OTHER THAN U.S. MILITARY CUSTOMERS AERONAUTICAL SERVICES ON AIRCRAFT ENGINES AIRCRAFT ENGINE PARTS AND ACCESSORIES
37281	0.310	31696	37281	AIRCRAFT PARTS AND ACCESSORIES, N.E.C.
37283	0.750	994	37283	RESEARCH AND DEVELOPMENT ON AIRCRAFT PARTS

NEW SIC	4-FIRM CR WEISS	CENSUS VALUE OF SHIPMENTS	OLD SIC	DESCRIPTION
37285	0.810	583	37285	AIRCRAFT PROPELLERS
37310	0.600	32007	37311	NONPROPELLED SHIPS, NEW CONSTRUCTION
			37312	SELF-PROPELLED U.S. MILITARY SHIPS, NEW CONSTRUCTION
			37313	SELF-PROPELLED NONMILITARY SHIPS, NEW CONSTRUCTION
			37314	REPAIR OF U.S. MILITARY SHIPS
			37316	REPAIR OF NONMILITARY SHIPS
37320	0.147	10311	37322	OUTBOARD MOTORBOATS, INCLUDING PREFABRICATED KITS
			37325	INBOARD MOTORBOATS, INCLUDING INBOARD-OUTDRIVE HOUSEBOATS
			37326	INBOARD-OUTDRIVE BOATS, EXCEPT HOUSEBOATS
			37327	ALL OTHER BOATS (SAILBOATS, ROWBOATS, CANOES, ETC.)
			37328	BOAT REPAIR
37430	0.543	22842	37431	LOCOMOTIVES AND PARTS (INCLUDES 37432, PASSENGER AND FREIGHT TRAIN CARS, NEW)
			37433	STREETCARS, PARTS AND ACCESSORIES FOR RAILROAD CARS AND STREETCARS, AND REBUILT PASSENGER AND FREIGHT TRAIN CARS
37511	0.700	3968	37511	BICYCLES AND PARTS
37512	0.650	1123	37512	MOTORCYCLES AND PARTS
37610	0.800	37053	37611	MISSILE SYSTEMS, EXCLUDING PROPULSION
			37612	SPACE VEHICLE SYSTEMS, EXCLUDING PROPULSION
			37613	RESEARCH AND DEVELOPMENT ON COMPLETE MISSILES
			37614	RESEARCH AND DEVELOPMENT ON COMPLETE SPACE VEHICLES
			37615	ALL OTHER SERVICES ON COMPLETE MISSILES AND SPACE VEHICLES
37640	0.730	7406	37645	COMPLETE MISSILE OR SPACE VEHICLE ENGINES
			37646	RESEARCH AND DEVELOPMENT ON COMPLETE MISSILE OR SPACE VEHICLE ENGINES
			37647	ALL OTHER SERVICES ON COMPLETE MISSILE OR SPACE VEHICLE ENGINES
			37648	MISSILE AND SPACE VEHICLE ENGINE PARTS AND ACCESSORIES
37690	0.520	8254	37692	MISSILE AND SPACE VEHICLE PARTS AND SUBASSEMBLIES, N.E.C.
			37694	RESEARCH AND DEVELOPMENT ON MISSILE AND SPACE VEHICLE PARTS AND COMPONENTS, N.E.C.
37920	0.200	12765	37921	RECREATION TYPE TRAILERS
			37922	CAMPING TRAILERS, CAMPERS AND PICKUP COVERS
37950	0.829	2851	37950	TANKS AND TANK COMPONENTS
37993	0.900	541	37993	GOLF CARTS, SELF-PROPELLED
37994	0.850	203	37994	SNOWMOBILES, SELF-PROPELLED

337

NEW SIC	4-FIRM CR WEISS	CENSUS VALUE OF SHIPMENTS	OLD SIC	DESCRIPTION
37999	0.200	4595	37999	OTHER TRANSPORTATION EQUIPMENT
38110	0.000	702	38110	ENGINEERING AND SCIENTIFIC INSTRUMENTS, N.S.K.
38111	0.350	5737	38111	AERONAUTICAL, NAUTICAL AND NAVIGATIONAL INSTRUMENTS
38112	0.200	3359	38112	LABORATORY AND SCIENTIFIC INSTRUMENTS
38113	0.450	1262	38113	SURVEYING AND DRAFTING INSTRUMENTS AND LABORATORY FURNITURE
38220	0.555	6581	38220	AUTOMATIC TEMPERATURE CONTROLS
38230	0.243	7947	38230	PROCESS CONTROL INSTRUMENTS
38240	0.000	8	38240	FLUID METERS AND COUNTING DEVICES, N.S.K.
38242	0.680	2077	38242	INTEGRATING METERS, NONELECTRICAL TYPE
38243	0.730	480	38243	COUNTING DEVICES
38244	0.820	701	38244	MOTOR VEHICLE INSTRUMENTS, EXCEPT ELECTRIC
38250	0.000	678	38250	INSTRUMENTS TO MEASURE ELECTRICITY, N.S.K.
38251	0.790	1695	38251	INTEGRATING INSTRUMENTS, ELECTRICAL
38252	0.450	8690	38252	TEST EQUIPMENT FOR TESTING ELECTRICAL, RADIO, AND COMMUNICATION CIRCUITS, AND MOTORS
38253	0.260	2234	38253	OTHER ELECTRICAL MEASURING INSTRUMENTS
38290	0.000	1124	38290	MEASURING AND CONTROLLING DEVICES, N.E.C., N.S.K.
38291	0.610	745	38291	AIRCRAFT ENGINE INSTRUMENTS, EXCEPT ELECTRIC
38292	0.250	1063	38292	PHYSICAL PROPERTIES TESTING AND INSPECTION EQUIPMENT
38293	0.500	945	38293	COMMERCIAL, METEOROLOGICAL, AND GENERAL PURPOSE INSTRUMENTS
38294	0.510	1982	38294	NUCLEAR RADIATION, DETECTION, AND MONITORING INSTRUMENTS
38320	0.390	5847	38321	OPTICAL INSTRUMENTS AND LENSES, EXCEPT SIGHTING AND FIRE-CONTROL EQUIPMENT
			38322	SIGHTING AND FIRE-CONTROL EQUIPMENT, MADE FROM LENSES, PRISMS, ETC., PRODUCED IN THE SAME PLANT
			38323	SIGHTING AND FIRE-CONTROL EQUIPMENT, MADE FROM PURCHASED LENSES
38410	0.307	9842	38410	SURGICAL AND MEDICAL INSTRUMENTS AND APPARATUS

NEW SIC	4-FIRM CR WEISS	CENSUS VALUE OF SHIPMENTS	OLD SIC	DESCRIPTION
38421	0.490	7820	38421	SURGICAL, ORTHOPEDIC, AND PROSTHETIC APPLIANCES AND SUPPLIES
38423	0.340	2260	38423	PERSONAL INDUSTRIAL SAFETY DEVICES
38424	0.670	500	38424	ELECTRONIC HEARING AIDS
38430	0.309	3523	38430	DENTAL EQUIPMENT AND SUPPLIES
38510	0.476	4835	38511 38512 38513	OPHTHALMIC FRONTS AND TEMPLES OPHTHALMIC FOCUS LENSES, INCLUDING CONTACT LENSES ALL OTHER OPHTHALMIC GOODS
38610	0.000	1607	38610	PHOTOGRAPHIC EQUIPMENT AND SUPPLIES, N.S.K.
38611	0.670	6165	38611	STILL PICTURE EQUIPMENT
38612	0.900	14551	38612	PHOTOCOPYING EQUIPMENT
38613	0.590	1916	38613	MOTION PICTURE EQUIPMENT
38614	0.800	1375	38614	MICROFILMING, BLUEPRINTING, BROWNPRINTING, AND WHITEPRINTING EQUIPMENT
38615	0.970	14276	38615	SENSITIZED PHOTOGRAPHIC FILM AND PLATES, EXCEPT X-RAY
38616	0.000	3764	38616	SENSITIZED PHOTOGRAPHIC PAPER AND CLOTH, SILVER HALIDE TYPE
38617	0.650	3062	38617	SENSITIZED PHOTOGRAPHIC PAPER AND CLOTH, EXCEPT SILVER HALIDE TYPE
38618	0.800	2862	38618	PREPARED PHOTOGRAPHIC CHEMICALS
38619	0.980	2976	38619	X-RAY FILM
38730	0.390	8808	38731 38734 38735 38737	CLOCKS WATCHES WITH IMPORTED MOVEMENTS WATCHES WITH DOMESTIC MOVEMENTS AND PARTS FOR ALL CLOCKS AND WATCHES WATCHCASES
39110	0.124	9818	39110 39111 39112	JEWELRY, PRECIOUS METALS, N.S.K. JEWELRY, MADE OF PLATINUM METALS OR CARAT GOLD JEWELRY, MADE OF PRECIOUS METALS, EXCEPT PLATINUM METALS AND CARAT GOLD
39140	0.422	3175	39141 39142	SILVERWARE, PLATED WARE, AND STAINLESS STEEL WARE FLATWARE
39150	0.075	3362	39151 39152	JEWELERS' FINDINGS AND MATERIALS LAPIDARY WORK AND DIAMOND CUTTING AND POLISHING
39311	0.660	1074	39311	PIANOS

NEW SIC	4-FIRM CR WEISS	CENSUS VALUE OF SHIPMENTS	OLD SIC	DESCRIPTION
39312	0.560	1883	39312	ORGANS
39313	0.640	546	39313	PIANO AND ORGAN PARTS
39314	0.400	1560	39314	OTHER MUSICAL INSTRUMENTS AND PARTS
39420	0.226	2779	39420	DOLLS AND STUFFED TOY ANIMALS
39440	0.291	15007	39440	GAMES, TOYS, CHILDREN'S VEHICLES, N.S.K.
			39441	GAMES, EXCLUDING TOYS
			39442	TOYS, EXCLUDING GAMES
			39443	BABY CARRIAGES AND CHILDREN'S VEHICLES, EXCEPT BICYCLES
39491	0.260	1677	39491	FISHING TACKLE AND EQUIPMENT
39492	0.460	2767	39492	GOLF EQUIPMENT
39494	0.380	1074	39494	PLAYGROUND, GYMNASIUM, AND GYMNASTIC EQUIPMENT
39495	0.340	8116	39495	OTHER SPORTING AND ATHLETIC GOODS
39510	0.439	3117	39510	PENS, MECHANICAL PENCILS, AND PENPOINTS
39521	0.520	631	39521	LEAD PENCILS AND CRAYONS
39522	0.550	1014	39522	ARTISTS' MATERIALS
39530	0.270	1634	39530	HAND STAMPS, STENCILS, AND OTHER MARKING DEVICES
39551	0.510	1500	39551	INKED RIBBONS, ALL TYPES
39552	0.460	1538	39552	CARBON PAPER, STENCIL PAPER, ETC.
39610	0.113	4417	39610	COSTUME JEWELRY AND COSTUME NOVELTIES, EXCEPT PRECIOUS METAL
39620	0.140	1018	39620	FEATHERS, PLUMES, AND ARTIFICIAL FLOWERS
39630	0.217	1031	39630	BUTTONS AND PARTS (EXCEPT OF PRECIOUS OR SEMIPRECIOUS METALS OR STONE)
39641	0.710	2545	39641	ZIPPERS AND SLIDE FASTENERS
39642	0.390	2657	39642	NEEDLES, PINS, FASTENERS (EXCEPT SLIDE), AND SIMILAR NOTIONS
39910	0.000	334	39910	BROOMS AND BRUSHES, N.S.K.
39911	0.240	605	39911	BROOMS

NEW SIC	4-FIRM CR WEISS	CENSUS VALUE OF SHIPMENTS	OLD SIC	DESCRIPTION
39912	0.450	1126	39912	PAINT AND VARNISH BRUSHES
39913	0.280	1864	39913	OTHER BRUSHES
39930	0.050	10892	39930	SIGNS AND ADVERTISING DISPLAYS, N.S.K.
			39931	LUMINOUS TUBING AND BULB SIGNS
			39932	NONELECTRIC SIGNS AND ADVERTISING DISPLAYS
			39933	ADVERTISING SPECIALTIES
39950	0.250	3879	39951	METAL CASKETS AND COFFINS, COMPLETELY LINED AND TRIMMED, ADULT SIZES ONLY
			39952	WOOD CASKETS AND COFFINS, COMPLETELY LINED AND TRIMMED, ADULT SIZES ONLY
			39953	OTHER CASKETS AND COFFINS AND METAL VAULTS
39960	0.881	3003	39960	HARD SURFACE FLOOR COVERINGS
39990	0.000	3175	39990	MANUFACTURING INDUSTRIES, N.E.C., N.S.K.
39991 *	0.660	1257	39991	CHEMICAL FIRE EXTINGUISHING EQUIPMENT AND PARTS
39993	0.730	816	39993	MATCHES
39994	0.350	1008	39994	CANDLES
39999	0.200	6216	39999	OTHER MISCELLANEOUS FABRICATED PRODUCTS, N.E.C. ESTABLISHMENT

* 39992 0.000 911 39992 Coin-operated amusement machines

Appendix 3   Industry matchings

The following industry matchings were used to determine whether the same two firms were ranked at the top of an industry in 1972 as in 1950. Industries were omitted if no reasonably close matching industry could be found in the other year, if fewer than two firms out of the 1,000 largest samples were reported in one year, or if they were one of the miscellaneous or not-elsewhere-classified categories. The industry numbers listed are our assigned numbers as given in Appendix 2.

1950	1972	1950	1972	1950	1972	1950	1972
20110	20110	20850	20850	22710	22710,20,90	24310	24310
210	210	900	170	910	910	330	520
220,50	220	910	994	930	930	440	410
230	230	920	790	940	940	910	910
240	240	950	870	950	950		
260	260	960	996	980	980		
310	910	970	970	990	990	25110	25110,20,40
331,2,4,5,8	330	980	980			210	210,20
336	332	991	991			310	310
337	322	992	992	23110	23110	410	410
340	340	993	993	210	210		
352	352	996	950	220	220		
353	353			230	230	26110	26110
354	354			270	270	120	210
371	920	21110	21110	280	280	411	410,11
372,73	370	210	210	340	350	412	412
410	410	310	310	350,60	370	414	413,14
420	470,30			410	410	510	420
430	430			420	420	610	430
510	510	22120	22810,20,30	910	910	710	510,20,30
520	520	130	110,210	920	920	740	550
610	610	230	840	930	930	910	450
710	650	410	410	940	940	930	493
720	660	510	510			992	492
730	670	520	520			993	540,1,2
810	860	530	530	24110	24110	994	471,72

1950	1972	1950	1972	1950	1972	1950	1972
820	820	540	540	210	210	996	495
830	830	550	590	220,320	350		
840	840	560	570	230,40,50	290		
27510	27510	28933	28444	32110	32110	33330	33330
710	710	934	445	210	210	415	395
820,30	820	941,993	710	290	294	418	397
910	910	942	994	312	315	517	510
920	530	950	950	410	410	526	530
930	930	970	791	540,50,90	590	527	540
940	940	980	991	610	610	910	129
		991	794	640	640	920	125,52,570
		992	792	691,2	690	930	126
28120	28121			710	710,20	995	991
190	193			720	750		
210	650	29110-19,20	29110	750	960		
230	210	510	510	810	810	34110	34110,20
240	220	520	520	910	910	211	211
250	230	990	990	922-27	920	212	212
260	920			930	930	220	232
342	349			950	950	230	230,31
413	414	30110	30110	970	970	240	233
415	410,11,13	210	210			250	250
421	412	310	310			291	297
423	423	992	696	33110	33120,1	292	292
424	424	993	695	120,21	122	293	293
510,30	510	994	697	122,3,4	123	295	294
520	160			126	124	391	333
710	730,40,62			130	130	395	334
210,20,60	20740	31110	31110	210	210	398	335
870	992	310	310	220	220	410	410
910	930	410	430,40,90	230	250	420	420
931	442	610	610	310	310	431	435,7,8,9
932	443	710	710	320	320	432	430
		720	720				
34433	34433	35312	35314	35710	35740	36214	36310
434	434	313	316	760	760	310	33570,76
440	440	315	320	791,92	810	410	36940-6
630	650,60,90	320	331	810	36330	510	410
	692,94,95,99	411	411-15	820	35820	612	511,12
680	710	421	470	830	36360	613	620-3
892	33150,51	422	420	840	36350	615	514
893	33156	423	460	851,52	36320	622	730
894	33157	425	493	853	35853	623	710
912,3,4	34120	431	440	855	855	624	720
930	930	433	452	856	852,6,7	640	610

1950	1972	1950	1972	1950	1972	1952	1972
940	520	511	511	860	860	910	910
950	510	512,14	512,13	890	890	920	920
960	992	513	514	910	34940		
970	970	520	520	920	34980		
		530	531,2	930	35620	37150	37150
		540	540			171	110,11
35110	35110	550	550–55			172	112
191	191,92	591	591	36110	36430,41–3	173	113
192	193	592	592	120	240	174	115
193	196	593	593	140	210,1,2,3,4	175	140
194	199	594	594		217,8,9	290	281
195	195	611	610,1,2	151	125	310	310
211	231	612	613	152	122	320	320
212	312,13	613,4	630	161	131	410,20	430
213,227	240	640	640	170	230	511	512
221	230–8	650	370	192	291	512	511
222	239	660	660,80	211	341		
310,17,19	318,19	672	672	212	391		
311,630	350,60	680,90	673	213	342,3,4		
38111,211	38111	39811	39911				
113	112	812	912				
212	242	813	913				
213	230	820	24994				
214	244	830	39993				
310	320	930	930				
410	410	990	991				
423	26471						
424	38421						
510	510						
612	611						
613	615						
614	616,17						
615	618						
616,17	613						
710	730						
39120	39150						
140	140						
390	314						
410,30	440						
420	420						
490	491,2,4,5						
510	510						
520	521						

1950	1972	1950	1972
530	530		
550	551,52		
630	630		
640	642		

Appendix 4   Assets acquired data (Chapter 7)

The basic listing of the number of mergers and sizes of acquired companies was obtained from the FTC overall merger series. This series was found to contain many errors: Some mergers appeared more than once, some mergers were reported that did not occur. The "histories" of each acquiring company as reported in *Moody's Industrial Manual* were used as a check against the FTC data to determine the year of acquisition, size of acquisition, and whether they did actually occur. The assets reported in the FTC Large Merger Series were substituted for those in the Overall Series whenever the two differed. When an acquired company was itself listed in *Moody's*, its assets in the year prior to its acquisition were used if no other figure was available.

For those mergers for which no assets figure for the acquired firm was reported, but the amount of cash or stock exchanged for the acquired company was reported, a consideration paid figure was used as the value of the assets acquired. In general, the consideration paid exceeds the book value of assets acquired. On a stock exchange acquisition, the consideration paid was computed at the midpoint of the stock's price range in the year of the merger.

When it was known that the assets of an acquired firm were subsequently sold – for example, following an antitrust decision – the acquisition was not recorded.

For most acquisitions of less than $10 million, no asset figure was reported. We approximated the assets acquired as follows: Over the period 1972–78, the FTC reported the number of mergers falling into the greater than $1 million and less than $10 million category, and the less than $1 million category. We assumed that the average merger between $1 and $10 million in assets equaled $5.5 million, the midpoint of this range, and the average of a merger of less than $1 million equals $0.5 million. Over this period, 85 percent of the mergers were under $1 million and 15 percent fell between $1 million and $10 million. The expected value of the assets acquired in a merger

346

for which the acquired firm's size was unknown was $1.25 million. Taking 1975 as the midpoint of the 1972–78 time period, we then scaled this $1.25 million figure back to our 1950–72 time period using the nonresidential investment component of the GNP price deflator. The appropriate, adjusted figure for each year was then used to determine an assets acquired figure for all mergers in a given year for which no assets figures are reported. Thus, for example, a 1967 acquisition of unknown size was estimated to have an expected size of $0.75 million. A company making 2 acquisitions of unknown size in 1967 was recorded as acquiring $1.5 million in assets. A company making 10 acquisitions of unknown size in 1967 was recorded as acquiring $7.5 million in assets.

Obviously, the figures for small acquisitions are open to substantial errors. Fortunately, these errors arise with respect to the smaller acquisitions so one may hope for some averaging effect, as when a company makes 10 acquisitions in a given year. But our assets acquired figures are subject to considerable errors in observation.

Some error also exists in the figures for the number of years in which an acquisition occurred. The FTC merger series was very sloppy in recording these, if one assumes the figures in *Moody's* to be accurate with respect to the date of acquisition. For companies making many acquisitions or very few, the numbers we have recorded for *NAQ*, number of years in which at least one acquisition occurred, should be reasonably accurate. When the FTC data report a company as making acquisitions in 1954, 1967, and 1968, the true *NAQ* figure must be either 3 or 2; that is, the only plausible error is that the two latter acquisitions both occurred in the same year, either 1967 or 1968. When a company is making three or more acquisitions per year, as some did, the incorrect recording of one or two dates will not affect the accuracy of the *NAQ* count. The biggest errors are most likely to occur in the middle ranges of acquisitions. Here, the most positive statement one can make, perhaps, is that the errors should truly be random.

Appendix 5   Mergers and market share: samples of merging companies

ACQUIRING COMPANY	ACQUIRED COMPANY	YEAR ACQ.	N O T E S
ALLEGHENY LUDLUM	TRUE TEMPER	67	
ALLIS CHALMERS	BUDA	53	
AMERICAN CAN	MARATHON	57	
" "	DIXIE CUP	57	
" "	METAL THERMIT	62	
" "	NORTHERN PAPER MILLS	52	ACQUIRED BY MARATHON
AMERICAN HOME PR.	EKCO PRODUCTS	65	
" "	BRACH & SONS	66	
AMERICAN RADIATOR	WESTINGHOUSE AIR B.	68	
" "	MULLINS MFG.	54	
AMERICAN TOBACCO	SUNSHINE BISCUIT	66	
" "	JERGENS, ANDREW	70	
" "	GORDON BAKING	56	
ARMCO STEEL	NATIONAL SUPPLY	58	
ATLANTIC OIL	RICHFIELD OIL	66	
BEATRICE FOODS	CREAMERIES OF AMERICA	52	
BORDEN	SMITH-DOUGLAS	64	
BORG-WARNER	YORK	56	
BUDD	CONTINENTAL DIAMOND	55	
BURLINGTON MILLS	LEES, JAMES	60	
" "	ERWIN MILLS	62	
" "	GOODALL-SANFORD	53	
" "	BLUMENTHAL, S.	57	
" "	MOORESVILLE MILLS	54	
" "	PACIFIC MILLS	53	
CAMPBELL SOUP	SWANSON	55	
CELANESE	DEVOE & RAYNOLDS	65	
CHRYSLER	BRIGGS	53	AUTO PROPERTIES ONLY
"	KING-SEELEY	68	" " "
CITIES SERVICE	COLUMBIA-CARBON	62	
" "	TENNESSEE	63	
COLGATE-PALMOLIVE	KENDALL	72	
CONE MILLS	DWIGHT MFG.	51	
CF & I	ROEBLINGS	51	
CONTAINER CORP	MENGEL	53	

348

ACQUIRING COMPANY	ACQUIRED COMPANY	YEAR ACQ.	NOTES
CONTINENTAL CAN	GAIR, ROBERT	56	
" "	FORT WAYNE C.P.	59	
" "	SOUTHERN ADV.BAG	54	ACQUIRED BY GAIR
CONTINENTAL OIL	AMER.AGR.CHEM.	63	
CORN PRODUCTS	BEST FOODS	58	
CROWN ZELLERBACH	GAYLORD CONT.	55	
EATON MFG.	YALE & TOWNE	63	
FORD	PHILCO	61	
GENERAL TIRE	BYERS, A.M.	56	
GOODYEAR RUBBER	MOTOR WHEEL	64	
" "	LEE RUBBER	65	TIRE BUSINESS ONLY
GULF OIL	WILSHIRE OIL	60	
HYGRADE FOODS	KINGAN	52	
INTERNATIONAL PAPER	LONG-BELL LUMBER	56	
INTERNATIONAL SHOE	FLORSHEIM SHOE	53	
KIMBERLY-CLARK	SCHWEITZER	57	
MEAD	WOODWARD IRON	68	
MORRIS, Ph.	MILPRINT	56	
"	AMER.SAFETY RAZOR	60	
"	MILLER BREWING	69	
MURRAY (WALLACE)	SIMONDS SAW	66	
NASH	WILLYS OVERLAND	52	BOUGHT FROM KAISER
"	HUDSON	54	in 1970
NATIONAL DISTILLERS	US INDUSTRIAL CHEM	52	
" "	BRIDGEPORT BRASS	61	
" "	BEACON	66	
NATIONAL LEAD	DOEHLER-JARVIS	52	
OLIN	MATHIESON CHEM.	54	
"	BLOCKSON CHEM.	55	
"	BROWN PAPERS	55	
OWENS-ILLINOIS	NATIONAL CONTAINER	55	
" "	LILY TULIP	68	
PHILLIPS PETROLEUM	OSWEGO FALLS	65	
PULLMAN	TRAILMOBILE	51	
REYNOLDS, R.J.	PERRICK & FORD	65	
ST. REGIS PAPER	RHEINLANDER PAPER	56	
" " "	ST.PAUL & TACOMA	56	
" " "	CORNELL WOOD PR.	59	
SCOTT PAPER	SOUNDVIEW PAPER	50	
" "	HOLLINGS & WHITNEY	53	
SOCONY-VACUUM	VIRGINIA-CAR.CH.	63	
SPERRY	REMINGTON RAND	55	
STRANDARD BRANDS	CLINTON FOODS	56	
" "	PLANTERS NUTS	60	
" "	CARTISS CANDY	64	

ACQUIRING COMPANY	ACQUIRED COMPANY	YEAR ACQ.	N O T E S
STEVENS, J.P.	UTICA & MOHAWK	52	
"	CHENEY BROS	55	
"	FORSTMAN	57	
"	KARAGHESIAN	63	
"	UNITED ELASTIC	68	
SUN OIL	MID-CONTINENT	54	
" "	SUNRAY	68	
UNION BAG	CAMP	55	
UNION CARBIDE	VISKING	55	
UNION OIL	PURE OIL	65	
WEST POINT	PEPPERELL	65	
WEST VIRGINIA P&P	HINDE & DAUCH	53	
" " "	US ENVELOPE	60	
WEYERHAEUSER	EDDY	57	
"	KIEKHAEFER	57	
"	CROCKER BURBANK	62	
"	DIERKS LUMBER	69	
WHEELING	PITTSBURGH	68	
YOUNGSTOWN S&T	EMSCO	55	
AMERICAN METAL	CLIMAX MOLY.	57	
AKZONA	INTERNATIONAL SALT	70	
ASHLAND OIL	UNITED CARBON	63	
BRISTOL-MYERS	MEAD JOHNSON	67	
CARRIER	AFFILIATED GAS	55	
"	ELLIOTT	57	
CERTAIN-TEED	KEARSBY-MATTISON	62	
CLUETT-PEABODY	VAN RAALTE	68	
COPPERWELD	SUPERIOR STEEL	56	
DAN RIVER	ALABAMA MILLS	55	
" "	WOODSIDE MILLS	56	
DIAMOND ALKALAI	SHAMROCK OIL	67	
" "	NOPCO	67	
DIAMOND MATCH	US PLAYING CARD	69	
" "	US PRINTING	59	
" "	GARDNER BOARD	57	
DRESSER	HARBISON-WALKER	67	
EAGLE-PICHER	OHIO RUBBER	52	
FMC	AMERICAN VISCOSE	63	
"	LINK-BELT	67	
GAF	RUBEROID	67	
GENERAL HOST	CUDALRY PACKING	71	
GOULD	SERVEL	67	
"	CLEVITE	69	
"	CENTURY ELECTRIC	72	
GREAT NORTHERN	NEEKOOSA	70	

ACQUIRING COMPANY	ACQUIRED COMPANY	YEAR ACQ.	NOTES
GREAT WESTERN	COLORADO MILKING	68	
HOUDAILLE	BUFFALO BOLT	57	
INTERLAKE	NEWPORT STEEL	56	
"	ACME STEEL	64	
KELSEY-HAYES	HEINTZ	57	
MASSEY	FERGUSON	53	
McGRAW-ELECTRIC	EDISON	57	
" "	NATIONAL ELECTRIC	58	
" "	AMERICAN LAUNDRY	60	
MERK	SHARPE-DOHME	53	
MIDLAND STEEL	SURFACE COMBUSTION	56	
" "	IND. RAYON	60	
" "	NATIONAL MALLEABLE	64	
SMITH, ALEX.	MOHAWK CARPET	55	
"	FIRTH	62	
NATIONAL GYPSUM	HURON PORTLAND	58	
REXALL DRUG	THATCHER GLASS	66	
SINGER	GENERAL PRECISION	68	
SQUIBB	LIFE-SAVERS	55	
"	BEECH-NUT	68	
STAUFFER CHEMICAL	CONSOLIDATED CHEM.	51	
" "	VICTOR CHEMICAL	59	
THOMPSON	UNITED CARR	68	
"	UNITED DRILL	68	
"	MARTIN ROCK	63	
TEXTRON	ROBBINS MILLS	54	
"	CAMPBELL	56	
"	AMERICAN WOOL	55	
"	SHEAFFER PEN	66	
"	GORHAM	67	
"	FAFNIR	68	
"	TALON	68	
"	SPENCER-KELLOGG	60	
UMM	A. JUILLIARD	52	
USM	FARREL	68	
WHIRLPOOL	SEEGER	55	
WHITE MOTOR	AUTOCAR	53	
" "	REO MOTOR	57	
" "	DIAMOND T	58	
" "	OLIVER	60	
US PLYWOOD	ASSOCIATED PLYWOOD	54	
" "	CHAMPION PAPER	67	
AMERICAN HARDWARE	EMHART	64	
" "	SAVAGE ARMS	57	
" "	PLYMOUTH	60	

ACQUIRING COMPANY	ACQUIRED COMPANY	YEAR ACQ.	NOTES
AMERICAN LIBERTY OIL	COSDEN PETROLEUM	63	
AMERICAN MAIZE	IND. SWISHER	66	
AMF	HARLEY-DAVISON	69	
PURITY BAKERIES	AMERICAN BAKERIES	53	
BATH INDUSTRIES	CONGOLIUM-NAIM	68	
CHAIN BELT	NORDBERG	70	
COOPER-BESSEMER	NICHOLSON FILE	71	
FALSTAFF	BALLANTINE	72	
FEDERAL MOGUL	BOWLER ROLLER	54	
FEDERAL PAPER BOARD	RIEGEL PAPER	72	
FOREMOST DAIRIES	GOLDEN STATE	53	
FOREMOST DAIRIES	EL DORADO	55	
GEORGIA PACIFIC	COOS BAY LUMBER	56	
" "	HAMMOND LUMBER	56	
" "	CROSSET LUMBER	62	
" "	SUTHERLAND PAPER	59	
" "	KALAMAZOO	67	
" "	PUGET SOUND	63	
INT. MINERALS & CH.	LAVINO	65	
KAYSER	HOLEPROOF	54	
KOEHRING	THEW SHOVEL	64	
LAMBERT	AMERICAN CHICLE	62	
"	" OPTICAL	67	
"	PARKE-DAVIS	70	
"	EVERSHARP	70	WET SHAVE BUSINESS O
MERGENTHALER	ELECTRIC-AUTOLITE	63	
NATIONAL ACME	CLEVELAND TWIST	67	
NAUMKEAG	LINEN THREAD	59	
"	BACHMAN UXBRIDGE	60	
"	BANCRAFT	61	
POTLATCH	NORTHWEST PAPER	64	
RELIANCE ELECTRIC	TOLEDO SCALE	67	
SCM	PROCTOR SILEX	66	
"	GLIDDEN	67	
WHITE SEWING MA.	APEX ELECTRIC	56	
" " "	BLAW KNOX	68	
" " "	GIBSON REGRIGERATOR	55	
" " "	HERCULES MOTOR	60	
" " "	PERFECTION ST.	54	
" " "	WHITIN MACHINE	65	
UNIVERSAL-CYCLOPS	DETROIT STEEL	70	
" "	REEVES STEEL	58	

B ≡ Backward vertical integration.

CONGLOMERATE MERGERS CONTROL GROUP

California Packing
Hershey
Timkin Roller Bearing
Heinz, H. J.
Kellogg
Fairmont Foods
Pepsi Cola
Utah-Idaho Sugar
Glenmore Distillers
Gerber Products
Savannah Sugar
Graniteville
Standard-Coosa-Thatcher
Dixie Mercerizing
Spartan Mills
Phillips-Jones
Blue Bell
Evans Products
General Fireproofing
Kroehler
Consolidated Paper
Sonoco Products
Arvey
Proctor and Gamble
Publicker
Avondale Mills
National Cylinder & Gas
Sun Chemical
Trico Products
Weatherhead
McCord
Bausch & Lomb
Robertshaw Control
Neptune Meter
Brunswick
Wurlitzer
Richardson
Sunbeam
Noblitt-Sparks
Crown Cork & Seal
Electric Storage Battery
Hammermill Paper
Hudson Pulp & Paper
Southland Paper
Dennison
Sorg Paper
Alton Box Board
Inland Container
Longview Fibre

St. Joe Paper
Waldorf Paper
Gulf States Paper
Textiles, Inc.
Greenwood Mills
Hanes Knitting
Springs Cotton Mills
C. H. Masland
Revere Copper & Brass
McLouth
Maytag
Harnischfeger
Motorola
Gen American Transportation
Fruehauf
Dana
Clark Equipment
Standard Railway Equipment

Cook Paint & Varnish
Mississippi Cottonseed Products
Quaker State Oil
Bird & Son
Lone Star Cement
Dayton Malleable Iron
Wyman-Gordon
Ladish
Coleman
National Pressure Cooker
Lamson & Sessions
Trane
Butler
Ceco Steel
Lennox Furnace
Cincinnati Milling Machine
Addressograph-Multigraph
Hobart
Outboard Marine
Harris-Seybold-Potter
Manitowac Shipbuilding
I-T-E Circuit Breaker
American Bosch
Emerson Electric
Lincoln Electric
Champion Spark Plug
Triangle Conduit & Cable
Todd Shipyards
American Sugar
U.S. Tobacco
American Snuff
Edward Hines Lumber
Simpson Logging
E. L. Bruce
Pacific Lumber
Hall Bros.
American Hard Rubber
Norton
Crompton & Knowles
Warner & Swasey
Tecumseh Products
DeLaval
SKF Industries
Ingersoll-Rand
Hoover
Oneida
A. E. Staley
Peter Paul
Bayu K

Parker Pen
Ex-Cello
Chicago Pneumatic Tool
F. M. Schaefer
American Thread

Rohm & Haas
Interchemical
Commercial Solvents
Cabot Carbon
S. C. Johnson
Mallinckrodt
Benjamin Moore
J. M. Huber
National Can

HORIZONTAL MERGERS CONTROL GROUP

California Packing
Standard Oil California
Timkin Roller Bearing
Fairmont Foods
Pepsi Cola
Glenmore Distillers
Savannah Sugar
Graniteville
Standard-Coosa-Thatcher
Dixie Mercerizing
Spartan Mills
Evans Products
Consolidated Paper
Sonoco Products
Arvey Corp.
Avondale Mills
Quaker State Oil
Bird and Son
Brown Shoe
Dayton Malleable Iron
Wyman-Gordon
Ladish
National Pressure Cooker
Lawson & Sessions
Hobart
Champion Spark Plug
Triangle Conduit & Cable
Todd Shipyards
Edward Hines Lumber
Simpson Logging
E. L. Bruce
American Hard Rubber
Peter Paul
Riegel Textile
Ludlow Mfg.
Chatham
Wiscassett Mills
Magee Carpet
Interchemical
Revever Copper & Brass
Alan Wood
McLouth
American Cast Iron
General American Transportation
Fruehauf
Dana
Clark Equipment
Standard Railway
F. M. Schaefer
American Thread

Trico Products
Weatherhead
McCord
Robertshaw Control
Richardson
Noblitt-Sparks
Hammermill Paper
Hudson Pulp & Paper
Southland Paper
Dennison
Sorg Paper
Alton Box Board
Inland Container
Longview Fibre
St. Joe Paper
Waldorf Paper
Gulf States Paper
Collins & Aikman
Reeves Bros.
Duplan
Mount Vernon-Woodberry
Textiles, Inc.
Greenwood Mills
Bibb Mfg.
Hanes Knitting
Springs Cotton Mills
C. H. Masland
M. Lowenstein

Notes

Notes

1   The persistence of firms

1 In recent years, actual or potential bankruptcies have been headline events. Thus, the figures for the 1950–72 period may not be representative of this newer, more severe economic environment. It should also be kept in mind, however, that many recent bankruptcies or threatened bankruptcies have, to an indeterminate degree, been legal strategems to win concessions from employees, plaintiffs in occupational injury cases, and the like. The use of bankruptcy as a mode of bargaining is definitely an innovation of the late seventies.
2 This result accords with those of Singh (1971, 1975) for the United Kingdom and Schwartz (1982) for the United States. In a couple of cases, it was not known which firm acquired which in a merger, and we designated the larger as the acquirer. In a couple of other cases, a company in the 1,000 largest was acquired by one outside the 1,000 largest, but we regarded the member of the 1,000 largest as the survivor to keep it in the sample. These classifications bias our figures slightly in the direction of a positive size-survival relationship. There are only about a half dozen cases of this type, however, not enough to affect the statistical relationship.

2   The persistence of profits above the norm

1 For additional discussion and critique of Brozen's work, see Wenders (1971a, b;), MacAvoy, et al. (1971), Winn and Leabo (1974), Qualls (1974), and McEnally (1976).
2 Data were obtained from the Standard and Poor's COMPUSTAT Tape and conform to its definitions thus,

$$\Pi_i = (INCOME\ (18) + INTEREST\ (15)/TOTAL\ ASSETS\ (6).$$

Where COMPUSTAT data were not available, but *Moody's* data were, the analogous definition based on *Moody's* data was used.
3 In about six cases, severe multicollinearity was observed in one of the higher-order polynomials in $1/t$ along with a higher $\overline{R}^2$. The estimates from the lower-order regression were used in these few cases, both because

355

they are less likely to be distorted by the multicollinearity, and because the standard errors that are particularly affected by this problem are used as weights in the subsequent work.

4 The estimate of λ exceeded 1 in seven cases. It was set equal to 0.95 for these firms.

5 Connolly and Schwartz (1984) test for the persistence of profit differences across firms by estimating probabilities that firms that start a 20-year time period a given distance from the mean converge to it. By and large, these results suggest that company returns do converge on the mean over time, but very slowly. Their conclusion is consistent with the interpretation offered here. It is also interesting that support for their regression-on-the-mean hypothesis is stronger for companies with initially below-average profits. Just as we found that, on the average, the coefficient on lagged profits is highest in the highest profit class, Connolly and Schwartz find some of the strongest evidence against the convergence-on-the-mean hypothesis in their top two profit groups. Firms in the highest group remain in the highest group with a significantly higher-than-expected probability. Firms in the second highest group enter the highest group with a significantly higher probability than predicted.

3   The persistence of market power

1 The C_4 figures are census values, with that for 1972 being adjusted by Leonard Weiss (1981) to account for regional and local market definitions and imports. The advertising intensity variable is the ratio of advertising to sales for 1963 reported on a three-digit level by the IRS. The patent figure is the average number of patents per year over the period 1966–68 reported by the NSF (1977), divided by 1967 Census of Manufacturing sales. The year 1963 was chosen as falling roughly in the middle of our sample period; the patent data are the earliest reported on an industry basis.

4   Profitability and market structure

1 The origins of this approach can be traced back to Fellner (1949) and Bain (1952). See also Bishop (1960), Cyert and De Groot (1973), Kuenne (1974), and Shubik (1980).

2 The number of firms drops out, since we have not explicitly constrained the sum of the demand schedules.

3 Richard Levin also kindly supplied me with demand elasticity estimates he made using an entirely different technique from that of Intriligator and DeAngelo. Levin's estimates do not cover all industries. The simple correlation between Levin's estimates and the Intriligator-DeAngelo estimates over those industries where both were available was − .04, further increasing one's uneasiness of the gain to be made from including external

estimates of demand elasticity in structure-performance studies.

It must be stressed that the reservations expressed are in no way meant as criticisms of the capabilities of the scholars making the estimates. Alas, obtaining demand elasticity estimates sufficiently comparable across industries to be of use in studies of the present kind seems beyond the limits of available data and estimating techniques. I have chosen not to make my own estimates because I did not feel I could do better.

4 We also substituted Pagoulatos and Sorensen estimates for the Intriligator-DeAngelo figures where the former were available. This measure performed even worse than the other.

5 No figures at all are given for unprogressive industries SIC 21, 23–27, 29, and 31. We assumed zero patent-to-sales ratios for these. (Other unprogressive industries had patent-to-sales ratios of 0.04–0.05 in comparison with some progressive industry ratios of around 1.0.)

6 The equations were estimated without restraining the intercept and the coefficient on market share to sum to one. Separate t-tests could not reject the hypothesis as implied by equation (4.33) that these two parameters sum to one for equations (1)–(3) using a 5 percent level, two-tail test. Equation (1) failed the test at the 10 percent level. However, equations (4)–(7) all failed the test at the 5 percent level.

7 Ravenscraft (1983) found the coefficient on market share became insignificant when an interaction term between market share and advertising was included.

5   The results in perspective

1 Some of the rise in Heinz's profits in the latter part of the 1960s and early 1970s is evidence of the averaging effect of mergers to be discussed in Chapter 8. It acquired Star-Kist Foods, a leading tuna packer, in 1963, which added to its income (*Business Week*, November 11, 1967), and Ore Ida, a frozen vegetable packer, in 1965. Ore Ida raised Heinz's sales 7 percent, but raised its profits 13 percent (*Moody's Industrial Manual* 1968).

2 Albeit there were many straws in the wind prior to the seventies suggesting the lack of robustness of the concentration-profits link. The pioneering, large-scale econometric investigation of the relationship was the study by Collins and Preston (1968). For 4 of the 10 industry groups they examined, concentration did not have a positive and significant relationship with price–cost margin at the four-digit level. George Stigler (1963) failed to find a positive relationship, but his findings were attributed to choice of time period (Kilpatrick 1968). Comanor and Wilson (1967) failed to find a positive partial correlation, but their finding was attributed to multicollinearity. As always in economics, evidence contradicting a reigning conventional wisdom must withstand far more scientific scrutiny than supporting evidence.

3 To my knowledge, the only models from which predictions for the sign of a market share–concentration interaction term have been formally

derived from the firm's profit-maximizing equilibrium conditions are the one employed here and its sister by William Long (1982). Given their similarities, it is not surprising that both models predict the same sign on the coefficient for this term. My thinking on how to model a firm's decisions in an oligopoly setting has been greatly influenced by William Long's work over the past decade.

6   Profitability and the firm's own advertising, patent activity, risk, and other characteristics

1 Data were collected by Rosemary Morley and Hugh Lederman from Leading National Advertisers.
2 The patent data were collected by Rosemary Morley.
3 Since we weight each observation by the reciprocal of the standard error of our estimate of projected profits, if failure to account for intangible capital results in a worsened fit to the time-series profits equation, then those companies having substantial variability in advertising and R&D over time receive less weight in our empirical work. Thus, the problem of ignoring intangible capital for these companies is mitigated.
4 Let α_i^* be firm i's projected profits after adjustment for intangible capital and α_i before adjustment. Then

$$\alpha_i^* = \frac{K_i \, (\alpha_i \Pi + \Pi) \, (\overline{K} + \overline{A}/\lambda_A)}{(\Pi \overline{K}) \, (K_i + A_i/\lambda_A)} - 1.$$

5 Although our measure of assets does not include "goodwill" assets created by advertising and inventive activity, it does include goodwill assets purchased as part of the acquisition of other firms to the extent that the economic value of these assets is reflected in the purchase price of these companies, and the purchase price is used to revalue the assets of the acquired company upon its acquisition and absorption into the acquiring firm's balance sheet. Thus, purchased intangible capital stocks are accounted for.
6 My deep gratitude goes to Carl Schwinn for estimating these βs.
7 The expected positive correlation between βs estimated on common shares and returns on common shares has been found. See, e.g., Jenson (1972).
8 See, e.g., Stigler (1963), Shepherd (1975), Winn (1977), Grabowski and Mueller (1978), Lawriwsky (1984), and for banks (Edwards and Heggestad (1973). Fisher and Hall's (1969) study is the one most frequently cited in support of a positive relationship.
9 The CAP model has been under continued attack in recent years. See, for example, Haim Levy (1983) and references cited therein.
10 See Jacquemin and Lichtbuer (1973), and Jacquemin and Saez (1976). Note also Marcus's (1969) response to Hall and Weiss. In personal con-

versation, Leonard Weiss has expressed doubt regarding his early findings with Hall, since he has been unable to reproduce the result.

11 The classic discussion of the market power advantages stemming from diversification is by Corwin Edwards (1955).

12 Assuming M-form organizational structures now go hand in hand with diversification, one can cite Oliver Williamson's (1970, 1975) arguments for the efficiency advantages of the M-form as justification for expecting a positive impact of diversification on profits.

Somewhat more indirectly, diversification could lead to more basic research, higher payoffs from one's research effort, and thereby in the long run greater profitability. On this, see Nelson (1959) and Grabowski (1968).

13 See Rhoades (1973) and Carter (1977). Subsequent work by Rhoades finds the reverse effect, however (Rhoades, 1974).

14 This measure of diversification was most exhaustively investigated by Berry (1975), although he used 1.0 minus the index we use.

15 These results do not bear directly on the hypothesis that multimarket contact between diversified firms facilitates cooperation, and thereby higher prices and profits, as put forward and tested recently by John Scott (1981, 1982). We have not undertaken the effort to measure multimarket contact.

7 Managerial control, profitability, and managerial compensation

1 Marris assumes it is the valuation ratio, the ratio of market to book value, that is the key variable in determining the threat of takeover, but, as he notes, the valuation ratio itself can be related directly to the profit rate.

2 Note the shift in Baumol's position between the 1959 and 1967 editions of *Business Behavior, Value and Growth*. Fama (1980) emphasizes the constraint on managerial discretion placed by the market for managers.

3 Of these, see Galbraith (1961). For a discussion of the founding of the SEC and resistance to it, see Parrish (1970).

4 The other obvious group from which companies wish to keep their market share and profit data secret is the antitrust authorities. If the only sources of profitability are efficiency and market power, one wonders which of these two sources companies wish to conceal.

5 The prediction of Jensen and Meckling (1976) that companies voluntarily reveal information that allows outsiders to estimate π^* and X seems so patently at odds with the evidence for so many companies regarding so many pieces of relevant information, that something must be wrong with the theory. The assumption that leads them to their erroneous prediction is that companies are continually dependent on the external capital market to raise investment funds. The largest corporations can and do rely on internal funds to finance investment. These large companies need not reveal information that might reveal managerial diversion of potential profits to induce the capital market to supply additional capital.

6 This criterion is used by Larner (1966) following Berle and Means ([1932], 1968). See, also, Kamerschen (1968); Monsen, Chiu, and Cooley (1968); Boudreaux (1973); and Palmer (1973a, b).

7 We write (7.7a) without intercept on the assumption that the management of a company with zero sales has no discretion to garner company revenues.

8 As noted above, the nonlinear specification (7.7b) gave slightly higher R^2s than the linear (7.7a). The latter's estimates would suggest relatively greater deviations for lower values of MC, and relatively smaller deviations for high MCs.

8   Mergers and profitability

1 This percentage could be arrived at, for example, by a company making 44 acquisitions each equal to 1 percent of its assets at the time of the acquisition, a single acquisition of 44 percent of its assets, or any combination summing to 0.44.

2 The number of years in which an acquisition took place, NAQ, introduced in Chapter 7 was also tried in place of GAQ. It performed analogously, but gave poorer statistical performance. Since this variable cannot be related easily to the averaging effect, no results for it are reported.

In all equations in Table 8.2, each observation is weighted by the reciprocal of the standard error of the estimate of the projected profits variables, as discussed in Chapter 4. Weighting the right-hand-side variables by the sales-to-assets ratio or the reciprocal of external demand elasticity estimates did not improve the statistical fit.

9   Mergers and market share

1 Perry and Porter (1983) have recently shown that the reduction in output for the merging firms may be so large that it makes a horizontal merger unprofitable for the merging companies even though it would raise industry profits. Salant, Switzer, and Reynolds (1983) demonstrate that some horizontal mergers that increase industry profits are unprofitable in the presence of modest fixed costs. We do not amend our model to allow for these possibilities because our focus is on the *effects* of mergers, not their determinants. We know that some mergers turn out to be unprofitable ex post, and wish to employ a model that allows for that possibility ex ante. The question of why firms might undertake mergers that turn out to be unprofitable is not addressed here.

2 Note that an acquired company having some sales in markets in which the acquiring had sales, and some in markets where it did not, appeared in both the conglomerate and horizontal merger samples. Its market share in each was calculated by aggregating over the j appropriate to each definition.

3 Because our reference point in selecting a sample is firms in existence

and relatively large in 1950, a far smaller percentage of our mergers took place in the late sixties than is true for the population of all firms in existence at each point in time. The unweighted mean year for a merger in the sample is 1961, virtually in the middle of the time period.

4 The procedure proposed by Gleijser (1969) was employed to test for the presence of heteroscedasticity, with M_{50}^{α} and S_{50}^{α} as likely scale variables, $\alpha = .5, 1, 2$.

10 The threads gathered and conclusions woven

1 See Clarke, Davies, and Waterson (1984) and Kessides (1984). The former study appears to assign firms to industries and treat all of their sales and profits as if they were from the industry to which the firm was assigned. This procedure is of questionable legitimacy even in the United Kingdom, but it is impossible in the United States, where diversification is more widespread.

The Federal Trade Commission's Line of Business data, which Kessides employs, are well suited for this type of study. Both his work and an earlier effort by myself (1980b) suggest that the figures for the 1974–76 period give sufficiently perplexing results that caution must be employed in their interpretation.

2 The number of papers proving this result in one form or another is immense, e.g., Lancaster (1975), Spence (1976a, b), Schmalensee (1978), Olivera (1973), von Weizäcker (1980) and Loury (1979).

References

Bain, Joe S., *Barriers to New Competition*, Cambridge: Harvard University Press, 1956.

———, *Price Theory*, New York: Henry Holt, 1952.

———, *Industrial Organization*, New York: Wiley, 1959.

Baumol, William J., *Business Behavior, Value and Growth*, New York: Macmillan, 1959; 2d ed. 1967.

Baumol, William J., Panzar, John C., and Willig, Robert D. *Contestable Markets and the Theory of Industry Structure*, New York: Harcourt, Brace, Jovanovich, 1982.

Ben-Zion, U., and Shalit, S. S., "Size, Leverage and Dividend Record as Determinants of Equity Risk," *Journal of Finance*, September 1975, *30*, pp. 1015–26.

Berle, Adolf A., and Means, Gardner C., *The Modern Corporation and Private Property*, New York: Commerce Clearing House, 1932; rev. ed., New York: Harcourt, Brace, Jovanovich, 1968.

Berry, Charles H., *Corporate Growth and Diversification*, Princeton: Princeton University Press, 1975.

Bishop, Robert L., "Duopoly: Collusion or Warfare?" *American Economic Review*, December 1960, *50*, pp. 933–61.

Bloch, Harry, "Advertising and Profitability: A Reappraisal," *Journal of Political Economy*, March-April 1974, *82*, pp. 267–86.

Bond, Ronald S., and Lean, David F., *Sales, Promotion and Product Differentiation in Two Prescription Drug Markets*, Washington, D.C.: Federal Trade Commission, 1977.

Bothwell, James L., Cooley, Thomas F., and Hall, Thomas E., "A New View of the Market Structure–Performance Debate," *Journal of Industrial Economics*, June 1984, *32*, pp. 397–418.

Bothwell, James L., and Keeler, Theodore E., "Profits, Market Structure, and Portfolio Risk," in Robert T. Masson and P. David Qualls, eds., *Essays on Industrial Organization in Honor of Joe S. Bain*, Cambridge: Ballinger, 1976, pp. 71–88.

Boudreaux, Kenneth J., " 'Managerialism' and Risk-Return Performance," *Southern Economic Journal*, January 1973, *39*, pp. 366–72.

Bowman, Edward H., "A Risk/Return Paradox for Strategic Management," *Sloan Management Review*, Spring 1980, *21*, pp. 17–31.

———, "Risk Seeking by Troubled Firms," *Sloan Management Review*, Summer 1982, *23*, pp. 33–42.

Boyle, Stanley E., "Pre-merger Growth and Profit Characteristics of Large Conglomerate Mergers in the United States, 1948–68," *St. John's Law Review*, Spring 1970, spec. ed. *44*, pp. 152–70.

Bresnahan, Timothy F., "Duopoly Models with Consistent Conjectures," *American Economic Review*, December 1981a, *71*, pp. 934–45.

———, "Departures from Marginal-Cost Pricing in the American Automobile Industry," *Journal of Econometrics*, 1981b, *17*, pp. 201–27.

Brodley, Joseph F., "Potential Competition Mergers: A Structural Synthesis," *Yale Law Journal*, November 1977, *87*, pp. 1–89.

———, "In Defense of Presumptive Rules: An Approach to Legal Rulemaking for Conglomerate Mergers," in Roger D. Blair and Robert F. Lanzillotti, eds., *The Conglomerate Corporation*, Cambridge, Mass.: Oelgeschlager, Gunn, and Hain, 1981, pp. 249–81.

Brown, Randall S., "Estimating Advantages to Large-Scale Advertising," *Review of Economics and Statistics*, August 1978, *60*, pp. 429–37.

Brozen, Yale, "The Antitrust Task Force Deconcentration Recommendation," *Journal of Law and Economics*, October 1970, *13*, pp. 279–92.

———, "Bain's Concentration and Rates of Return Revisited," *Journal of Law and Economics*, October 1971a, *14*, pp. 351–69.

———, "The Persistence of 'High Rates of Return' in High-Stable Concentration Industries," *The Journal of Law and Economics*, October 1971b, *14*, pp. 501–12.

Buchanan, James M., Tollison, Robert D., and Tullock, Gordon, eds., *Toward a Theory of the Rent-Seeking Society*, College Station: Texas A&M Press, 1980.

Burch, Philip H., Jr., *The Managerial Revolution Reassessed*, Lexington, Mass: Heath, 1972.

Buzzell, Robert D. and Farris, Paul W., "Marketing Costs in Consumer Goods Industries," in Hans B. Thorelli, ed., *Strategy and Structure-Performance*, Bloomington: Indiana University Press, 1977, pp. 122–44.

Cable, John, "Market Structure, Advertising Policy and Intermarket Differences in Advertising Intensity," in K. Cowling, ed., *Market Structure and Corporate Behavior*, London: Gray Mills, 1972, pp. 111–24.

Carter, John R., "In Search of Synergy: A Structure-Performance Test," *Review of Economics and Statistics*, August 1977, *59*, pp. 279–89.

———, "Collusion, Efficiency and Antitrust," *Journal of Law and Economics*, October 1978, *21*, pp. 435–44.

Caves, Richard E., Porter, Michael E., Spence, Michael, with Scott, John T., *Competition in the Open Economy*, Cambridge: Harvard University Press, 1980.

Caves, Richard E., and Yamey, Basil S., "Risk and Corporate Rates of Return: Comment," *Quarterly Journal of Economics*, August 1971, *85*, pp. 513–17.

Chevalier, Jean-Marie, "The Problem of Control in Large American Corporations," *Antitrust Bulletin*, Spring 1969, *14*, pp. 163–80.

Ciscel, David H., and Carroll, Thomas M., "The Determinants of Executive

Salaries: An Econometric Survey," *Review of Economics and Statistics*, February 1980, *62*, pp. 7–13.

Clarke, Darral G., "Econometric Measurement of the Duration of Advertising Effect on Sales," *Journal of Marketing Research*, November 1976, *13*, pp. 345–57.

Clarke, Roger, Davies, Stephen, and Waterson, Michael, "The Profitability-Concentration Relation: Market Power or Efficiency?" *Journal of Industrial Economics*, June 1984, *32*, pp. 435–50.

Collins, Norman, and Preston, Lee, *Concentration and Price–Cost Margins in Manufacturing Industries*, Berkeley: University of California Press, 1968.

Comanor, William S., and Leibenstein, Harvey, "Allocative Efficiency, X-Efficiency and the Measurement of Welfare Losses," *Economica*, August 1969, *36*, pp. 304–9.

Comanor, William S., and Scherer, F. M., "Patent Statistics as a Measure of Technical Change," *Journal of Political Economy*, May-June 1969, *77*, pp. 392–98.

Comanor, W. S., and Wilson, T. A., "Advertising, Market Structure and Performance," *Review of Economics and Statistics*, November 1967, *49*, pp. 423–40.

———, *Advertising and Market Power*, Cambridge: Harvard University Press, 1974.

Connolly, Robert A., and Hirschey, Mark, "Specification Uncertainty and the Robustness of Structure-Performance Relations," University of North Carolina at Greensboro working paper, December 1983.

Connolly, Robert A., and Schwartz, Steven, "The Intertemporal Behavior of Economic Profits," 1984, photocopy.

Cowling, Keith, "On the Theoretical Specification of Industrial Structure-Performance Relationships," *European Economic Review*, 1976, *8*, pp. 1–14.

Cowling, K., and Waterson, M., "Price–Cost Margins and Market Structure," *Economica*, August 1976, *43*, pp. 267–74.

Cubbin, John, "Apparent Collusion and Conjectural Variations in Differentiated Oligopoly," *International Journal of Industrial Organization*, June 1983, *1*, pp. 155–63.

Cubbin, John, and Leech, Dennis, "The Effect of Shareholding Dispersion on the Degree of Control in British Companies: Theory and Measurement," *Economic Journal*, June 1983, *93*, pp. 351–69.

Cyert, Richard M., and DeGroot, Morris M., "An Analysis of Cooperation and Learning in a Duopoly Context," *American Economic Review*, March 1973, *63*, pp. 24–37.

Dansby, R. E., and Willig, R. D., "Industry Performance Gradient Indexes," *American Economic Review*, June 1979, *69*, pp. 249–60.

Demsetz, H., "Accounting for Advertising as a Barrier to Entry," *Journal of Business*, July 1979, *59*, pp. 345–60.

———, "Two Systems of Belief about Monopoly," in Harvey J. Goldschmid,

H. M. Mann, and J. F. Weston, eds., *Industrial Concentration: The New Learning*, Boston: Little, Brown, 1974, pp. 164–84.

———, "Industry Structure, Market Rivalry, and Public Policy," *Journal of Law and Economics*, April 1973, *16*, pp. 1–9.

Dewey, Donald, "Mergers and Cartels: Some Reservations about Policy," *American Economic Review*, May 1961, *51*, pp. 255–62.

Dodd, P., and Ruback, R., "Tender Offers and Stockholder Returns: An Empirical Analysis," *Journal of Financial Economics*, December 1977, *5*, pp. 351–74.

Donsimoni, Marie-Paule, Geroski, Paul, and Jacquemin, Alexis, "Concentration Indices and Market Power: Two Views," *Journal of Industrial Economics*, June 1984, *32*, pp. 419–34.

Duetsch, Larry L., "Structure, Performance, and the Net Rate of Entry into Manufacturing Industries," *Southern Economic Journal*, January 1975, *41*, pp. 450–65.

Edwards, Corwin D., "Conglomerate Bigness as a Source of Power," The National Bureau of Economic Research Conference report, *Business Concentration and Price Policy*, Princeton: Princeton University Press, 1955, pp. 331–59.

Edwards, Franklin R., and Heggestad, Arnold, "Uncertainty, Market Structure, and Performance in Banking," *Quarterly Journal of Economics*, August 1973, *87*, pp. 455–73.

Fama, Eugene F., "Agency Problems and the Theory of the Firm," *Journal of Political Economy*, April 1980, *88*, pp. 288–307.

Fama, Eugene F., and Miller, Merton H., *The Theory of Finance*, New York: Rinehart & Winston, 1972.

Federal Trade Commission (FTC), *Value of Shipments Data by Product Class for the 1,000 Largest Manufacturing Companies of 1950*, Washington, D.C.: Government Printing Office, 1972a.

———, *Economic Report on Conglomerate Merger Performance*, Washington, D.C.: Government Printing Office, 1972b.

———, *The United States Steel Industry and Its International Rivals: Trends and Factors Determining International Competitiveness*, Washington, D.C.: Government Printing Office, 1977.

———, *Statistical Report on Mergers and Acquisitions, 1978*, Washington, D.C.: Government Printing Office, 1980.

Fellner, William, *Competition Among the Few*, New York: Alfred A. Knopf, 1949.

Firth, Michael, "Takeovers, Shareholder Returns, and the Theory of the Firm," *Quarterly Journal of Economics*, March 1980, *94*, pp. 315–47.

Fisher, Franklin M., and McGowan, John J., "On the Misuse of Accounting Rates of Return to Infer Monopoly Profits," *American Economic Review*, March 1983, *73*, pp. 82–97.

Fisher, I. W., and Hall, G. R., "Risk and Corporate Rates of Return," *Quarterly Journal of Economics*, February 1969, *83*, pp. 79–92.

Galbraith, John K. *The Great Crash, 1929*, Boston: Houghton Mifflin, 1961.

366   **References**

Gale, Bradley J., "Market Share and Rate of Return," *Review of Economics and Statistics*, November 1972, *54*, pp. 412–23.

Gale, Bradley J., and Branch, Ben S., "Concentration versus Market Share: Which Determines Performance and Why Does it Matter?" *Antitrust Bulletin*, Spring 1982, *27*, pp. 83–106.

Gaskins, Darius W., Jr., "Dynamic Limit Pricing: Optimal Pricing under Threat of Entry," *Journal of Economic Theory*, September 1971, *3*, pp. 306–22.

Geroski, P. A., "Specification and Testing the Profits-Concentration Relationship: Some Experiments for the UK," *Economica*, August 1981, *48*, pp. 279–88.

———, "Simultaneous Equations Models of the Structure-Performance Paradigm," *European Economic Review*, 1982a, *19*, pp. 145–58.

———, "The Empirical Analysis of Conjectural Variations in Oligopoly," 1982b, photocopy.

Gleijser, H., "A New Test for Heteroscedasticity," *Journal of the American Statistical Association*, March 1969, *64*, pp. 316–58.

Goldberg, Lawrence G., "The Effect of Conglomerate Mergers on Competition," *Journal of Law and Economics*, April 1973, *16*, pp. 137–58.

Gollop, Frank M., and Roberts, Mark J., "Firm Interdependence in Oligopolistic Markets," *Journal of Econometrics*, August 1979, *10*, pp. 313–31.

Gorecki, Paul K., "The Determinants of Entry by New and Diversifying Enterprises in the Manufacturing Sector, 1958–63," *Applied Economics*, June 1975, *7*, pp. 165–74.

Grabowski, Henry G., "The Determinants of Industrial Research and Development," *Journal of Political Economy*, March-April 1968, *76*, pp. 292–306.

———, "The Effects of Advertising on the Interindustry Distribution of Demand," *Explorations in Economic Research*, Winter 1976, *3*, pp. 21–75.

Grabowski, Henry G., and Baxter, N.D., "Rivalry in Industrial Research and Development: An Empirical Study," *Journal of Industrial Economics*, July 1973, *21*, pp. 209–35.

Grabowski, Henry G., and Mueller, Dennis C., "Imitative Advertising in the Cigarette Industry," *Antitrust Bulletin*, Summer 1971, *16*, pp. 257–92.

———, "Industrial Research and Development, Intangible Capital Stock, and Firm Profit Rates," *Bell Journal of Economics*, Autumn 1978, *9*, pp. 328–43.

Greer, Douglas, "Advertising and Market Concentration," *Southern Economic Journal*, July 1971, *38*, pp. 19–32.

Hall, M., and Weiss, L., "Firm Size and Profitability," *Review of Economics and Statistics*, August 1967, *49*, pp. 319–31.

Harris, Frederick H., deB., "Market Structure and Price-Cost Performance under Risk," University of Texas, Arlington, 1983, photocopy.

———, "Growth Expectations, Excess Value, and the Risk-Adjusted Return to Market Power," *Southern Economic Journal*, July 1984, *51*, pp. 166–79.

Hart, P. E., and Prais, S. J., "The Analysis of Business Concentration," *Journal of the Royal Statistical Society*, 1956, *119*, pp. 150–81.

Hay, Donald A., and Morris, Derek J., *Industrial Economics*, Oxford: Oxford University Press, 1979.

Hay, George, and Untiet, Charles, "Statistical Measurement of the Conglomerate Problem," in Roger D. Blair and Robert F. Lanzillotti, eds., *The Conglomerate Corporation*, Cambridge, Mass.: Oelgeschlager, Gunn, and Hain, 1981, pp. 163–91.

Headen, Robert S., and McKie, James W., *The Structure, Conduct, and Performance of the Breakfast Cereal Industry: 1954–1964*, Cambridge: Arthur D. Little, 1966.

Hirschey, Mark, "The Effect of Advertising," *Journal of Business*, April 1981, *54*, pp. 329–39.

———, "Market Power and Foreign Involvement by U.S. Multinationals," *Review of Economics and Statistics*, May 1982a, *64*, pp. 343–6.

———, "Intangible Capital Aspects of Advertising and R&D Expenditures," *Journal of Industrial Economics*, June 1982b, *30*, pp. 375–90.

———, "Inventive Output, Profitability and Economic Performance," University of Wisconsin, Madison, 1982c, photocopy.

Houthakker, H. S., and Taylor, L. D., *Consumer Demand in the United States*, 2d ed., Cambridge: Harvard University Press, 1970.

Ijiri, Yuji, and Simon, Herbert A., *Skew Distributions and the Sizes of Business Firms*, Amsterdam: North-Holland, 1977.

Imel, Blake, and Helmberger, Peter, "Estimation of Structure-Profit Relationships with Application to the Food Processing Sector," *American Economic Review*, September 1971, *61*, pp. 614–27.

Jacquemin, Alex P., and Lichtbuer, Michel Cardon de, "Size Structure, Stability and Performance of the Largest British and EEC Firms," *European Economic Review*, December 1973, *4*, pp. 393–408.

Jacquemin, Alex, and Saez, Wistano, "A Comparison of the Performance of the Largest European and Japanese Industrial Firms," *Oxford Economic Papers*, July 1976, *28*, pp. 271–83.

Jensen, M. C., "Capital Markets: Theory and Evidence," *Bell Journal of Economic Management Science*, Autumn 1972, *3*, pp. 357–98.

Jensen, Michael C., and Meckling, William H., "The Theory of the Firm: Managerial Behavior, Agency Costs and Ownership Structure," *Journal of Financial Economics*, October 1976, *3*, pp. 305–60.

Johnston, J., *Econometric Methods*, 2d ed., New York: McGraw-Hill, 1972.

Kamerschen, David R., "The Influence of Ownership and Control on Profit Rates," *American Economic Review*, June 1968, *58*, pp. 432–47.

Kamien, Morton I., and Schwartz, Nancy L., "Limit Pricing and Uncertain Entry," *Econometrica*, May 1971, *39*, pp. 441–54.

———, "Conjectural Variations," *Canadian Journal of Economics*, May 1983, *16*, pp. 191–211.

Kessides, Ioannis N., "A Model of Differentiated Oligopoly: Some Empirical Results," Washington, D.C.: Federal Trade Commission, 1984, photocopy.

Kilpatrick, Robert W., "Stigler on the Relationship Between Profit Rates and

368   **References**

Market Concentration," *Journal of Political Economy*, June 1968, 76, pp. 479–85.

Kuenne, Robert E., "Towards an Operational General Equilibrium Theory with Oligopoly: Some Experimental Results and Conjectures," *Kyklos*, 1974, 27, pp. 792–820.

Kuh, Edwin, *Capital Stock Growth: A Micro-Economic Approach*, Amsterdam: North Holland, 1963.

Kwoka, John, "The Effect of Market Share Distribution on Industry Performance," *Review of Economics and Statistics*, February 1979, 61, pp. 101–9.

Kwoka, John E., Jr., and Ravenscraft, David J., "Collusion, Rivalry, Scale Economies and Line of Business Profitability," Washington, D.C.: Federal Trade Commission, 1982, photocopy.

Laitner, J., " 'Rational' Duopoly Equilibria," *Quarterly Journal of Economics*, December 1980, 95, pp. 641–62.

Lambin, Jean Jacques, *Advertising, Competition and Market Conduct in Oligopoly Over Time*, Amsterdam: North Holland, 1976.

Lancaster, Kelvin, "Socially Optimal Product Differentiation," *American Economic Review*, September 1975, 65, pp. 567–85.

Larner, Robert J., "Ownership Control in the 200 Largest Nonfinancial Corporations, 1929 and 1963," *American Economic Review*, September 1966, 56, pp. 777–87.

Lawriwsky, Michael L., *Corporate Structure and Performance*, London: Croom Helm, 1984.

Lester, Richard A., "Shortcomings of Marginal Analysis for Wage-Employment Problems," *American Economic Review*, March 1946, 36, pp. 63–82.

Levy, Haim, "The Capital Asset Pricing Model: Theory and Empiricism," *Economic Journal*, March 1983, 93, pp. 145–65.

Lewellen, Wilbur G., *Executive Compensation in Large Industrial Corporations*, New York: Columbia University Press, 1968.

Lewellen, Wilbur G., and Huntsman, Blaine, "Managerial Pay and Corporate Performance," *American Economic Review*, September 1970, 60, pp. 710–20.

Lindenberg, Eric, and Ross, Stephen, "Tobin's q Ratio and Industrial Organization," *Journal of Business*, January 1981, 54, pp. 1–32.

Long, William F., "Market Share, Concentration, and Profits: Intra-Industry and Inter-Industry Evidence," Washington, D.C.: Federal Trade Commission, 1982, photocopy.

Long, William, and Ravenscraft, David, "The Usefulness of Accounting Profit Data: A Comment on Fisher and McGowan," *American Economic Review*, June 1984, 74, pp. 494–500.

Loury, Glenn C., "Market Structure and Innovation," *Quarterly Journal of Economics*, August 1979, 93, pp. 395–410.

MacAvoy, Paul W., McKie, James W., and Preston, Lee E., "High and Stable Concentration Levels, Profitability and Public Policy: A Response," *Journal of Law and Economics*, October 1971, 14, pp. 493–9.

Machlup, Fritz, "Marginal Analysis and Empirical Research," *American Economic Review*, September 1946, *36*, pp. 519–54.

Mandelker, Gershon, "Risk and Return: The Case of Merging Firms," *Journal of Financial Economics*, December 1974, *1*, pp. 303–35.

Manne, Henry G., "Mergers and the Market for Corporate Control," *Journal of Political Economy*, April 1965, *73*, pp. 110–20.

Marcus, Matityahu, "Profitability and Size of Firm: Some Further Evidence," *Review of Economics and Statistics*, February 1969, *51*, pp. 104–7.

Marris, Robin, "A Model of the 'Managerial' Enterprise," *Quarterly Journal of Economics*, May 1963, *77*, pp. 185–209.

———, *The Economic Theory of Managerial Capitalism*, Glencoe: Free Press, 1964.

Marris, Robin, and Mueller, Dennis C., "The Corporation, Competition, and the Invisible Hand," *Journal of Economic Literature*, March 1980, *18*, pp. 32–63.

Martin, Stephen, "Market, Firm, and Economic Performance: An Empirical Analysis," Washington, D.C.: Federal Trade Commission, 1982, photocopy.

Marvel, Howard P., "Collusion and the Pattern of Rates of Return," *Southern Economic Journal*, October 1980, *47*, pp. 375–87.

McEachern, William A., *Managerial Control and Performance*, Lexington, Mass: Heath, 1975.

McEnally, Richard W., "Competition and Dispersion in Rates of Return: A Note," *Journal of Industrial Economics*, September 1976, *25*, pp. 69–75.

McGuckin, Robert, "Entry, Concentration Change, and Stability of Market Shares," *Southern Economic Journal*, January 1972, *38*, pp. 363–70.

McMillan, John, "Collusion, Competition and Conjectures," June 1982, photocopy.

Meeks, Geoffrey, *Disappointing Marriage: A Study of the Gains from Merger*, Cambridge, England: Cambridge University Press, 1977.

Monsen, R. Joseph, Chiu, J. S., and Cooley, D. E., "The Effect of Separation of Ownership and Control on the Performance of the Large Firm," *Quarterly Journal of Economics*, August 1968, *82*, pp. 435–51.

Monsen, R. Joseph, Jr., and Downs, Anthony, "A Theory of Large Managerial Firms," *Journal of Political Economy*, June 1965, *73*, pp. 221–36.

Mueller, Dennis C., "Patents, Research and Development, and the Measurement of Inventive Activity," *Journal of Industrial Economics*, November 1966, *15*, pp. 26–37.

———, "A Theory of Conglomerate Mergers," *Quarterly Journal of Economics*, November 1969, *83*, pp. 643–59.

———, "The Persistence of Profits above the Norm," *Economica*, November 1977a, *44*, pp. 369–80.

———, "The Effects of Conglomerate Mergers: A Survey of the Empirical Evidence," *Journal of Banking and Finance*, December 1977b, *1*, pp. 315–47.

———, "Do We Want a New, Tough Antimerger Law?" *Antitrust Bulletin*, Winter 1979, *24*, pp. 807–36.

————, ed., *The Determinants and Effects of Mergers: An International Comparison*, Cambridge: Oelgeschlager, Gunn, and Hain, 1980a.

————, "Economies of Scale, Concentration, and Collusion," Washington, D.C.: Federal Trade Commission, 1980b, photocopy.

————, *The Determinants of Persistent Profits*, Washington, D.C.: Federal Trade Commission, 1983.

National Science Foundation (NSF), *Science Indicators 1976*, Washington, D.C.: Government Printing Office, 1977.

Nelson, Phillip, "Information and Consumer Behavior," *Journal of Political Economy*, March/April 1970, *78*, pp. 311–29.

Nelson, Richard R., "The Simple Economics of Basic Scientific Research," *Journal of Political Economy*, June 1959, *67*, pp. 297–306.

Nelson, Robin C., "Cereals Snap, Crackle, Sometimes Lay Bombs," *Printer's Ink*, June 24, 1966, *292*, p. 19ff.

————, "Cereals: Marketing's Survival School," *Printer's Ink*, March 1970, *298*, p. 32ff.

Netter, Jeffry, M., "Excessive Advertising: An Empirical Analysis," *Journal of Industrial Economics*, June 1982, *30*, pp. 361–73.

Nyman, S., and Silberston, A., "The Ownership and Control of Industry," *Oxford Economic Papers*, March 1978, *30*, pp. 74–101.

Olivera, Julio H. G., "On Bernoullian Production Sets," *Quarterly Journal of Economics*, February 1973, *87*, pp. 112–20.

Orr, Dale, "The Determinants of Entry: A Study of the Canadian Manufacturing Industries," *Review of Economics and Statistics*, February 1974, *56*, pp. 58–66.

Pagoulatos, Emilio, and Sorenson, Robert, "A Simultaneous Equation Analysis of Advertising, Concentration and Profitability," *Southern Economic Journal*, January 1981, *47*, pp. 728–41.

Palmer, John P., "The Profit-Performance Effects of the Separation of Ownership from Control in Large U.S. Industrial Corporations," *Bell Journal of Economics and Management Science*, Spring 1973a, *4*, pp. 293–303.

————, "The Profit Variability Effects of the Managerial Enterprise," *Western Economic Journal*, June 1973b, *11*, pp. 228–31.

Parrish, Michael E., *Securities Regulation and the New Deal*, New Haven: Yale University Press, 1970.

Peles, Yoram, "Rates of Amortization of Advertising Expenditures," *Journal of Political Economy*, September/October 1971, *79*, pp. 1032–58.

Peltzman, S., "The Gains and Losses from Industrial Concentration," *Journal of Law and Economics*, October 1977, *20*, pp. 229–63.

Perry, Martin K., "Oligopoly and Consistent Conjectural Variations," *Bell Journal of Economics*, Spring 1982, *13*, pp. 197–203.

Perry, M. K., and Porter, R. H., "Oligopoly and the Incentive for Horizontal Merger," 1983, photocopy.

Peterson, Shorey, "Corporate Control and Capitalism," *Quarterly Journal of Economics*, February 1965, *79*, pp. 1–24.

Pindyck, Robert S., and Rubinfeld, Daniel L., *Econometric Models and Economic Forecasts*, New York: McGraw-Hill, 1976.

Porter, Michael E., "Consumer Behavior, Retailer Power and Market Performance in Consumer Goods Industries," *Review of Economics and Statistics*, November 1974, *56*, pp. 419–36.

Posner, Richard A., "The Social Cost of Monopoly and Regulation," *Journal of Political Economy*, August 1975, *83*, pp. 807–27.

Qualls, P. David, "Stability and Persistence of Economic Profit Margins in Highly Concentrated Industries," *Southern Economic Journal*, April 1974, *40*, pp. 604–12.

Ravenscraft, David J., "Structure-Profit Relationships at the Line of Business and Industry Level," *Review of Economics and Statistics*, February 1983, *65*, pp. 22–31.

Rhoades, Stephen A., "The Effect of Diversification on Industry Profit Performance in 241 Manufacturing Industries," *Review of Economics and Statistics*, May 1973, *55*, pp. 146–55.

Rhoades, Stephen A., "A Further Evaluation of the Effect of Diversification on Industry Profit Performance," *Review of Economics and Statistics*, November 1974, *56*, pp. 557–9.

Roberts, Mark J., "Testing Oligopolistic Behavior," *International Journal of Industrial Organization*, December 1984, *2*, pp. 367–83.

Salamon, Gerald L., "Accounting Rate of Return, Measurement Error, and Tests of Economic Hypotheses: The Case of Firm Size," University of Iowa, 1983, photocopy.

Salamon, Gerald L., and Moriarty, Mark M., "The Use of Accounting Rate of Return in Tests of Economic Hypotheses: Evidence from the Advertising-Profitability Issue," University of Iowa, 1984, photocopy.

Salant, S. W., Switzer, S., and Reynolds, R. J., "Losses from Horizontal Merger: The Effects of an Exogenous Change in Industry Structure on Cournot-Nash Equilibrium," *Quarterly Journal of Economics*, May 1983, *98*, pp. 185–99.

Sant, Donald T., "A Polynomial Approximation for Switching Regressions with Applications to Market Structure-Performance Studies," Federal Trade Commission Staff Working Paper, Washington, D.C.: February 1978.

Saxonhouse, Gary R., "Estimated Parameters as Dependent Variables," *American Economic Review*, March 1976, *66*, pp. 178–83.

Scherer, F. M., *Industrial Market Structure and Economic Performance*, 2d ed., Chicago: Rand McNally, 1980.

——, *Industrial Market and Economic Performance*, 2d ed., Chicago: Rand McNally, 1980.

——, "The Breakfast Cereal Industry," in Walter Adams, ed., *The Structure of American Industry*, New York: Macmillan, 1982, pp. 191–217.

——, "Mergers Sell-Offs and Managerial Behavior," paper presented at the Conference on the Economics of Strategic Planning, sponsored by the Columbia Business School, 1984a.

——, "Narrative Summary of the Case Studies," 1984b, photocopy.

Scherer, F. M., Beckenstein, A., Kaufer, E., and Murphy, R. D., *The Economics of Multiplant Operation*, Cambridge: Harvard University Press, 1975.

Schmalensee, Richard, "Entry Deference in the Ready-To-Eat-Breakfast Cereal Industry," *Bell Journal of Economics*, Autumn 1978, *9*, pp. 305–27.

———, "Product Differentiation Advantages of Pioneering Brands," *American Economic Review*, June 1982, *72*, pp. 349–66.

———, "Do Markets Differ Much?" *American Economic Review*, June 1985, *75*, pp. 341–52.

Schwartz, Steven, "Factors Affecting the Probability of Being Acquired: Evidence for the United States," *Economic Journal*, June 1982, *92*, pp. 391–8.

Schwinn, Carl R., "Tobin's *q* Ratio and Industrial Organization: Further Results," Federal Trade Commission, Working Paper No. 104, Washington, D.C., 1983.

Scitovsky, T., "A Note on Profit Maximization and Its Implications," *Review of Economic Studies*, 1943, *11*, pp. 57–60.

Scott, John J., "Multimarket Contact: A New Look at a Classic Sample," Dartmouth College, 1981, photocopy.

———, "Multimarket Contact and Economic Performance," *Review of Economics and Statistics*, August 1982, *64*, pp. 368–75.

Sharpe, William F., "Capital Asset Prices: A Theory of Market Equilibrium under Conditions of Risk," *Journal of Finance*, September 1964, *19*, pp. 425–42.

Shavell, Steven, "Sharing Risks of Deferred Payment," *Journal of Political Economy*, February 1976, *84*, pp. 161–8.

Shepherd, William G., "The Elements of Market Structure," *Review of Economics and Statistics*, February 1972, *54*, pp. 25–37.

———, *The Treatment of Market Power*, New York: Columbia University Press, 1975.

Sherman, Roger, and Tollison, Robert, "Technology, Profit Risk and Assessments of Market Performance," *Quarterly Journal of Economics*, August 1972, *86*, pp. 448–62.

Shubik, Martin, *Market Structure and Behavior*, Cambridge, Mass.: Harvard University Press, 1980.

Simon, Herbert A., "The Compensation of Executives," *Sociometry*, March 1957, *20*, pp. 32–5.

Simon, Herbert A., and Bonini, Charles P., "The Size Distribution of Business Firms," *American Economic Review*, September 1958, *48*, pp. 607–17.

Singh, Ajit, *Take-overs: Their Relevance to the Stock Market and the Theory of the Firm*, Cambridge: Cambridge University Press, 1971.

———, "Take-overs, 'Natural Selection' and the Theory of the Firm," *Economic Journal*, September 1975, *85*, pp. 497–515.

Smiley, Robert, "Tender Offers, Transactions Costs and the Theory of the Firm," *Review of Economics and Statistics*, February 1976, *58*, pp. 22–32.

Smith, Richard Austin, *Corporations in Crisis*, Garden City, N.Y.: Doubleday, 1963.

Solomon, Ezra, "Alternative Rate of Return Concepts and Their Implications for Utility Regulation," *Bell Journal of Economics*, Spring 1970, *1*, pp. 65–81.

Spence, Michael, "Product Differentiation and Welfare," *American Economic Review*, May 1976a, *66*, pp. 407–14.

———, "Product Selection, Fixed Costs, and Monopolistic Competition," *Review of Economic Studies*, June 1976a, *43*, pp. 217–35.

Stauffer, Thomas R., "The Measurement of Corporate Rates of Return: A Generalized Formulation," *Bell Journal of Economics*, Autumn 1971, *2*, pp. 434–69.

Steiner, Peter O., *Mergers: Motives, Effects, Policies*, Ann Arbor: University of Michigan Press, 1975.

Stigler, George J., *Capital and Rates of Return in Manufacturing*, Princeton: Princeton University Press, 1963.

Stiglitz, Joseph E., "Incentives and Risk Sharing in Sharecropping," *Review of Economic Studies*, April 1974, *41*, pp. 219–55.

Sullivan, Timothy G., "The Cost of Capital and the Market Power of Firms," *Review of Economics and Statistics*, May 1978, *60*, pp. 209–17.

Sutinen, J.G., "The Rational Choice of Share Leasing and Implications for Efficiency," *American Journal of Agricultural Economics*, November 1975, *57*, pp. 613–21.

Sweezy, Paul M., "Demand under Conditions of Oligopoly," *Journal of Political Economy*, 1939, *47*, pp. 568–73.

Telser, L.G., "Advertising and Competition," *Journal of Political Economy*, December 1964, pp. 537–62.

Thomadakis, Stavros, "A Value-Based Test of Profitability and Market Structure," *Review of Economics and Statistics*, May 1977, *59*, pp. 179–85.

Tullock, Gordon, "The Welfare Costs of Tariffs, Monopolies, and Theft," *Western Economic Journal*, June 1967, *5*, pp. 291–303.

Ulph, David, "Rational Conjectures in the Theory of Oligopoly," *International Journal of Industrial Organization*, 1983, *1*, pp. 131–54.

Weiss, Leonard W., "Econometric Studies of Industrial Organization," in Michael Intriligator, ed., *Frontiers of Quantitative Economics*, Amsterdam: North-Holland, 1971, pp. 362–411.

———, "The Concentration-Profits Relationship and Antitrust," in H. J. Goldschmid, H. M. Mann, and J. F. Weston, eds., *Industrial Concentration: The New Learning*, Boston: Little, Brown, 1974.

———, "Corrected Concentration Ratios in Manufacturing–1972," Washington, D.C.: Federal Trade Commission, 1981, photocopy.

Weiss, Leonard, and Pascoe, George, "Some Early Results of the Effects of Concentration from the FTC's Line of Business Data," Washington, D.C.: Federal Trade Commission, 1981, photocopy.

———, "The Extent and Permanence of Market Dominance," paper presented at E.A.R.I.E. meetings, August 1983.

Weizäcker, C. C. von, *Barriers to Entry*, Berlin: Springer-Verlag, 1980.

Wenders, John T., "Profits and Antitrust Policy: The Question of Disequilibrium," *Antitrust Bulletin*, Summer 1971a, *16*, pp. 249–56.

————, "Deconcentration Reconsidered," *Journal of Law and Economics*, October 1971b, *14*, pp. 485–8.

Weston, J. Fred, "The Nature and Significance of Conglomerate Firms," *St. John's Law Review*, Spring 1970, spec. ed., *44*, pp. 66–80.

Weston, J. Fred, "Diversification and Merger Trends," *Business Economics*, January 1970, *5*, pp. 50–7.

Weston, J. Fred, and Mansinghka, S. K., "Tests of the Efficiency Performance of Conglomerate Firms," *Journal of Finance*, September 1971, *26*, pp. 919–36.

White, Laurence J., "Searching for the Critical Industrial Concentration Ratio," in Stephen Goldfeld and Richard E. Quandt, eds., *Studies in Non-Linear Estimation*, Cambridge: Ballinger, 1976, pp. 61–75.

Williamson, Oliver E., *The Economics of Discretionary Behavior: Managerial Objectives in a Theory of the Firm*, Englewood Cliffs, N.J.: Prentice-Hall, 1964.

————, "Hierarchical Control and Optimum Firm Size," *Journal of Political Economy*, April 1967, *75*, pp. 123–38.

————, *Corporate Control and Business Behavior: An Inquiry into the Effects of Organization Form on Enterprise Behavior*, Englewood Cliffs, N.J.: Prentice-Hall, 1970.

————, *Markets and Hierarchies: Analysis and Antitrust Implications*, New York: Free Press, 1975.

Winn, Daryl N., "On the Relations between Rates of Return, Risk, and Market Structure," *Quarterly Journal of Economics*, February 1977, *91*, pp. 157–64.

Winn, D. N., and Leabo, D. A., "Rates of Return, Concentration and Growth–Question of Disequilibrium," *Journal of Law and Economics*, April 1974, *17*, pp. 97–115.

Worcester, Dean A., "Why 'Dominant Firms' Decline," *Journal of Political Economy*, August 1957, *65*, pp. 338–47.

Index

375

DATE DUE

GAYLORD			PRINTED IN U.S.A.